Fred Jones

Tools *for* Teaching

Second Edition

Discipline • Instruction • Motivation

Fredric H. Jones, Ph.D.

with

Patrick Jones and Jo Lynne Jones

Illustrations by Brian T. Jones

Fred Jones Tools for Teaching – Discipline, Instruction, Motivation

Executive Producer: Jo Lynne T. Jones
Production and Web Design: Patrick Jones
Illustrations: Brian T. Jones

ISBN: 978-0-9650263-2-1
Library of Congress Catalog Control Number: 2007925215

printed in China
2nd Edition
00 01 02 03 04 05   12 11 10 9 8 7 6 5 4 3 2 1

Fredric H. Jones & Associates, Inc.
103 Quarry Lane
Santa Cruz, CA 95060
tel: (831) 425-8222   fax: (831) 426-8222
info@fredjones.com   www.fredjones.com

Awards for
Tools for Teaching, First Edition

2002 Finalist
Association of Educational Publishers
Golden Lamp Award

2001 Finalist
Independent Publishers
IPPY Award

Awards for
Tools for Teaching, Video Toolbox

2002 Winner
Two Telly Awards
for Video Excellence

Awards for
Tools for Teaching, Parent Edition DVDs

2005 Winner
Just for Mom Foundation
Mom's Choice Award

Preface

Over twenty years ago, I published two books with McGraw-Hill entitled, *Positive Classroom Discipline* and *Positive Classroom Instruction.* I thought they should be published as textbooks. But McGraw-Hill said, "There is no point in publishing a textbook for a course that no one is offering." I couldn't fault their logic on that point.

A lot has changed since then. Teachers routinely receive courses in classroom management as part of their training. During my workshops young teachers say things such as, "Oh, you are *the* Fred Jones. You were in my college textbook. I thought you were dead."

I procrastinated in updating these first two books because, frankly, it is very hard to write books and travel at the same time. I rationalized, "They're not dated. Fundamentals never change." Actually, that was only a half-truth. Fundamentals don't change, but my understanding of them certainly does.

I have never given a workshop without returning home knowing more than I did when I went out. New insights come from stories that teachers tell me, from discussions over lunch, or perhaps from answering a question that forces me to think on my feet in a new way. And, of course, I read constantly. I may be thinking about some aspect of body language only to read an article about interpreting facial expressions or the body language of dominance and submission. Suddenly a few more pieces of the puzzle fall into place.

I realized how much my understanding of classroom management had grown when I finally sat down to write *Tools for Teaching.* Discussions of key aspects of classroom management such as Meaning Business and Responsibility Training were on an entirely different level than those contained in *Positive Classroom Discipline* and *Positive Classroom Instruction.* They were more thorough and clear.

Now it is five years later, and my daughter, Anne, the college librarian, tells me, "Libraries won't order any reference book with a copyright date more than five years old. You need to revise *Tools for Teaching.*" "But, it's just fine the way it is," I replied. "Too bad," she said. So, I began revising. For starters I added six pages to Chapter 1 and completely rewrote Chapter 2. So much for the notion that it's just fine the way it is.

As before, the sections on Meaning Business and Responsibility Training have undergone significant improvement. Getting kids to *stop* doing what you *don't* want them to do and *start* doing what you *do* want them to do will always represent central issues in child management. But the most significant enhancement is the chapter on Say, See, Do Teaching which more clearly integrates interactive learning, continuous assessment, and immediate feedback during the teaching of each lesson.

This book describes the fundamental skills of being a classroom teacher. It contains all of the lessons that I have learned over the years. It is my gift back to the profession.

Contents

Acknowledgements

I credit my wife Jo Lynne with much of my interest in classrooms. Throughout my years in graduate school she was a classroom teacher, and every night when she came home from work, we had a 1-hour "debriefing" – like the astronauts have when they return from space. During our debriefings I relived every trauma and gratification of the day, and by Thanksgiving, her students were members of the family. After years of debriefings I became very interested in classrooms. When I began my classroom management research, Jo Lynne was a collaborator, and she has been my partner ever since.

Jo Lynne was the kind of teacher who did several hours of work each evening to prepare for the next day. Knowing how hard dedicated teachers work has been a crucial consideration in the development of the classroom management methods contained in this book. It is not enough for a technique to succeed. It must also be affordable in terms of the teachers' time and energy.

I must also acknowledge a large debt to my family. I come from a family of teachers and have always appreciated the competence and dedication that goes into being a teacher. In addition, my parents' blending of love and firmness helped me to see discipline management in child rearing as an extension of nurturance.

Our son Patrick has been my partner in preparing this manuscript. I wanted it to have the spontaneous, conversational character of a workshop. To accomplish this, I dictated major portions of the manuscript. Patrick would type a section as I repeatedly stopped and started, and then we would read it on the computer screen. Patrick was very patient and helpful. I remember one time dictating a paragraph on verbosity. After we read it over, I said to Patrick, "What do you think?" He said, "Dad, you don't want to know." I reread it and cracked up.

Our son, Brian did all of the cartoons and graphics for the book. He was finishing course work at San Francisco Art Institute just as Patrick and I were beginning the manuscript. Brian has cartooning in his blood. The timing was perfect. I said to Brian, "How would you like your first job to be drawing 60 or 70 cartoons for my new book? We are going to do it in full color." It was not a hard sell.

I wish to thank Hans Miller, my mentor at UCLA, who gave me my foundation in behavior management. I am also indebted to a series of outstanding graduate students at the university of Rochester – Robert Eimers, William Fremouw, Andrew Burka, Richard Cowen, Herbert Weis, and Kenneth Docteur as well as undergraduate Steve Carples. They were partners in the research that validated many of the procedures contained in *Tools for Teaching*.

I would also like to thank my daughter, Anne, for her careful proofreading. And I am especially grateful to Virginia Rossi, Dorothy Derge-Elb, Wendy Kent, and my daughter-in-law Monique Jones for keeping the office running during the months of rewriting.

The Study Group Activity Guide

Web Site: www.fredjones.com

In this age of cyberspace, a book can be much more than the pages between a cover. As soon as the book manuscript was completed, we started to write a study guide that would allow teachers to conduct training of the highest quality at their school sites. The resulting *Study Group Activity Guide* is provided for **free** at our web site.

Study Group Activity Guide

The *Study Group Activity Guide* structures twelve 45-minute after school meetings during which teachers master the skills contained in *Tools for Teaching*. Each meeting includes:

- reading assignments with focus questions
- sharing and problem solving
- performance checklists
- skill building activities

Thorough protocols are provided for each skill building exercise. These protocols contain every prompt and clarifying remark used by Dr. Jones during his workshop. Skill building activities include not only the practice of discrete management skills but also simulations of more complex classroom management dilemmas.

In addition, coaching skills are described in detail so that participants can help each other "learn by doing." During peer coaching, teachers employ Say, See, Do Teaching and Praise, Prompt and Leave so that skill practice is safe and comfortable. In addition, a Group Problem Solving Process is provided so that participants can develop strategies for managing difficult problems as they arise.

Parent Edition: Facilitator Handbook

A series of DVDs has been developed to help parents apply the skills of *Tools for Teaching* in the home. The book, *Tools for Teaching,* and the DVDs, *Tools for Teaching: Parent Edition,* serve as primary resources for parent training.

To structure skill training with parents, a *Facilitator's Handbook* has been posted on the web site with handouts for each of 10 meetings. As with the *Study Group Activity Guide,* it is provided free of charge.

Other Web Resources

While Study Group meetings include sharing, the web site also provides opportunities for teachers to share their ideas and experiences with colleagues worldwide. Sections of the web site devoted to sharing include a Preferred Activity Bank, applications of Bell Work, tips for substitute teachers, a message board, and a college report page.

In addition, our web site contains resources for structuring systematic staff development at the school site. Under the heading, "Creating Change In Education," you will find sections on "The Principal's Role" and "Reducing the Risk of Change."

Tools for Teaching Videos

Tools for Teaching: The Video Toolbox

Skill Building

While *Tools for Teaching* describes the skills of classroom management, skill building will be greatly facilitated if teachers can see the skills being modeled. The *Video Toolbox* augments *Tools for Teaching* by giving you a front row seat at one of Dr. Jones' workshops. You will see him explain procedures, model key skills, and demonstrate skill building exercises.

The Video Toolbox

The *Video Toolbox* contains eight DVDs:

- An Overview Disc
- Six Discs containing video for each of the twelve training sessions
- A Coaching Disc

Toolbox Format

The *Video Toolbox* provides the visual modality for each of the twelve training sessions structured in the *Study Group Activity Guide*. In addition to providing trainees with workshop footage of Dr. Jones, the *Video Toolbox* also provides the anticipatory set for each skill so that trainers can focus on the practice exercises.

The *Video Toolbox* also contains an Overview Disc and a Coaching Disc. The **Overview Disc** (enclosed) outlines the entire *Tools for Teaching* program along with workshop highlights and teacher interviews. The **Coaching Disc** models every skill building exercise step-by-step for review by coaches prior to training along with simulation activities for trouble-shooting difficult management situations. In addition, Dr. Jones presents a Group Problem Solving Process that makes bringing classroom problems to the study group a safe and rewarding experience for trainees.

Tools for Teaching: Parent Edition

Title One and Title Two Parents

School districts who are using *Tools for Teaching* in the classroom have requested help with parent training since all Title One and Title Two grants now require a parent outreach component. In pilot work, parents eagerly read *Tools for Teaching* and immediately put the skills to work at home. To augment *Tools for Teaching*, Parent Edition DVDs were developed in which Dr. Jones explains and models key skills prior to coaching parents through skill building exercises. The Parent Edition videos are available in both English and Spanish.

The Parent Edition

The Parent Edition contains three DVDs that focus on those topics that cause parents the most concern:

- **Meaning Business**: How to get your kids to stop doing what you don't want them to do.
- **Teaching Responsibility**: How to get your kids to do what you want them to do when you ask them to do it.
- **Building Values**: How to teach your kids right from wrong.

Research and Development

Validation of Procedures

Research was carried out by Dr. Jones while on the faculties of UCLA and the University of Rochester to validate the main procedures described in *Tools for Teaching*. The following summaries provide a thumbnail sketch of work published in major peer reviewed journals.

Major Findings

Jones, F. H. and Miller, W. G.; The effective use of negative attention for reducing group disruption in special elementary school classrooms. Psychological Record, 1974, 24, 435-448.

As a result of skill training, disruptions decreased by 56% and the ignoring of disruptions dropped by 73.5%. A three month follow-up showed that teachers were still using the skills.

Jones, F. H. and Eimers, R.; Role-playing to train elementary teachers to use a classroom management "skill package." Journal of Applied Behavior Analysis, 1975, 8, 421-433.

Following training, "talking to neighbors" decreased by an average of 73% while "out of seat" decreased by an average of 72%. During the same period, academic productivity during seat work increased 29% for the middle third of the class and 76% for the bottom third of the class.

Jones, F. H., Fremouw, W., and Carples, S.; Pyramid training of elementary school teachers to use a classroom management "skill package." Journal of Applied Behavior Analysis, 1977, 10, 239-253.

Teachers were trained in skills of Limit Setting (Tier 1) and were then coached to train colleagues (Tier 2). For Tier 1 teachers "talking to neighbors" was reduced by 44% – 87% as a result of peer training. "Out of seat" followed a similar pattern with reductions ranging from 50% – 74%. Peer training produced results for the Tier 2 teachers comparable to results obtained for the Tier 1 teachers who had been trained by the authors. In addition, all Tier 1 teachers showed increases in student productivity.

Burka, A. A. and Jones F. H.; Procedures for increasing appropriate verbal participation in special elementary classrooms. Behavior Modification, 1979, 3, 27-48.

Training teachers in basic classroom management skills (Skill Training 1) reduced classroom disruptions during group discussions by 83% and increased appropriate verbal participation (AVP) by 244%. Training teachers in skills of discussion facilitation (Skill Training 2) reduced classroom disruptions by 95% overall while further increasing AVP by 604% overall.

Cowen, R. J., Jones, F. H., and Bellack, A. S.; Grandma's rule with group contingencies, cost-efficient means of classroom management. Behavior Modification, 1979, 3, 397-418.

During small group instruction, students could earn Preferred Activity Time for "on task" behavior. "Talking to neighbors" was reduced by 52% – 80% and "out of seat" was reduced by 72% – 85%. In addition, "off task behavior" was reduced by 41% – 60%

Section One

Building a Classroom Management System

Chapter One

Learning from the "Natural" Teachers

Succeeding in the Classroom

Focus on Teachers

This book is for teachers. I want teachers to enjoy teaching.

I know teachers who thrive in the classroom. They are energized by teaching. I have heard them say, "I can't wait until school starts." These teachers, however, are a distinct minority.

Most teachers are exhausted by the end of the day. Almost a third of new teachers quit by the end of their second year on the job. Many who stay suffer from burn-out.

Most of the stress of teaching comes from getting students to do things. Managing the behavior of young people is no easy job, as any parent can tell you. Managing a whole classroom full of young people is the subject of this book.

Focus on Students

This book is for the students. For students to learn, they must enjoy learning. They must look forward to entering the classroom in the morning.

Some teachers create just such classrooms. They make learning an adventure. There is excitement in the air.

It is no mystery to the parents who these teachers are. They can see how one teacher causes their child to love school while another teacher causes the same child to

Preview

- All of our efforts to improve education come down to the classroom. Whether or not lessons come alive and students learn depends upon the teacher's skill.
- In some fortunate classrooms, both the teacher and the students look forward to getting to school in the morning. This book describes how to produce such classrooms.
- Many of the lessons in this book were learned in the classrooms of gifted or "natural" teachers. As a result, the procedures described are practical and down to earth.
- Natural teachers do not work themselves to death. Instead, they put the students to work.
- Effective management saves you time and effort. As a result, you have more time for learning and enjoyment in the classroom, and more energy after you get home.

complain and fall behind. Parents know that the key to success in the classroom is the teacher.

Focus on Classrooms

All of our efforts to improve education come down to the classroom. National policies and state mandates and district guidelines must be translated into better teaching practices, or they are of no use.

Whether or not lessons come alive and students learn depends upon the teacher's skill. Whether or not the students are even on task depends on the teacher's ability to manage the group.

This book is about classroom management. It is a description of the skills that exceptional teachers use to make classrooms come alive.

Enjoying Teaching

Learning by Doing

Students learn by doing. They like being active. Even more, they like being *interactive.*

Students enjoy learning when the process of instruction engages all of their senses. When the students enjoy learning, teachers enjoy teaching.

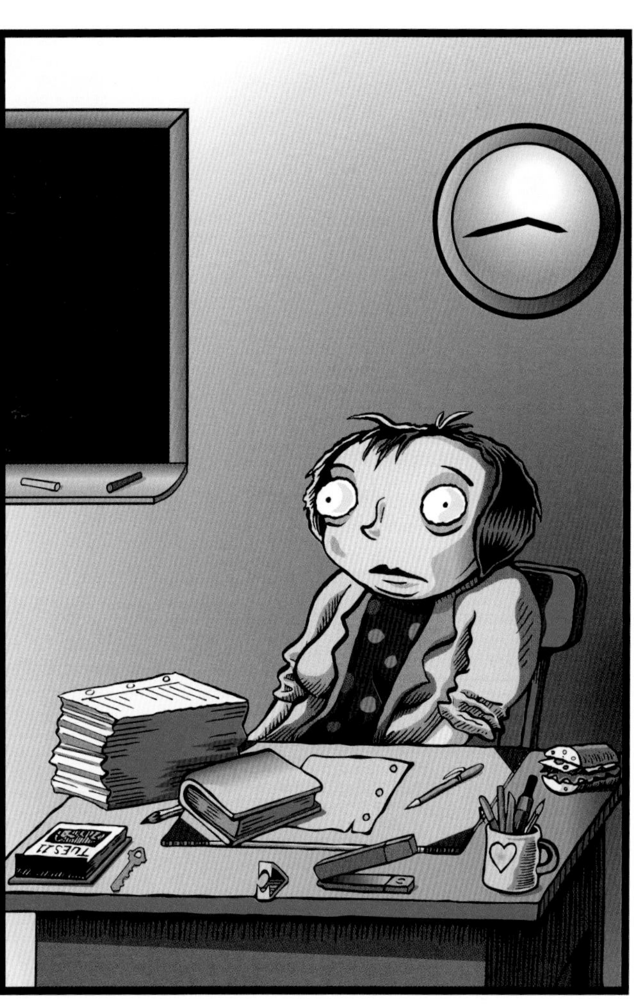

You are on your toes all day long.

Reducing "Goofing Off"

Within the classroom, the main impediment to learning by doing is *not doing*. The many ways of *not doing* are known to us all from experience – whispering to the kid sitting next to us, passing notes, sharpening pencils just to be out of our seats, doodling, dawdling and gazing out the window. We will refer to these pleasures of the flesh collectively as "goofing off."

Teaching a lesson would not be so hard if the students would just pay attention and get to work. It is the *goofing off* that wears you down.

Working Yourself to Death

While trying to deal with goofing off, you have to get the kids to do one thing after another all day long – hand papers in, pass papers out, get into groups, line up, sit down, pay attention, take turns. How about the students who sit helplessly with their hands raised day after day and say, "I don't understand how to do this!"? How about the students who say, "This is stupid!"?

After school you have parent conferences, committee meetings, and paper grading. You are on your toes all day long, and then you keep working into the evening. You can *run yourself ragged.*

But, some of our colleagues find the job *energizing.* These teachers do not work themselves to death. They work *smart,* not hard.

Lessons from Natural Teachers

We Have a Problem

The year was 1969, and I was asked to consult at a private school for emotionally, behaviorally, and learning handicapped junior-high-age students. All of them had been "removed" from the Los Angeles Unified School District. I had just been given a free ticket to the all-star game of classroom goof-offs.

On my first visit, I observed four classrooms, two in the morning and two in the afternoon. The two I observed in the morning were a shock.

As I approached the first classroom, I could hear yelling. As I entered, I saw only empty chairs. I looked to my left and saw, to my amazement, nine kids crouched *on top* of the coat closet staring at me. I thought, "What an unusual lesson format."

Then, a half-dozen other kids poured out of the coat closet. They were armed with items of clothing with which they began pelting the students above. One student leapt from on top of the coat closet to wrestle a classmate to the floor.

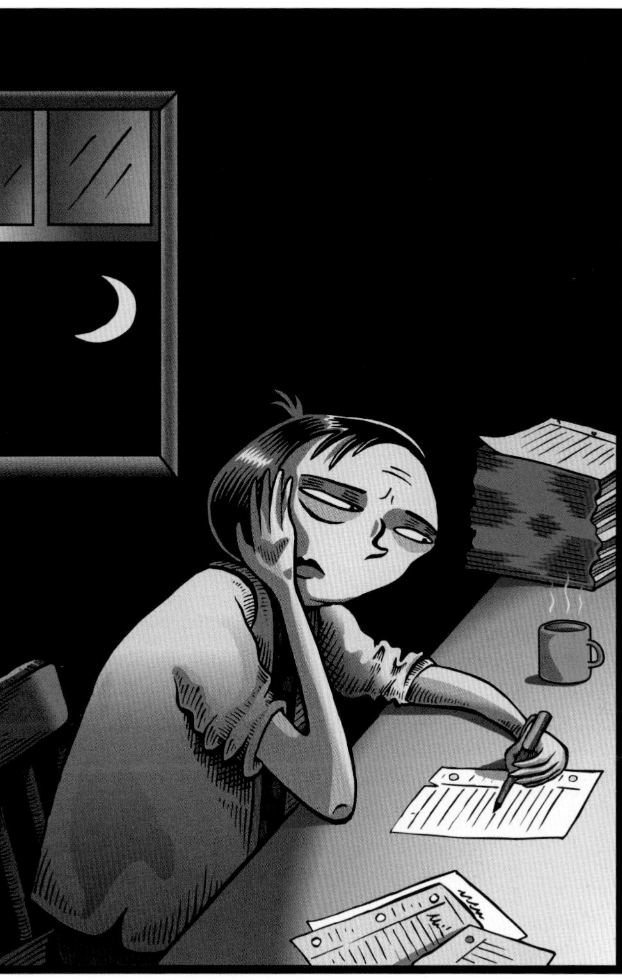

Then, you keep working into the evening.

In front of this scene was a male teacher who was donating his body to the betterment of young people – his stomach lining, his dental work, and his circulatory system – as many of us do. With arms folded, teeth clenched and a look of grim desperation he shouted,

"Group!"

This worried me. I am a clinical psychologist by training, and I had spent years working with groups – group process, group dynamics, group communication, group problem-solving. I didn't see any *group.*

Then, the teacher said,

"I am simply going to *wait* until you *all* settle down!"

I didn't know how long he had been waiting. It was November.

The second classroom I visited that morning was almost as bad. A young female teacher was leading a class discussion. I could tell because everyone was talking. Who do you think was talking louder than any of the students?

> "Class. There is absolutely *no excuse* for all of this noise!... Class!..."

By the end of the morning, I desperately wanted to leave. But, since I had promised, I stuck it out past lunch.

Observing Two "Naturals"

After lunch I watched the students who had been on top of the coat closet enter a new teacher's classroom. The teacher greeted them warmly at the door. The students took their seats as they entered, looked at the chalkboard where an assignment was posted, and went to work.

When the bell to begin class rang, only one or two looked up. The students worked on a math assignment for about ten minutes. Then there was a lesson transition. The teacher said,

> "I want you to place your papers here on the corner of my desk. If you need to sharpen pencils, now is the time to do it. Get a drink of water if you need to, and return to your seats."

I thought, "This is where chaos sets in."

However, the students did as the teacher instructed and were back in their seats ready to go in *41 seconds.* The teacher then conducted a group discussion in which the students *took turns.* Since the faculty at UCLA couldn't do that on the best day of their lives, I was thoroughly impressed. Throughout the class period these students behaved like any well-mannered group of kids.

I might have written this experience off as a fluke had not the second teacher of the afternoon gotten similar results with the refugees from that morning's group discussion. She had her own style, of course, but, with apparent ease, she got respectful behavior and good work.

As far as the management of goofing off is concerned, I observed three characteristics of these teachers that I will never forget.

- They were not working hard at discipline management. In fact, they were not working very hard at all.
- They were relaxed.
- They were emotionally warm.

At the very least, I learned that discipline management did not have to be humorless or stressful or time-consuming. You certainly do not have to wait until December to smile. Rather, these teachers had the simple luxury of enjoying the process of teaching.

How could two classes that were so out of control in one setting look so normal in another setting? I returned to these classrooms for several days hoping to discover the secret. All I saw was two "naturals" making it look easy. I scheduled a meeting on Thursday afternoon to find out how they did it.

They Didn't Have a Clue

These two teachers could not have been more generous in their efforts to help me understand their teaching methods. Unfortunately, they did not help very much.

I said, "How do you get the kids to behave so well?"

They both said, "You have to *mean business.*"

First Impressions of Naturals

- **They were not working hard at discipline management. In fact, they were not working very hard at all.**
- **They were relaxed.**
- **They were emotionally warm.**

I said, "Right! But exactly how do you mean business?"

They said, "On the first day of school the classroom will either belong to *you* or it will belong to *them*. God help you if it belongs to them."

I said, "Right! But how do you do it?"

They said, "Frankly, a lot of it has to do with *expectations*. Their behavior will not exceed your expectations. If you do not expect them to behave and to learn, they won't."

I said, "Right! How do you get them to do that?"

They said, "Well, a lot of it has to do with your *values*. If you value every child as a learner…"

I said, "*Wait!* Give me credit for good values and high expectations. I want to know *what to do*. Imagine that I am a substitute teacher taking over your class tomorrow morning. You obviously have the students in a groove. I don't want to lose it. I'm standing in front of your class. Now, what do I do?"

"Oh, yes," they said. "I see. Hmm. Well, I can tell you this much. You had better mean business."

On that day I learned something remarkable about these natural teachers. They could not tell me what they were doing if their lives depended on it. They had no technology of management. They had *good instincts*.

The last thing in the world that a teacher will ever have is 'extra' time.

The Classroom Through New Eyes

The Behavior Modification Revolution

The reason this private school for the behaviorally "challenged" had called us at UCLA was because we were behavior management hot-shots. At that time we were in the throes of the "behavior modification revolution." We had learned that consequences govern the rate of behavior, and we were setting up management programs to fix all kinds of problems – acting out, social isolation, you name it.

Problems of Cost

I was not impressed with the behavior modification revolution. Perhaps it was because I come from a family of teachers – mother, sister, aunts, cousins. When we get together, it is like a staff development conference.

Growing up in such a family, I learned certain things about the teaching profession without anyone ever having to tell me. Prominent among them were:

- Teachers work twice as hard as the general public will ever imagine.
- The last thing in the world that a teacher will ever have is "extra" time.

I knew from the beginning that if I came up with some hot new classroom management procedure that cost the teacher *time* – for planning or record keeping – I could forget it. For any system of classroom management to be truly helpful, it must *save* time.

The problem with our fancy behavior modification programs was *cost.* We were designing individualized management programs. Each program required planning conferences, data collection, specialized contingencies, and constant monitoring.

The good news was that these programs worked. The bad news was that they cost an arm and a leg. I once calculated that implementation of one of my "B-Mod" programs consumed about 20 minutes of the teacher's time each day. There goes the planning period. And the teacher had at least a dozen other problems in the class that were just as serious.

Management At No Cost

Suddenly I was looking at teachers who could get the students – all of them – to shape up and do what was expected at *no* cost. There were no formal behavior management programs, no stressful confrontations, and very little energy spent in getting kids to do things. They made it look easy.

I had to find out what was going on. If the naturals couldn't give me specifics, I would find out myself. I would study classrooms until I understood them. I would compare typical teachers with the naturals until I could explain the difference. I had just begun a new career.

A Hard Look at Reality

Typical Classrooms

Tools for Teaching is based on thousands of hours of classroom observation, state of the art research, and hundreds of mini-experiments in which procedures were tested and fine-tuned by teachers in the field. Let me telescope these observations in order to pinpoint where teachers typically have the most difficulty.

- **Squandered Time**: A typical class period is not on task until 5-7 minutes after the bell rings. It is called "settling in." Students hand in their homework, sharpen pencils, and get out their materials as the teacher takes roll.

  A lesson transition averages about 5 minutes in length. Students move desks, get into groups, shuffle papers, and sharpen pencils. It is break time for the students, and they are in no hurry to get back to work.

  In a 50 minute class period, settling in and one lesson transition will consume a minimum of 10 minutes – 20% of learning time. If the teacher has 2 lesson tran-

Eighty percent of the goofing off in any classroom is "talking to neighbors."

sitions, coming and going will consume 30% of learning time.

- **Passivity**: As the teacher presents the lesson, the students sit. Perhaps, they pay attention and take notes – or not. At the secondary level lesson presentation often takes 20-30 minutes. This pattern is becoming more common at the elementary level.

  Apart from being exhausting for the teacher, this pattern of "teacher active, students passive" maximizes cognitive overload to say nothing of the students' restlessness and inattention. Goofing off in the back of the room is rampant.

- **Goofing Off**: After the lesson presentation when the students are supposed to "work independently on today's lesson," a common pattern emerges. A handful of students sit with arms waving in the air waiting for help. They are the same students every day – the *helpless handraisers*.

  The teacher services the helpless handraisers one at a time by tutoring them through the lesson that was just presented to the group. These tutoring interactions average four and a half minutes in duration with a range of 3-8 minutes.

  When the teacher begins tutoring, they lose the class. In five seconds goofing off ignites. In ten seconds it spreads throughout the classroom. Eighty percent of goofing off is "talking to neighbors." Fifteen percent of goofing off is "out of seat."

> **The most widespread management procedure in real classrooms is nag, nag, nag.**

The overall picture that emerges is one of massive time-wasting. Rather than being "out of control," the typical classroom is simply *inefficient* due to dawdling, passivity, and *goofing off.* Goofing off kills more learning time and generates more teacher stress than all of the "serious" disruptions that are the subject of the school discipline code.

Most of the teachers' exhaustion, apart from doing six matinees a day, comes from dealing with the *frequent, small* disruptions that characterize goofing off. It has a familiar sound.

Nag, Nag, Nag

Have you ever heard teachers use the following words when dealing with everyday student misbehavior?

"All right class, there is absolutely *no excuse* for all of this *talking!* When I look up, I expect to see people *working!* There is an assignment on the board, and we have ten minutes until the bell rings, so let's get something *done!*"

or

"Where are you going? Would you please *take your seat?* I am sick and tired of looking up only to see you wandering aimlessly around the room!"

or

"What are you *playing with?* Let me have that! You may have this back at the end of the period. Right now, would you please turn around in your seat, put your feet on the floor, and get to work?"

I have just given three examples of the most widespread behavior management procedure in education – *Nag, nag, nag.* No job is more perfectly suited to making a *nag* out of an idealistic young person than trying to get a room full of kids to do one thing after another all day long.

No one wants to nag. Rather, it creeps up on you.

The Stages We All Go Through

If *talking to neighbors* will be your most common classroom disruption, the logical question of classroom management is, "*What are you going to do about it?*" Answering this question over and over all day long is something we were not prepared to do when we entered the teaching profession. Instead, we must figure out for ourselves.

We all progress through the same learning curve. It is one of the main reasons that our first year of teaching is so exhausting. We pass through four predictable stages.

Stage 1: As Green as Grass

Imagine that it is the first day of your teaching career. As the saying goes, you are *as green as grass.*

It is the undying hope of the green teacher that if you just love your students and are nice to them, they will be nice to you and everything will turn out fine. This is the sweet dream of the uninitiated. It will get a smile from your more experienced colleagues.

You are, however, crystal clear about what you are *not* going to do.

> "I am not going to *nag* my students. I *hate it* when teachers do that!"

Thus, with a smile on your face and love in your heart, the ball game begins. Five minutes into the first lesson you look up to see two kids on the far side of the room *talking* instead of paying attention. Can you *believe* it?

Green teachers, not wanting to nag, say to themselves:

> "I'll just ignore that problem for now. Maybe the students will get back to work."

You may even remember the words of some professor who extolled the use of *extinction* in the classroom.

> "Ignore the problem behavior while it is occurring and systematically reinforce competing appropriate behavior as soon as it occurs. *Catch them being good.*"

So you ignore the talking for the moment. The students, naturally, keep talking. Unfortunately, the rest of the class can see this, and they can certainly see that you are doing nothing about it. Not surprisingly, they conclude, "*If they can talk, so can I.*"

Soon the noise level rises. Suddenly two students are out of their seats and wandering around the room.

You are losing control of the class! You say to yourself, "*I have to do something!*" We will refer to this realization as *losing your innocence.*

But do what? In all of your teacher training you were never prepared for this moment.

Stage 2: Do Something!

You bag extinction. You swing into action. You stand, turn toward the offending students and say their names.

> "Tyrone. Roberta."

They respond with that familiar look of mild surprise and total innocence. We will call it "smiley face." Green teachers often mistake smiley face for repentance.

You watch and wait, looking your most serious. Tyrone and Roberta seem to get back to work. You return to helping your student. What do you think Tyrone and Roberta will be doing ten seconds from now?

If you say their names *again*, you may be able to observe the various stages of *pseudo-compliance* – the basic "fake-out moves" that all students master. In order, they are:

- **Smiley face:** They give you the look of the repentant angel, as if asking, "*Who, me?*"
- **Book posing:** They open their books and look back at you as though to ask, "*Does this fulfill the requirements of formal education?*"
- **Pencil posing:** They get out a pencil and touch it to paper before looking back at you as though to say, "*Look, I'm writing.*"
- **Pseudo-scholarship:** They start to write with furrowed brow, but look up periodically to see if you are still tracking their behavior.

It certainly looks like compliance from where you stand. But when you turn away from the disruptors, Tyrone and Roberta resume their conversation.

How many times will you endure pseudo-compliance before it finally gets under your skin? When you find yourself getting *upset* by the disruption on the far side of the room, you have entered phase three of your apprenticeship: *Sick and Tired!*

Stage 3: Sick and Tired

The students know when you have finally become *sick and tired*. That is when the *serious* nagging begins.

You turn with a look of grim determination. You put your hands on your hips, grit your teeth, cock your head forward, raise an eyebrow, and draw in a breath before saying the students' names – but with an *edge* on your voice:

"Tyrone! Roberta!"

It sounds as though something *heavy* is finally coming down. But what? You still have no clear strategy.

When forced to say *something* when we really don't know what to say, we are very likely to engage in a unique form of nagging known as *silly talk*. The following examples recount some of the silly things that teachers say in the heat of the moment.

"Roberta, what are you supposed to be doing?" (Students know what they are supposed to be doing.)

"Roberta, this is the second time I've had to talk to you." (They are keeping count.)

"Roberta, am I going to have to come over there?" (They know you don't want to.)

Once again the students' conversation resumes as soon as you turn away. How long must you put up with this foolishness before *enough is enough?* This brings you to phase four: *Laying Down the Law!*

Stage 4: Laying Down the Law

You stand slowly, square up with your best *sick and tired* look and march over to Tyrone and Roberta. It is time to deal with this nonsense *once and for all.* In so doing, you pull half of the class off task as all eyes follow you. After you arrive, you get to have a *silly conversation.*

"I am sick and tired of looking up to see nothing but talking over here."

"Okay."

"I expect to see some work being done on these papers. Do you understand?"

"Okay."

"And, when I come back over here, I want to see something accomplished."

"Okay."

"All right then."

Having taken a firm stand for all that is right and good, you trudge back across the classroom with all eyes following. With one last sick and tired look at Tyrone and Roberta, you resume helping the poor student who has been patiently waiting. What do you think Tyrone and Roberta will be doing in twenty seconds?

How long must you put up with this foolishness before "enough is enough"?

Getting Nowhere

Right Back Where You Started

When you look up to see Tyrone and Roberta talking again, it will no doubt dawn on you that *you are right back where you started.* After you repeat this melodrama several times, you may eventually "throw in the towel." Two basic patterns emerge:

- **Save the trip and just nag**: There is a certain logic to support this move. If you are going to fail, fail cheap. The trip across the room is a lot of work for nothing. No doubt this is why nagging is the most widespread discipline management technique in education.
- **Give up**: When a teacher finally decides to just give up, they usually announce it in the teachers' lounge with a self-justifying pronouncement. I will call it the "Policeman Speech."

  "I did not go into teaching to be a *policeman.* I am not going to spend all of my time and energy dealing with one little disruption after another all day long. I will certainly deal with situations in which a student is way out of line, but I am *not* going to stop my lesson every thirty seconds for chit-chat on the far side of the room. Blah, blah, blah."

Both of these responses belong to well-intentioned teachers who have been defeated. They have finally accepted the fact that they cannot win.

Look at the cost-benefit ratio. It costs you an arm and a leg to stop what you are doing and deal with each example of "goofing off." The students, on the other hand, have only to face forward in their seats *temporarily* in order to be in compliance. It is hard for you and easy for them.

Waiting You Out

If you think that you can bring "law and order" to the frontier by chasing each little bandit all over the territory, let me remind you of some realities that might bring a note of sobriety to your calculations.

- There are many of them, and only one of you.
- You are older, and you tire more easily.
- They send in "fresh troops" every year.

Being calculating by nature, students know that you will wear out before they do. Some students even seem to be entertained by watching it happen.

Any time that you are working harder at discipline management than the students, you will eventually lose. They simply will wait you out and then resume their normal classroom social life.

Dying by Inches

Going through the four stages of the learning curve like previous generations of teachers will cause you to get old and tired before your time. You are not only working too hard, but you are also dying by inches.

When you are dying, it is sort of interesting to see how close you are to being dead. Inquiring minds want to know. The following stages represent a well-worn path from frustration to "throwing in the towel."

Exhaustion – You are constantly dealing with discipline.

Futility – It doesn't get any better no matter how hard you try.

Cynicism – You can't do anything with these kids.

Resentment – It finally becomes them against you.

Rationalization – Here come the self-justifications.

- It's just the way kids are at this age (i.e., the hormone hypothesis favored by junior high teachers).
- It's the homes these kids come from.
- It's the television and the video games. They have the attention span of gnats.
- I don't really have any *major* problems.
- The noise doesn't really bother me *that* much.
- It's *my* job to teach. It's *their* job to learn.

Stress Management

Teaching is a stressful job. So, part of the job is managing stress. The naturals experience a *minimum* of stress. Most of their colleagues are exhausted at the end of the day.

The bottom line in stress management is simple. You have to manage stress moment by moment, class period by class period *on the job.* You cannot allow yourself to be stressed all day long and then somehow undo it once you get home.

You can try. The usual candidates are, 1) rest – lots of luck if you have kids, 2) exercise – lots if luck if you have kids, and 3) a glass of Chardonnay. But, the damage has already been done.

We have to get smart like the naturals instead of working ourselves to death. There has to be an easier way to do this job – one that is better for *us* and better for the *kids.*

Chapter Two

Focusing on Prevention

Classroom Management Is Complicated

Getting Things Done

Classroom management is the business of getting kids to do what you want them to do. If the teacher is good at it, a lot gets done and kids enjoy coming to class. If the teacher is not so good at it, kid's goof off and waste a lot of time while the teacher becomes stressed. When the teacher becomes stressed, nobody has a good time.

A Real Challenge

Teachers and parents constantly deal with the same issues. How do you get kids to *do* what you want them to do when you ask them to do it. How do you get kids to *stop doing* what you don't want them to do? How do you get kids to cooperate? How do you get them to be nice to each other? How do you teach them to address you respectfully without argument or backtalk?

I will ask workshop participants, "How many of you are parents?" Most hands will go up. I will then ask, "Is being a parent an easy job?"

The response is a mixture of laughter and groans. Everybody knows that being a parent is one of the most challenging jobs on earth. It takes all of the intelligence and energy that you can muster. It takes never ending love and patience even when you are exhausted. It is all day, every day.

Can you think of anything more challenging than being a good *parent*? I can.

Preview

- This chapter is an overview of the topics described in the book.
- This book focuses on the fundamental skills of classroom management. These skills replace working hard with working smart.
- Instructional practices focus on making learning interactive while replacing helpless handraising with independent learning.
- The management of motivation focuses on helping students to internalize values of hard work and conscientiousness. Incentives for productivity combine enjoyment with accountability.
- Discipline management focuses on 1) making cooperation and responsible behavior a matter of routine, and 2) setting limits in a nonadversarial fashion through mobility, proximity, and the body language of meaning business.

Managing a Classroom Is Harder Than Parenting

Being a parent is a *piece of cake* compared to managing a classroom. For one thing, you have years to love your own children and teach them to be good kids.

That is a luxury you do not have in the classroom. In the classroom you have *other people's* kids. These "other people" will send you a room full of youngsters whose personality traits range from exemplary to highly inappropriate.

Some parents teach their children that *no means no*, but not all of them do. Some parents teach their children that *if a job is worth doing, it's worth doing right*, but not all of them do. Rather, some people raise kids who *don't* make their beds, *don't* clean their rooms, *don't* set the table, and *don't* pick up their clothes.

It's not that these parents don't *want* their kids to be responsible and well behaved. They are doing the best they can, but they don't know how to get results. They lack the necessary skills.

So, they make a lot of "rookie errors" as their kids are growing up. They are inconsistent when they attempt to say "no" to misbehavior. They nag instead of teach. They tell their kids to do something but don't follow through to make sure that it gets done. Attempts to get cooperation get an argument instead.

Over time these kids often learn to avoid work by being contrary. They master procrastination, heel dragging and, their favorite – doing a job so sloppily that parents finally throw up their hands and say, "You know, it's just easier to do it *myself!*"

These kids will show up to your class on the first day of school. You will then ask them to do more work in *one day* than they do at home in a *month*. And you will want it:

- finished on time
- done correctly
- written legibly
- with a good attitude.

Lots of luck!

In every classroom you start out with a motley crew.

A Motley Crew

Add to this the usual assortment of characters that show up to any classroom on the first day of school – a handful of helpless handraisers, a couple of kids who can't stop talking, a bully, a social isolate, several students with learning disabilities, and one who is hyperactive. Even with a lot of good kids, you start out with a motley crew.

To this motley crew you do not just teach curriculum. You teach civilization. You teach your students to follow rules, to be responsible, to get along with each other, to show respect, and to value achievement through hard work.

Making Up for Lost Time

In many cases you have to make up for lost time. You have to train kids to cooperate who are quite uncooperative at home. You have to train kids to be respectful who backtalk their parents. And, you have to do it quickly. The longer it takes you to make up for lost time, the more stress your body will absorb.

How will you succeed – by "winging it" like their parents did? Are you kidding? You will need some serious, high-tech, industrial-strength classroom management skills.

The Management of Goofing Off

Focusing on Discipline

Tools for Teaching began with the observation of natural teachers who could make good students out of kids who were jumping off of the furniture in other classrooms. From the beginning, therefore, our understanding of classroom management focused on discipline.

While students jumping off of furniture is obviously extreme, extensive observations of regular classrooms showed this to be simply an exaggerated version of the norm. In classrooms goofing off is the eternal enemy of time-on-task.

In the classroom life of children, goofing off is a given. Kids naturally talk. They don't naturally study. Managing a classroom requires that you replace the normal social life of young people with rigorous work for hours on end.

Every teacher, therefore, is a "disciplinarian" by necessity. Any classroom has the potential to be a problem classroom. Whether the class develops its full potential depends on how it is managed.

Avoiding Exhaustion

As we well know, getting a roomful of young people to quit goofing off long enough to get some work done can be a prescription for exhaustion. The number of teachers who attend burn-out workshops would indicate that we have a lot to learn about "cost containment" in the management of discipline.

Yet, the natural teachers that we observed made it look easy. They were spending very little time and energy dealing with disruptions. Rather, their time and energy went into teaching – the fun part of the job. How could they get so much good behavior and time-on-task out of so many highly disruptive students while remaining calm, cool, and collected?

"There is an easy way to do everything," as the saying goes. Apparently, these natural teachers had found it. They could not explain it, and I could not see it, but knowing that it was possible kept us going.

If there is a concern that pervades *Tools for Teaching*, it is *exhaustion* – *your* exhaustion. How do you teach a classroom all day long, day after day, without working yourself to death? It's not obvious, but it *is* possible.

Research and Development

Useful Procedures

There is a huge literature on classroom management and discipline. Over the years, I have thrown out almost all of it.

The problem was not that the procedures didn't work. The problem was that they were *impractical.* They cost the teacher too much in terms of time and energy.

Time and energy are *finite.* All of the time and energy that goes *into* discipline management comes *out of* instruction.

My objective was not to saddle the teacher with expensive management programs. My objective was to drive the cost of discipline management as close to *zero* as possible.

A Useful Procedure Must Produce:

- **Better behavior**
- **More learning**
- **Less hassle for the teacher**

Along the way I threw out most of my own ideas too. To be kept, a procedure had to meet three simple criteria:

- Better behavior
- More learning
- Less hassle for the teacher

Believe the Teacher

At this point I was aided by my coming from a family of teachers – a collection of parents, aunts and *great* aunts who were quite sure of themselves. I naturally assumed from early childhood, therefore, that if a teacher told you that something was *so*, it was *so.*

Consequently, in years of working with teachers, rather than telling them what *should* work, I let them tell me what *did* work. We would get together after the kids went home to go over that day's "trial and error." If something did not work or was impractical, the teachers would tell me so in no uncertain terms. They might say, "It's all well and good Dr. Jones, but I don't have time during the day to fool around with all of that record keeping." If that was the verdict, I accepted it and went back to the drawing board.

At least I had the sense not to tell experienced teachers that they should "go the extra mile" for my sake or for the kids' sake. They were already going the extra mile and then some. Rather, I knew from the naturals that running yourself ragged was not the answer.

A Long Journey

While "goofing off" was our initial focus, you cannot get very far with classroom discipline without understanding instruction and motivation. And while we learned a lot through trial and error, entire areas of management had to be constructed from scratch.

How, for example, do you teach an entire class to be responsible? Parents scratch their heads over how to teach a single child to be responsible. But an entire class – the whole motley crew? And how do you do it *fast?* You don't have a decade to create a responsible ten-year-old. You need responsible behavior *now.*

While the natural teachers gave us our start, I never met a teacher who was using more than a portion of the skills described in *Tools for Teaching* prior to training. When you do it all, you will have amazing power.

A Profile of Classroom Management

The Classroom Through New Eyes

After about 15 years the pieces of *Tools for Teaching* began to coalesce into a unified picture. The pieces of the classroom management puzzle fall into three broad areas:

- **Instruction** – maximizing the rate of learning while making independent learners out of helpless handraisers
- **Discipline** – getting students to quit goofing off and get busy
- **Motivation** – giving students a reason to work hard while being conscientious

The natural enemy of working the crowd is the helpless handraiser.

Although guided by theory, the "how to" of classroom management was perfected by trial and error in the field. Years of trial and error have produced a management program with the following characteristics:

- **Specificity** – *Tools for Teaching* deals with specifics rather than generalities. It answers the question, "What do I *do?*" by walking you through each procedure step-by-step. In addition, the Study Group Activity Guide gives you detailed protocols for practicing each skill.
- **Economy** – The procedures in this book have one characteristic in common – they produce dramatic results while *reducing* the teacher's workload. For example, constant Limit Setting is replaced by Meaning Business, and individualized behavioral programs are replaced by a single program that trains the *entire class* to be responsible.
- **Prevention** – In making management affordable, "An ounce of prevention is worth a pound of cure." *Tools for Teaching*, therefore, is primarily about prevention. Prevention encompasses every aspect of classroom life – discipline, instruction, and motivation – and redefines each one. Prevention, therefore, functions as our unifying theme and provides *Tools for Teaching* with its unique perspective.

To give you an overview of *Tools for Teaching*, I will summarize each of the three major areas of classroom management – discipline, instruction, and motivation. Consider it an advance organizer.

Instruction

Working the Crowd

The easiest way to prevent goofing off is *location*. When students are *near* the teacher, they tend to be on their best behavior.

Effective teachers make an art form out of *working the crowd* – otherwise known as "management by walking around." Rather than spending all of their time in the front of the classroom, they put the students to work and walk among the students as they supervise.

To make working the crowd as easy as possible, we will have to rearrange the furniture in the classroom. The optimal room arrangement allows you to get from any student to any other student in the fewest steps.

Helpless Handraisers

Once teachers focus on working the crowd, they immediately confront the natural enemy of working the crowd – the *helpless handraisers*. Every classroom seems to have five or six helpless handraisers who constantly demand the teacher's undivided time and attention – especially during Guided Practice.

During Guided Practice, the teacher tutors each helpless handraiser – a process that takes an average of four-and-a-half minutes. Unfortunately, the teacher pays a very high price for tutoring these needy students. In *ten seconds* the classroom becomes noisy. For the sake of tutoring, the teacher loses control of the class.

In addition, the teacher's time and attention reinforce help-seeking itself. For this reason, helpless handraising becomes chronic for the five or six most needy students. Their dependency is inadvertently shaped into a learning disability.

To keep the class from being rowdy during Guided Practice, the teacher must make independent learners out of their helpless handraisers. Achieving this will impact every aspect of instruction.

- **The Verbal Modality:** How, exactly, do you help a student who is stuck? It must be brief or the teacher will lose the benefits of working the crowd.

  Corrective feedback must be reduced to a simple prompt that answers the question, "What do I do next?" This pattern of giving corrective feedback is called "Praise, Prompt, and Leave." Praise, Prompt, and Leave reduces the average duration of corrective feedback from four-and-a-half minutes to thirty seconds.

- **The Visual Modality:** A helping interaction of thirty seconds is brief but not brief enough. The teacher will lose the class in ten seconds.

  The only way to reduce the duration of corrective feedback further is to *substitute pictures for words.* Good graphics provide the students with a picture for each step of performance. This *set of plans,* called a Visual Instructional Plan (VIP), prepackages the information normally contained in the teacher's explanations.

  The teacher can now give corrective feedback by pointing out a critical feature of one of the steps in

If working the crowd is to have a chance, we must free the helpless handraisers from their dependency on the teacher.

the VIP. This will reduce the duration of helping interactions to 5-10 seconds.

In addition, a VIP is the crucial "halfway house" in weaning the helpless handraisers. Needy students learn that, if they want the teacher's attention, they must produce some work. For help with the assignment, they must rely on the VIP. The students refer to the VIP as often as necessary until they gain confidence and no longer need it.

- **The Physical Modality:** Efficient verbal and visual prompts will only take us halfway to our goal of creating independent learners. The most direct way of minimizing the need for corrective feedback *after* the lesson is to teach the lesson correctly in the first place.

  We learn by doing. Effective teaching, therefore, must exploit the physical modality. Making learning physical has much to do with the *packaging* of student activity.

  There are two basic ways to package the activity of learning. The first is:

  Input, Input, Input, Input – ***Output***

  This characterizes most teaching, especially at the secondary level. The second pattern is:

  Input, **Output**, *Input,* **Output**, *Input,* **Output**

  With the second pattern, output is immediate which eliminates most problems of forgetting. In addition, it is fast moving and interactive, which maximizes student involvement.

As you can see, the prevention of discipline problems reconfigures the process of instruction. Effective teachers structure the lesson as *Input,* **Output**, *Input,* **Output**, *Input,* **Output.** The students are active rather than passive, and teachers continually monitor and adjust the students' performance as they work the crowd.

What separates the natural teachers from their colleagues is *not* the curriculum. The difference is in *process* – the *organization* of learning activity. Naturals focus on the building of correct performance, whether it is the mastery of a skill or the expression of a concept.

Discipline

Consequences and Cost

When a problem occurs, there must, of course, be consequences. Therefore, the traditional wisdom of discipline management focuses upon consequences. But consequences can be extremely *expensive.* The appearance of success is often an illusion.

For example, imagine that a student in your class pulls some stunt, and you deal with it. As a result of your intervention, you do not see that behavior for the rest of the day. Would you conclude that what you did was effective? Most teachers would.

But suppose that the same student does the same thing tomorrow and you respond in the same way with the same result. Once again, the student does not repeat the problem behavior for the rest of the day. Would you conclude that your technique had worked for a second time? Most teachers would.

But suppose that the same student pulls the same stunt for the third day in a row, and you respond in the same way with the same result. Are you having doubts yet?

Meaning Business

In addition to solving a problem, consequences need to be cheap. With our natural teachers, when a student got out of line, a simple look put an end to the problem. That was *cheap!* How did they do that?

Rather than using traditional consequences, our natural teachers simply "meant business." It was so subtle that, for a long time, we could not even see it.

When we finally cracked the code, we realized that Meaning Business was a combination of *calm, commitment,* and utter *consistency* that taught the students that "no" *always* means "no" and that consequences would *always* be delivered.

Once this understanding was established, the teacher could signal the students to "cool it" using progressively smaller cues until a word, a look, a pause, or ultimately, the teacher's mere presence was enough to enforce limits. Rather than providing consequences, the teacher *became* the consequence. When the teacher walked into the classroom, the management program arrived.

This made perfect sense to me. My mother and father meant business. I knew that look. I knew from an early age that "no meant no" and that, while we could always talk something over, arguing was not an option.

Meaning Business is conveyed to the students primarily through the teacher's body language. The students read you like a book. They know what they can get away with and how far they can push you at any moment.

When learning to mean business, you will learn to read and speak a new language – body language. You will have to practice until you are good at it. Providing practice to mastery is the purpose of the Study Group Activity Guide.

Responsibility Training

Getting students to stop doing what you don't want them to do is only half of discipline management. The other half is getting students to do what you want them to do *the first time you ask.*

How do you train students to be responsible? The management system that achieves this goal is called Responsibility Training. Responsibility Training represents a significant advance in technology and a great economy for the teacher because it trains the *entire class* to be responsible for very little effort. It can save large amounts of learning time by simply eliminating dawdling.

Omission Training

Unfortunately, there is usually at least one student in any class who will ruin any group management program just to prove that he or she can. How do you succeed with the highly alienated and oppositional student?

Responsibility Training can save huge amounts of learning time by eliminating dawdling.

Omission Training is a specialized incentive system for dealing with these alienated and oppositional students. It can be added to Responsibility Training at almost no cost to the teacher.

Omission Training provides a powerful reason for the alienated student to work *with* the group rather than *against* the group. As a by-product, these alienated students, who are often highly unpopular, are rapidly accepted into the peer group.

Omission Training is your response of choice for extremely difficult students. It is a win-win solution to a management dilemma that often appears to have no solution. It will eliminate most of your office referrals.

The Backup System

In discipline management, when push comes to shove, there is the School Discipline Code – the teacher's Backup System. While necessary, the Backup System is also extremely expensive. At the very least it requires the involvement of both teachers and administrators. Incident reports and meetings with parents after school run up the price even more.

While aggressive or dangerous behavior may require the use of the Backup System, in practice most office referrals are for repeated goofing off and insolence that finally has teachers "at their wit's end."

For teachers who are at their wit's end, the office offers only respite, not remedy. The same teachers will send the same students to the office all year long.

For the vast majority of office referrals, the only effective remedy is effective classroom management. It is therefore cost-effective for administrators to invest in training the faculty in *Tools for Teaching.* Only by reducing the steady stream of office referrals can administrators finally devote their time to instructional leadership.

A Criterion for Success

To help clarify success and failure in providing consequences, we need a *criterion of success.* Here is a simple, down to earth criterion:

If a procedure is working,
the problem should go away.

While this criterion may seem stringent, it is the only price a teacher can afford to pay in the long run. The alternative is to manage the same problems from the same students using the same consequences all year long.

The more you use an *effective* procedure, the *less* you should need to use it. For example, Meaning Business begins with setting limits and providing consequences, but eventually your mere presence enforces your rules.

Consequently, as the school year progresses, discipline management should take up less and less of your time until you finally work yourself out of a job. Eventually, your time and energy can be devoted to instruction without interruption. Hence, our maxim:

Any discipline management technique that is working
should self-eliminate.

Motivation

Why Should I?

Students who do not care about the lesson can be just as frustrating to the teacher as students who disrupt or constantly seek help. These are the students who say:

"Do we have to do this?"

"This stuff is dumb."

Before an unmotivated student will work hard, the teacher must answer one simple question, "Why should I?" The answer to that question is known as an *incentive.* Any classroom teacher will have to know a thing or two about the design of incentive systems.

Building a Work Ethic

Some students have internalized standards that motivate them to work hard and to be conscientious. However, many, if not most, of our students do not.

How do you train students to be hard working and conscientious? For starters, they will have to have something to work for – something they want – something in the not too distant future. Call it a *preferred activity.*

But for students to learn to be conscientious, you must be able to check their work *as it is being done.* Only then can you hold them to high standards. Otherwise, they learn to do quick, sloppy work in order to finish the assignment as quickly as possible.

How can you be free to check students' work while it is being done? First, you must wean the helpless handraisers who monopolize your time during Guided Practice so you can devote your time to checking work.

Once you can check work while it is being done, you can then provide a Criterion of Mastery for students to meet in order to be done with the assignment. When they meet your Criterion of Mastery, you can excuse them to do their preferred activities.

In order for you to build a work ethic in your students, you must become a provider of preferred activities. You *must* have fun in the classroom. As teachers learn during training: *no joy, no work.*

Tools for Teaching Is a System

Basic Characteristics of a System

To begin with, "system" has to be one of the most overused words in education. *Everything* is a system. So, for clarity's sake, let's describe what we mean by a *system.*

- It gives you the pieces you need.
- The pieces fit together like a puzzle.
- The whole is greater than the sum of its parts.

Tools for Teaching is a system – a comprehensive system of classroom management. It began in classrooms where students were jumping off of furniture and evolved over time to include discipline, instruction, and motivation.

Our objective has always been shaped by that first experience – a desire to replace goofing off with time-on-task. It is not surprising, therefore, that the most practical way to organize *Tools for Teaching* is in terms of discipline.

Areas of Discipline Management

- Classroom Structure
- Limit Setting
- Responsibility Training
- The Backup System

Discipline management can best be organized under four major headings beginning with prevention and ending with the management of severe behavior problems. The four areas of discipline management are as follows:

1. **Classroom Structure** (i.e. Prevention)
    - Room arrangement and working the crowd
    - All of instruction
    - All of motivation
    - Classroom rules, routines, and standards
    - Procedures for the first day and week of school
2. **Limit Setting** (i.e. Meaning Business)
3. **Responsibility Training**
4. **The Backup System**

In this schema prevention plays the dominant role. Prevention brings the process of instruction front and center. As the system unfolds, most of the hallowed objectives of teaching – independent learning, the integration of modalities, high standards, learning to be responsible – are brought within the teacher's grasp.

As you read *Tools for Teaching,* your cognitive map of classroom management will develop. As it does, you will realize that there is no "big answer," no "silver bullet" for "shaping kids up." Rather, there are many skills. The more of them you master, the better your life in the classroom will be.

Nor is there a "bag of tricks" through which to rummage when in need of an answer. Rather, there is systematic problem solving. Here's how it works.

Keep It Cheap

A room full of students can keep the teacher in high gear all day long. To avoid exhaustion, discipline management has to be *cheap.* Here are some of the characteristics of the management system that define cost:

- Classroom Structure is *cheaper* than Limit Setting.
- Limit Setting is *cheaper* than Responsibility Training.
- Responsibility Training is *cheaper* than the Backup System.

Here is a criterion to use when choosing a procedure:

Always use the cheapest remedy.

Choose the procedure that is the least work, requires the least planning, and, hopefully, requires no paperwork. When solving a problem, therefore, always begin with Classroom Structure because prevention is always cheaper than remediation. If the problem is not yet eliminated, go to Limit Setting. If the problem is still not eliminated, go to Responsibility Training and then to the Backup System.

Management Is Cumulative

Another characteristic of the system is that it is cumulative. Each procedure is built upon a foundation of management provided by the system. The foundation must be in place for any procedure to work properly. The system functions as follows:

- The Backup System is *built upon* Responsibility Training.
- Responsibility Training is *built upon* Limit Setting.
- Limit Setting is *built upon* Classroom Structure.

To take a simple example, if you do not train the class to walk quietly through the halls during the first week of school, you will have to set limits on the noise they make during the second week of school.

And, since the system is cumulative, you can't try procedures in any order just because they look interesting. Responsibility Training, for example, may look like a wonder cure, but it needs Classroom Structure and Limit Setting in order to succeed.

Focusing on Fundamentals

Tools for Teaching describes the fundamentals of classroom management. Fundamentals are basic to everything you do, and they never change.

Take Meaning Business as an example. It is conveyed primarily through body language, and the human race has only one body language. You can either master it in order to create learning, or you can spend your career one step behind the students who read you like a book.

Working the crowd is another example. The biggest single variable that governs the likelihood of students goofing off in your class is their physical distance from your body. You can either exploit mobility and proximity to create time-on-task, or you can pay the price.

Teaching in small chunks with immediate performance and feedback (*Input, Output – Input, Output*) is another example. If you teach to the brain the way it is built, learning will be relatively rapid and errors relatively infrequent.

Mastery of the fundamentals also allows you to adapt to the unpredictable. Without that mastery, you are constantly forced to scramble in order to solve problems in the heat of the moment. *That* is hard work.

Some of our most typical feedback from teachers is:

"I have energy at the end of the day. I have a life after school."

It is the undying hope of green teachers that, if they love their students and are nice to them, everything will turn out fine.

"I have recouped the time that the students used to waste. I now have time for the enrichment activities and learning games that students love."

"Why didn't I get this twenty years ago?"

Paradigm Shifts

A paradigm shift is a change in your entire frame of reference for analyzing a problem and its solution. A paradigm shift can be hard to wrap your mind around.

Tools for Teaching is a long series of paradigm shifts. But, they are gentle and sensible shifts. You won't have to fight them. In fact, they often affirm the solutions to classroom management problems that you have developed on your own over the years. As workshop participants often say at the end of three days:

"Dr. Jones, it's just a big collection of common sense."

Discipline Dreams

"It's Simple"

When teachers and administrators begin their training in discipline management, they are usually looking for "the answer." They say things like:

"What is the key to your program?"

"What is the trick to keeping kids on task?"

"What is the *one thing* that is most important for a teacher to keep in mind?"

Love without expertise is powerless.

Even after decades of teacher training, I am still taken aback by such questions. We are dealing with a topic that is far more complex than being a parent. We are attempting to rear a room full of other people's children while simultaneously teaching them academic skills and the basics of civilization.

Yet, people keep looking for the answer in a "one-liner." It takes time to develop a cognitive map for something as complex as classroom management. Until the cognitive map is developed, we are prone to categorical thinking.

"Love Is Enough"

Every good teacher wants to have a positive classroom atmosphere. However, wanting to be positive and pulling it off under pressure are as different as day and night. They are separated by a deep chasm that can only be bridged by the mastery of the requisite skills.

As mentioned earlier, it is the undying hope of green teachers that, if they just love their students and are nice to them, everything will turn out fine. This is the sweet dream of the uninitiated.

Success requires expertise. Without expertise, the struggle to manage the motley crew will leave you exhausted, and your patience will be the first casualty.

Love without *expertise* is powerless. To succeed, you will need them both in equal measure.

Section Two

Exploiting Proximity

Chapter Three

Working the Crowd

Preview

- The most basic factor that governs the likelihood of students goofing off in the classroom is their physical distance from the teacher's body.
- Effective teachers work the crowd. They know that "either you work the crowd, or the crowd works you."
- By using mobility and proximity as tools of management, teachers constantly disrupt the students' impulse to be disruptive.
- Since these teachers are typically supervising the students' work as they move about the room, they get discipline management for free.
- Working the crowd provides the perfect camouflage for setting limits on disruptions. Since teachers move continually among the students, they can move close to the disruptive students without embarrassing them in front of their peer group.

Physical Proximity

Where Does Goofing Off Start?

I'll bet you already know the most important single fact about the management of goofing off in the classroom. After all, you spent the whole first part of your life calculating the odds.

Look at the diagram to the right – a typical classroom with the teacher's desk in the front. The "X" marks the spot where the teacher is standing helping a student who is stuck. Imagine you are that teacher.

Now, place your finger on the spot in the classroom where goofing off is most likely to begin.

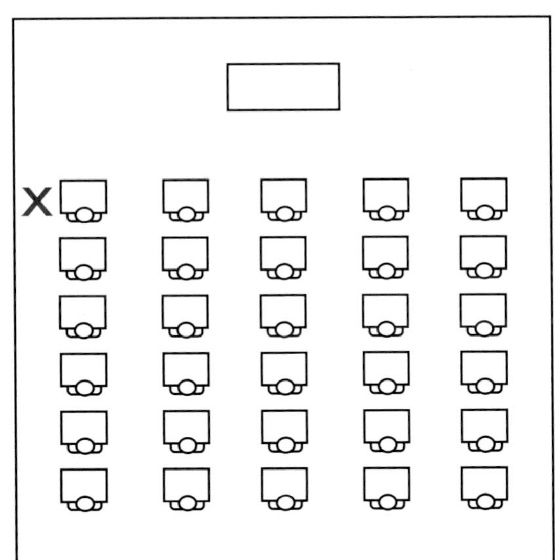

You Know How It Works

Chances are, you put your finger on the corner of the room that is farthest from the teacher. You've played the game. You know how it works.

When the teacher is standing near you, you cool it. If you are not working, you at least make it *look* as though you are working. But, when the teacher is on the far side of the room, well, that is a different story.

The most basic factor that governs the likelihood of your goofing off in the classroom is your *physical distance from the teacher.* The closer the teacher is, the *less* likely you are to goof off. The farther away the teacher is, the *more* likely you are to goof off.

Proximity and Mobility

Watching Natural Teachers

When you watch natural teachers, you do not see very many things that you would label as "management techniques." Rather, you see a room full of students who are busy working.

While the students work, the teacher *walks.* The teacher meanders around the classroom supervising the students' work in a most unremarkable fashion.

If you were to ask a naive observer what the teacher was doing, the answer would probably be, *"Nothing."* The observers might occasionally see the teacher lean over to help a student. But typically it looks as though the teacher is just "cruising" around. Only after you watch a lot of classrooms and note the differences between the effective and ineffective teachers does the importance of this cruising become apparent.

"Either you work the crowd, or the crowd works you."

Crowd Control

Once a discipline problem occurs, management cannot be truly cheap. When a problem occurs, you must stop and deal with the problem or declare "open season" on yourself. If you stop and deal with the problem, it will take time and energy, and it will pull you away from instruction.

Consequently, before we get into complicated discipline management techniques, think in *simple* terms. In a classroom there are roughly 30 students. That is a *crowd.* The most basic level of discipline management is *crowd control.*

Crowd control does not create a perfect classroom. Rather, crowd control gets *most* of the students to do *most* of what they are supposed to be doing *most* of the time. If teachers can get most of the management they need cheaply through crowd control, they can then afford to give their undivided attention to the few problems that are left over.

Working the Crowd

The most basic technique of crowd control is called "working the crowd." Anyone who earns a living in front of a crowd will come to understand working the crowd. Singers, comedians, teachers and preachers – they all work the crowd. They know that *either you work the crowd, or the crowd works you.*

Entertainers will work the crowd with *movement, eye contact* and *energy*. If they feel that they are losing part of the room, they will work that area all the harder.

If, for example, people at a table are talking instead of paying attention, performers will direct everything to that table until they have eye contact. Thereafter, they will focus on that table as often as necessary to keep from losing it. If they were to allow that table to "slip away," they might lose the table next to it and perhaps the table next to it as well. Soon they would be playing to the backs of people's heads over the din of conversation.

Natural teachers instinctively work the crowd. They have an innate sense of being "in contact" with the students. They use the proximity of their bodies as an instrument of management. They *move.*

Calculating the Odds

All students have computers in their brains dedicated to answering the question,

Is the coast clear?

Psychological Distance

Zones of Proximity

Think of every student in the classroom as having a computer whirring in the back of his or her brain dedicated to answering one simple question, *"Is the coast clear?"* This computer is operating at all times, even though it may not be at a conscious level. It calculates such things as how far away the teacher is, which direction the teacher is facing, and whether the teacher is preoccupied.

Next, imagine a teacher walking among the students. Picture three *zones of proximity* surrounding the teacher's body in concentric circles. We will use the colors of a stoplight to represent these three zones: *red, yellow* and *green.*

- **Red**: The *red* zone is a circular area around the teacher roughly eight feet in radius. Using the stoplight as our analogy, *red* means *stop.*

  Students in the red zone cool it. Their computer says, "Goofing off now would be really stupid. You would get nailed." Very few problems occur in the red zone.

- **Yellow**: Outside of the red zone is the *yellow* zone. The yellow zone extends another six feet in every direction. *Yellow* signals *caution.*

  In the yellow zone students act much the way students in the red zone act – as long as the teacher is facing in their direction. But if the teacher should become distracted by helping a student for a little too long, especially if the teacher's back is turned, the computer says, *"The coast is clear."* Suddenly a part of the student's brain wakes up – the part that likes to goof off.

- **Green**: Outside of the yellow zone lies the *green* zone – *green* as in *go!* When students in the green zone look up to see that the teacher is on the far side of the room, particularly if the teacher is preoccupied, the little computer in the back of the brain gets excited and says, *"Why not?"*

  Students in the green zone, however, do not start goofing off immediately. They need a little time to size up the situation. After they notice that the coast is clear, they need to cook up a plan and to cast an eye about for an accomplice.

The longer students are in the green zone, the more likely goofing off becomes. Imagine students in the back half of the classroom of a teacher who spends all of his or her time standing in the front. These students will spend the whole semester in the green zone. Oh my!

Disrupting Disruptions

As effective teachers work the crowd, they constantly cause the zones to change. Imagine students who look up to see that they are in the green zone. But just when their computers signal, *"Coast clear,"* the teacher looks their way and begins to casually stroll in their direction.

"Dang!" says the computer. *"I hate it when that happens! Oh, well, back to work."*

When a teacher is working the crowd, two or three steps will switch a student from the green zone to the yellow zone or from the yellow zone to the red zone. Thus, through *mobility*, the teacher is constantly disrupting the students' impulse to disrupt.

Kids feel safer goofing off in the green zone.

Of course, neither the teacher nor the students monitor these calculations at a conscious level. It is *subconscious* – at the edge of awareness.

When I asked teachers who worked the crowd why they continually moved among the students, they would say, "To see how they are doing." They would look at me as though it were the most obvious thing in the world.

But I asked the question because I wanted to know whether their use of proximity to manage goofing off was conscious or instinctive. I found that it was instinctive.

So I asked the students, "What is the purpose of the teacher's moving around the classroom while you are working?" They responded, "So I can get help if I need it."

Only when you watch these same students in the classroom of a teacher who does *not* work the crowd, do you come to appreciate the subconscious calculations of the classroom. By the time these previously well-behaved students have been in the green zone for five minutes, they become living proof of the statement, *either you work the crowd, or the crowd works you.*

Working the Crowd from the Front

Working the Near and Far Zones

Let's imagine that you are talking to the class from the *front* of the room. When you are in the front of the class, you work the crowd just like an entertainer would work a room in Las Vegas. You continuously move, and you direct your energy and eye contact with a purpose.

Eye contact is effective at a distance, whereas proximity is effective at close range. Since you worry about the students on the far side of the room, you will direct most of your eye contact toward the *green* zone. You will let physical proximity take care of the *red* zone.

It is best to make eye contact with *individuals* on the far side of the room. Don't just scan an area. Make eye contact for about a second. Then, move on to another target and then another as you teach.

Interspersed between these moments of eye contact with students on the far side of the room are more fleeting "scans" of students in the red and yellow zones. Thus, while you do make eye contact with everyone in the room, most of your time and attention is directed to the far side.

As you talk, you walk. Your general pattern of movement is roughly an arc as pictured below.

This general pattern of movement accomplishes several goals simultaneously. *First,* you constantly change the zone in which a student is sitting so that no one is in the green

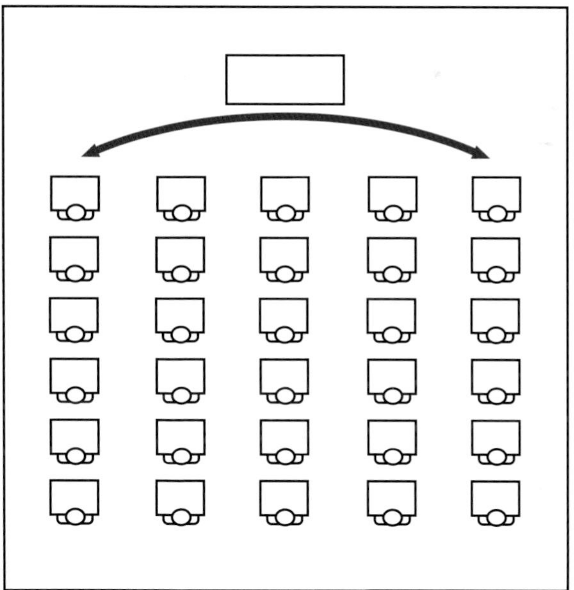

Even when you are in the front of the class, you move.

zone very long. *Secondly*, you constantly change everyone's visual field by forcing them to watch a moving target. If you stand still, you create a stationary target, a "talking head," and the brain "zones out" in a matter of seconds. *Finally*, you provide yourself with *camouflage* should you need to set limits on a student who is goofing off.

Camouflage for Setting Limits

Camouflage is an important concept when dealing with students who are goofing off. You want to get them back on task, but you do not want to embarrass them in front of the group. Your normal pattern of movement creates the perfect camouflage needed to "work" individual students without it being blatant.

Imagine, for example, that you catch two students goofing off on the far side of the room. These students suddenly become the two most important people in the room.

Of course, you could stop and ask the students to get back to work. This would be about as subtle as an entertainer stopping in the middle of a song and saying to the patrons of the lounge, "Group, I am simply going to wait until I have your undivided attention."

Rather than embarrassing the student, you can use *finesse*. Without breaking your train of thought as you talk to the group, turn toward the whisperers and move slowly toward them. Typically they will notice you because students keep an eye on the teacher when goofing off.

You now have eye contact with the disruptors. Talk directly to them as you stroll a step or two in their direction. Then, pause and half turn as you continue addressing the group as though nothing special were happening. This is your normal pattern of moving, pausing, and scanning. Repeat this process until you are addressing the group while standing near the disruptors. You may want to stand near them a little longer than usual. A knowing look might be in order.

Having "disrupted the disruption," you can now begin to move away as you continue your lesson. However, when you scan toward the disruptors, make eye contact with them for that extra half-second. This reminds the students that you are still thinking about them.

To an old pro, all of this would take place with hardly a conscious thought. But when first starting out, remember that working the crowd is *work*. Think of yourself as an Australian sheepdog that must constantly keep its charges from wandering off.

Three Rules of Movement

- Constantly change the zones of proximity so that no one is in the green zone for very long.
- Stimulate the brain to attend by constantly changing everyone's visual field.
- Use movement as camouflage for dealing with disruptive students.

Working Inside the Crowd

Mixing with the Audience

While teachers can work the crowd from the front of the room, they can work the crowd more intimately if they place themselves among the students. Even entertainers will move off stage to mingle with the audience if they want more intense contact.

I have often seen good teachers walk among the students while they explain a concept or act out a part, gesturing dramatically as students watch wide-eyed. You can read a story as you cruise among the desks. You can facilitate a discussion as you move. If you need to write periodically on the chalkboard or overhead, you can do so and then work the crowd as you explain your point.

During Guided Practice

The most frequent occasion for a teacher to move among the students is during Guided Practice. Working the crowd enables the teacher to supervise students as they work on an assignment.

Teachers who work the crowd in this fashion cannot imagine *not* doing it. They say, "How else would you know what the students are doing? You have to check their work, especially at the beginning of an assignment, or they could do it all wrong, and you would never know."

These teachers are "monitoring and adjusting" while getting discipline management for free. You might wonder why any teacher would *not* work the crowd. Yet, most do not.

Obstacles to Working the Crowd

When something that is as sensible and beneficial as working the crowd fails to happen, there has to be a reason. Something must be blocking common sense. The most common reasons are:

- **Years of Modeling**

  My junior high, high school, and college teachers all lectured from the front of the room. Yours probably did too. When you entered teaching you had over a *decade* of modeling that predisposed you toward teaching from the front. Without it being conscious, this reservoir of experience defines both your expectations and your comfort zone. To overcome this pattern requires a conscious commitment.

- **The Overhead Projector**

  Another common factor that inhibits working the crowd is the *overhead projector.* Rarely do teachers who are using an overhead get more than three steps away from it. It is as though they were tethered to the machine. They take a step or two while making a remark to the class, and then they head back to the projector to make their next point.

  One simple way of using an overhead projector while working the crowd is to quit doing all of the work yourself. Let one of your students write on the transparency. Make it a privilege. Assign a different person to do it every week.

- **The Furniture**

  While the overhead projector can present a formidable barrier to working the crowd, it is not the main barrier. The main barrier to movement is the furniture. We will spend the *entire* next chapter dealing with that topic.

Body Language Is Subtle

As we describe working the crowd, we are beginning to learn about body language. Body language gets much more complex as the teacher attempts to remediate disruptions that are already in progress. In subsequent chapters on Meaning Business, for example, we will learn how to deal with even those disruptions that escalate into back talk and beyond.

Yet, the simple interactions described in this chapter reveal a key characteristic of body language in discipline management. Body language allows the teacher to use *finesse* to *protect* students from embarrassment while dealing effectively with their goofing off. If you protect students, they will cut you some slack. But, if you embarrass them, they will get revenge.

Chapter Four

Arranging the Room

Barriers to Mobility

Tripping over the Furniture

Once the importance of mobility and proximity become clear, the next logical step is to make working the crowd as easy as possible. Are there any obstacles that you need to overcome?

Look around a typical class and you will see a whole room full of obstacles. The biggest impediment to working the crowd in a typical classroom is the *furniture.*

The Custodial Room Arrangement

The most common room arrangement in education is pictured in the diagram to the right. Now, ask yourself, "Who arranged the furniture in this classroom?"

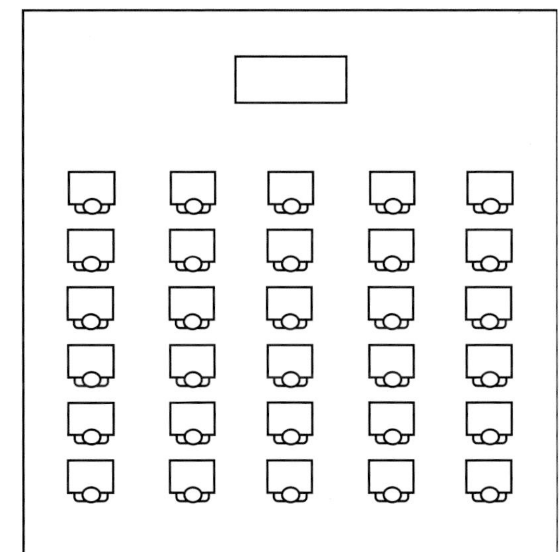

Who arranged the furniture in this classroom?

Preview

- The biggest obstacle to working the crowd in a typical classroom is the furniture.
- The custodial room arrangement makes cleaning easy, but it creates barriers to movement.
- The best room arrangement allows the teacher to get from any student to any other student in the fewest possible steps.
- Teachers can increase proximity by removing their desks from the front of the room and moving the students' desks forward.
- Teachers need walkways. These are not little, narrow walkways, but rather, boulevards.
- The most efficient pattern of movement takes the form of an interior loop. This general pattern can be adaptable to a wide variety of teaching situations.

During training, teachers respond without hesitation, "The custodian!"

Now, ask yourself, "What is the custodian's vested interest in the arrangement of furniture?"

During training, teachers respond, "Cleaning."

Unfortunately, the room arrangement that is *best* for cleaning is the *worst possible* room arrangement for classroom management.

Right Back Where You Started

Imagine that you are standing at the "X" in the diagram to the right as you help a student who is stuck. You look up to see two students *goofing off* in the far corner. What are you going to do about it?

If you ignore the talking, other students will take note and say to themselves, "Oh great! I wanted to talk too." We call this *declaring open season on yourself.* You need to *do* something. But, what?

Previously we described the usual options. After some nagging and a warning comes the trip across the classroom (see diagram) to "lay down the law." You remember the silly conversation that follows.

> "I am *sick and tired* of looking up to see nothing but talking over here... blah, blah, blah."

The students are contrite when you are standing over them, but their repentance is short-lived. How long do you think it will take them to start talking again after you leave?

The day may come when you decide to save yourself the trip across the classroom in favor of a few well chosen words. Think of nagging in this situation as a labor saving device. At least it saves you a trip across the room for nothing.

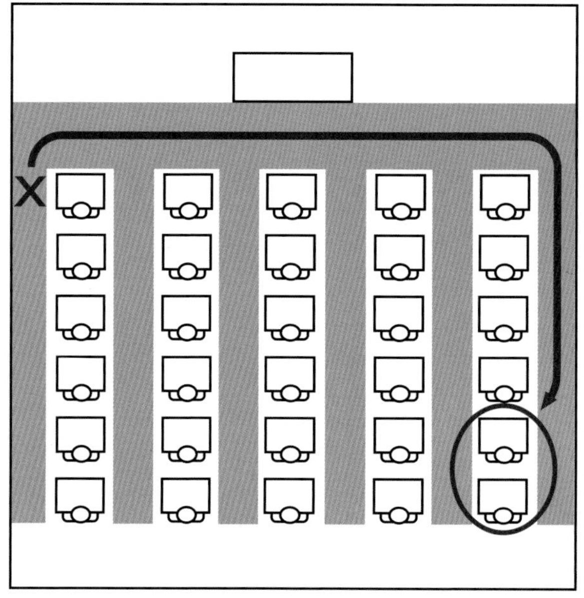

Walking across the room is usually an expensive response to a small problem.

Arranging the Room for Teaching

Imagine teenage bodies at the desks in the diagram above. With normal crowding, students' feet reach to the chair in front.

Consequently, the custodian's room arrangement creates *five impermeable barriers* between the left side of the room and the right side. How will you work the crowd? How will you move toward students who are goofing off without hiking around the periphery? During training, teachers learn the following maxim:

Anything that you do not arrange to your advantage, somebody else will arrange to their advantage, and it won't be to your advantage.

Attempting to work the crowd with the custodian's room arrangement will be so frustrating that you may give up the whole idea.

The first element of Classroom Structure for which you must take full responsibility is room arrangement. You will need to rearrange the furniture in your classroom to facilitate mobility and proximity. Your objective is to work the crowd. To save steps you must carefully analyze space, distance, and movement.

The Teacher's Desk

Move It

The first step in room arrangement is to get your desk away from its traditional location in the *front* of the classroom. Where should the desk go?

Most teachers just shove it into the corner so they can conveniently lay things on it. Other teachers place it at the side of the room or in the back – it doesn't much matter.

Why move your desk? Because, it costs you *eight feet of proximity* with every student in the classroom!

I used to carry a tape measure with me when I visited classrooms. With the teacher's desk in the front, the distance from the chalkboard to the students in the front row is roughly thirteen feet.

Now, stand in front of a colleague who is seated, and imagine that you are conversing with him or her. Make it a comfortable conversational distance. Look down to see how far your knee is from your colleague's knee. It is usually about three feet.

Next, imagine that you are addressing the class. Add another two feet to the conversational distance described above. This extra space gives students to the side a decent viewing angle for the overhead projector or writing on the board.

You are now approximately five feet from the desks of the students in the front row. Compared to when your desk was in the front, you are now *eight feet* closer to every student in the class.

The Cost of Eight Feet

Is eight feet important? In terms of the zones of proximity described in the previous chapter, it is the difference between the *red* zone and the *green* zone.

To feel the difference, stand about thirteen feet from a group of your colleagues who assume the role of typical students who would love to chit-chat in class. Ask them, "Would you start if I were standing here?"

Next, walk toward them until you are standing five feet away. Have them imagine that they are the same students. Now, ask them, "Would you? Could you?"

You will find that when you are thirteen feet away, the students feel free to goof off. But when you are five feet away, they "cool it." This is a tremendous increase in power for simply moving a piece of furniture.

This experiment will give you a feeling for the close relationship between proximity and goofing off. In your classroom, *eight feet* is the difference between *prevention* and *remediation* whenever you are standing in the front of the classroom.

Leaving Your Comfort Zone
I must warn you that, when you first bring the students forward, you may feel a bit claustrophobic. It takes a few hours in the classroom for your comfort zone to readjust. But you will soon come to appreciate the intimacy and control that proximity provides.

The Students' Desks

Analyzing the Use of Space
I will show you some sample room arrangements. Do not jump to the conclusion that they are "correct." They are generic examples that demonstrate key features of room arrangement as they relate to working the crowd.

These room arrangements make mobility easy. Once you become familiar with them, you will be able to rearrange your own classroom in a way that is best for you.

As we look at space, think of teachers in one of two different places. The *first* is standing in front of the classroom as they address the group or facilitate a discussion. The *second* is walking among the students supervising written work during Guided Practice. A good room arrangement must serve the teacher well in both of these situations.

> **"The objective of room arrangement is to create walkways."**

Compact Room Arrangement
Let's start with the fairly traditional room arrangement pictured on the following page. In this diagram the teacher is in the front of the room, and the students are separated and facing forward.

For starters, you only need *two aisles* running from the front of the classroom to the back rather than the four or five aisles that the custodian typically provides. As a result, you can make the room arrangement more compact by placing desks where several of the custodian's aisles used to be.

Think of the rows of desks as running *from side to side* rather than from front to back, as in the custodian's room arrangement. There are now eight students in the front row rather than the five or six that the custodian would place there.

In addition, these students are much closer to you than they were before you moved your desk to the corner. We are following two strategies to make the room arrangement more compact. We are *moving the students forward* and *packing them sideways.*

Spacing Desks

Now, imagine yourself positioning the second row of desks. *First,* sit in a chair in the second row and relax your legs (bent, not straight out in front of you). *Second,* with a tape measure, measure eighteen inches from your toe to the back leg of the chair in front of you. That distance will provide you with an adequate walkway.

When you first look at the distance separating the first row from the second row, it seems huge. How can you afford that kind of space in a crowded classroom? The extra space that we need for wide walkways will come from the space we *saved* by moving the students forward and by packing them sideways.

Making Walkways

The most important feature of room arrangement is *not* where the furniture goes, but, rather, where the furniture *does not go.* The objective of room arrangement is to create *walkways* in order to make mobility easy. I do not mean little, narrow walkways. I mean *boulevards.*

I want you to be able to stroll down the boulevards without kicking students' feet, tripping over backpacks, or being blocked because a student is tall. In addition, I do not want you to pull students off task because they are worried about being stepped on.

The diagram pictured above has four rows running from side to side with eight students per row for a class of thirty-two students. We can now work the crowd with easy access to every student.

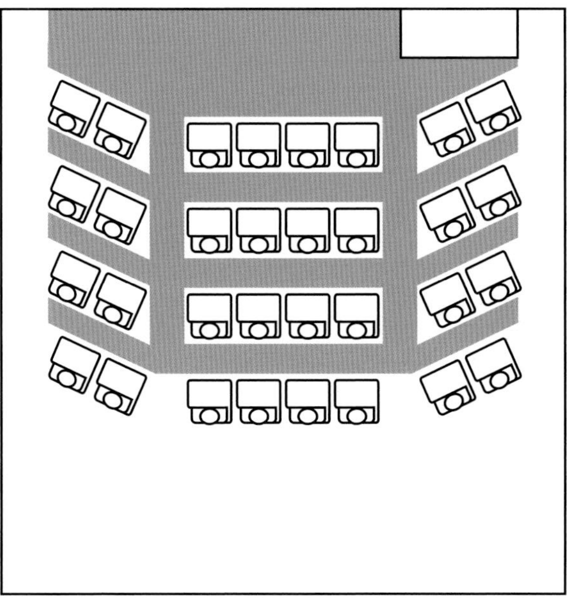

The space for walkways is created by bringing the students forward and packing them sideways.

Generic Room Arrangements

Proximity and Supervision

Imagine yourself working the crowd during Guided Practice as you supervise written work. To supervise written work, you must be able to *read* it. How far can you be from students and still read their work.

With normal eyesight, you can read the work of the student sitting on the aisle as well as the next student over. But you cannot read the work of the third student over because the writing appears too small.

Normal eyesight limits you to supervising *two students to your right and two students to your left* as you work the crowd.

This fact will play a major role in determining the placement of furniture and walkways in your room arrangement.

An Interior Loop

What is the shortest distance you can walk that would allow you to read the work of every student in the class? It is pictured in the diagram below to the left. We will call this pattern of movement an *interior loop.*

As you work the crowd along this interior loop, every student is within two seats of an aisle. In addition, you are only a few steps from any student in the class. As you work the crowd, no student will be in the green zone for very long.

Imagine standing at the edge of this room arrangement. You would pay a high price for being in this location very long. An interior loop allows you to *avoid the periphery of the room* where you are cut off from the students on the far side.

Mobility with Overcrowding

What if you have more than thirty-two students? Where will you place the overflow?

Don't make a fifth row! The middle section of that row would usually be in the green zone. Instead, place the extra students at the *ends* of the two walkways that run from front to back. These locations are the most accessible to you as you work the interior loop.

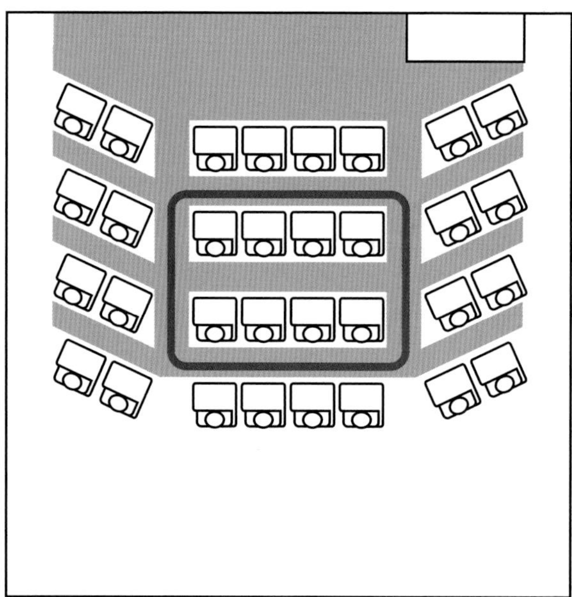

An interior loop allows you to work the crowd with the fewest steps.

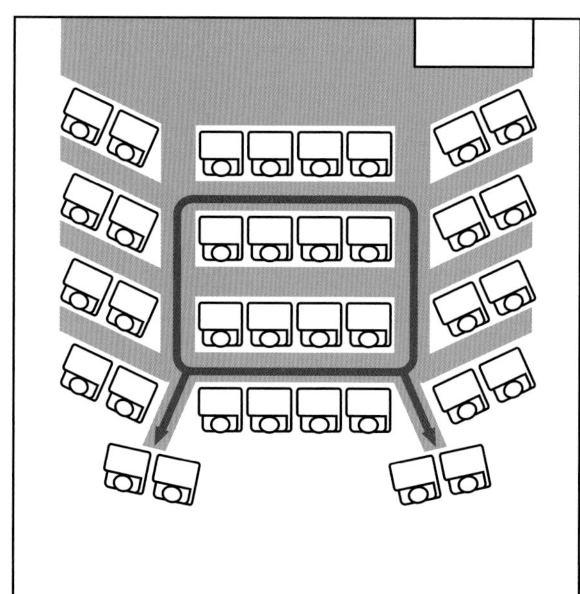

With overcrowding, you may need to use an interior loop with ears.

Of course, you will need to take a step or two out of the loop to see how these students are doing. This produces the elaborated pattern of movement shown on the previous page. We'll call it *an interior loop with ears.*

The placement of "ears" will depend on the idiosyncrasies of your classroom. You will find that one of these ears is no trouble, and two is doable. But, if you have three of them the whole idea begins to collapse because you are in the ears as much as you are in the interior loop.

Cooperative Learning

With the room arrangements on the preceding page each section of every row is laid out in even numbers. This facilitates interactive learning with partner pairs. This arrangement is also very flexible. You can create groups of four by saying,

> "Would rows *one* and *three* please turn your desks around so that we may get into our cooperative learning groups."

Each partner pair combines with the one behind to create a foursome or "study square."

The diagram to the right shows a completely different room arrangement for groups of four. We refer to it as the "wagon wheel." You will see that it is not all that different, however, when you begin to work the crowd. You will find your *interior loop with ears* soon enough.

Basic Patterns

You may have to rearrange your room several times before you get it the way you want it. The goal is efficiency. The optimal room arrangement *allows you to get from any student to any other student with the fewest steps.*

I have rearranged many classrooms over the years, and the most efficient room arrangements tend to fall into two basic patterns. The *first* is rectilinear or "grid" (previous page). The *second* is curvilinear or "wagon wheel" (above).

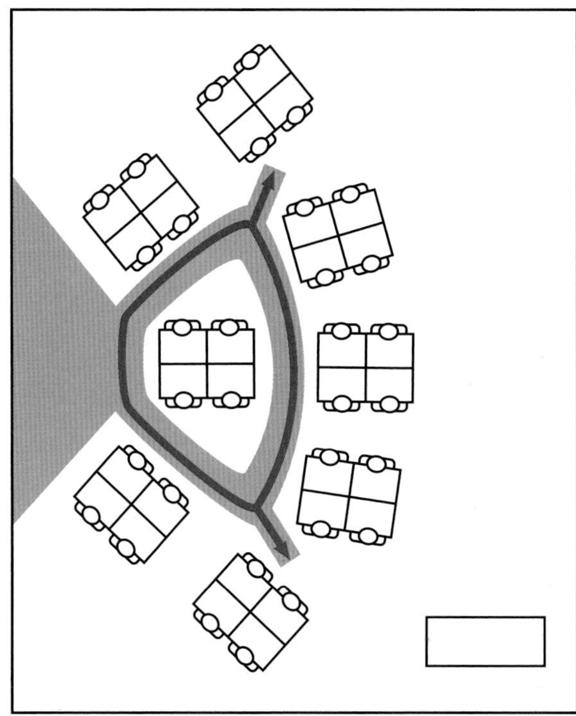

An interior loop with ears fits a wide variety of furniture configurations.

Long rectangular rooms such as portables usually work best with a "wagon wheel" with the front of the room on the long wall (above). If the front of the room is on the short wall where the architects usually place it, the whole back half of the classroom will be in the green zone. If your portable is set up in this way, change it even if it means relocating the chalkboard. If you can't get permission, you can always apologize later.

After you have rearranged your classroom, walk around to see if you can get to every student easily, and count your steps. It is not uncommon for a teacher to show me a diagram like the one at the top of the following page and say,

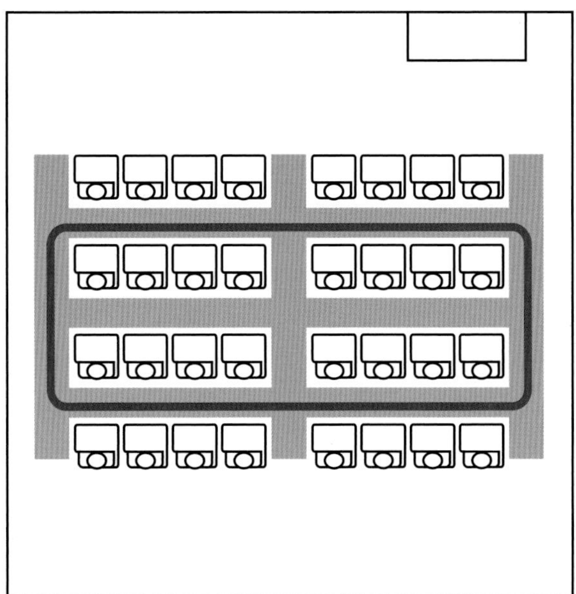

Beware! A central aisle creates a peripheral loop and increases the distance you walk by 60 percent.

"I think my room arrangement is close to what you are describing. I have a central aisle that allows me to get around the room fairly easily."

Beware of a central aisle! The weakness of this room arrangement becomes apparent when you picture yourself supervising written work during Guided Practice. The distance you must walk in order to read the students' work (loop above) is *60 percent longer* than an interior loop. In addition, half of this loop is on the periphery.

Variations on Room Arrangement

There are patterns of room arrangement other than the "grid" and the "wagon wheel" that work beautifully. The common element is that they make mobility and proximity easy for the teacher. Here are some examples.

"Double E"

The arrangement pictured below works well with large tables. It is called a "double E" because it resembles two capital E's back to back. The teacher can easily stroll the central area between the two E's while facilitating a group discussion or supervising work stations such as lab tables.

Computer Labs

Another variation that many teachers use is the "horseshoe" or "U." It is practical in most special education classrooms and with the small groups typical of resource rooms.

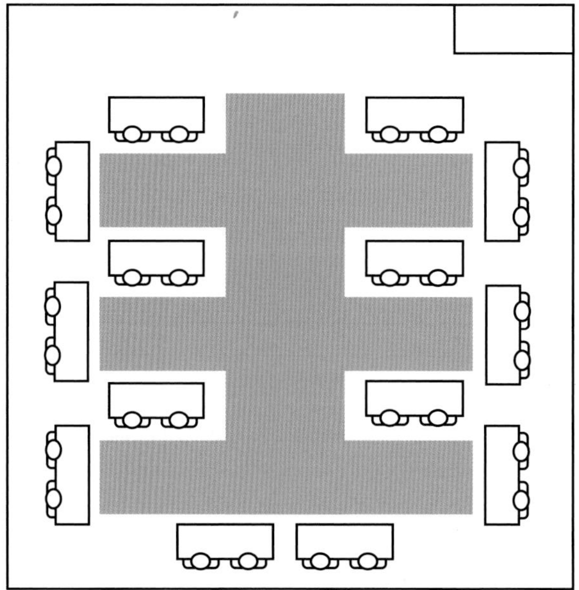

The "Double E" works well with two-person desks.

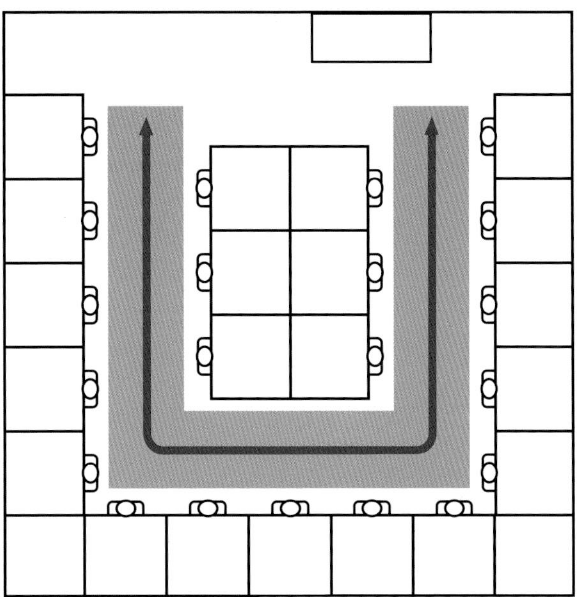

A "U" shaped arrangement works for computer labs.

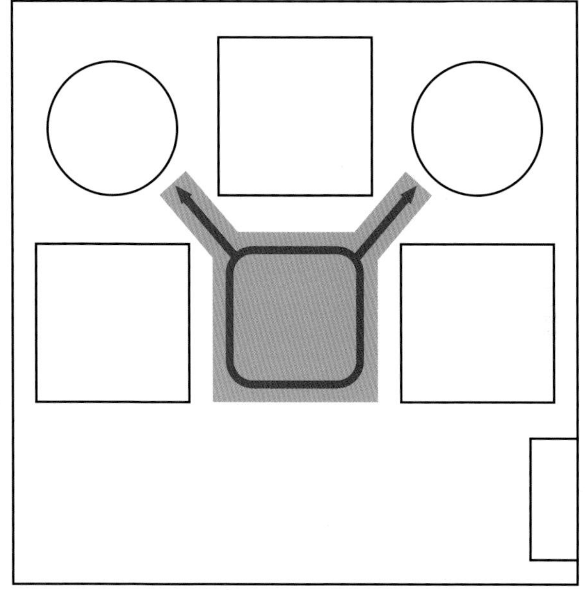

A variation on the "U" facilitates supervision during rehearsal for instrumental and choral music.

With normal size classes, however, the "U" is so large that, when teachers are supervising students on one side of the room, they are cut off from students on the other side. However, this design can work when students are at workstations. The diagram above shows a computer lab with additional workstations placed in the interior part of the "U." Using this arrangement, the teacher can look over students' shoulders with a minimum of walking.

Instrumental and Choral Music

Instrumental and choral music teachers often ask for ideas that might help them during rehearsals. They feel cut off from the students in the back where most of the fooling around occurs.

These teachers typically use the same room arrangement during rehearsal that they use for a concert. This arrangement, however, is poorly suited for rehearsal where you want to hear subunits clearly while working the crowd.

One practical solution is to arrange the subunits of the ensemble around three sides of an open square as shown above. Vocal music teachers often report that they can hear the altos and sopranos clearly for the first time, and band teachers like the separation between brass and woodwinds. Walkways to the percussion and rhythm instruments (circles) facilitate instruction while making it easier for the teacher to set limits on noise making.

Play With Your Room Arrangement

The examples of room arrangement provided in this chapter should be viewed as food for thought rather than as prescriptions. Rooms are different, lesson formats are different, and teacher preferences are different.

Rather than thinking of a room arrangement as being right or wrong, think of it as an attempt to cut your overhead. Remember, your objective is to get from any student to any other student with the fewest possible steps. Play with your room arrangement until you find what works best for you.

Mobility with Small Groups

Elementary Classrooms

During training, teachers ask, "What do you do about room arrangement when you are seated at a table working with a small group?" The answer is usually, "Nothing."

The purpose of room arrangement is to facilitate *mobility* and *proximity*. If you already have proximity without moving, you needn't go any further.

The same logic applies to primary teachers who are seated while reading to students at their feet. Management of minor disruptions can usually be accomplished by simply stopping, turning toward the disruptors, and waiting until they become quiet.

Reading Groups

Teachers of reading groups typically sit with the students in a circle while having each student read aloud in turn. This time honored format has two disadvantages:

- **Low time-on-task:** If there are eight students in the reading group, only one of them is reading while seven out of eight are passive. How can we increase the ratio of students who are actively engaged in reading without sacrificing teacher supervision?
- **Performance anxiety:** Some students get nervous when they have to read out loud. They block due to anxiety which causes other students to giggle. This causes the student who is reading to block all the more.

"The purpose of room arrangement is to facilitate mobility and proximity."

One way of alleviating these problems is to have the students work in partner pairs with one student reading while the other listens. Another approach is to have all of the students "whisper read" by themselves.

With both of these formats, the teacher can supervise by moving around the periphery of the group while leaning down to listen to the reading of individual students. The teacher will hear one student at a time just as well as before.

Once up and about, the teacher can then cruise among those students not in the reading circle from time to time. When the teacher is mobile during small group instruction in this fashion, goofing off and time-on-task are within normal limits.

Small Group Instruction with the Teacher Seated

Mobility during small group instruction is not always an option. Sometimes the teacher must remain seated in order to work intensely with students. The management of small group instruction hits the wall as soon as the teacher sits down.

Within seconds "talking to neighbors" triples and time-on-task drops by over half. Traditionally, educators have accepted this high level of goofing off as the unavoidable price of working intensely with a small group. It could be argued, however, that the cost of this format exceeds the benefit.

How can the teacher relinquish working the crowd in order to work intensely with small groups without paying such a high price in goofing off? This will require an entirely new technology that goes above and beyond working the crowd. This technology will be described in detail in a later section entitled Responsibility Training.

People Issues

Teacher Inertia

Over the years I have repeatedly seen resistance on the part of experienced teachers to changing their room arrangements. I suppose this inertia is not surprising. We all resist changing what is familiar, especially when it alters our "comfort zone."

This resistance is so great that, if you train your colleagues, you will probably want to break into "furniture moving squads," go to each participating teacher's classroom in turn and say, "Where do you want the furniture?"

Your colleague will often give you a funny look as though surprised that he or she must actually change things. But, after a pause, he or she will usually say, "Let's start with my desk."

"The optimal room arrangement allows you to get from any student to any other student with the fewest steps."

Without your "furniture moving squads," over a third of trainees never rearrange their furniture. This is a fatal omission. Without a proper room arrangement, working the crowd becomes extremely difficult. In addition, without working the crowd, many of the skills of effective classroom management described in subsequent chapters cannot be implemented.

The Custodian's Cooperation

Teachers who rearrange their furniture without having a talk with the custodian are asking for resistance. I have known teachers who rearranged their furniture on Monday only to find it back in rows on Tuesday.

For one thing, the room arrangements pictured in this chapter are more difficult to clean than rooms arranged in traditional rows. But, perhaps more importantly, nobody likes to have their world changed without being consulted.

If you want the custodians to put out extra effort to give you an optimal room arrangement, treat them like colleagues. Have a joint planning meeting with teachers and custodians to share the rationale for the changes and discuss the details of implementation. Treat the custodians like professionals, and they will probably respond as professionals.

Section Three

Creating Independent Learners

Chapter Five

Weaning the Helpless Handraisers

Preview

- Most lessons go smoothly until Guided Practice when the teacher is met with hands waving in the air. They are the same students every day.
- While the teacher tutors the helpless handraiser, the noise level in the class rises. Soon the teacher must stop to reprimand.
- No discipline management program can succeed if teachers lose control of the class each time they help a student.
- In addition, students will not become independent learners if the teacher constantly reinforces helpless handraising with time and attention.
- How can we help a student who is stuck without reinforcing helplessness? Only by answering this question can we replace helpless handraising with independent learning during Guided Practice.

Typical Lesson, Typical Day

Bop 'til You Drop

I have spent years observing teachers at all grade levels in every subject area trying to isolate those things that get in the way of teaching and learning. In nearly every classroom one pattern emerges day after day that makes teachers want to scream.

At the beginning of the lesson when the teacher is presenting new material, students have a high level of attending and a low rate of goofing off. They seem to enjoy watching the teacher work out. Call this portion of the lesson "Bop 'til You Drop."

While teachers often find five matinees a day exhausting, it is easy compared to what comes next. The hard part of the lesson begins with Guided Practice. That is when the teacher attempts to put the *students* to work.

Guided Practice

Imagine a math lesson. Can you remember these timeless words as the teacher transitions from Input to Guided Practice?

> "Class, if there are no more questions, would you please open your books to page sixty-seven? As you can see, the problems at the top of the page are like the ones we've been doing together. We have 20 minutes until the bell rings. Let's do problems one through six, and I'll be coming around to see how you are doing.

"If you are having difficulty with any of the problems, look at my example on the board. Go through the steps, and try to do it on your own. If, however, you are still having difficulty, you may raise your hand, and I will help you as soon as I can."

These words hardly leave the teacher's mouth before hands start waving in the air. I ask teachers, "Are they the same students every day?" They just roll their eyes.

The teacher then goes to the first hand waver and asks, "Where do you need help?"

The student says, "I don't know what to do here."

The teacher says, "What part don't you understand?"

The student responds, "All of it."

I'll bet you recognize this student. I'll bet you have more than one in your class.

At this point, the teacher begins a process of *tutoring*, walking the student through the lesson one step at a time. As the teacher tutors, the noise level in the room rises.

"I'll be around to help you as soon as I can."

Holler 'Em Down

At *five* seconds there is whispering. At *ten* seconds there is talking all over the room. At *fifteen* seconds you can hear loud voices and laughter, and one or two students are out of their seats.

As the noise level reaches a crescendo, the teacher turns to address the class. The words are only too familiar.

"*Class!* There is altogether too much talking in here! You all have work to do, and the assignment is up on the board. I cannot be everywhere at once. If you are having difficulty with the first problem, go to the second problem."

The teacher resumes tutoring. The noise level rises. The teacher addresses the group once again with a tone of irritation.

"All right class, this is the *second* time I've had to talk to you! When I look up, I expect to see people working instead of fooling around. Robert, would you *please* take your seat."

The teacher resumes tutoring. The noise level rises.

"Class! There is absolutely *no excuse* for all of this noise. I am sick and tired of looking up to see… blah, blah, blah… nag, nag, nag."

A teacher in Texas told me with an impish grin, "Dr. Jones, I have another name for nag, nag, nag. I call it 'Hollerin' 'em down.'" She made me proud to be from the midwest where we love the unvarnished truth and haven't lost our sense of humor towards life's darker side.

"Holler 'em down" indeed. Walk the halls of any school, and you will hear teachers hollerin' 'em down. There is no profession more perfectly suited to making a nag out of an idealistic young person than trying to manage a room full of kids. No one wants to nag, of course, but sometimes…

Instant Replay
When the teacher finishes tutoring the first student, they look up to see arms waving. When they arrive at the second handraiser, they say, "I'm sorry you had to wait. Show me where you are having difficulty."

The student says, "I don't know what to do here..."

The teacher then tutors the second student. By the time the teacher has finished, the handraisers on the far side of the classroom will have been waiting for over ten minutes! What do you think they have been doing during this time? By tutoring instead of working the crowd, the teacher has declared "open season" for goofing off.

When Guided Practice is finally over, the teacher will be tired from tutoring helpless handraisers through the same lesson a half-dozen times. To compound the teacher's exhaustion, tonight he or she will have to grade papers because, during Guided Practice, they were too busy tutoring to monitor the work of the rest of the class.

We Have a Pattern

The picture of Guided Practice painted above is one of the most predictable patterns of student-teacher interaction in education. Ask yourself these questions about the helpless handraisers in your classroom:

Are They the Same Students Every Day?
Any teacher could give you their names.

How Many Are in a Typical Class?
The national average is five or six.

How Long Does Helping Take?
Tutoring interactions usually consume three to seven minutes (Mean: 4.23 minutes. Standard Deviation: 1.27 minutes). It is difficult for a teacher to tutor in less than three minutes, since half of the time is spent in prompting and checking for understanding as the student works.

The Kindergarten Laboratory

We will use kindergarten as our laboratory for understanding those dynamics of any classroom that foster chronic dependency and help-seeking. Using kindergarten as our laboratory allows us to see patterns easily because the kids have not gotten "slick" yet.

Hang in there if you teach high school. *Nothing changes.*

You Can Spot Them a Mile Away
Kindergarten teachers have demonstrated the ability to predict, after only one day of school, which students will "bomb" in math and reading when they reach first grade. Experienced teachers can often spot them as they entered the room. How do they know?

One test is to look down in order to see who is clinging to your legs and crying uncontrollably. Teachers refer to these students as "immature." However, the term used in the teachers' lounge is "babies."

What are the chief characteristics of immature behavior that stick out like a sore thumb in a kindergarten classroom?

- They are clingy and want constant attention.
- They do not follow verbal instructions.
- They do not do what they are supposed to do unless you are standing over them and helping them.

The reason that kindergarten teachers can spot the babies a mile away is because they exhibit the level of immaturity typical of a three-year-old. Their social-emotional development is lagging behind their physical development by nearly *half of their life span.*

Toddler Behavior
Toddler behavior is primitive. They are still at a symbiotic stage of social-emotional development which explains why they are so clingy.

In addition, they are not yet civilized. Think of your children when they were three years old. Ask yourself:

- Did they share? *Yeah, right!*
- Did they take turns? *In your dreams!*
- What did they do if they didn't get their way? *They cried, hit, bit, tantrummed, or whacked their little playmate over the head with a Tonka truck.*

Most children will have outgrown toddler behavior by the time we ship them off to school. But, not *all* of them.

The Sociology of the Classroom

The following sociological realities drive the help-seeking behavior in *any* classroom. Continue to imagine kindergarten.

Everybody Wants Your Body

Your loving and caring time and attention are the most powerful reinforcers in the classroom.

Some Want It More Than Others

While everybody wants your body, the babies *need it.* They need it in the *worst way.*

There Is Never Enough Teacher to Go Around

The fact that you are in short supply creates *competition* among the baby kids – competition for your body.

There Is a Pecking Order

Competition for your body creates a *pecking order.* Among the students who want your body it is "survival of the fittest." The most ruthless competitors will win.

The Cast of Characters

The Squeaky Wheel Gets the Grease

Picture yourself as the kindergarten teacher. Imagine the *clinginess* of toddlers. Ask yourself:

- Will they share your *body?*
- Will they take turns for your *body?*
- What will they do if they cannot get your *body?*

The answer to the last question is, *"Whatever it takes."* Their objective is to get your undivided attention, and they will be as "immature" as they need to be in order to get it.

While the teacher helps the first student, the helpless handraisers wait.

The Same Characters Every Year

First year teachers are amazed at the odd assortment of characters that populate their classrooms. But more experienced teachers realize that they will get the same cast of characters year after year.

The classroom is a social ecosystem. A social ecosystem is analogous to a biological ecosystem. There are niches in which creatures specialize to compete for limited resources.

The reason the cast of characters never changes is because the niches of the ecosystem never change. Most of these niches are populated by students who want the teacher's body. Do you recognize any of these characters?

- **The Clinger** – What is the most direct way to monopolize the teacher's body? Grab it, of course!
- **The Student Who Does Not Listen Carefully to Instructions** – What do you do with students who were "zoning out?" Will you have to spend some extra time with them in order to get them started?

- **The Student Who Falls Out of His or Her Chair** – Ask your secondary teachers, "Are they are still doing it in junior high?"

Avoiding Ridicule

As these "clingers" get older, they eventually realize that they are paying a high price for their babyishness. The peer group gets tired of their antics. The other students often ostracize them and call them names.

Consequently, during first or second grade as their social I.Q.s improve, the clingers begin to clean up their act. They learn to *look* less babyish even if they are not.

How can immature students avoid looking like babies in the upper grades while monopolizing as much of the teacher's body as possible? They'll have to alter their game plan.

Handraisers may have to wait for ten or fifteen minutes.

Helpless Handraising

Fortunately for these students, there is a perfect way of monopolizing the teacher's body that avoids looking like a baby. It is, of course, *helpless handraising.*

In addition to avoiding peer disapproval, helpless handraising also gets a sympathetic response from the teacher. It is the perfect ruse. These students appear to be hungering and thirsting after knowledge while doing absolutely nothing.

Handraising Is Hard

Since the helpless handraisers are scattered around the classroom, some will be on the opposite side of the room from where the teacher begins tutoring. As mentioned earlier, these students will have to wait *ten minutes* or more before the teacher even gets to them.

This creates a severe dilemma for these helpless handraisers on the far side of the room. How can they hold their arms up for *ten minutes* or more? They are faced with a problem of sheer endurance!

Fear not. These students are up to the challenge.

The Four Basic Positions

As handraisers tire, their handraising typically deteriorates through the following four positions:

1. **The Beginning Position:** Helpless handraisers begin with their arms held straight up. We will call this the *beginning position.* The problem with the beginning position is that the blood drains from the arm. The student experiences mild numbness followed by a pin-prickling sensation all over the hand.
2. **Half-Mast:** One day while waiting, the helpless handraiser looks up to see a classmate modeling a perfect solution to the dilemma. The discomfort can be remedied by lowering the arm and providing a bit of support. This produces hand raising position number two, *half-mast.*
3. **The Broken Wing:** While an improvement, half-mast still requires the student to hold up his or her arm for an extended period. Less work is required if you rotate the arm a quarter turn and relax. This produces position number three, the *broken wing.*
4. **Out Cold:** While some students can maintain the broken wing indefinitely, others lose their "train of thought." When the teacher finally arrives, the student is *out cold.*

Helping the Helpless Handraisers

"I Don't Know What to Do Here."

When beginning to work with a helpless handraiser, the teacher typically asks, "Where do you need help?"

The student responds, "I don't know what to do here."

The teacher says, "What part don't you understand?"

The student responds, "All of it."

Cluelessness

Being clueless is a very shrewd strategy. If the student were to respond, "I don't understand what to do on step five," the teacher would explain step five and be gone in 30 seconds.

To be so specific would be a tactical error on the part of helpless handraisers. The more they know, the quicker the teacher leaves. To monopolize the teacher's body, it is best to be clueless.

Why should helpless handraisers even pay attention during the lesson presentation? If they did, they would have to *fake* being clueless. If they "zone out," they can get the same result at no effort.

Learned Helplessness

"I Have Seen the Enemy, and It Is Us."

Giving the needy student several minutes of your undivided time and attention during Guided Practice provides a powerful incentive for seeking help. By repeatedly helping the same students day after day, we inadvertently create the most widespread learning disability in American education – *learned helplessness.*

No other disability occurs at a consistent rate of five to six per classroom nationwide. Students will never grow up if we reinforce them daily for remaining infantile.

Trying to Fix the Problem

Almost everything we have done in the past 40 years to deal with problems of helplessness and passivity in the classroom has only made it worse. These "cures" include:

- **Hustle**

  When dedicated teachers confront a problem, their first response is usually to *work harder.* What if, for example, you were to hustle so you could consistently help *eight* students during Guided Practice instead of the normal *five.* How many chronic help-seekers would you have?

  Oops! You will have exactly the number of chronically helpless students that you can help chronically.

- **Teachers' Aides**

  What do you think would be the most predictable by-product of adding an untrained instructional aide to a classroom?

  Oops! We double the number of helpless students that can be serviced. Of course, I am not opposed to instructional aides. But they will need to be trained.

The Beginning Position

Half Mast

The Broken Wing

Out Cold

- **Special Education**

  Can special education ever cure regular education? Imagine, for example, that you had five failure-to-thrive students in fourth grade. All of them were tested, and two of them qualified for special placement. How many would be left?

  Oops! Remember, there is a *pecking order* in the classroom, and there is never enough teacher to go around. If there are five slots for chronic help-seekers, and two of these slots are vacated, number six and seven in the pecking order will move up to occupy the vacated slots.

Creating Independence

Helping Is Tricky

How do you help students without making them increasingly helpless? It's tricky.

You can look in vain for this topic in the curriculum of teacher training. Yet, as mentioned earlier, tutoring helpless handraisers during Guided Practice is the source of most of the teacher's chronic headaches.

- **Discipline:** Why shouldn't students in the green zone chit chat when they know that the teacher will be preoccupied with tutoring on the far side of the room for the next five minutes?
- **Instruction:** Why should students pay attention to the lesson and then *fake* not understanding when they can zone out and achieve the same result?
- **Motivation:** Why should students get to work when they can play helpless and have the teacher do the work for them?

A Full Scale Weaning Program

The babies in kindergarten stick out like a sore thumb. If their issues of dependency are not dealt with soon, they will become chronic. By the time they reach fifth grade, they will have patterns of learned helplessness that are over a half-decade old.

You will not be able to reverse such chronic patterns of behavior with only a few minor adjustments. Helpless handraisers *like* being taken care of, and they won't give it up without a *fight.*

To *wean* the helpless handraisers, we will have to redesign the process of instruction from the ground up to build independent learning. Furthermore, our weaning program must be *airtight.* If there are six ways to beat the weaning program and we fix five of them, all of the babies will remain helpless in the way left open to them.

In the following chapter we will begin to build our weaning program. We will start with the pivotal question: *How do you help a student who is stuck?*

Chapter Six

Praise, Prompt, and Leave: The Verbal Modality

Preview

- How do we help a student who is stuck? Typically we find out what they don't understand, and then we show them what to do.
- This process takes several minutes. During this time we not only reinforce helplessness, but we also produce cognitive overload.
- To fit the limitations of auditory memory, corrective feedback must be brief. It must answer the question, "What do I do next?"
- Since our eye immediately finds things in the visual field that do not "belong," we have a natural tendency to focus on the error.
- Beginning corrective feedback by focusing on the error makes the student defensive. In addition, the error rarely provides any useful information.
- We will organize corrective feedback into three steps: Praise, Prompt, and Leave.

Cognitive Overload

Common Sense

How do we help a student who is stuck? The whole human race gives corrective feedback the same way. We might think of it as "human nature" or "common sense."

Imagine helping a student with a math problem. We check through the work to find the difficulty. We explain what the student does not understand, we guide him or her through an example, we check for understanding, and with a parting note of hope, we tell the student that the following problems will be similar to this one.

This helping interaction will take several minutes. And if we paraphrase or answer a question, it will take a few minutes more. As mentioned previously, tutoring in this fashion causes big management problems. For starters, the teacher:

- reinforces helplessness
- loses the class

But there is another problem caused by giving corrective feedback in the form of tutoring – a far more serious problem when we consider the students' ability to learn from our help. That problem is *cognitive overload.*

Cognitive overload occurs when we try to put too much "stuff" into the student's head at one time. Cognitive overload will be the subject of this chapter.

In One Ear and Out the Other

The common sense strategy for helping students could be paraphrased as follows:

Find out what they don't understand, and then show them how to do it.

Unfortunately, this strategy does not reflect how the brain works. To put corrective feedback into proper perspective, we need to focus on *long-term memory*, and, in particular, long-term memory in the *auditory modality.*

To make a long story short, *we have very limited long-term memory in the auditory modality.* Just ask yourself the following questions:

- Have you ever been introduced to someone only to have that person's name slip your mind before the end of the conversation?
- Have you ever forgotten a set of directions that you've just been given by the time you've gotten to your car?
- Have you ever forgotten a phone number by the time you've found a piece of paper to write it on?

These universal experiences convince most of us that we have some kind of memory problem. In fact we do, but we share it with the rest of the human race. While long-term *visual* memory may be great and long-term *kinesthetic* memory may be good, long-term *auditory* memory will get you lost on the way to my house.

Of course, we have only known this for thousands of years. Hence the saying, "In one ear and out the other."

Exploiting Short-Term Memory

Most of what we hear during the day goes in one ear and out the other. It sticks around long enough to make conversation possible, but it soon fades. Very little of what we learn will be stored in long-term memory, and for that we must pay a price. Let's examine the price.

Short-term memory is free. And it is nearly total recall. The only problem is that it does not last very long. But at least we're not out a lot of effort. It is simply a by-product of perception.

Long-term memory, on the other hand, requires a great deal of work, particularly with the subjects we study in school. Remember all of the studying we did for those tests in college? Remember studying the same material for the mid-term? Remember cramming it again for the final? Had we been forced to take the final again a month later without studying, we would have flunked it cold.

How much long-term memory can you count on as you instruct students during corrective feedback? The simple answer is, "None." You don't have *time* to create long-term memory. You must exploit *short-term* memory because that's all you have.

Since we hit cognitive overload in only a few sentences, we can safely teach only *one step* of the task. But it won't last long, so put students to work *fast* before they lose what you just gave them.

This may sound sensible. But it's *not* the way teachers usually behave.

Teaching "The Whole Thing"

Let's return to helping our student with the math problem. Imagine that the math problem has *eleven* steps. The student is stuck on step number *seven* (diagram below). How do we usually go about helping this student?

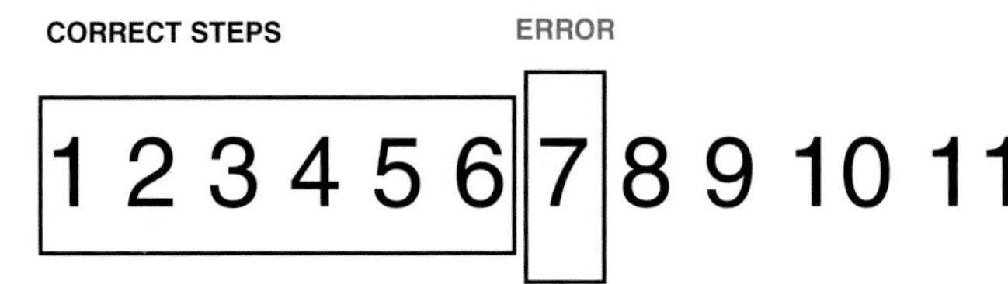

First, we help the student by teaching step number *seven*. If the student understands, we are typically encouraged to proceed to step number *eight*. And, if the student continues to "get it," we will often walk the student through the remainder of the problem before leaving. After all, we know we won't be back.

What demands have we made on long-term memory by walking the student through the remainder of the calculation? During our helping interaction we will spend several minutes asking the student to encode, store, decode, and perform *five steps of new learning*.

What are the odds that the student can "keep it all straight?" Not much considering that we learn *one step at a time*. Teaching all the way to the end of the task (steps 8-11 in this case) would represent cognitive overload to a factor of roughly *500 percent*.

Getting "Faked Out"

How could such a gross overestimation of the student's ability to "keep it all straight" go unrecognized by the teacher day after day? My best explanation is that we are *faked out*. We are faked out by the confusion of short-term memory with long-term memory.

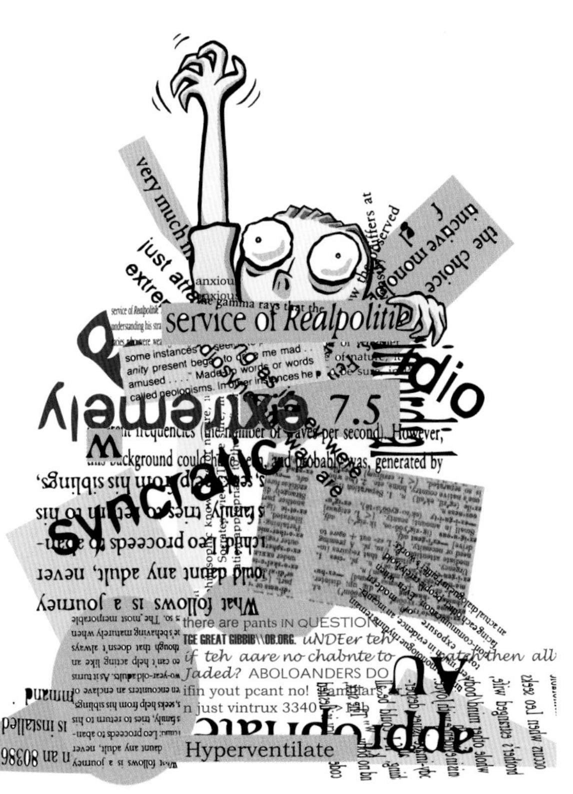

It is easy to drown the student in cognitive overload with our explanations.

Short-term memory is quick and easy, whereas long-term memory is built slowly through hard work. But they both *feel* the same. You either remember or you don't. As teachers, however, it is important for us to know which one is operating.

Let's return to our typical helping interaction with the math student. Imagine that you show the student how to do all of the steps of the problem as described earlier. Since you are teaching one step at a time, the student "gets it." You feel good and the student feels good. You feel confident enough to leave, and the student is ready to start the next problem. Everyone experiences "closure." But that closure is based on short-term memory.

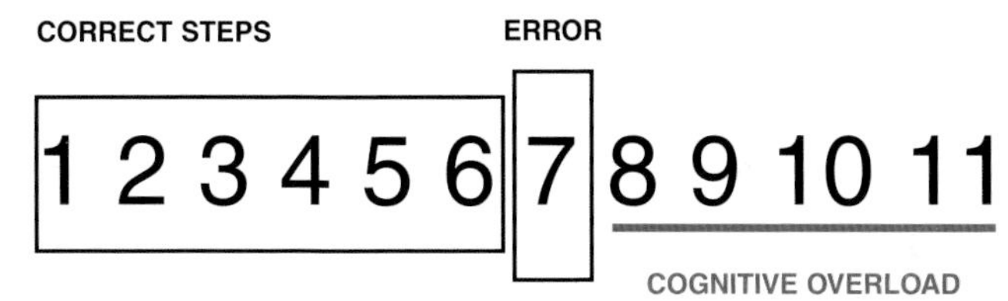

Cognitive overload will show itself clearly only in the light of forgetting. After you leave, the student must copy the next problem and solve it by doing steps one through six. By the time the student gets to step seven – the new learning – *two minutes have passed.*

Now, the student is reaching for *long-term memory*. But we didn't build long-term memory. The student, therefore, finds that many details of solving the math problem have faded. Stuck again!

How can the math student explain this confusion? Other students in class seem to be able to do this stuff, and they didn't have extra help. The most obvious explanation is that, *I must be S-T-U-P-I-D.*

Simplifying Corrective Feedback

One Step at a Time

We are going to do radical surgery on the traditional method of giving corrective feedback. We are going to have to cut it down to size. We must align it with what the brain can actually do.

The brain's natural capacity is captured in that ancient truism: *All learning takes place one step at a time.* All learning takes place one step at a time for one simple reason. That's about all you can "keep straight" long enough to reach the second ancient truism of learning: *We learn by doing.*

A Simple Prompt

Do not approach corrective feedback with a fancy model of instruction. And, do not engage in complex dialogue. Keep it short and simple.

When stripped of its excess baggage, corrective feedback can be reduced to a simple answer to a simple question: *"What do I do next?"*

In learning theory the answer to this question is called a *prompt.* The heart of corrective feedback is a good prompt.

Our Achilles heal is *verbosity.* We love to explain things. We yackety, yackety, yack, and if the kid doesn't get it, we yackety yack some more. We act as though the student had unlimited recall. Instead, just get to the point.

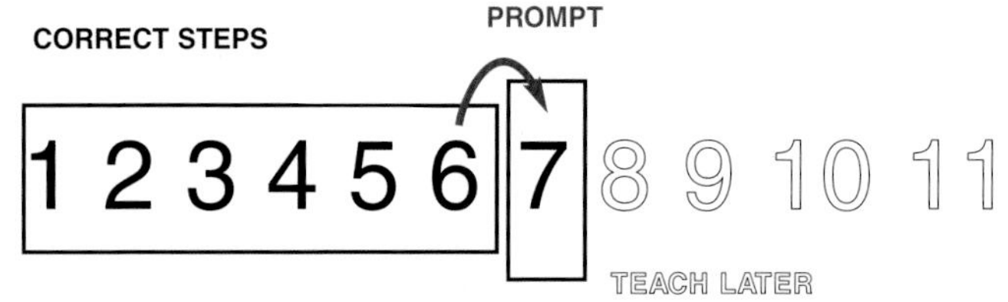

Remember:

- *Simplicity* is *clarity* is *brevity* is *memory.*
- Teaching need never be more difficult than taking students from where they are to wherever you want them to be – *one step at a time.*
- In order to progress, all the student needs to know is *what to do next.*
- Be *clear.* Be *brief.* Be *gone.*

The Negative Side of Corrective Feedback

Human Nature Is Biology

When everybody does the same thing in the same way, we are dealing with a behavior that has a strong biological component. No amount of training could produce that degree of uniformity. We refer to these common traits as "human nature."

The way in which we give corrective feedback is just such a behavior. We ask, "Where are you stuck?" Then, we try to help.

In order to pinpoint the biological component in giving corrective feedback, look at the picture to the right. What catches your eye? The little *blue beastie*?

When we scan a pattern, our eye is captured by anything that breaks the pattern. Our brain stops and says, "What's *that* doing there?"

The Eye Finds the Error

When you look at a piece of work that is part right and part wrong, which part catches your eye – the part that is right or the part that is wrong? During training, everyone answers, "the part that is wrong."

Let me assure you that this behavior has nothing to do with personality traits such as negativism or fault-finding. This piece of behavior is built-in.

Finding the "thing that does not belong" in the visual field has to do with survival. The thing that does not belong in the visual field may be the thing that could "eat you up."

We, therefore, filter out the familiar and focus on the unexpected. This operation takes place instantaneously.

When giving corrective feedback on a piece of schoolwork like our math problem, therefore, we scan past the part that is right – the part that matches our expectation – and *stop at the error.* Having found the error, we are now ready to give corrective feedback.

Our Emotional Response

When we see something that is surprising or upsetting, we have an emotional response – the *fight-flight reflex.* The classroom version of this response is mild compared to a life-threatening situation, but it contains the same physiological components – a tensing of muscles and a tiny shot of adrenaline.

The *mild* version of the fight-flight reflex is called *exasperation.* Have you ever looked at a student's paper to see the wreckage of your lesson and had a sinking feeling?

"Simplicity is clarity, is brevity, is memory"

Typical Openers

What you see is what you *say.* If you are looking at the error and begin to speak, you will be talking about the error.

What pops out at such times are patterns of speech that we have been hearing all of our lives. They are so common that we do not even stop to analyze them. I will refer to these remarks as "typical openers."

I will list five of the most common openers. But they will not sound like much – just the background noise of life.

To hear them with fresh ears, I want you to imagine that you are *failing* my class. Your self-esteem is *nil.* You are *vulnerable.*

These are the kids who really hear the openers. The strong students don't seem to mind them nearly as much. To further help you hear the message implied by these openers, I will paraphrase.

- **Ask Them** – Ask the student where he or she is having difficulty.

"Okay, Billy, show me where you are having your difficulty."

This hardly sounds like a hurtful message. It even sounds helpful. See how invisible these openers are? Now, let's paraphrase:

"Okay, Billy, how did you mess it up this time?"

By focusing upon the error as we try to help, we trigger one of the most frightening facets of Billy's already shaky self-concept – the thought that he just *might* be *S-T-U-P-I-D.* Upon this experience we will attempt to build learning. Lots of luck!

- **Tell Them** – Sometimes it is not worth asking students where they are having difficulty because they seem lost. In such cases, we usually just jump in.

  "Okay, Billy, let's look here at this first problem. Yesterday, you'll remember, we were adding fractions with *like* denominators. Today the denominators are *different.* We will have to begin by finding a common denominator. Do you remember how we do that? Let's look at our example on the board."

  Let's paraphrase to see how it sounds to Billy.

  "Okay, Billy, let's look at the very first thing you were supposed to do today - finding the common denominator. Do you remember how to do that? Apparently not. So, let's look at my example which is on the board in front of you as plain as day."

- **"Yes… But" Compliment** – Wouldn't it be better if we used *praise?* Unfortunately, when you begin with the error, praise won't save you. All you get is a sugar-coated failure message known as a *yes… but compliment.* Yes… but compliments always follow the same form – *first* the good news, *then* the bad news.

  "You are off to a good start, Billy. You have found your lowest common denominator. You have checked it and inserted it into the equation. Great! Now, let's look at the numerator. Do you remember what I said about "adjusting the numerator?" Let's look at step number five."

  Do you want to hear it from Billy's point of view?

  "Okay, Billy, you have done the first part right. We spent all day yesterday and the day before on that. Now, I want you to look at 'adjusting the numerator.' That's the operation I tried to teach you today. Do you remember anything about it?"

  It is impossible for us to interpret remarks as anything but critical when they focus upon our shortcomings. You have been on the receiving end.

  For example, has a supervisor ever given you feedback after having visited your classroom? It usually begins with the "good news."

  "Today, when I was in your class, I saw some real strengths that I want to share… blah, blah, blah."

  You know what part is coming next, don't you? Shall we call it "Needs improvement" or "Areas of potential growth?" Why don't we just call it, "Things I didn't especially like."

- **S & M** – "S & M" does not stand for sado-masochism. This is a classroom, after all. "S & M" stands for "Sighs and Moans" – the sighs and moans of martyrdom.

  When we have a fight-flight reflex, even the mild one we call exasperation, muscles tense. One of these muscles is the diaphragm. We breathe in wearily. Then, after we fill our lungs, we speak.

  To hear the sigh, breathe in deeply, and then gently exhale as you say,

  (Sigh) "Okay, let's see here…"

  or simply,

  "Hmmmmm…"

  The teacher may as well look to the heavens and say, "Why me, Lord?"

- **Zaps and Zingers** – Sometimes, as a result of repeated exasperation (particularly with the same students day after day) the thin veneer of civilization finally cracks. Frustration boils to the surface, and we "let fly."

Zaps and zingers refer to *sarcasm.* All sarcasm can be paraphrased as, *"I don't understand how you could be so stupid!"*

Let's look at some common examples in the order of increasing exasperation and imagine how they might make Billy feel.

Okay, Billy, let's go over this *one more time.*

Billy, we just went over this *at the board*!

Billy, I don't understand *why* you are still having difficulty with this.

Billy, I want you to *pay attention* this time.

Billy! Where were you *ten minutes ago*?

Criticism Makes People Defensive

Frankly, it does not matter which typical opener you use. They all begin the process of corrective feedback by rubbing the student's face in his or her inadequacy. Would you be surprised if the student's attitude toward learning was less than enthusiastic?

Let me ask you a question about corrective feedback that might bring it closer to home. Have you ever tried to give "corrective feedback" to a spouse or loved one? Have you ever noticed how easily they get *defensive* no matter how you phrase it?

"Dear, you know this is for your own good…"

"Honey, I wouldn't tell you this if I didn't love you…"

These words hardly leave your lips before they begin to bristle. Corrective feedback is indeed a tricky business.

Vulnerable Students Get the Most Failure Messages

Who do you think receives corrective feedback most often, the top third of the class or the bottom third of the class? Who do you think has the lowest self-esteem, the top third of the class or the bottom third of the class?

> **The degree of error is irrelevant. If the student is on square one, teach square one.**

Students with the least self-confidence receive *ten times* as much corrective feedback as the top third of the class. In addition, they tend to be *sensitive* to failure messages, whereas, the stronger students often take them in stride.

Students begin public education with many beliefs about themselves which they bring from home. But, there is one important facet of self-concept that must be learned at school. Either I am *smart* with school work, or I am *stupid.* Giving corrective feedback in the natural, common-sense fashion will polarize this perception for any struggling student.

A New Perspective on Error

Consider the following when your eyes are drawn to the shortcomings in a student's performance: *There are a million ways to mess up anything. Each is as useless to remember as the next.*

Why spend precious instructional time going over something with students that you a) *don't* want them to remember, and b) *never* want them to repeat? Not only does it make the students feel defensive, but it also overloads short-term memory with throw-away information.

Corrective Feedback in Detail

Teaching one step at a time sounds simple, but as they say in sports, "There are levels to the game." Swinging a baseball bat may seem simple until you find yourself in a slump. Then you will learn how much a good batting coach can see in that swing.

So, let's slow things down and look at corrective feedback in detail. A lot is going on both cognitively and emotionally.

Your Physical Response

When you look at a piece of work that is part right and part wrong, you will see the part that is *wrong* first whether you want to or not. You will also have a fight-flight reflex that may range in intensity from the imperceptible to real exasperation. The question is, *"What do you do about it?"*

First, take a *relaxing breath.* During this relaxing breath you will *not* be ready to formulate a plan of action. Rather, you will be mildly exasperated and focused on the error. This relaxing breath will calm you and allow time for the fight-flight reflex to come and go.

Second, take *another* relaxing breath. During the second relaxing breath, take a fresh look at the task. Scan the student's work with fresh eyes, and ask yourself, *"What has the student done right, so far?"*

Third, starting from this point, ask yourself, *"What do I want the student to do next?"*

Your Verbal Response

The heart of corrective feedback is the prompt which answers the question, *"What do I do next?"* However, there are some additional elements that you may wish to consider along with the prompt.

- **Praise** – The label "Praise" simply serves as a reminder to focus upon what the student has done *right so far* rather than upon what the student has done *wrong.* Rather than being gratuitous "nice, nice talk," praise describes one or two aspects of the student's performance in simple, declarative sentences. Its purpose is to:
  - *focus* the student's attention on that portion of their performance that is relevant to the upcoming prompt.
  - *review* what the student has done right so far so that it is in the forefront of his or her awareness as you begin the prompt.

  Let's look again at our graphic of the math problem containing an error. Which step would be the most useful to review as the bridge to teaching step seven? During training, teachers respond in unison, *"Step six."*

  CORRECT STEPS ERROR

  1 2 3 4 5 6 7 8 9 10 11

  Knowing what we know about auditory memory, would it be useful to review steps one through six? Trainees respond, *"No!"*

  Praise is most useful the *first time* you help a student. However, praise is usually superfluous the *second time* you help that student because he or she is already focused. Since praise is competing for short-term memory with the prompt, *dump* it and go straight to the prompt. The less said, the better.

- **Prompt** – All modalities of learning can be exploited to increase the clarity of a prompt. Prompting with

Beware as you transition to the prompt.

the *visual* and *physical* modalities will be the subject of subsequent chapters.

For now, let's focus upon what we *say* as we begin the prompt. Beware of the following words as you transition from praise to the prompt:

- But
- However
- Instead of

You can watch the student's face drop as you utter these words. Your attempt to help has just become a *yes... but compliment.* Now the student is waiting for the other shoe to drop.

Begin the prompt with the following phrase, and you will pass through the transition safely:

"The next thing to do is..."

- **Leave** – When you give a student a prompt, it would be logical to check for understanding before you leave. If your instincts tell you that this would be a wise thing to do, then, by all means, do it.

  But, as usual, I am preoccupied with the *helpless handraisers.* They constantly exploit corrective feedback for *attention* rather than learning. For clingers, you have to play the game differently. Leave *before* you see the student carry out the prompt.

  Your instincts may tell you to check for understanding, but, with helpless handraisers, that is usually a bad idea. Leave, because, if you stay, you:

  - signal that you think they may need more help
  - offer your body as the reinforcer if they seek help

Make a helpless handraiser an offer like that, and you *know* what the outcome will be. Leave because you really have no choice.

Deal with your worry about this student's success by giving a *more effective prompt,* not by staying to check for understanding. The following chapters on the *visual* and *physical* modalities of instruction deal with more effective prompting.

Prompting Variations

Praise, Prompt, and Leave is the simple, generic pattern for giving corrective feedback. It is better to stay with this simple version at the beginning, lest you slide back into verbosity. As you become more comfortable, however, you may find the following elaborations useful.

Leave because you really have no choice.

Question Asking

Should you ever ask the student a question? Giving a simple prompt does not leave much room for dialogue. Well, sometimes it is helpful to ask a question, and sometimes it isn't.

Beware of *beginning* corrective feedback with a question. It is one of the most common ways that teachers "get started" when helping a student.

However, there are potential problems to consider when beginning corrective feedback with a question:

- **It takes time** – Dialogue usually takes at least a minute. During that time you are not working the crowd. The predictable outcome will be time off task and noise.
- **It produces verbosity** – The best way to guarantee that you talk for three minutes is to talk for one minute. And, of course, verbosity produces cognitive overload.
- **It sets the student up for failure** – While there are many sophisticated questioning strategies in the literature, I rarely see them used in the classroom. Rather, I usually observe a series of *leading* questions.

  Teachers often refer to this as the "Socratic method." However, most of the time leading questions are questions leading nowhere. The teacher is simply fishing. When the student fails to grasp the teacher's drift, the student feels even more stupid.
- **It plays into the helpless handraisers** – While some dialogue with curious students may yield rich dividends, to helpless handraisers it provides a golden opportunity to be needy. They will play it like a violin.

An alternative use of questioning is in checking for understanding *after* the prompt. The student can answer the question because you just supplied the information.

Discussion Facilitation

The skills of facilitating a group discussion are an extension of Praise, Prompt, and Leave. They enable the teacher to guide the discussion while creating a degree of safety that encourages the quiet students to talk.

Imagine that a given student's comment is mediocre – somewhat off the point or partially incorrect. Our normal focus would to be on the error. If, however, we direct attention to the student's shortcoming, we will not get any more participation from *that* student in the future. As an alternative, use the following sequence:

1. **Selective reinforcement** – Take the best and leave the rest.
2. **Key issue** – Where does the student's comment lead? You get to choose. By highlighting a particular key issue, you can guide the discussion without taking it over.
3. **Open-ended prompt** – Direct the key issue to the class in the form of an open-ended question. Direct it to the student who gave the mediocre response if you wish to engage him or her in idea building.
4. **Wait time** – Give time for the wheels to turn after a prompt. When you speak, you shut down student participation.

Discrimination Training

Can the teacher *ever* point out the student's error? Well, sometimes.

Pointing out the error at the *beginning* of acquisition usually does more harm than good. In addition to wasting time and creating defensiveness, it strengthens the error through repetition.

The situation is reversed when the error is *already* well learned in the form of misinformation or a bad habit. In this case we must engage in *discrimination training*.

Discrimination training focuses upon discriminating *correct* from *incorrect* performance as a prelude to replacing old learning with new learning. We must place both ideas into the student's awareness simultaneously in order to contrast critical features.

Athletic coaches do this all of the time since their corrective feedback is usually triggered by seeing the athlete do something wrong. This chapter does it in order to help us discriminate the proper way of giving corrective feedback from the widespread habits of 1) tutoring students who raise their hands during Guided Practice, and 2) beginning corrective feedback by focusing on the error.

By bringing error to a conscious level, discrimination training walks a fine line with the student's emotions. If it is done skillfully, it can open the door to learning. But, if it is done poorly and arouses the student's defensiveness, it closes that door.

Painless Prompts

Initiating and Terminating Requests

As a means of getting closure on corrective feedback, consider a prompt as simply a request for behavior. There are two basic kinds of requests: *initiating* requests and *terminating* requests.

Initiating Requests

An initiating request asks a person:

- **to do** something
- to do something **more**

An initiating request is emotionally *safe* because it carries **no implied judgement**. You can ask anybody to do anything, to turn cartwheels or quack like a duck, and it carries no implication that what this person was doing previously was wrong.

Terminating Requests

A terminating request asks a person:

- **not to do** something
- to do something **less**

A terminating request is emotionally *dangerous* because it always carries an **implied judgement**.

"Don't swing at a pitch when it's over your head!"

"How many times do I have to ask you not to leave your clothes on the floor?"

"Don't drive so fast!"

Terminating requests are *natural.* They are the verbal component of a fight-flight reflex. We see a problem, and we respond instinctively. Since this pattern is natural rather than learned, it is not subject to forgetting. But it makes a poor prompt because it makes the person defensive without telling him or her what to do.

Initiating requests are *not natural.* They represent a learned pattern that takes a lot of *practice.* Since this pattern is learned, it is subject to forgetting. For as long as we live, it will be easy for us to slip back into focusing on the error and giving a terminating request, especially when we are tired or upset.

Shaping

Shaping is the name given by learning theory to the basic process of instruction. Shaping is *the prompting and reinforcing of successive approximations of task completion.*

A given instance of corrective feedback is simply one step in the shaping process. Instruction always comes down to the same basic question: *"What do I do next?"*

Chapter Seven

Visual Instructional Plans: The Visual Modality

Preview

- An efficient verbal prompt takes the teacher about 30 seconds.
- Unfortunately, it only takes the class 10 seconds to get noisy.
- We must reduce the duration of corrective feedback to less than 10 seconds, and we must reduce the verbosity that creates cognitive overload.
- If words are getting us into trouble, eliminate the yackety yak. After all, a picture is worth a thousand words.
- In order to wean the helpless handraisers, we must replace verbal prompts with visual prompts to create clarity while reducing the duration of the interaction.
- A Visual Instructional Plan (VIP) is a lesson plan in visual form. It is a string of visual prompts that provides a clear set of plans for correct performance.

Problems with Corrective Feedback

Increasing Efficiency

Our objective is to make independent learners out of helpless handraisers so that you can be free to work the crowd during Guided Practice. As long as you are preoccupied with tutoring the helpless handraisers instead of working the crowd, goofing off will be rampant, helplessness will be reinforced, and the rest of the class will receive no supervision at all.

To accomplish our objective we must *wean* helpless handraisers from their chronic pattern of helplessness, dependency, and passivity. Step *one* is to reduce the *duration* of helping interactions.

Praise, Prompt, and Leave – or more commonly, just Prompt and Leave – reduces the duration of the helping interaction through sheer efficiency. We answer the question, "What do I do next?" simply and clearly and then put the student to work before he or she has time to forget the prompt. We solve problems of cognitive overload, forgetting, and the reinforcement of learned helplessness in one fell swoop. Beautiful!

Close, But No Cigar

Years of training teachers to do Praise, Prompt, and Leave in a variety of subject areas has given me a clear picture of how long it takes to help a student who is stuck when you are efficient. The average is 30 seconds. The range is roughly 15-45 seconds, and if the student asks a question, you are over a minute before you know it. On average, therefore, we decreased the duration of corrective feedback from four-and-a-half minutes to half-a-minute – *an 89% reduction*!

Unfortunately, this is a classic example of, "Close, but no cigar." Praise, Prompt, and Leave takes 30 seconds, but you lose the class in *ten seconds*! Praise, Prompt, and Leave is too long by a factor of *three*.

But this is just the first of many problems with Praise, Prompt, and Leave that forced the further development of our instructional methodology. Verbosity proved to be a far more intransigent problem than I had imagined.

Backsliding into Verbosity

During training to do Praise, Prompt, and Leave, I would spend the better part of a day doing "prompting exercises." The trainees would practice efficient prompting using math, science, language arts, and social studies examples. Teachers would struggle with their verbosity, but eventually almost everyone would learn to prompt efficiently in one or two sentences.

Unfortunately, when I had the opportunity to visit their classrooms a month or two later, I found that half of them had slipped back into habits of yackety, yackety, yack. Why? We had worked so hard!

Habit Strength

One problem was *habit strength*. In a nutshell, a behavior that you have repeated 10,000 times has more habit strength than a behavior you have repeated 100 times. It coincides perfectly with the characterization of an old habit as having a "deep groove."

During training, we were attempting to replace habits of speech that were three or four *decades* old with habits that were three or four *hours* old. On the basis of habit strength, which patterns of speech do you think would win out over the following months?

Yet, while habit strength posed a formidable problem, the biggest problem resided not in the teachers but, rather, in the students. The helpless handraisers were constantly seducing the teachers into staying longer in order to tutor.

Wallowing Weaners

Every classroom in the country has a handful of "weaners" – the helpless handraisers that we are trying to *wean* from habitual patterns of learned helplessness. These students have a routine that "works" for them. They do nothing until you finally get to them, and then they watch as you do their assignment.

They are not about to give up this pampered lifestyle without a *fight* – certainly not in order to become *independent learners*. That's work!

Consequently, when you try to wean them, *weaners fight back*. I have seen weaners use some very primitive tactics in order to keep the teacher from leaving – like grabbing them and shouting, "Wait!"

Helpless handraisers have a routine that "works" for them.

But, most of the time, weaners use more sophisticated verbal skills.

When weaners fight back, their primary tactic is *wallowing*. The refrain of the wallowing weaner is, "Yeah, but."

- "Yeah, but I don't understand what to do on this next part."
- "Yeah, but that's not what you said at the board."
- "Yeah, but you didn't explain that."
- "Yeah, but I still don't understand."
- "Yeah, but I'm going to play helpless as long as I can to keep you here forever."

The refrain of the wallowing weaner is, 'Yeah, but ...'

Worried Teachers Hover

The final reason that trainees tended to backslide into verbosity was that, being caring teachers, they *worried* about the students who chronically struggled. To a nurturing teacher who worries in this fashion, a simple verbal prompt seems so cold and brief.

Watch these teachers as they attempt to leave a wallowing weaner, and you will be treated to a bit of visual comedy. They give the prompt, and then they look at the student hesitantly. They straighten up and look back at the student a second time.

Their body language is saying, "How can I be *sure* that you don't need more help. I just *don't know*. After all, I didn't really spend much time with you."

This hovering is an open invitation to wallowing. No weaner worth his or her salt will miss such a blatant cue. And once they murmur, "Yeah, but," it seems so cold-hearted to continue walking away. But, then, *co-dependency is a two-way street.*

Beyond the Verbal Modality

Wean to What?

After watching my trainees backslide, I concluded that I was blocked – at least temporarily. Then one day, as I watched a teacher tutoring a helpless handraiser on a math assignment, I saw the teacher point to the board and say, "…then do step four, just like my example on the board."

When I looked at the board, I had an epiphany! What I saw is pictured below. It was the teacher's *example on the board*. I recognized it instantly. It was just like the example my fifth grade teacher put on the board years before.

Since I grew up with examples on the board like this, I never gave them a second thought. It was your standard visual aide – no big deal.

But, when the teacher said, "…then do step four, just like my example on the board," I looked at the board as the student would. That's when I had my epiphany.

I could not see step four. It was buried. The individual steps of the calculation were nowhere to be seen.

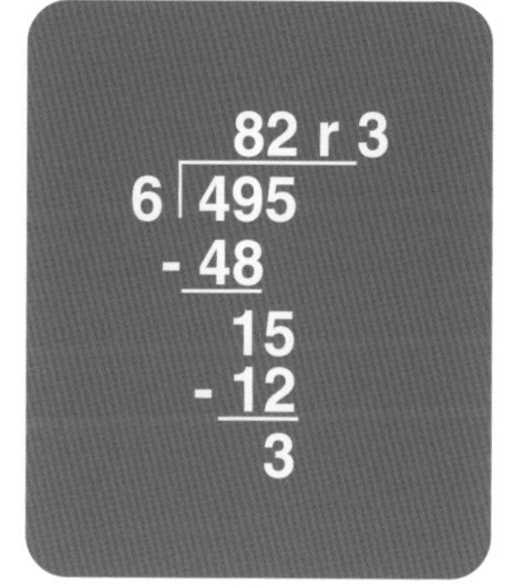

A summary graphic hides the individual steps of a lesson.

Opening the Door to Wallowing
Imagine that you are a helpless handraiser trying to monopolize the teacher's body. The typical "example on the board" would give you an excellent excuse to raise your hand and say, "I don't understand what to do here."

As I watch teachers constructing their examples on the board in the traditional fashion, I am reminded of a standard scene from old-time western movies. The outlaws are being pursued across the rocky badlands by the posse. One of the outlaws dismounts and breaks off a piece of sagebrush to obliterate the tracks of their horses over the rocks so the posse can't follow.

With our summary graphics, we also *obliterate the trail* so the students cannot follow. All they have left is their memory of your verbal presentation. This gives every helpless handraiser a green light for wallowing.

A New Perspective on Graphics

Summary Graphics
I will call the traditional "example on the board" a *summary graphic* because it summarizes the steps of the calculation. Teachers usually build their summary graphic progressively as they go through the steps of the calculation.

Rather than being a good visual aid, it *omits* most of the information that might come from the visual modality. The students are left with a single picture of how the problem should look when it is completed. But, there is no path to follow.

For strong students this is no big deal, but for weaker students it is disastrous. Some will seek help while others will fail in silence.

Building a Model Airplane
To get a new perspective on the visual modality of instruction, let's step out of the classroom for a moment. Imagine that you are shopping for a birthday present for a ten-year-old. As you pass a hobby shop, you notice model airplanes in the window. You decide to buy one.

On the box you see a picture of that model built by a professional. It is *perfect.* There are no flaws – no bent decals or glue dripping down the side. Your *example on the board* is like the picture on the box.

But, when you give the model to a kid, he or she quickly opens the box to see what's inside. On top of all of the parts is a *set of plans* for putting the airplane together. Kids need a set of plans because they have never made one of these things before.

A Set of Plans
The objective of a *set of plans* is to be utterly clear to someone who has never done this task before. What format does it follow?

- One step at a time
- A picture for every step
- Minimal reliance on words

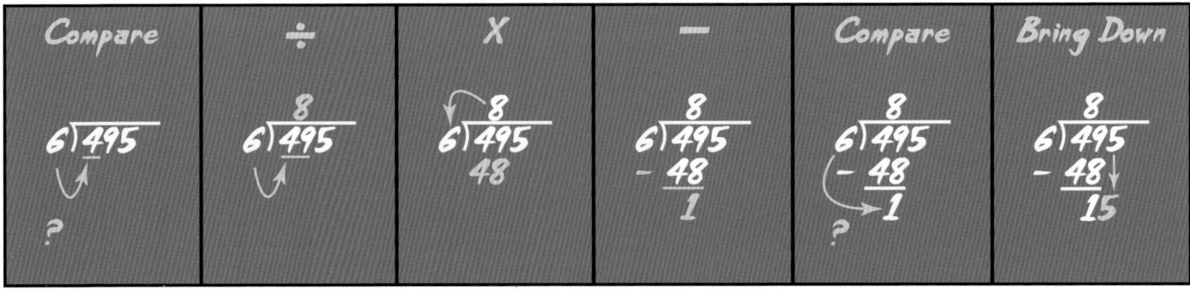

A Visual Instructional Plan (VIP) shows each step of the lesson.

The model airplane company understands that they will never know the kid who tries to build the model airplane – age, IQ, reading ability, or mother tongue. But they know that if this model doesn't go together right the first time *without a teacher in the room,* the kid will never buy another one.

Consequently, they have been forced to answer the question, "What do I do next?" clearly and without language. They had no choice but to use *pictures.* After all, a picture is worth a thousand words. This format has worked well for generations.

A Lesson Plan Is a Set of Plans for the Student

Think of a lesson plan as a set of plans for building something. It may be a calculation, a sentence, a paragraph, an essay, or a wooden bench in shop class.

A lesson plan is for the *student* – the person who has to "put this thing together." While it may also be of use to the teacher's supervisor or to a substitute, these are secondary functions. First and foremost, it is for the *student.* If it does not help the student learn, it is for the most part a waste of time.

If the student cannot do the assignment from your set of plans, then, by default, the student is thrown back on the only other resource in the classroom. That resource is *you.* Once a needy student gets your time and attention, they will want to keep it.

Visual Instructional Plans (VIPs)

A String of Visual Prompts

I will refer to a lesson plan with clear stepwise graphics as a Visual Instructional Plan or "VIP." It is little more than a *string of visual prompts.* It provides the student with a permanent record of your instruction that can be referred to at will.

Sticking with our long division example for the time being, imagine providing a separate picture for each step. The VIP might look like the illustration to the left.

Next, just to get the feel of it, let's look at an example from algebra (below). Remember multiplying two binomials?

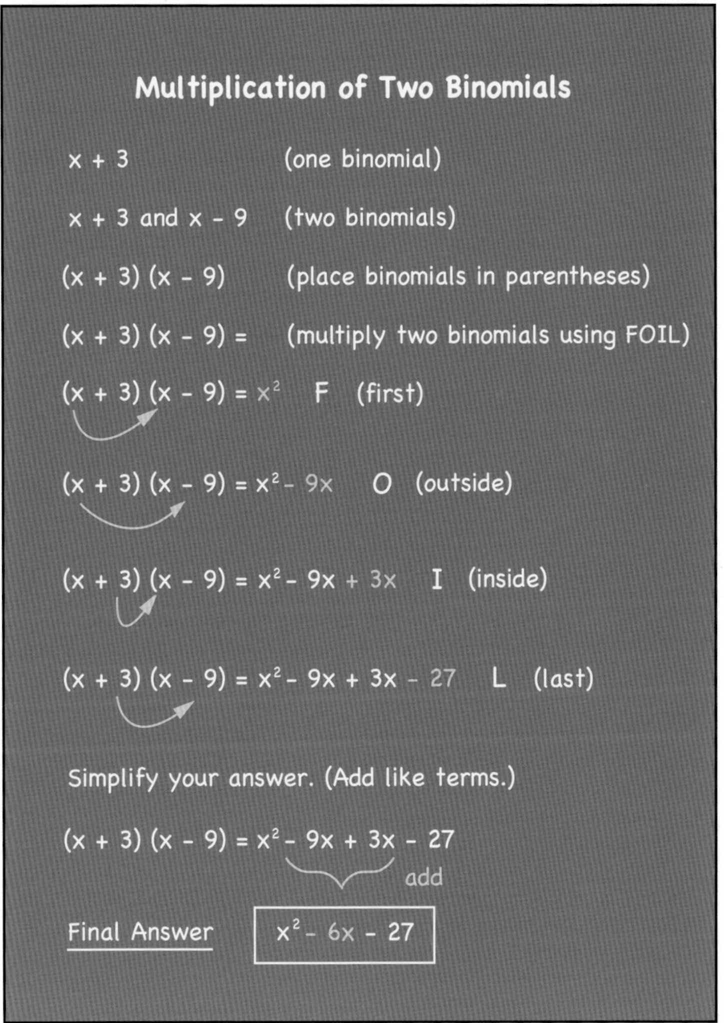

Multiplication of Two Binomials
x + 3 (one binomial)
x + 3 and x - 9 (two binomials)
(x + 3) (x - 9) (place binomials in parentheses)
(x + 3) (x - 9) = (multiply two binomials using FOIL)
(x + 3) (x - 9) = x² F (first)
(x + 3) (x - 9) = x² - 9x O (outside)
(x + 3) (x - 9) = x² - 9x + 3x I (inside)
(x + 3) (x - 9) = x² - 9x + 3x - 27 L (last)
Simplify your answer. (Add like terms.)
(x + 3) (x - 9) = x² - 9x + 3x - 27
add
Final Answer
x² - 6x - 27

Geometry Class

Let's stick with math a bit longer because it is so clearly stepwise and graphic. Below is an example from geometry class – Using a Compass to Draw a Hexagon. As with any good prompt, simplicity produces clarity.

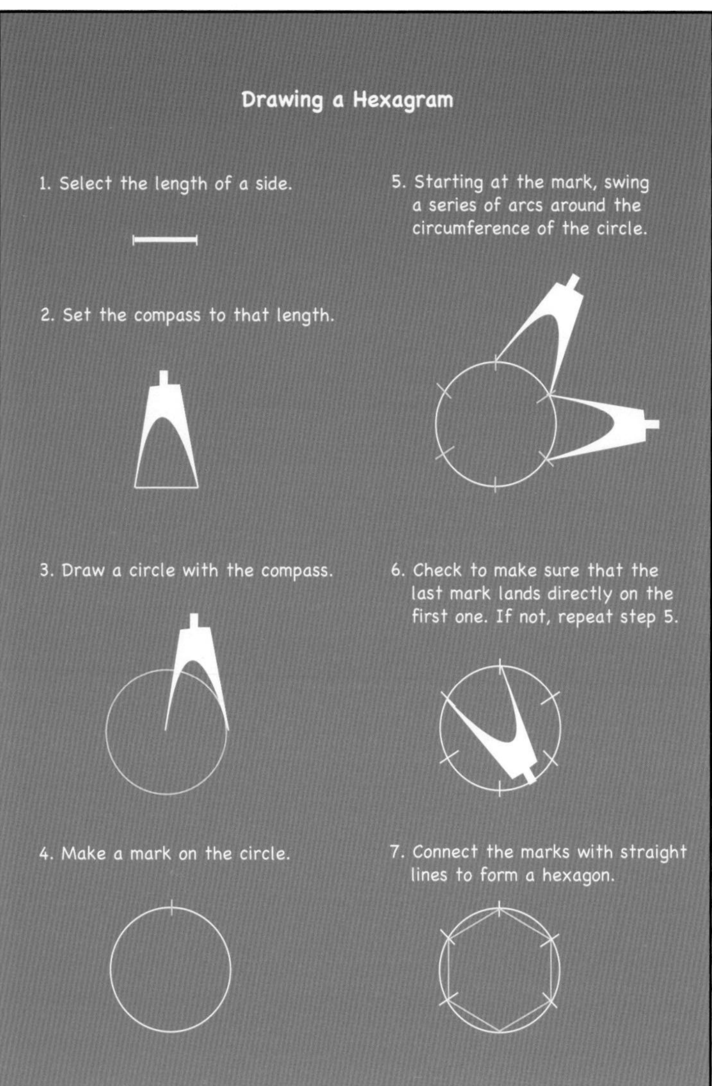

Drawing a Hexagram
1. Select the length of a side.
2. Set the compass to that length.
3. Draw a circle with the compass.
4. Make a mark on the circle.
5. Starting at the mark, swing a series of arcs around the circumference of the circle.
6. Check to make sure that the last mark lands directly on the first one. If not, repeat step 5.
7. Connect the marks with straight lines to form a hexagon.

Art Class

Below is an example of a VIP from art class – Line Perspective Drawing. Of course, a VIP is not a substitute for teaching. You would involve students in the step by step activity of learning as you always have.

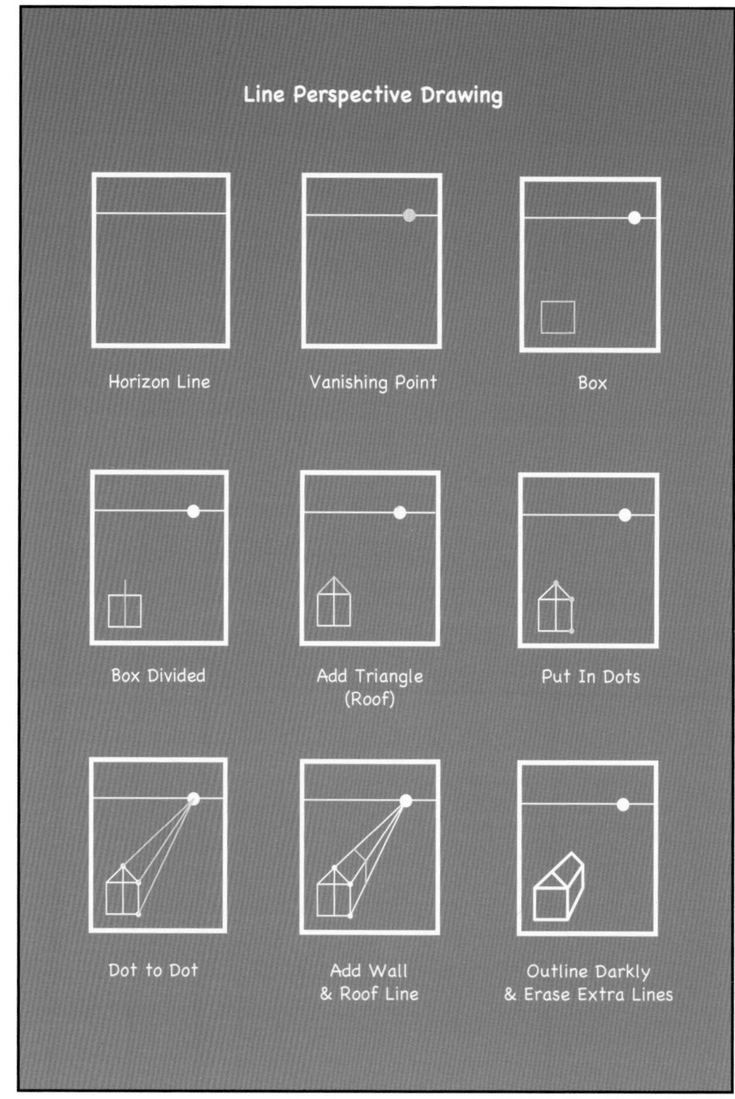

Beware! Old habits are hard to break. We grew up watching teachers make summary graphics. To help in making a separate picture for each step, tell yourself to *step to the right.* Each time you take a step, you will be faced with a blank section of chalkboard. This will prompt you to draw a new picture.

VIPs for the Primary Grades

A common question asked by primary teachers is, "What do you do if the students cannot read?" The easy answer is, "Omit words." Pictured below is a lesson plan for a classroom procedure – carrying a chair properly.

For students who cannot read, omit words.

To appreciate the use of this lesson plan, imagine that you have taught the students how to carry a chair properly, complete with modeling and practice. A few days later you see a student dragging a chair across the room. Before that student can whack another kid in the shins with a chair leg, you intervene.

Since you expect such mistakes in the days following training, you post the VIP shown above where it can easily be seen. Rather than having a verbal interaction with the student, you might simply stop the child, point to the graphic and wait. Usually, nothing would need to be said.

VIPs Accelerate Learning

VIPs dramatically accelerate learning. The VIP of long division was developed during a workshop in twenty minutes by a fifth grade teacher. When I talked to him the following year, he said,

> "Last year I spent the entire first semester on long division, and by December, I still had a half-dozen kids who couldn't do it. This year, with good graphics, we all mastered single-digit division in one week and double-digit the following week."

By accelerating learning, VIPs greatly reduce your level of frustration. It is hard to feel a sense of accomplishment when one handraiser after another says, "I don't get it."

Many teachers post the VIPs for each subject on the bulletin board so students can refer to them if they have forgotten something from yesterday or the day before. You can even give a student extra credit for making you a neat copy for posting.

Some teachers have been able to use these VIPs to simplify working with students who have been absent. Make two or three of your best students your "catch-up committee," and have them tutor the student who has been absent using the VIP.

VIPs Aid Weaning

Reducing the Duration of a Prompt

When the teacher is helping a student during Guided Practice, the noise level becomes loud in ten seconds. Therefore, the teacher must give students all of the help they need *clearly* and *thoroughly* in less than ten seconds.

When faced with this necessity, you will realize that there is only one way out. Your explanation must be *prepackaged.*

How can you prepackage an explanation. Once again, when faced with necessity, you will realize that there is only one way out. You must *substitute pictures for words.*

With adequate graphics, the teacher can point out a critical feature of one of the steps and be gone. It is not uncommon for a prompt to sound like this:

> "Look at Step Four up on the board. That is what you do right here. Do the rest of the problems through step four. I'll be back in a minute, and we'll go to step five."

After teachers develop an economy of speech during training, the next skill is to make prompts open-ended. Give students a job that keeps them busy until you get back.

A Halfway House for Weaning

You cannot wean a helpless handraiser by simply removing the help. If you try to go "cold turkey" with chronic help-seekers, they will increase the intensity of their help seeking.

Rather, you must wean the student from your body to a *body substitute.* A VIP is a body substitute. It answers the question, "What do I do next?" in your absence. Only when we combined efficient prompting with a VIP were we able to "turn the corner" on wallowing.

A lesson plan is nothing more than a string of visual prompts.

Shaping Independence

With a VIP you can begin to put help-seeking on extinction. Rather than operating a simple extinction program, you will operate a program known as DRO – differential reinforcement of other behavior. You systematically replace the behavior you don't want with the behavior you do want. This "other behavior" is independent work.

A VIP with an efficient verbal prompt allows you to reduce social reinforcement for help-seeking to a few seconds. Then you can give more generous attention after the student has followed the prompt. Students quickly learn that they can still "get your body," but they will get very little if they *don't* try and much more if they *do* try.

If you return to a student who is still doing nothing after you have given a prompt and worked the crowd, reduce social reinforcement to zero. Simply point to the VIP and give the student "a look" as you keep moving.

Reducing Performance Anxiety

While help-seeking is habitual with some students, the help-seeking itself has an emotional trigger. That trigger is performance anxiety. As soon as the student feels a twinge, their hand shoots up in order to get help.

VIPs help to reduce chronic help-seeking by reducing performance anxiety. At any time the student can look up and see exactly what to do next. This has a calming and reassuring effect. It helps the student focus on the task instead of initiating their task avoidance routine.

Once students relax and learn that they can still bask in your attention when they produce some work, weaning speeds up. Eventually, students wean *themselves* from the VIP. They glance at it as long as they need to, and when they no longer need to, they quit glancing up.

Types of VIPs

Pictures

The VIPs presented so far are nothing more than a list of steps with a picture for each step. Pictures are most useful for tasks which involve computation or physical performance. I saw a good one recently at a public swimming pool – three pictures for mouth-to-mouth resuscitation that left little doubt as to what to do.

But not all lessons lend themselves to pictures. By this point in a workshop the social studies teachers are usually feeling antsy, and someone raises a hand to say,

> "I teach history and government. We deal with *concepts*. I don't see how VIPs apply to us. How do you draw a picture of a concept?"

Outlines

Actually, you have been drawing pictures of concepts since elementary school. An outline is a picture of a concept.

An outline provides a string of visual prompts for the development of an idea. It tells the student what to do next just like a picture would. It provides a conceptual framework to guide them, for example, as they write an essay.

A common practice in the humanities, unfortunately, is to simply *assign a topic* for a paper. A topic by itself provides the absolute minimum of structure. However, replacing it with an outline causes many teachers to balk and say, "You've just written the paper for them."

This is a natural perception which I have shared. Before passing judgement, however, ask yourself, "Is this paper a contest to see who is the smartest, or is it an attempt to teach as much as possible to as many as possible?"

I had to ask myself that question at the beginning of my teaching career at the University of Rochester. I assigned a paper to my graduate seminar. I was shocked at the papers I received. Whole areas were missing from almost every paper. What they wrote was well done, but not one of them was complete. Why?

It was difficult to attribute the poor outcomes to laziness or stupidity since I was dealing with doctoral students at one of the top universities in the country. Stripped of easy rationalizations, I had to examine *my* contribution in order to explain the high degree of variability in quality.

As I ruminated, it occurred to me that I had provided no structure whatsoever for their work. Instead, I had simply assigned a topic. I was blindly following a pattern modeled by almost every teacher I had as I was growing up.

In order to change, I had to confront my own feelings. If I told them *exactly* what I wanted, was I "giving them the answer?"

This topic became the subject of our seminar, and it became clear how silly it was for me to expect graduate students to have a complete cognitive map of a topic that I had been studying for fifteen years. Of course they left out whole areas.

Consequently, I developed an outline for the paper that I wanted to receive. Once I started, I got on a roll. I provided the headings, the subheadings, the major questions to be addressed, and my favorites references for each section of the paper.

The papers I received were beautiful. The students worked very hard. Rather than "doing the work for them," I had simply specified the work that I wanted them to do.

When approaching an outline for a paper, be thorough. Be complete. Don't hold back. You're not doing their work for them. You're giving them a road map. As the old saying goes, *"If you don't know where you're going, you're not too likely to get there."*

Mind Maps

Mind maps combine the information of an outline with the clarity of a picture in an easy-to-read diagram. A mind map is literally any graphic that shows someone how to organize an idea, solve a problem, or perform a series of operations. The graphic to the right is a mind map of mind mapping.

Most descriptions of mind mapping focus on clarifying the relationship between main ideas and secondary ideas. But in mind mapping, necessity is the mother of invention. Sometimes mind maps illustrate a linear sequence with no secondary ideas at all, something that could just as easily have been presented in the form of a list.

The illustration on the following page shows a variety of schema for mind maps. You are probably familiar with all of them. No doubt you have made some of your own that were far more complex.

Nevertheless, social studies teachers often struggle to build mind maps that are appropriate for representing concepts. Fortunately several excellent resources are available including Mapping Inner Space: Learning and Teaching Visual Mapping (Nancy Marqulies), Mind Mapping (Joyce Wycoff), The Mind Map Book (Tony and Barry Buzan), and Use Both Sides of the Brain (Tony Buzan).

VIPs vs. Simple Visual Aids

It is important to discriminate VIPs from other common types of visual aids. Over the years teachers have developed many devices for representing performance in graphic form. Many of them are far too cryptic to serve as VIPs.

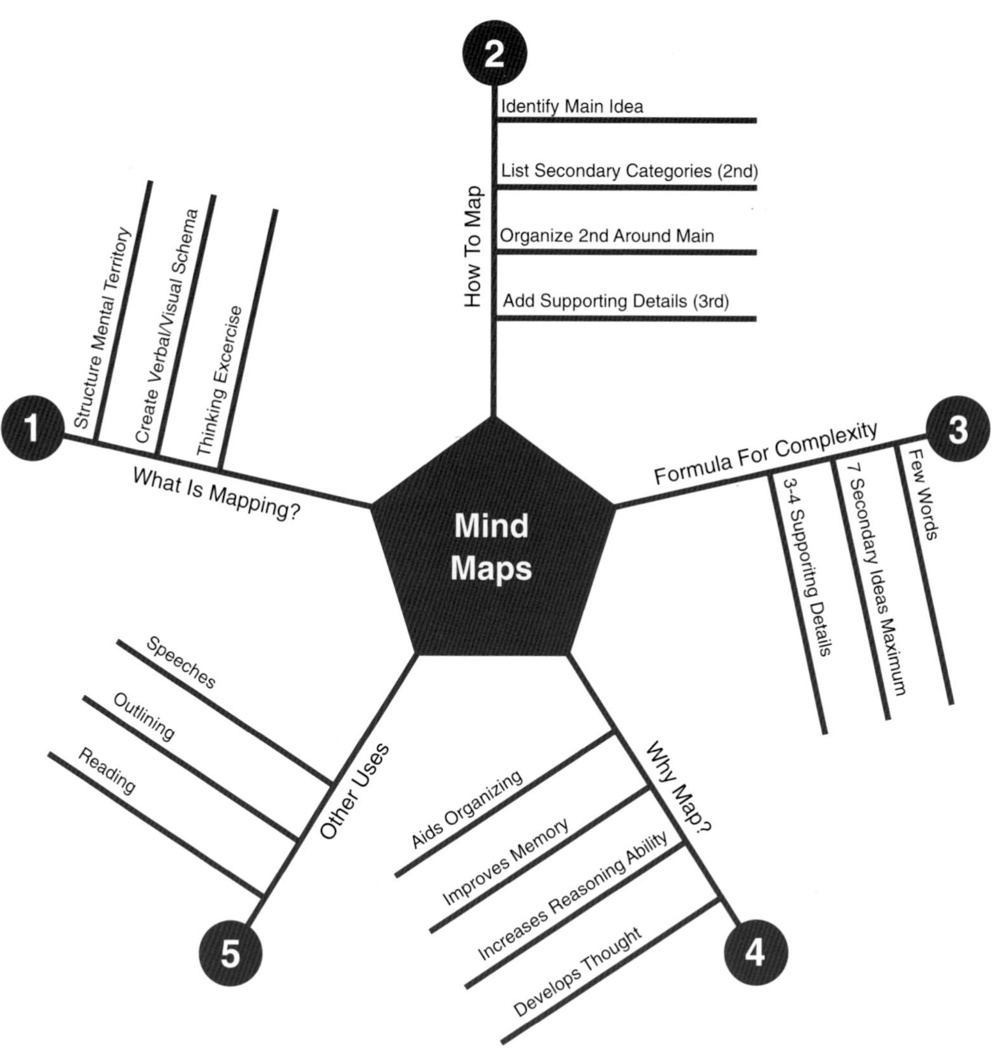

A mind map shows someone how to organize an idea, solve a problem, or perform a series of operations.

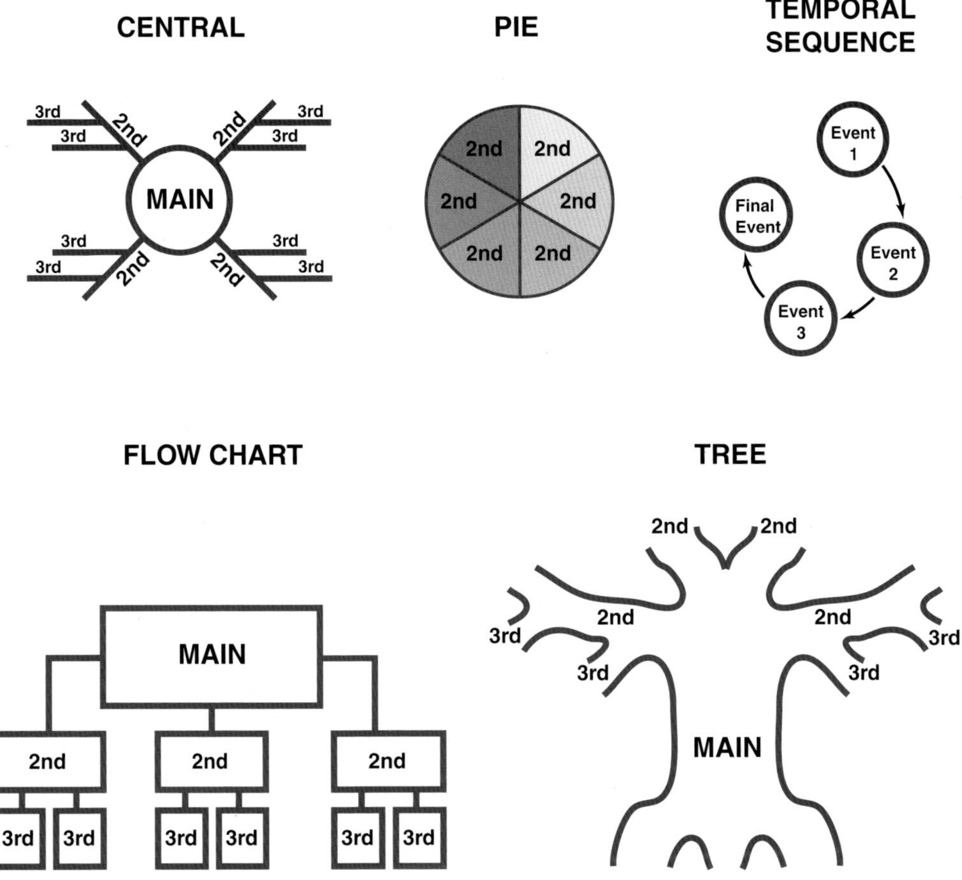

In mind mapping, necessity is the mother of invention.

Our algebra VIP provides an example. High school math teachers will say, "I use F-O-I-L to help the students remember the sequence of multiplying two binomials."

F-O-I-L is a convenient memory device that would be of help when reviewing for the mid-term. But, it omits most of the information needed for initial acquisition.

Long division provides another example. Teachers have traditionally summarized the computation with the four symbols pictured below. It would be more accurate to think of this graphic as a *vestige* of a VIP rather than the VIP itself.

Task Analysis and Performance

Task analysis is the term commonly used in education for dividing a task into the steps of performance. I have learned that logic alone is not a reliable guide to performing a task analysis. You can logically divide any task into any number of steps.

To be useful, the steps into which you divide the task must align with what you want the students to *do*. They must correspond to *meaningful acts.*

In order to see the task with the fresh eyes of new learning, actually manipulate the equipment, do the calculation, or walk yourself through performance. From the student's vantage point, keep asking yourself, "What do I *do* next?"

Chapter Eight

Say, See, Do Teaching: The Physical Modality

Preview

- With effective verbal and visual prompts, we are halfway to our goal of weaning the helpless handraisers.
- By teaching the lesson right the first time so that mastery is the natural outcome, we can prevent most of the helplessness.
- Both comprehension and long-term memory are maximized when we integrate the verbal, visual, and physical modalities of learning.
- Integration occurs when all modalities are used simultaneously. Teaching one step at a time with all three modalities produces a series of Say, See, Do Cycles.
- Structured Practice slowly walks the students through these cycles often enough so that they approach automaticity before Guided Practice.

Continuing the Weaning Process

Our goal is to wean helpless handraisers from their chronic pattern of help-seeking in order to make them independent learners. Our objective is to replace tutoring of several minutes duration which reinforces helplessness with brief, yet rich helping interactions. Effective verbal and visual prompts, however, take us only halfway to our goal.

The focus of this chapter will be to reduce the *need* for corrective feedback during Guided Practice to an absolute minimum. To take the next step in weaning, we will need to deal with the *physical* modality of teaching and learning.

The most direct way of minimizing the need for corrective feedback *after* the lesson is to teach the lesson effectively in the first place. How do you teach a lesson so that mastery is the natural outcome of instruction?

Teaching for Mastery

Goals of Instruction

The twin goals of instruction are *comprehension* and *long-term memory*. We want the students to get it and to keep it.

Comprehension and long-term memory are two sides of the same coin. They occur simultaneously and for the same reason – the integration of learning modalities.

In most classroom work, we teach to three modalities: auditory, visual, and physical. I will refer to the *verbal* modality when I wish to focus on the activity of the classroom teacher. I will refer to the *auditory* modality when I am focusing on the students reception of verbal input. The verbal modality of teaching should match the students ability to process auditory input.

Comprehension

The strength of the *verbal* modality is its unique ability to convey information and ideas. The efficiency of the verbal modality in this regard can seduce us into relying on it too heavily during instruction.

When we teach by talking, we rapidly load information onto the auditory modality in which storage is poor. There is good reason for saying, *"In one ear and out the other."*

The *visual* modality, in contrast, seems capable of producing immediate comprehension almost effortlessly. Hence the saying, *"A picture is worth a thousand words."*

The *physical* modality produces a unique depth of understanding. Hence the saying, *"We learn by doing."*

This understanding of learning is not new. A Chinese proverb states it most succinctly:

I hear, and I forget.

I see, and I remember.

I do, and I understand.

To create comprehension and long-term memory, you must integrate Say, See, and Do.

Long-Term Memory

The auditory, visual, and physical modalities, as we know from experience, have quite different capacities for storage. While the *auditory* modality is extremely limited, the *visual* modality is nothing short of phenomenal.

When we sleep, we dream so realistically that we sometimes wake thinking that we were actually there. Our minds can conjure up sights decades old in holographic color at the equivalent of thirty frames a second – a movie from the past.

The *physical* modality is somewhere between the auditory and visual modalities in terms of memory. As with auditory memory, significant practice is required to get results. Nevertheless, once skills are acquired, the "feel" stays with us. "Once you learn to ride a bicycle, you never forget how."

Combining Modalities

We have three learning systems, each with its own strengths and weaknesses. We can maximize both comprehension and long-term memory by *integrating* all three systems.

The brain simply constructs and decodes *patterns.* If all three modalities can be "welded together" into a *single pattern,* the student can profit from the strengths of each modality – *three for the price of one!*

This integration is crucial for learning in the auditory modality. While auditory memory by itself is weak, it can be made stronger by locking it into a pattern that includes visual and physical memory – *the strong carry the weak.*

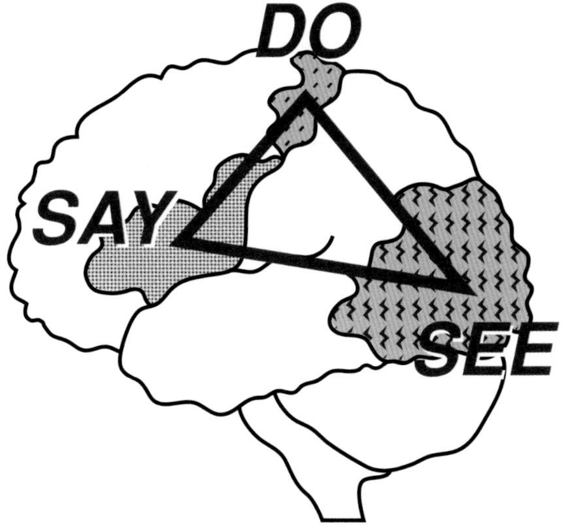

We weld the three modalities into a single pattern by using them simultaneously.

How do we weld all three modalities together? Simple – *use them simultaneously.* Whatever neurons are firing at a given instant become integrated into a single pattern. That is why we learn by doing.

The diagram to the left represents this welding together or linking of modalities. For simplicity's sake, let's refer to these three modalities as *say, see, and do.*

Say, See, Do Teaching

We already know that we *learn by doing* and that we *learn one step at a time.* Put these two notions together and you get a simple, yet powerful model for the process of teaching.

This model is comprised of the repetition of a unit which we will call a "Say, See, Do Cycle." A Say, See, Do Cycle integrates one "chunk" of input as follows:

- Let me explain what to do next
- Watch as I show you
- Now, you do it

The cycle is repeated as often as necessary in order to complete the lesson. The presentation of the lesson would be interactive by its very nature.

We will call this pattern of instruction "Say, See, Do Teaching." It is depicted in the figure to the right above.

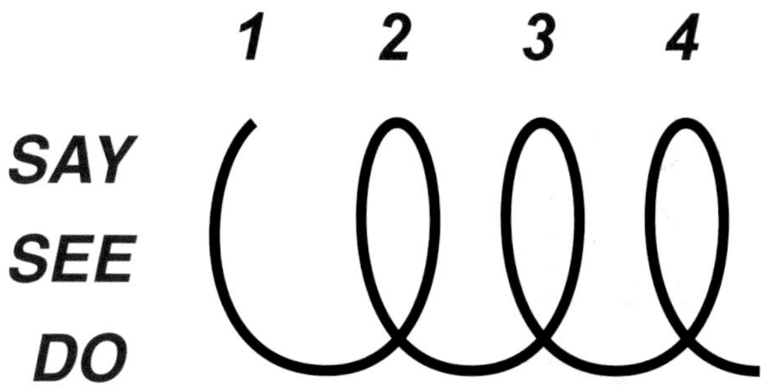

We learn by doing one step at a time in a series of Say, See, Do Cycles.

Say, See, Do Teaching Is Fundamental

Do not leap to the conclusion that Say, See, Do Teaching is *direct instruction* as opposed to *inquiry* or that it is *induction* as opposed to *deduction.* Say, See, Do Teaching is more basic than any of these and is contained in all of them.

All good teaching focuses on learning by doing. The alternative is passivity. When planning a lesson you must constantly ask yourself, "What do I want the students to do with this chunk of material?"

The verb "do" forces us to make concepts into activities. If you want your students to explore and discover, for example, what skills will they need and what methodology will they employ?

In addition, do not leap to the conclusion that Say, See, Do Teaching is for *whole group* instruction or *small group* instruction or *individualized* instruction. It is for all of these. The whole point of classroom management is to bring the precision and support of individualization to a larger group while keeping goofing off to a minimum.

Packaging Instruction

Two Basic Structures

A surprising amount of instructional methodology has to do with packaging. How do we package the activity of learning?

There are only two basic ways to package a lesson. You are familiar with both of them.

Bop 'til You Drop

The first one looks like this:

Input, Input, Input, Input – ***Output***

This is the model we all grew up with. It characterized my junior high, my high school, and my college. The teacher does the *Input, Input, Input, Input* – the lesson presentation. After the input comes output by the students – maybe.

Think back to your high school history, government, and math classes and those college lectures. How many times did you sit through a 20, 30, or 40 minute presentation before doing anything. My own kids reported that even in high school the entire 50 minute class period was often taken up by the teacher's presentation with the homework assignment being given hurriedly right before the bell.

From the teacher's perspective lecturing is *exhausting*. It requires that you do *five matinees a day*. For this reason my name for the traditional method of packaging a lesson is "Bop 'til You Drop." If people in show business were asked to do five matinees a day, there would be a general walkout.

Of course, Bop 'til You Drop produces serious problems with cognitive overload and forgetting. The students are literally in a state of enforced passivity throughout the presentation. Let's say your presentation lasts only twenty minutes. By the time you reach output, what you said at the beginning of the presentation is twenty minutes old and has been overlaid with twenty minutes of additional material.

The cartoon on the facing page depicts my statistics professor during my first semester in graduate school. He scribbled equations furiously while talking over his shoulder. In eight weeks he taught 24 new Ph.D candidates that we were stupid and, very likely, on the verge of failure.

Doing five matinees a day is exhausting.

Input, Input, Input, Input can produce serious problems with cognitive overload and forgetting.

Before a test there was so much anxiety in the air that our normal talkativeness was replaced with a tense silence.

Even if output is a group discussion which requires less precise recall than math, what kind of discussion do you get after twenty minutes of cognitive overload? Does everyone participate in idea building? Fat chance! The "A" students will do all of the talking while everyone else tries to disappear. Call on one of the students who is avoiding eye contact and see what you get.

"What do you think about that, Harold?"

"I dunno."

Say, See, Do Teaching

The second way of packaging a lesson looks like this:

Input, **Output,** *Input,* **Output,** *Input,* **Output**

After you provide a manageable amount of input, the students immediately *do* something with it. Then you give the students another "chunk" of input, and the students do something with that. This process is repeated as the students *learn by doing one step at a time.*

When output immediately follows input, most problems of cognitive overload and forgetting are eliminated. In addition, it allows you to monitor students' work while it is being done so you can give quick and precise corrective feedback.

Students like this approach to teaching. They would much rather *do* something than sit passively and be "talked at."

As a means of summarizing the advantages of this approach to teaching, workshop participants repeat the following words:

It is not your job to work yourself to death while the students watch.
It is your job to work the students to death while you watch.

My name for this method of packaging a lesson is "Say, See, Do Teaching." My nickname for it is "the baby Sam theory of learning." I got this notion from watching my daughter Anne feed my grandson, Sam, when he was 6 months old. She was feeding him yogurt mixed with apple sauce. She would put some in his mouth, and he would gum it and swallow it. Then she would put a second spoonful in his mouth, and he would gum and swallow that. She repeated this process over and over. I thought, "Anne, you are so clever!"

It is particularly clever when you consider the alternative. What if she had placed a spoonful of apple sauce and yogurt into Sam's mouth and then, before he could gum and swallow it, she placed a *second* spoonful in his mouth. Then, before he could gum and swallow that, she stuffed in a *third* followed by a *fourth.* What would Sam have done with this input? Chances are, he would have either choked on it or spit it out. Feeding knowledge to students is an apt analogy for what we do in the classroom.

The diagram below compares the forgetting of input with Say, See, Do Teaching and Bop 'til You Drop. A *learning* curve is on the left side and a *forgetting* curve is on the right side. It's fitting to place them side-by-side since the only predictable outcome of learning is forgetting.

As we all know, retention drops as a function of time. In the auditory modality it drops like a stone. The "X" at the top of the forgetting curve shows where performance occurs with Say, See, Do Teaching. The "X" at the bottom of the forgetting curve shows where performance occurs with Bop 'til You Drop Teaching.

Focusing on Performance

Say, See, Do Teaching Is Coaching

Imagine that you were a sixth grade basketball coach showing kids how to bend their knees to play defense. You

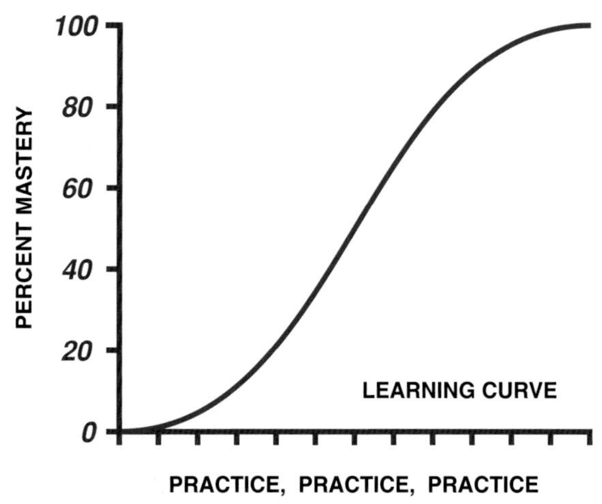

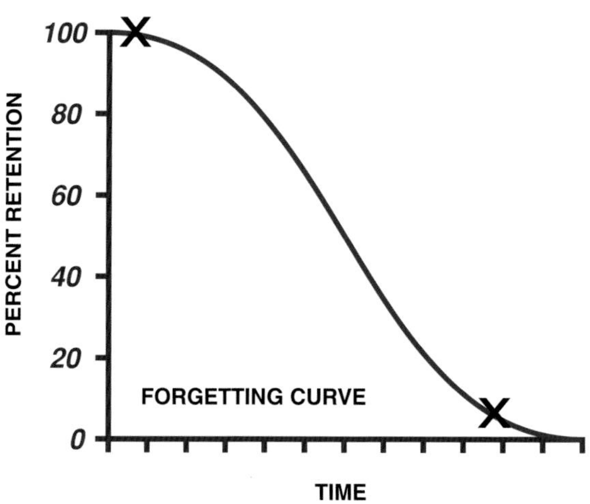

Say, See, Do Teaching places performance at the top of the forgetting curve. Bop 'til You Drop Teaching places performance at the bottom of the forgetting curve.

Only perfect practice makes perfect.

would model the stance and then say, "Now, let's see you do it." If you saw a kid with knees only slightly bent – the typical error – you would immediately step in and do something about it.

You might say, "I am going to put my hand on your shoulder. Keep bending your knees as long as I'm pushing down… There, that's it. That's how defense feels."

Watching a student perform a skill incorrectly is your cue to give corrective feedback. You give most of your corrective feedback during *initial acquisition,* not later. You have high standards as you coach because anything else is a waste of time. In fact, it is *worse* than a waste of time.

Good coaches know that you walk a razor's edge when you teach someone to perform a skill. There is no neutral ground upon which to land. If your trainee does not learn to do "it" right, he or she learns to do it wrong. The only alternative to a good habit is a bad habit. Bad habits, however, are very hard to break.

Coaches, therefore, are perfectionists. In the words of Vince Lombardi, legendary coach of the Green Bay Packers:

Practice does not make perfect.
Only perfect practice makes perfect.

Of course, you know better than to expect one trial learning. After having constructed correct performance, you would repeat that performance, slowly at first, watching like a hawk in order to spot any error. You would correct errors as you went to keep them from being repeated.

With additional practice, speed and fluidity would gradually develop. But a good coach makes sure that correct performance is *never* sacrificed for speed. *Teaching* something means teaching your students to do it *right.* To coach Lombardi's dictum you can add the words of John Wooden, legendary UCLA basketball coach:

You haven't taught until they have learned.

The Good Old Days

Trying to teach a class with the involvement and precision of coaching has always been a preoccupation of effective teachers. I grew up with the most time-honored solution – three walls of slate chalkboards with erasers and chalk for each student lying in a chalk tray. Throughout my grade school years I did almost all of my lessons "at the board" – vocabulary, arithmetic, sentence structure, verb tense. We were rarely at our desks except for group work.

A half-dozen times a day I would hear the teacher announce the beginning of a lesson by saying,

"All right class, let's all go to the board."

If the lesson was math, she would write a problem on the board, and we would copy it. Then she would say,

"Class, let's do this first problem slowly so that we all get it."

The teacher would briefly explain and model step one, and then we would do step one. She could check our work as it was being done from the front of the class. She could easily read it since it was written large in chalk.

Corrective feedback was given immediately, often by way of partner pairs standing next to each other.

> "Robert, would you check your partner's multiplication on that last step."

We would walk through the steps of the problem with continual monitoring and corrective feedback so that there was little worry about getting it wrong. We were thoroughly engaged, but, since kids love to write with chalk, it was hardly work. The teacher coached the class through the new skill just as a basketball coach might coach a team through a new play.

After completing the first problem we would erase and do another problem. The process would be the same, but we would pick up the pace a bit since we were now familiar with the steps. Then we would erase and do another, then another, then perhaps another. By this time we were "in the groove." Then the teacher would say,

> "Let's do one last problem, and then we'll take our seats."

At our seats we would do another five or six problems as the teacher circulated – what is now called Guided Practice. But we didn't need much guidance since we had already done a number of problems correctly at the board. All but one or two students were at Independent Practice by the time we took our seats. To stay busy, the teacher checked our work as it was being done.

Bring Back the Chalkboards

The use of chalkboards has gone out of style since I was a kid. I visited my old elementary school recently, and it had been renovated. The slate chalkboards had been hauled to the dump and replaced with coat hooks and bulletin boards.

Learning theorists have a tendency to denigrate the old in order to make way for the new, and in so doing often "throw the baby out with the bath water." Sending kids to the chalkboard has been demonized because "students suffer embarrassment when they make mistakes in front of their peers."

Never in my growing up was a student sent to the board alone, and embarrassment was hardly an issue. Rather, the teacher's continuous monitoring and prompting prevented us from doing it wrong.

The teacher could check our work from the front of the class since it was written large and in chalk.

You will need ways of doing Say, See, Do Teaching that are simple and convenient.

This format provided the involvement and precision of one-on-one coaching – the ideal of group instruction. Working at the board also prevented a lot of squirrely behavior since it enabled us to get out of our seats, stretch our legs, and do something. Besides, writing with chalk was fun.

Say, See, Do Teaching can occur whenever you make learning physical. I read an article years ago in which a teacher taught inner city kids spelling by having them stand up and form each letter with their bodies. Spelling review resembled cheerleading practice.

Say, See, Do Teaching formats can be beautifully creative. But you will also need ways of doing it that are convenient and cheap. These will be your "bread and butter" teaching formats that you use day in and day out.

The Three Phase Lesson Design

It is helpful to have a simple model for packaging the presentation of a lesson from beginning to end. It allows us to do a quick check during lesson preparation to see if anything has been left out. We will continue to imagine math as our lesson prototype since it is the perfect combination of conceptual complexity and physical expression.

Lessons, regardless of the subject area, tend to have three phases. Like a play, they have a beginning, a middle, and an end. The beginning is *setting the stage*. The middle is *acquisition* – the initial acquisition of skills and concepts. The end is *consolidation* – coaching and practice to mastery with "variations on a theme" being optional.

Setting the Stage

Setting the stage represents the preliminary business of the lesson: a series of decisions by the teacher as to what the students need to have in mind before they encounter the new material. The items listed below are typical. Any combination of these may be present in any given lesson, and you may wish to add a few items of your own:

- **Raising the Level of Concern**: Why is this lesson important?
- **Review and Background:** What skills from yesterday need to be rehearsed? What information is needed to create a context for today's lesson?
- **Goals and Objectives:** Where will this lesson take us? What will we learn? You might wish to present a "preview of the coming attraction" called an *advance organizer.*

Acquisition

Acquisition is the label we will give to the middle part of the lesson – the meat and potatoes. This is the main event. During Acquisition we put the new stuff into the students' heads.

During Acquisition we teach to all three modalities, and we maximize their integration. The labels below are common names for the elements of the Say, See, Do Cycle.

- **Explanation (Say):** What do we do next? It is a prompt – one step. The less said the better.
- **Modeling (See):** What does this step look or sound like? Modeling is a broad term in learning theory that is synonymous with "demonstration." It allows the students to experience correct performance, be it a computation, an athletic skill, the phrasing of a passage of music, or the proper pronunciation of a word.
- **Structured Practice (Do):** What does correct performance feel like? The purpose of Structured Practice is to build correct performance without building bad habits. It is practice that is so highly structured that the likelihood of error is driven to near zero.

Consolidation

Consolidation in most cases is synonymous with practice, practice, practice. It perfects and solidifies new learning while committing it to long-term memory.

There is, of course, no end in the quest for perfection. How many times must a professional musician practice a passage or a professional basketball player practice a shot before it is mastered to his or her satisfaction?

Yet, even at the level of normal classroom learning, performance must become second nature. We must achieve what Dr. Benjamin Bloome refers to as "automaticity."

- **Guided Practice:** Guided Practice is practice at a level of Acquisition that requires *feedback from a coach* in order to maintain correct performance. Error readily invades performance, and it often goes undetected by a new learner. Without the supervision of a coach, bad habits can creep into performance where they are then inadvertently practiced to mastery.
- **Independent Practice:** With Independent Practice you are *your own coach.* First, you must be able to discriminate error as soon as it occurs. Then, you must be able to reinstruct yourself in order to correct the error.
- **Generalization and Discrimination:** Generalization and discrimination constitute the "fine tuning" of a lesson. *Generalization* refers to teaching variations on a theme. In mathematics, there might be variations of a procedure. In the humanities, there might be different interpretations of a historic event from varying perspectives. *Discrimination* refers to delineating correct from incorrect performance.

Consolidation should not be confused with "drill and kill." We can all remember doing math problems at our seats long after the point of diminishing returns had been reached. Over the years, however, almost all repetition has been stigmatized as drill and kill. It is hard to find a new teacher who is comfortable with the level of repetition that constitutes Structured Practice and Consolidation.

Yet, common sense tells us that mastery requires enough repetition to produce comfort and fluency. If we do not provide that repetition under controlled conditions with feedback, it will occur haphazardly or not at all.

The diagram below shows the Three Phase Lesson Design in its entirety. Acquisition is the main event with Say, See, Do at center stage. Note also the repetitions of the skill (R1, R2, etc.) during Structured Practice to make performance nearly automatic *prior* to Guided Practice. Consequently, there should be only occasional need for corrective feedback *during* Guided Practice.

The Three Phase Lesson Design

Setting The Stage

Raising The Level Of Concern

Review And Background

Goals And Objectives

Acquisition

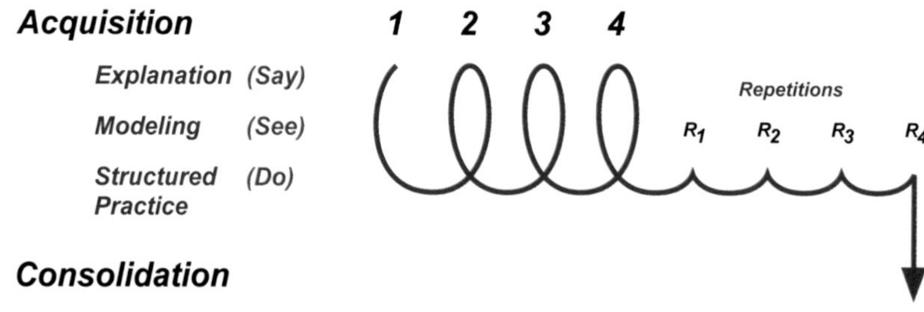

Consolidation

Guided Practice

Independent Practice

Generalization And Discrimination

Structured Practice

Structured Practice Preempts Bad Habits

One of the most noticeable characteristics of lesson presentation when you watch an effective teacher, regardless of the subject area, is that Structured Practice comprises the bulk of the lesson. Only during Structured Practice do we have enough control over performance to produce perfect practice. If we "pay our dues" during Structured Practice, students should need relatively little help during Guided Practice.

Walk through Slowly

The traditional method of "getting it right the first time" is to *slow down* and walk students through performance one step at a time. With continual monitoring and corrective feedback, students feel support as they gradually gain confidence. With additional repetitions, students' performance becomes increasingly fluid and automatic.

With a musical instrument, for example, the teacher would have the student play the passage slowly at the beginning in order to play it "cleanly." Once it was played cleanly, the student could slowly increase speed as long as he or she maintained a clean and fluid performance. If students speed up too soon, errors immediately creep in, and the passage become "ragged."

Students, of course, always want to go for speed too soon. They want to play "hot licks" like their heroes. The eternal struggle of the teacher or coach is to slow students down until they can increase speed without increasing error.

Say, See, Do with Concepts

Performance in the Humanities

It is common to regard concepts as fundamentally different from physical skills when it comes to teaching. Social studies teachers will say, "You have to approach the teaching of ideas entirely differently." This is a misconception.

While history is "conceptual" in nature, it is no more so than mathematics or playing a musical instrument. All skills are simply conceptual operations that are:

- expressed through performance
- perfected through feedback
- made permanent through repetition

Social studies teachers can be seduced into thinking that their subject is uniquely "conceptual" if they rely heavily on Bop 'til You Drop Teaching. When input is divorced from output, teachers tend to drift into a "mentalistic" model of learning – the notion that understanding occurs as a direct result of input. This is another misconception.

We do not create understanding directly. We create it *indirectly*. Understanding is a by-product of experience.

Our job as teachers is to create that experience. Without *doing* something with conceptual input *quickly*, it will simply dissipate – another example of "in one ear and out the other."

In the humanities, therefore, the central question of Say, See, Do Teaching is, "How do you *do* a concept?" There are a limited number of answers to that question. You can:

- **Talk** – anything from quickly paraphrasing a concept with a partner to an English-style debate.
- **Write** – anything from a quick in-class essay to a dissertation.
- **Perform** – anything from some role playing in class to acting out a scene in Shakespeare to a medical school internship.

Partner Teaching

Partner teaching is one of your "bread and butter" Say, See, Do Teaching formats. The procedures described below are simple and can be used in any subject area. It is, however, uniquely suited to producing performance with concepts during a class period.

First, divide the class into partner pairs. This is a subtle process in which the teacher pairs strong with weak while avoiding best friends, worst enemies, and other combinations that just won't work. Partner pairing will determine your seating arrangement since you will want to get in and out of partner teaching frequently.

To begin input, explain a "chunk" of the concept and say, "Teach your partner." Partner A teaches Partner B complete with explanation and demonstration just like you did. Then have Partner B teach Partner A in the same fashion. Repeat this process as you move on to the next step and the next.

The first time you use partner teaching, however, practice with a piece of review material. The real lesson is, "How do we behave during this format?" All of your corrective feedback will be aimed at training the students to implement partner teaching properly. The errors of greatest concern to you are "format errors."

The most common format errors are 1) parallel play, and 2) lazy teaching. In parallel play the partners are doing the task side-by-side, but nobody is talking. In lazy teaching, one person is explaining while the other person is doing. Both of these short-cuts reduce the integration of modalities.

Corrective feedback might sound like this:

"Who is the teacher?"

"I am."

"Good. As you explain it, *show* her how to do it just as I did in front of the class. When you are finished, switch so your partner becomes the teacher."

In addition to being interactive, this format is very efficient since there is no down time. Students are either teaching or being taught. It not only structures step-by-step performance of ideas through verbalization, but it also functions as a pre-writing activity.

Clear Writing Is Clear Thinking

Writing and rewriting are the crucibles in which the fragments of ideas that pass for understanding in our consciousness are forged into clarity. Clear writing is clear thinking. We are all, therefore, teachers of English composition.

When writing becomes a process rather than an assignment, it fits very nicely into the Say, See, Do framework. Think of partner teaching as the Say, See, Do Cycles of the lesson. This could be followed by a ten minute in-class essay to integrate the material while it is fresh.

Structured Practice might take the form of Read Around Groups (RAGs) in which students groups take turns reading the papers of other groups, selecting the best one, and marking strong passages in the margin. The class might then construct a "rubric" listing the key features of a well-written essay. Guided Practice would be the writing of a second and third draft.

Problems of Scale

Coaching and Classroom Chaos

Coaching the performance of a skill provides a model of teaching to high standards that we can all understand. In coaching, continuous monitoring, immediate corrective feedback, and high standards are integral to acquisition.

The problem for a *classroom* teacher is one of scale. How can you replicate the involvement, precision, and support of coaching in a class of thirty students?

Having a room full of students all doing something can be noisy. All of that *doing* can spin out of control and become a discipline management nightmare. And, if the students are all *doing* at the same time, how do you deal with all of the different mistakes that are being made simultaneously?

Expensive Trade-Offs

One way of simplifying your job and reducing potential chaos, especially if you lack "bread and butter" Say, See, Do Teaching formats, is to eliminate the *doing*. The room really settles down when you have the kids sit quietly.

If you do this long enough, however, it may warp your understanding of the learning process. You might end up adopting a bogus theory of learning.

Bogus Theories of Learning

During your years as a teacher, you will run across many bogus "theories" of teaching and learning. They will not be labeled and attributed to some great theorist, however, because nobody would want to own them.

But, they are all around you, and they can easily seep into your thinking. It would be worthwhile to do some discrimination training at this point as a way of inoculating you against the more common bogus theories.

The Viral Theory of Learning

The Viral Theory of Learning assumes that students acquire learning the same way that they acquire chicken pox – by being *exposed* to it. The Viral Theory of Learning comes to the fore whenever we are trying to teach too much material in too little time. You will hear colleagues say things like,

"We can't spend too much time on this topic, but I want the students to know that it's out there."

"We have to at least mention it because it's going to be on the standardized test."

The Professor Harold Hill Theory of Learning

Professor Harold Hill was the main character in Meredith Willson's musical, *The Music Man*. "Professor" Hill was the flim-flam artist who sold expensive band instruments and uniforms to parents in nineteenth century small town America only to skip town before teaching the kids how to play. But when Professor Hill missed his train out of town, he was cornered by angry parents and hauled in front of a room full of bedecked kids with their horns. Professor Hill was forced to put his "think method" into practice then and there. He turned to his "students" and implored desperately, "Now THINK! Just THINK!"

The "think method" is not limited to Broadway. It is alive and well in schools all over the country. I know of a teacher who recently chided her class for using the same tired adjectives in all of their sentences.

"I want you to use some more colorful adjectives when you write – not the same ones over and over. Be creative."

However the teacher had not spent one minute of class time expanding the students' repertoire of adjectives. I could just picture her standing in front of the class and saying,

"Now class, think! Just THINK!"

Bop 'til You Drop

Of course, the world champion of bogus teaching methods is Bop 'til You Drop. The obvious shortcomings of this approach have hardly gone unnoticed by educators. It has been decades since I first heard this saying:

Teaching is not talking, and learning is not listening.

But this insight has hardly swept the nation by storm. To the contrary, Bop 'til You Drop is still the norm in secondary and post secondary education.

One by-product of this widespread use of Bop 'til You Drop is that, by the time you take your first teaching job, you will have lived with it for a solid decade A decade of modeling will have a profound impact on your approach to instruction whether you want it to or not.

The popularity of Bop 'til You Drop is not without reason. In addition to your having grown up with it, Bop 'til You Drop is seductive. It seems as though it *ought* to work. After all, once we get information as far as the ear, we are so close to the brain. Just another inch or two... Besides it saves all of that planning time required to come up with something for the students to do.

Yet, the greatest appeal of Bop 'til You Drop may be that very thing we find most appalling – the utter passivity on the part of the students. When you make students active in the classroom, you have to manage that activity. If you are not highly skilled at management, the activity can run amok. For teachers with little training in discipline management, talking to passive students is far less stressful than constantly struggling to keep the lid on. It may be their way of avoiding being the nag they don't want to be.

Covering the Material

No Time for Mastery

The umbrella term for teaching *too much* curriculum in *too little* time is "covering the material." It is teaching in fast forward. Unfortunately, if you don't teach correctly, the students don't learn correctly.

To a frightening degree systematic skill building has been replaced by "covering the material" in American education. I've gotten into a habit over the years of asking the following question when having lunch with sixth grade teachers,

> "What percentage of students in your class have their times tables down *cold* through 12?"

The reason I first asked this question was because the teachers were complaining about their students' math skills. I chose time tables because it is simple rote learning – not something conceptually "deep" that some kids couldn't get. And it is prerequisite to everything that follows in the math curriculum.

The answers I received were shocking, but they have been echoed dozens of times by sixth grade teachers in every part of the country. In the suburbs the rate is 25-35%. Downtown it is 10-15%.

When I was in third grade, the whole class mastered their times tables in three weeks. During that time we lived and breathed times tables. We didn't just drill. That's no fun. We had teams, we had races, we had our names posted around the room with a bar taped below announcing each new times table that we had mastered. We did time tables hop scotch on the playground.

How can a kid learn long division without knowing the times tables? How can a kid want to pursue math? Kids instinctively avoid those areas in which they lack confidence. We ask ourselves, "Why don't more students pursue math and science in college?" The simple answer is that we lost most of them by the end of third grade.

So Much To Learn

Of course there is always a good reason for speeding up. In my son's calculus class, which contained the 24 best math students in the high school, his study group was getting A's and B's until March. Then they all suddenly pulled D's on the test.

My wife, Jo Lynne, and I had a conference with the math teacher. She said,

> "We have to cover all of this material because it's going to be on the Advanced Placement test which is given in May. We simply *have to* pick up the pace."

How failing to learn calculus would prepare someone for the AP test was beyond us, but the teacher was adamant. Some parents hired tutors, and other parents wrung their hands as their kids drowned.

Slow Down!

If I were to give one simple prescription for increasing learning in American education, it would be, "Slow down!" What is the point of covering a lot of material if it goes past the students in a blur? It is better to have 10 lessons learned than 100 lessons forgotten. Madeline Hunter had a saying about covering material:

> "If your objective is to cover the material, cover it with dirt because it's dead."

Of course, this notion runs counter to the prevailing winds in American education. Just look at the state curriculum guides or the thickness of a high school text book. To cover all of that material would require that we bop very fast indeed.

Dump the Students and Speed Up!

The problem with Say, See, Do Teaching is the *doing*. The doing slows you down something fierce! It takes *time* to do stuff. An effective teacher will spend more time with output than with input.

If you want to speed things up significantly in order to cover more material, there's only one way to do it. You have to *get the students out of the learning process.*

Eliminate all of that time consuming "learning by doing," and you can hit curriculum overdrive. Then, the amount of material you cover in a semester is limited only by how fast you can bop. Why, if we "floor it," we might even cover *everything that's important*!

Everything That's Important

I read an article some time ago in which the author collected all of the topics that various "experts" thought were "essential knowledge" for a high school student. When combined these topics represented seven and a half years of education.

When I read the list I was appalled! It left out all kinds of things that I thought were essential. They didn't learn squat about the Greeks and the Romans. The Renaissance was over before it got started. Why, those kids wouldn't know Caravaggio from DiMaggio. Seven and a half years of high school, and the kids are still ignorant!

Or, could it be that we are pointed in the wrong direction? Perhaps our job is to take a carefully selected *sample* of knowledge and use it to teach the kids *first* to think and *then* to express their thoughts clearly in spoken and written form.

Pressure to Bop

It's Going to Be on the Test

During a workshop, teachers sometimes experience consternation when they realize that teaching properly will slow them down. They say, "But it's all going to be on the standardized test!"

I try to comfort them by explaining that no kid ever got a lower score on a test by learning more. I tell them that administrators don't hassle effective teachers. They are too busy cleaning up the messes made by ineffective teachers. But teachers these days have been pushed by "leaders" with a life-long devotion to the Viral Theory of Learning to the point where they are running scared.

Teaching to the Top

Bop 'til You Drop can produce learning, truth be told, but only for the top students. They read the assignment, take notes, and study for the test. These efforts outside of class provide the "do" for learning by doing.

If, however, you wish to reach the many rather than just the few, you will have to take a more active role in structuring the work that produces learning. And you will have to do it during class time.

If you send students home without having achieved mastery in class, and if the kid cares about doing homework, six hours later he or she will be sitting at the kitchen table trying to figure it all out. This is where *cultural double jeopardy* comes into play.

If the student's parents are "learning oriented," they will at least sit down with their kid as I did with my sons, look at the algebra assignment, and repeat these time honored words.

> "Well... Hmmmm... It's been a long time since I've seen one of these."

When I could, I helped. When I couldn't, as in calculus, I hired a tutor. But, one way or another, I was not about to stand by and watch my child drown.

If, however, the kid's parents are not "learning oriented," lots of luck! This is one of many reasons why kids from the bottom quarter of the socio-economic spectrum are six times more likely to drop out of high school than kids from the top quarter.

Homework

What, then, do you send home for homework? It's simple – something the kid can succeed in doing.

The function of homework is Independent Practice. If the students are at an earlier phase of acquisition, don't send the work home. Either wait until the students have achieved mastery in class, or have them do some review.

When to Bop

I do not mean to imply that all "bopping" is bad. I know that exceptional teachers are made out of ham. I know how much fun it is to strut your stuff. It doesn't have to end.

Just keep in mind that students remember stories, not lists of facts. Stories stick in the mind because the listener supplies the visual modality through imagination.

Good story telling pays its greatest dividends at the *beginning* of the lesson when you are Setting the Stage. Once you have "set up" the lesson and are ready for the "new stuff," it is time to slip back into Say, See, Do mode.

Mastery, Helplessness, and Weaning

You Get What You Pay For

The three-phase lesson design gives us a simple language for describing the teaching process. If this process is carried out thoroughly, *mastery* should be the natural outcome.

But insofar as the process is abbreviated, *failure* will be the outcome. The students' casualty rate on a lesson is a good index of the degree to which the teaching process has been abrogated.

Missing Lesson Parts

The part of the lesson that is most commonly omitted is Structured Practice. Taking mathematics as our model once again, it is not uncommon to see a teacher walk the class through only one or two examples before going to Guided Practice. It is equally common to see the teacher model all of the steps of the computation on the board, pausing only for questions, and then go straight to Guided Practice before the kids do a single problem.

Weaners Think Like Lawyers

When students arrive at Guided Practice on cognitive overload from the teacher's input, help-seeking will be the predictable outcome. Cognitive overload is the first cousin of learned helplessness.

The helpless handraisers will be waving their arms in the air as soon as the teacher says, "Let's get to work." As we say during training:

All the chickens come home to roost in Guided Practice.

Like lawyers, weaners must have a case.

Weaners would like you to spend as much time with them as possible, of course. But, they want your *nurturance,* not your scorn for having done nothing. They want to enroll your helping instincts.

To do this, they must think like lawyers. They must *have a case.*

Skillful weaners, therefore, are sophisticated consumers of teaching. They can tell a faulty product when they see one. They know when a step of the task analysis has been left out. They know when a step is too big. They know when the teacher has assumed too much. They know when they have a good case for seeking help.

When weaners have a good case, they will pursue it with zeal. With their hands waving helplessly in the blue, they will nail you for five minutes of individualized attention.

Preempting Helplessness

The dividends of teaching a lesson thoroughly go beyond the acquisition of learning. Teaching thoroughly provides the *preventative* component in our *weaning program for helpless handraisers.*

Teaching the lesson thoroughly ruins the weaner's case for help-seeking. How can a weaner say, "I don't understand how to do this," after you have walked him or her through several correct performances?

Weaners may, of course, give help-seeking one last try out of pure habit. But, having laid the groundwork for weaning with both thorough teaching and a good VIP, you are in a position to give scant attention for helplessness and generous attention for effort.

With thorough teaching, therefore, you work yourself *out of a job* during Guided Practice. With incomplete teaching, you work yourself *into a job* during Guided Practice.

The Proper Function of Guided Practice

With students working away and helpless handraisers weaned, you have the luxury of pausing, taking a deep breath, and asking yourself, "What should I really be doing with my time during Guided Practice?"

Here's a thought. You could free up your evening for lesson planning by doing your paper grading during Guided Practice. By checking the work *as it is being done,* you could hold the students to high standards just like any good coach. Checking the work while it is being done, however, opens the door to an even greater dividend – the systematic management of motivation.

Section Four

Raising Expectations

Chapter Nine

Creating Motivation

Preview

- The management of productivity in the classroom focuses on building *diligence* (working hard) and *excellence* (working conscientiously).
- In order to get more and better work, we must answer the basic question of motivation, "Why should I?" The answer to this question is called an *incentive.*
- A simple incentive is the juxtaposition of two events: a task and a preferred activity. The best preferred activities in the classroom combine fun with learning.
- Since preferred activities can only be given after the task has been completed correctly, work must be checked as it is being done.
- Say, See, Do Teaching plus the weaning of helpless handraisers frees the teacher to check work in the classroom during Guided Practice rather than at home.

Beyond Weaning

A successful weaning program must build independent learning so that the teacher's time is no longer consumed during Guided Practice with tutoring the helpless handraisers. Once the teacher's time is liberated, possibilities open up for the management of *motivation* and *accountability* that were not previously available.

This chapter will focus on *motivation* – the building of *diligence* in the classroom. The following chapter will focus on *accountability* – the building of *excellence* in the classroom.

What tools can the teacher bring into play in the classroom to give students a reason to be diligent – to work hard? For many students, working hard on school assignments is a novel idea. How can the teacher build a good work ethic in these students – one that is often lacking?

Focus on Motivation

During training, teachers express as much frustration with students who *won't do anything* as with students who disrupt. These are the apathetic students who say:

"Do we have to do this?"

"This is boring."

"We did this last year."

"This stuff is dumb."

How do you motivate the student who simply *does not care?* Motivation is a very complex topic. There are many reasons for the failure of students to apply themselves in school. A few of them we can control, but most of them we cannot.

Things We Do Not Control

A student's attitude toward learning is largely a function of *enrichment in the home environment.* One of the largest single correlates of success in reading during first grade is the amount the child has been read to *before* first grade. Contrast a home in which snuggling with children and reading is a daily nurturing ritual with a home in which books are not present and neglect is the norm. However, you have no control over the student's home life.

Abusive child rearing practices can also seriously handicap a child in school. A child raised by the "yell and hit" method of parenting is likely to harbor a deep resentment toward adult authority. That resentment will be transferred to the teacher once the child comes to school. There are few handicaps to learning greater than a habitual passive-aggressive response to the teacher's instruction. However, you cannot quickly alter the child's personality.

A student's attitude toward learning is also a function of the *ills of society.* Drugs, violence, and constant danger stunt a child's imagination and dreams. However, we cannot wait until the ills of society have been cured before we begin to teach.

A student who has been allowed to substitute *television and video games* for reading may show a short attention span and little interest in classroom tasks. However, you will not have influence over the child's access to video.

We do have some control over the curriculum, but this is not a book about the *content* of instruction. This is a book about the *process* of instruction. What elements of the instructional process do we control that might increase the students' motivation to learn?

Things We Do Control

We do control the students' experience of learning in our classrooms? We can affect the students' willingness to work if we create a learning experience that has crucial elements of motivation built into it.

Our management of academic productivity will focus on two things:

- *Quantity* of work or diligence
- *Quality* of work or excellence

Ideally, we would like the students to *work hard* (diligence), and we would like them to *work conscientiously* (excellence). If we can gain some leverage over these two aspects of performance, we can go a long way toward overcoming disadvantages that children bring from outside of the classroom.

A Dynamic Tension

When students work on a task, quantity and quality are constantly in dynamic tension. If students work too fast, quality suffers. But if they obsess, quantity suffers.

Ideally, we would like students to work as fast as they can *short* of becoming sloppy – to push hard without pushing *too* hard. This balance point between diligence and excellence

Productivity

The management of productivity in the classroom focuses on:

- Quantity – diligence or "working hard"
- Quality – excellence or "working carefully"

is different for each student depending on his or her ability, and it varies from one subject to another.

Discovering Our Own Limits

We have all gone through a process of discovery in learning our own limits with various types of tasks. We have gone too rapidly and made mistakes. And, we have gone too slowly and failed to finish. We try to function somewhere between *haste makes waste* and *get on the ball and hustle!*

By pushing ourselves, we learn that we can accomplish much more than we might have thought possible. When we have a deadline, for example, we focus our attention and mobilize our resources. When we want to do something badly enough, we usually can.

But, we must *want to.* To learn our limits we must *push* ourselves. Finding out what we can accomplish in different areas when we really try is part of discovering who we really are.

Incentives

Why Should I?

Before we will push ourselves to define our own capabilities, we must have a reason to do so. We must have a good answer to the question underlying any discussion of motivation: "*Why should I?*"

Why should I get to work right now? Why should I concentrate so hard? Why should I keep working when I would love to take another break? Why should I stay up late studying when I would love to just "hit the sack?"

Incentives answer the question, 'Why should I?'

Without a good reason, we will effortlessly slip into our comfort zone. Our minds will wander and our hands will slow down as we unconsciously reduce stress.

Any answer to the question, "Why should I?" is called an *incentive.* The term "incentive" is interchangeable with the term "reinforcer." Incentives or reinforcers produce work. You may *offer* a person a reward for doing something, but until they are willing to *work* in order to obtain it, you cannot say that the reward functioned as a reinforcer.

Incentives Drive Decision Making

Life is full of incentives. Showing interest in what a person says can serve as an incentive for that person's continuing to talk to you. A parent's love and approval can serve as an incentive for a child's cooperation.

The opposite of an incentive is a *disincentive.* While incentives give you a reason to do something, disincentives give you a reason to stop.

For example, a child might be sent to a piano teacher only to discover that, because of a lack of any natural ability, progress is agonizingly slow and the price of that progress is agonizingly high. The toil might provide a disincentive for continuing with the piano.

A second child, being gifted, might find that progress is rapid and adulation from proud parents comes at a very reasonable price. This child might find practicing the piano reinforcing. Thus, an activity that is a disincentive for one child may serve as an incentive for another child.

Incentives are, therefore, a matter of *cost* and *benefit*. An experience in which the benefit outweighs the cost tends to be repeated.

Incentive Systems

We call an incentive along with the structure for delivering it an *incentive system*. When teachers plan ways of getting students to work hard or be conscientious, they are designing incentive systems.

Types of Incentive Systems

Informal Incentive Systems

Most incentive systems in family life are *informal*. The universal incentive in child rearing is *love*. Love is both a bond and a motivator. Children who love their parents will often do things to please their parents.

One of the most important jobs of parents, therefore, is to spend a lot of time giving affection to their children – to cuddle and play, to rough-house and horsey ride, to snuggle and read stories. These "good times" serve many purposes – bonding, brain development, and emotional growth to name a few.

One purpose, however, is to establish the parents as powerful reinforcers in their children's lives. Most of the cooperation that parents eventually get from their children will be based upon all of the emotional "money in the bank" that has been stored up over the years.

As soon as you are ready for bed, it will be story time.

If, for example, you ask your twelve-year-old to carry the groceries in from the car, and he or she says, "Okay," realize that your child has just given you a gift. But you have paid for it with all of the love and good times that you and your child have shared over the years. You have just received a small dividend check from your account in the bank.

Formal Incentive Systems

Some incentive systems in life are *formal.* They represent an agreed upon exchange of goods and services. Your paycheck is such an incentive.

Around the house, most of the formal incentive systems that we use as parents are simply routines to get the kids to do things. These routines are well understood in advance.

The one I remember most clearly from my childhood was "the bedtime routine." My mother would say:

> "All right kids, it is 8:30 – time to get ready for bed. Time to wash your face, brush your teeth, and get your pajamas on. As soon as you are in bed, it will be story time. But, lights out at 9:00."

As you can see, the terms of the arrangement were no mystery. The faster we moved, the more time we had for snuggles and stories.

Formal incentives and informal incentives work together. No matter what the formal incentive, we always try harder for someone we love and respect.

Formal Incentives in the Classroom

In the classroom teachers will need both informal and formal incentives to motivate students. Students will naturally work harder for teachers they like.

However, formal incentives will play a more prominent role in the classroom than they do in family life. For one thing, the students don't know you, much less love you, on the first day of school. And, for another thing, some students resent you just because they resent any adult authority who tries to tell them what to do. For these reasons, any teacher will need to develop technical proficiency in the design and implementation of formal incentive systems.

Classroom Incentive Systems

Simple and Complex Incentive Systems

Incentive systems can be simple or complex. A simple incentive system provides a reinforcer in exchange for a specified behavior. However, incentive systems can be complex depending upon the number of bonus clauses, penalty clauses, and fail-safe mechanisms that are built in.

Incentive systems for *discipline* management in the classroom tend to be relatively complex in order to get *everyone* to cooperate with the teacher – even the most disruptive students. These will be discussed in a later section of the book entitled, "Building Responsible Behavior." Incentive systems for *academic productivity,* the subject of this chapter, are relatively simple.

Formal Incentives in the Classroom

Formal incentives will play a more prominent role in the classroom than they do in family life. For one thing, the students don't know you, much less love you, on the first day of school. And, for another thing, some students resent you just because they resent any adult authority who tries to tell them what to do.

Grandma's Rule

Simple classroom incentive systems are straightforward applications of Grandma's Rule which says:

You have to finish your dinner before you get your dessert.

Effective parents and teachers have always been instinctive incentive managers. They have a knack for pairing chores with treats in order to get the work done.

Traditional Incentives

When I was a kid in grade school, I had teachers who used Grandma's Rule. They would come by my desk, look at my work, and say:

> "I think you know how to do this, Fred. When you complete that example, you may place your paper on my desk and then work on your art project for the remainder of the period."

I was thrilled! I loved working on art projects!

Most of my teachers were really into "projects." We did science projects, art projects, current events projects.

My teachers did not have to stop what they were doing in order to get us started on our projects. The projects were already organized so that teachers could simply excuse us and continue working with the rest of the class.

For example, all of my elementary classrooms had an easel in the back with three jars of tempera paint in the primary colors and a few well worn brushes. Every week we painted a new mural on the chalkboard depicting the theme of our social studies unit or the coming holiday. I can remember working on the horses for the wagon trains going west, the sails of the Nina, Pinta, and Santa Maria, and the turkeys in the Thanksgiving scene.

My sixth grade teacher, Miss Bakey, had a different system. She had us all bring a shoebox from home to serve as our "project box." We put our names on the boxes and filled them with the materials needed for an art or science project. All of the project boxes were lined up on a shelf beneath the window casements where we could easily find them when we finished our assignments.

You have to finish your dinner before you get your dessert.

The Problem with Traditional Incentives

The problem with these traditional and rather "seat of the pants" incentive systems was that the same seven or eight kids always got to paint the murals and work on science projects. They were the "smarties" who finished early. Everyone else worked until the bell rang.

While I loved doing these projects, as far as incentive management is concerned, these systems were naive and backwards. The kids who already had a good work ethic got all of the "goodies." Those who needed a reason to try harder almost never received an incentive.

My teachers probably weren't thinking about incentives, anyway. They were probably just trying to keep us busy. Rather than providing incentives for those in need of some motivation, our projects served more as "sponge activities" – learning activities to soak up time that would otherwise have been wasted. To make the transition from a sponge activity to a cost-effective classroom incentive system that serves the many rather than just the few, we will need to learn a lot more about the technology of incentive management.

Incentive System Design

Dinner and Dessert

A simple incentive system, as described by Grandma's Rule, is the juxtaposition of two events – a task (dinner) and a reinforcer or "preferred activity" (dessert).

- **Dinner** – the thing I *have* to do
- **Dessert** – the thing I *want* to do

The heart of an incentive system is the preferred activity which answers the question, "Why should I?" It gives the student something to look forward to in the not-too-distant future. It should be fun. Hence, the truism of incentive management: *No joy, no work.*

Criterion of Mastery

While the heart of an incentive system is the *preferred activity*, there is an additional, equally important element: the *criterion of mastery*. Every lesson in the classroom is a learning experiment. Any learning experiment needs a working definition of when mastery has taken place.

A criterion of mastery is typically stated in terms of *consecutive correct performances*. How many *in a row* do the students have to do *correctly* before you can relax and say, "They've got it!" It is a judgement call, of course. Too few feels "thin," and too many feels like we're beating it to death.

Criteria of mastery for complex human learning typically range from five out of five to ten out of ten. This is a sensible range that you can use in the classroom. Notice, however, that criteria of mastery are *not* stated in the form of a percentage, such as:

> "When you pass your post-test with a score of 80% or above, you may proceed to the next unit."

While this example represents common practice in education, I would not recommend it. I would doubt if anyone reading this book would equate a 20% error rate with the normal meaning of the word "excellence." Would you buy a car built to that criterion, or would you call it a piece of junk?

Criterion of Mastery and Guided Practice

In the classroom, the criterion of mastery is typically employed during Guided Practice. As the students do the assignment, the teacher works the crowd while checking the students' papers.

Students must meet the criterion of mastery before they can be excused to do their preferred activities. The transition to Guided Practice for a math assignment might sound like this:

"Class, I would like you to open your books to page 127 and look at the practice set on the top of the page. As you can see, the problems are very familiar. We have done the first four of them together.

"We have twenty minutes until the bell. I will be coming around to check your work and to answer any questions. As soon as I mark five in a row correct, you may hand in your paper and work on your projects for the remainder of the period."

Checking students' work during Guided Practice is straightforward in a subject like math where the teacher can carry an answer key. Interactions with students might sound like this:

"That one is correct, and so is that one. You have three in a row correct. Two more and you can go work on your project."

Dynamic Tension Revisited

Keep in mind, a criterion of mastery is stated in terms of *consecutive correct performances*. In the previous example the student had to have *five in a row* correct in order to gain access to his or her preferred activity. If that student were to do three problems correctly and then make an error on the fourth, they would have to start over.

Thus, the more problems a student completes correctly, the more they have to lose should they become sloppy. As the student's total of correct problems grows, they gain a greater and greater vested interest in doing the next one *carefully*.

The precondition of having high standards is the teacher's ability to check students' work as it is being done.

By having a criterion of mastery paired with preferred activities, the teacher creates the dynamic tension between speed and accuracy that trains students to work fast while being conscientious. In this way students learn to explore the limits of their abilities.

Continuous Work Check and High Standards

Having an incentive system for diligence is inseparable from having high standards. If the teacher were to allow students to work on their projects as soon as they finished *without* first checking the work, they would precipitate a disaster. The student would rush through the assignment as rapidly as possible, heedless of error, in order to get to the preferred activity as soon as possible. This is called a *speed* incentive.

The precondition of having high standards, therefore, is the teacher's ability to check the student's work *as it is being done* – typically during Guided Practice. Being free to check work during Guided Practice requires that the teacher's time and attention *not* be occupied by distractions – like tutoring helpless handraisers.

For this reason our weaning program for helpless handraisers had to precede our discussion of motivation. You could characterize the chapters preceding this one as, "everything you can possibly do to make yourself unemployed during Guided Practice so you can check the students' work."

Having high standards, therefore, is the *culmination* of classroom management. It is not where you begin.

Incentive Management Reality Check

A Sordid Past

Education has had a love-hate relationship with incentives in the classroom. In the 1960's many educators were anti-behavioral. In the 1970's, after accepting the notion that reinforcers produce motivation, educators went "hog wild."

Teachers were encouraged to offer "rewards" for everything under the sun, and administrators passed out so many certificates of merit at awards assemblies that trash cans became stuffed with them. The "hog wild" era of rewards in the classroom produced abuses as well as a strong reaction against those abuses.

Misconceptions bread anti-misconceptions with more heat than light being generated. Some theorists, wary of the overuse of points, tokens, treats, and meaningless "awards," decided that all incentives were bribery. They were to be eliminated.

This reaction is a classic example of "throwing the baby out with the bathwater." Teachers need a way of managing motivation in the classroom, particularly with students who just don't care.

Rather than turning our backs on incentives, we need to learn to do it right. It would be useful, therefore, to take a moment to clear away the underbrush so we could see the topic clearly.

"Bribery is the definition of malpractice in incentive management."

Bribery

In order to exploit incentives while avoiding their abuse, we need to understand bribery. Are all incentives bribes? To eliminate confusion, it will be helpful to first categorize formal incentives as either *proactive* or *reactive*.

A **proactive** incentive system is an exchange of rewards for work that is established *in advance*. These exchanges are routine events in family life that give parents some leverage in getting their kids to do things. For example:

- As soon as you are ready for bed, we'll have story time.
- As soon as you've finished your homework, you can watch TV.
- As soon as you've finished practicing the piano, you can go outside to play.

A **reactive** incentive system, on the other hand, is an exchange that is established *in the heat of the moment*. Imagine a situation in which a father wants some cooperation from his son but doesn't know how to get it. The child says, "No" and won't budge. Frustration sets in.

The father *reacts* to this dilemma in the heat of the moment by offering the child a reward for cooperation. This *reactive* incentive constitutes a *bribe*. Take, for example, the following argument:

Father: "Billy, I want you to clean your room."

Billy: "I don't want to."

Father : "Now, I want that room cleaned. It is a mess!"

Billy: "I want to go outside and play!"

Father : "Not until you get this room cleaned!"

Billy: "I'm not doing it!"

Father : "Oh, yes you are!"

Billy: "You can't make me!"

Father : "Listen, I'll give you fifty cents when this room is clean, and then you can go outside and play."

By digging in his heels and saying "No," Billy has just shaken fifty cents out of the money tree.

Unfortunately, when you use incentives incorrectly, they blow up in your face and give you the *opposite* of what you wanted. In this example, the father has just reinforced Billy for *noncooperation* rather than cooperation.

By digging in his heels and saying "No," Billy has just shaken fifty cents out of the money tree. If he had simply cleaned his room without an argument, he wouldn't have gotten a penny. What do you suppose will be going through Billy's mind the next time mom or dad ask him to do some chore around the house?

To put it simply, bribery is the definition of *malpractice* in incentive management. Nobody who is well trained in the technology of incentive management would even consider offering an incentive in this fashion.

Incentives Are Unavoidable

Incentives Are Everywhere

The notion that you can turn your back on incentive management is both comical and costly. Incentives are unavoidable Any way in which you schedule work during a class period will produce an incentive system of some kind. You have three choices. One of these three will happen with your knowledge or without it.

Incentives for Speed

Employing a criterion of mastery requires that you have enough time to check the work *as it is being done.* As mentioned earlier, if you excuse students to do their preferred activities *without* first checking their work, you create a *speed incentive* which trains students to work "fast and sloppy."

Incentives for Dawdling

If you are unable to check work as it is being done and do not wish to create a speed incentive, you are left with few options. You could always excuse the "smarties" to do preferred activities. That is what my teachers did. But the rest of the class will have to work *until the bell rings.*

Unfortunately, this creates a *dawdling incentive* for the rest of the class. Students say to themselves, "Why work yourself to death if it doesn't get you anywhere?" Students who must work until the bell rings will eventually learn to slow the rate of work in order to fill the time.

Incentives for Diligence

If you 1) *offer* a preferred activity and 2) *utilize* a criterion of mastery as you 3) *check* the students' work, you have it all – hard work and high standards. This, of course, is our goal.

Parts of the Package for Building Motivation

Incentive Options	Task	Work Check	Preferred Activity
Speed	X		X
Dawdling	X		
Diligence and Excellence	X	X	X

You have three classroom incentive options.

No Escape

You may as well get used to it. Everything you do in the classroom creates an incentive system of some kind. You get effective management or you get mismanagement depending on whether you have the whole package or just part of the package (table, below left).

As you can see, accountability is the most critical logistical hurdle that a teacher must overcome in order to build diligence and, with it, excellence. Work check must be *quick* and *cheap* so that it can be done while the students are working on the assignment. The entire next chapter will be devoted to this topic.

Checking Written Work

At this point in training someone will say,

> "I see how this works with math. But I teach social studies, and apart from group discussions, most of our in-class work involves writing. There is no answer key for writing. What am I supposed to do?"

In fact, you do have an answer key for writing whether you know it or not. You carry the standards for written work in you head, and you reserve the right to excuse students to do their preferred activities when they meet your standards. Furthermore, those standards can be quite individualized.

Praise, Prompt, and Leave during writing is usually just a brief directive for improving a sentence or paragraph. As the student's writing approaches what you consider to be a good effort, you might say,

> "We have this last paragraph in good shape now. All it needs is a little more pazazz. Go to the thesaurus and find 'upgrades' to these three adjectives. Then, after I check it, you may hand it in and work on your project."

A Final Note

Our discussion of incentives for diligence and excellence does not imply that I actually believe it will always be possible. I know how rushed and chaotic classroom life can be.

But, at least, you know your options. If you cannot have a proper incentive system for diligence and excellence, an incentive for dawdling is usually the "default mode." If it happens occasionally, it is not the end of the world. If you can provide incentives for diligence and excellence frequently, you can still have a major impact on your students' work ethic.

Preferred Activities

Keep It Cheap

Preferred activities are the fun part of the incentive system. They give students a reason to hustle.

In addition to being desirable, however, preferred activities must be cheap. They must be readily available, easy to use and represent a reasonable amount of prep time for the teacher.

Preferred activities are usually organized and ready to go *before* the lesson starts. The teacher will not have time to stop what he or she is doing during Guided Practice in order to get each student started on a separate preferred activity.

The "project box" that my sixth grade teacher used was very efficient. We spent most of one class period early in the grading period organizing our project boxes. For that investment, the teacher was free to teach without having to continually stop during Guided Practice to answer the question, "Now, what do I do?"

"Anything that the students eagerly look forward to can serve as a preferred activity."

Types of Preferred Activities

The range of preferred activities available to a teacher in the classroom is quite broad and varied. Literally anything that the students eagerly look forward to can serve as a preferred activity. Many would come under the heading of "enrichment activities." The following suggestions only scratch the surface.

Art Projects: In addition to the tempera paint murals on the chalkboards of my childhood classrooms, I can remember innumerable art projects accompanying social studies and science units.

We sketched and painted everything from wild animals to cell structure, from maps with rivers and mountains to villages of thatched huts. We drew igloos and log cabins.

We would decorate the room. Every upcoming holiday or back-to-school night provided the teacher with preferred activities. We would decorate walls and bulletin boards. To this day I cannot understand why a teacher would spend valuable time creating bulletin boards when the net result is to preempt a wonderful preferred activity.

My high school French teacher was particularly clever. She assigned each of her five huge casement windows to a different class period. Each class had the job of transforming one casement into a beautiful stained-glass window.

Preferred activities should be cheap, readily available, and easy to use.

Our teacher surrounded us with examples from the cathedrals of France, and she taught us how the artisans built the windows. Our materials were colored cellophane and electrician's tape. We went through all of the stages of construction from drawing the life-size cartoons to "leading" the "glass." We rushed to complete our daily assignments so that we could get to work on our windows.

Music Projects: When the teacher does whole-group instruction, the class can have a whole-group preferred activity. Our foreign language classes were particularly well suited for doing this since so many drills and dictations were group activities.

When we completed our stained-glass windows in French class, we moved right along to French folk songs. I can still sing some of them. We had to practice so that we could serenade the school before the spring break.

Listening centers make great preferred activities. Some teachers use listening centers to teach music appreciation. Other teachers put on background music to make whole-group preferred activities even more enjoyable. Sometimes small groups of students rushed to complete their assignments in order to work up a routine for a student talent show.

Learning Projects: One question that I was never asked in school was, "What do you want to know?" Children are curious by their very nature. This truism even applies to students who may not be very curious about the subjects contained in our normal curriculum.

Having students describe their special interests will help you identify relevant learning projects. It may be dwarf stars or race cars, but whatever the topic, it can become a research project.

Preferred activities, therefore, provide the teacher with an avenue for teaching research skills on a topic that the student is motivated to explore. The student could also prepare a presentation to the class as part of the project, complete with visual aids.

Interest Centers and Computer Centers: Interest centers are ready-made preferred activities. In addition, access to computers or special equipment of any kind can be a powerful motivator.

Learning Games: Almost anything in the curriculum can be taught in the form of a game. Books of games have been published for learning everything from history to the multiplication of fractions. Books of learning puzzles and mind benders are also available for different grade levels.

Reading and Writing for Pleasure: Having students read their library books is a time-honored preferred activity. Journal writing is another traditional favorite. Other teachers have the students work on a class newspaper.

Helping the Teacher: Students who finish their work early are natural candidates for peer tutoring. Training the class to use Praise, Prompt, and Leave gives students a valuable teaching skill.

Some students like to help the teacher with work check, writing test questions, developing materials for interest centers, or even helping the teacher search for good preferred activity games and puzzles. You can often find a bright student with artistic ability who will make beautiful VIPs for you before you teach the next lesson.

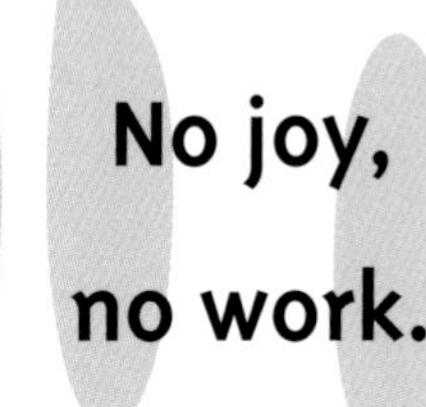

Extra Work: Using preferred activity time to build up extra credit is particularly appealing to some students. Memorizing poetry, doing more advanced assignments, or preparing a special class presentation are examples.

Some students want to do their homework during preferred activity time. These are often the high achievers whose after school hours are taken up with extra-curricular activities.

Scheduling Preferred Activities

Lesson-by-Lesson

The simplest way to schedule preferred activities is on a lesson-by-lesson basis. Grandma's Rule implies the juxtaposition of two activities, one that you have to do (the task) and one that you would rather do (the preferred activity).

These two activities are most commonly scheduled back-to-back. When you finish the first activity (correctly, of course), you can work on the second activity until the period is over.

Sometimes, however, this arrangement leaves the teacher and the students feeling as though the day is too chopped up, with never enough time to really get into the preferred activity. In such situations, the teacher may want to consider a *work contract.*

Work Contract

A work contract is simply a preferred activity that follows the completion of a *series* of tasks. Teachers in self-contained classrooms might leave the end of the day open for preferred activity time once all of the day's assignments have been completed. Teachers in a departmentalized setting might have preferred activity time once a week on Friday.

One clever way of organizing a weekly work contract is called "Freaky Friday." Friday, of course, is the day on which all of the week's assignments must be completed. Explain the rules of Freaky Friday to the class as follows:

> "Class, tomorrow we are going to have Freaky Friday. Let me remind you how it works. Before you can start Freaky Friday, all of your assignments for the week must be completed and turned in. Only then can you participate.
>
> "For Freaky Friday, I will put seven assignments on the board. You may choose any four of them and omit any three. When you have completed your four assignments to my satisfaction and handed them in, you may work on your project for the *rest of the day.*"

Some teachers have two lists, column A and column B, with the core subjects in column A. Students must choose two assignments from column A and two from column B. This device prevents students from avoiding all of the subjects that are more demanding.

It is hard for adults to appreciate how sweet it is for young people to have control over their own destiny. One teacher who had implemented Freaky Friday had a parent storm into her classroom after school and say,

> "I understand from my son that students get to do whatever they want all day Friday. Is that true? The children only work during four days of the week?"

The parent was slightly misinformed, of course. The child simply said that, "We get to do whatever we want on Fridays." In the excitement over getting to exercise freedom of choice, the student failed to clarify that "anything we want" included a full day's worth of academic work. But, how sweet it is to choose.

A Sense of Fun

You cannot have preferred activity time without having fun. Some teachers just have a sense of fun. They bring it with them into the classroom and find ways of making it happen.

But, implementing preferred activity time must also be affordable for the teacher. Work check must be cheap, organization must be simple, and a repertoire of preferred activities must be readily at hand.

Using preferred activities becomes much easier when the faculty members work together to gather preferred activity ideas and materials in a central "PAT Bank." Discovering more and more ways of making learning fun is a hallmark of our professional growth as teachers.

By understanding incentive systems, we can have our fun with learning and get motivation for free. Having fun with learning is, therefore, one of the main avenues to raising standards in education. Remember the maxim of incentive management: *No joy, no work.*

PAT Bank

Using preferred activities becomes much easier when the faculty members work together to gather preferred activity ideas and materials in a central "PAT Bank."

Chapter Ten

Providing Accountability

Preview

- Incentive systems require continuous work check to ensure that students work carefully rather than just quickly.
- Quality control requires designing the work process so that excellence is the natural outcome.
- Say, See, Do Teaching and the creation of independent learning provide the new "production process" upon which the pursuit of excellence can be built.
- Quality control requires that the product be built right the first time. This occurs during a lesson in the form of thorough Structured Practice and continuous work check during Guided Practice.
- When work becomes too complex to scan and check rapidly, it is time for the teacher to get help. Training students to check their own work conscientiously solves the problem.

Building Excellence

Accountability and Excellence

To students, incentive systems are all about preferred activities. For unmotivated students, preferred activities usually provide the only reason for putting any serious effort into an assignment. These students need short-term goals.

But, as we learned in the previous chapter, there is another key element in the process of building motivation – the criterion of mastery. The criterion of mastery requires that the work be done *correctly* which requires that work be checked as it is being done. You cannot build diligence unless you simultaneously build excellence.

Quality Control

In education we talk endlessly about building excellence and raising standards. Our ability to talk about excellence would seem to be inversely proportional to our ability to produce it.

The primary work environment of children is school. Their work ethic will be shaped by their experience in the classroom.

In the classroom we will try to replace laziness with hard work and sloppiness with conscientiousness. It is natural for us to want higher standards for our students than many students want for themselves. If unmotivated students do not learn good work habits in our classrooms, they will probably go through life as we found them.

If we are to be builders of excellence rather than just talkers of excellence, we must understand how excellence is built. Excellence will be produced in our classrooms in exactly the same way that it is produced at Caterpillar or Hewlett-Packard or Intel. The building of excellence is called *quality control.*

The goal of quality control is to train students to come up to our standards rather than for us to lower our standards to match their pre-existing work ethic. To achieve this goal we must spend some time learning about the technology of quality control.

Excellent Work from Ordinary People

The Typical Work Force

It is a rare student who wakes up in the morning and says wistfully, "Maybe today they will finally teach me how a bill becomes a law." In fact, many students, in spite of our "anticipatory set," haven't a clue as to the ultimate purpose of many of the lessons we teach.

Some students will go along with us and try their best regardless. Others, however, will take a more utilitarian approach to learning. They will habitually ask the motivational question, *"Why should I?"* Until they get a satisfactory answer, they will remain unmoved by our efforts.

The random assortment of personalities that walks into the classroom every day is known outside of educational circles as "the typical work force." Some are "gung-ho," some are "heel draggers," and most are somewhere in between. To be successful we must get good work from all of them.

Where Does Excellence Come From?

Part of the reason that some students do their best resides in your *lesson.* Obviously, relevant lessons are better than irrelevant ones, and interesting lessons are better than boring ones.

But if you think that the primary source of motivation is in the ability of your lesson to grab the students' souls, keep in mind that the typical work force produces widgets day after day without having a deep love of widgets. In some places they produce excellent widgets, and in other places they produce defective widgets.

Part of the reason that some students might do their best resides in the *student.* Some students learn at an early age that, "If something is worth doing, it is worth doing *right.*"

The Goal of Quality Control

The goal of quality control is to train students to come up to our standards rather than for us to lower our standards to match their work ethic.

But if you think that the primary source of motivation is the work ethic of your students, keep in mind that the craftsman seeking perfection is the exception rather than the rule. In the classroom, as in the automobile factory, you will have to produce excellence with the typical work force, or you will not produce excellence.

Organizing the Work Force

Both the captains of industry and classroom teachers, therefore, will have to work with the same raw material, the human species with all of its quirks. The question that will confront any leader is, "How do you organize a typical work force to produce excellent work?"

The Locus of Quality Control

Quality control can take place at any work site in either of two places during the production process:

- ***In-Production Quality Control*** – during production
- ***Post-Production Quality Control*** – at the end of production

In-Production Quality Control

Imagine that a worker at an automobile factory, call him Joe, has the job of connecting some electric wires that go from the radio to the rear speakers. To do so, Joe must connect three wires: the *blue* wire on *top*, the *yellow* wire in the *middle*, and the *red* wire on the *bottom*.

However, Joe is new to the job. Instead of doing the job correctly, he puts the red wire on the top and the blue wire on the bottom.

On the production line, a quality control supervisor, call her Carol, walks from station to station checking the work. As she carefully watches the new worker, she notices the error in wiring.

What would follow, ideally, would be a short, painless, and efficient teaching interaction that would correct the error. Carol might say,

> "On these speaker wires, the blue one goes on top and the red goes on the bottom. I'll sketch a diagram on this 3-by-5 card so you can double check."

Types of Quality Control

In-Production Quality Control

- *Quick (Praise, Prompt, and Leave)*
- *Continuous*
- *Preventative*
- *Cheap*

Post-Production Quality Control

- *Slow (Tear down and rebuild)*
- *Delayed*
- *Remedial*
- *Expensive*

In this example, corrective feedback has taken the form of Prompt and Leave with a VIP for quick reference. Teaching has been quick and efficient with little reason for defensiveness. And the job will probably be done right for the rest of the day.

Just as importantly, Carol has done very little work. She has insured that the person responsible for the wiring does the work and does it *right*. She is free to continue walking the production line.

Post-Production Quality Control

Imagine that the error in wiring was *not* fixed during production. At the *end* of the production line, the *post-production* quality control staff takes over.

In the automobile factory these specialists are the quick diagnosis and quick-fix artists. They have a long checklist, and they go through the car piece by piece to make sure that everything works.

Imagine that the inspector, Raymond, is going through his checklist. He tests the ignition, the headlights, and the radio in rapid succession. He turns the fader knob to the rear speakers, and everything goes dead.

"This is the third one of these we've had this morning!" he explodes. He turns off the ignition and begins his diagnostic procedure. Finding the problem, he reverses the wires that were installed backwards and hops back into the car to recheck the rear speakers.

Post-Production Quality Control Is Expensive
As you can see, the post-production quality control specialist has a far more complex and time consuming job than the in-production supervisor. Rather than investing only a few seconds in corrective feedback, the post-production specialist must *diagnose the problem, take the unit apart, and rebuild it.*

Consequently, post-production quality control is labor-intensive, time-consuming, and exasperating. It also has no effect on the production process. Rather than preventing problems, it only remediates them. New errors are being made as the old ones are being fixed.

This comparison of cost and benefit between in-production and post-production quality control leads to one of the cardinal rules of quality control:

It is always cheaper to build it right the first time.

As the saying goes:

If you don't have time to build it right the first time, when will you have time to fix it?

You may wish to consider these sayings the next time you take a stack of papers home to grade.

Zero-Defects Production

Excellence Is the Primary Product
Zero-defects production is a term from quality management in industry. It refers to designing the entire production process from the ground up so that *excellence is the primary product.* Assessment is built into *each step* of the production process. Workers are trained not only to do the job, but also to check the job and certify it before passing it along. In-production quality control supervisors simply *augment* the check routines of the workers in a joint effort to build it right the first time.

Errors are, therefore, detected and corrected immediately. An often cited example is the fact that workers on the Toyota production line can pull an overhead cable to stop the production process any time they see something wrong. Every worker is part of a *culture of excellence.*

Post-production quality control is labor-intensive and exasperating.

Excellence Is Not an Add-On

In contrast, naive attempts by top management to improve quality usually focus upon upgrading supervision of the *existing production process.* But the workers are not trained and integrated into the quality control effort. As a result, there is still a large reliance upon post-production quality control, and the quest for excellence "hits the wall" long before the error rate reaches the target that defines excellence.

Workers must be trained to function as an integral part of the quality control process. Production workers at Toyota, for example, receive 500 hours of training just so they can function as members of a quality control circle. That training includes a course in statistics so they can tell whether a defect is the result of a random error or a systematic error.

It is always cheaper to build it right the first time.

Zero-Defects Production in the Classroom

Quality Control During the Lesson

You might think of *Tools for Teaching* so far as a text on zero-defects production in the classroom. To see how all of the pieces of the quality control puzzle fit together, let's return to our math lesson at the board to see the whole picture at a glance.

- **Say, See, Do Teaching:** We have walked the students through the computation one step at a time, checking their work after every step.
- **Structured Practice:** We have walked the students through three or four additional examples of the computation. While the pace gradually quickens, we are still able to check their work after every step. We are creating *perfect practice,* and the students are approaching *automaticity.*
- **Visual Instructional Plan:** A VIP for the lesson is clearly visible. During Guided Practice, the students will be able to review prior instruction at any time by simply glancing at the VIP.
- **Guided Practice:** During Guided Practice students start working "on their own." We work the crowd in order to supervise "production," but very few students need any help. Many students are already at Independent Practice, and needy students have a very weak case for clinging.
- **Praise, Prompt, and Leave:** If a student does need help, we can use Praise, Prompt, and Leave in conjunction with our VIP in order to be gone in seconds. If a helpless handraiser tries to cling, we can immediately switch into an extinction program.
- **In-Production Quality Control:** During Guided Practice we should be relatively *unemployed.* Having been freed from the burden of tutoring helpless handraisers, we can now do in-production quality control by checking students' work as it is being done.
- **Incentives for Diligence and Excellence:** Since work can now be checked as it is being done, we can employ a criterion of mastery to give students access to preferred activities without creating a speed incentive. Having a near-term goal gives students a reason to work hard.

Dividends After School

With work check done in class for the most part, the after-school hours that you devote to teaching can now be invested where they will yield the greatest return. Better to invest that time in planning tomorrow's instruction rather than in doing yesterday's clerical work.

Of course, some work will go home. Final drafts of essays must be read with words of praise written in the margins, or students will feel that you don't care. And, some paper grading may be left over due to the interruptions and distractions typical of life in the classroom. But at least the bulk of your effort can be directed toward the future rather than the past.

The Traditional Approach To Work Check

The Paper Grading Trap

American education has a folklore concerning the production of excellence that, unfortunately, has little to do with either motivation or the production of excellence. Teachers take papers home to grade in the hope that this added effort will somehow translate into better learning. Students throw most of these papers into the wastebasket.

The students are trying to teach us a lesson about quality control. When we accept a student's work, we clearly signal that the production process is over. In the students' minds, they are *done* with the assignment. Rekindling their enthusiasm for that same task tomorrow will be like raising Lazarus from the dead.

In addition, by accepting faulty work, the teacher has already taught the students that mediocre work is acceptable. After all, you accepted it. This common error in quality control is expressed in the following rule:

The standard of excellence on any job site is defined by the sloppiest piece of work that you will accept.

Going Over the Papers in Class

Many teachers, in an attempt to keep last night's paper-grading from going to waste, go over the assignment again in class the following day item by item. This is both *very* boring and *very* inefficient – a process guaranteed to render most of the class comatose.

"Would anyone like me to go over problem number *one* from yesterday?"

Imagine that half-a-dozen students actually cared. This means that twenty four students out of thirty *don't care*. Such an exercise would not create a very good time-on-task ratio – 1 in 5. A rowdy classroom will be the teacher's reward.

The harder you work, the less excellence you can produce.

Bopping Is Costly

The problems with paper grading described above are all part of the expense of post-production quality control. Post-production quality control is an unavoidable by-product of Bop 'til You Drop Teaching because you have no time to check the students' work in class.

With Bop 'til You Drop, you work hard presenting the lesson, and then, due to cognitive overload, you work even harder during Guided Practice as you tutor the helpless handraisers. Since you are too busy during Guided Practice to check work, paper grading will consume your evening.

In contrast, Say, See, Do Teaching makes work check easier. Having eliminated the need for tutoring, helping

interactions during Guided Practice are few and brief. This frees the teacher to spend time with students who want to learn. Work check can be done "on the fly" as part of working the crowd. We will refer to this pattern of work during Guided Practice as "cruising and checking."

If you want to make accountability *expensive,* do it after the lesson is finished (post-production). If you want to make accountability *affordable,* do it in class while the work is being done (in-production).

The chronic overwork of bopping compared to Say, See, Do Teaching creates the following irony:

The harder you work,
the less excellence you can produce.

The less you work,
the more excellence you can produce.

Checking Complex Work

Checking Takes Time

When you do help an individual student during Guided Practice, you must always *check their work* as a prelude to giving corrective feedback. Since chit-chat spreads across the room in 10 seconds, work check must be done quickly.

Complexity Slows You Down

Your ability to check work as you move among the students is largely a function of the *visual complexity* of the work. If the work becomes sufficiently complex, work check bogs down.

If work check bogs down, you lose your ability to work the crowd and check work. This undermines your ability to utilize a criterion of mastery. As a result, incentives for diligence and excellence move out of reach.

In order to gain speed with visually complex work, we will have to become more efficient. *One* method is for *you* to become more efficient. A *second* method is to utilize *students* to check work as part of the quality control process.

Checking Work Yourself

Answer Keys

Let's return to math due to its stepwise nature and visual clarity. After we examine work check with math, we can move to more complex assignments like writing.

I mentioned in the previous chapter that a teacher might check math during Guided Practice by carrying an *answer key.* Traditional answer keys, however, won't do the job.

Let's return to our description of the biologically natural way of giving corrective feedback from chapter six. To review, our eye is naturally drawn to the error, and when we speak, we tend to focus on the error.

Traditional answer keys are perfectly aligned with this natural way of doing things. They simply list the correct answer for each problem.

Checking work has always been synonymous with checking the problems that are *wrong*– literally, with a red check mark. Checking work in this fashion discourages students and omits any information that might improve performance. It's like saying to the student,

"You messed up. Try again."

A traditional answer key leaves us hamstrung when we attempt to do Praise, Prompt, and Leave. For Praise, Prompt, and Leave we need to be able to see the part of the problem that is right and the part that is wrong *before* we get to the final answer. The part that is *right* would provide the *praise* statement, and the part that is *wrong* would provide the *prompt.*

You could do these checking operations in your head, of course, but it would take too long, and you might make an error. Both of these problems would only get worse as the work became more complex.

Check Masters

To check the body of the problem quickly and accurately, you will need a new kind of checking aid – a *check master.* A check master shows the *entire* problem including the answer. Work check then becomes a series of quick scans which note *matches* and *mismatches* as in the following example of triple digit multiplication.

Student's Work		Check Master
276		276
x598		x 598
2208	match	2208
2474	mismatch	2484
1380	match	1380
164948		165048

Give corrective feedback as follows:

- **Match**: praise
- **First Mismatch**: prompt

Your helping interaction might sound like this:

"You have multiplied your 5 and 8 correctly. Double check your 9 multiplication, and re-add. I'll be back in a minute."

Making Check Masters

Since text book companies don't publish check masters, where do you get them? You can prepare them yourself in advance, but this would consume precious lesson planning time. There has to be a simpler way.

If you can, have the kids do it. If the advanced math group is capable of checking their own work, they can provide all of your check masters. If that solution is not practical, find some bright kid with good penmanship who will do it the day before for extra credit.

Keep a file with check masters and VIPs for each lesson together. It will be ready for next semester.

Having Students Check The Work

Getting Help

When you feel defeated by either the volume or complexity of the work check, it is time to *switch strategies.* If you cannot keep up, it is time to *get help.*

Where is the handiest source of free labor in a classroom? The *students,* of course! Work check that would take one person thirty minutes might take thirty people one minute. Teachers have always exploited this logic by having the students exchange papers for grading.

But, you must train the students to check work *carefully* and *honestly*. How do you organize the class to do this?

After all, we wouldn't want students helping out their buddies, would we?

"Keep 'Em Honest" in Math Class

Kids are competitive by nature. We can use this trait to teach them to be both conscientious and honest. To do this we will play a game called "Keep 'Em Honest."

> **The standard of excellence on any job site is defined by the sloppiest piece of work that you will accept.**

Divide the math class into two teams. Each person on team A is paired with a person on team B. Have these pairs place their desks side by side.

Write a math problem on the board, and give the students a time limit for doing the problem.

"All right, class, you have two minutes for this next problem. Ready? Go!"

Give the students a warning as time runs out.

"Class, you have fifteen seconds."

When time runs out, go through the following check routine.

- "Time! Exchange your papers."
- "The answer is…"
- "Grade them and return them."
- "How many got it right on team A?" (students raise their hands)
- "How many on team B?"
- "The score is now ____ to ____ ."
- Alright, class, for the next problem you have three minutes…"

Would students on team A let students on team B have extra time to work on the problem? Fat chance! They'll say, "I'll take that!" and grab the paper.

Would anybody on team A cheat for anybody on team B? Not likely!

After the papers are returned, would students on team A let their counterparts on team B hold up their hands if they didn't get it right? What do you think?

The whole routine takes seconds, and each team keeps the other team honest. The teacher tallies the number of correct answers for each team at the end of each problem and adds that number to each team's total score. With every additional problem the score mounts and the tension builds.

Whenever school work is presented in the form of team competition, students think it is a game rather than an assignment. Everybody wins. The students have fun, and you have *no papers to take home.*

Group Competition

Having students check each other's work conscientiously as a by-product of team competition provides us with a general pattern that can be applied to a wide variety of situations. You could, for example, have each of your cooperative learning groups be a team. You might even have the teams form a league with league standings.

Post scores for each team based on how well they do on any given assignment. For work check on that assignment, pair the teams randomly. Let's call one of the pairings team A and team B.

Have team A and B exchange papers so that each individual on one team is responsible for scoring the work of an individual on the other team. Provide a scoring protocol so that the students' grading will be up to your standards. Score as follows:

- All correct answers by each team are worth 1 point.
- Any error that team A finds in the work of team B counts as one additional point for team A.
- Papers are then returned for double checking. Any *error in checking* made by one team gives 2 additional points to the other team.
- Total team points for the assignment are computed by adding the points gained through work check to the points gained for correct answers.

Once again, the students will check work conscientiously while keeping each other honest. This model can be applied to any subject, even a foreign language class.

Foreign Language Class

A high school foreign language teacher complained to me of her "lost weekends." She described filling her car with students' language notebooks three times a semester, and getting nothing done all weekend except grading six weeks worth of language assignments.

To reduce her workload while making work check more relevant, I suggested reorganizing the class into work-groups. She divided the room into groups of four with a student in each group who could serve as team leader. She then had the leaders drill their group members for the upcoming test. Test scores jumped.

She then developed a *competition* between the groups. Review prior to the test became far more task-oriented and intense. Again, test scores jumped.

Next, she developed a VIP for each type of language exercise contained in the notebooks. She drew the VIPs on butcher paper and posted them so that the students had a good visual guide as they checked work.

The last step in problem solving was to implement the Keep 'Em Honest format for work check. She had the teams exchange language notebooks for checking and double checking.

It worked like a charm. The teacher said, "Last week we checked the notebooks in twelve minutes flat! No more 'lost weekends!'"

Quality Control Circles

Building Work Groups

There are many students turning in many assignments, and there is only one teacher. If you are going to monitor work as it is being done, you will need some help.

Teaching students to check their own work should be part of any lesson. How else would students know whether or not they are doing it right?

In industry, workers are organized into quality control circles in order to implement quality management on a day-to-day basis. As mentioned earlier, workers receive extensive of "in-service training" so they will have the tools to function as part of a quality control team.

The same logic applies to the classroom. If the students understand the assignment, they should be able to check it. The ability of students to check their own work is, in fact, a crucial part of any meaningful definition of mastery. This is as true for written work as it is for computations.

Often our work groups are already organized for cooperative learning or laboratory work. Having these groups help with work check simply represents an extension of their responsibilities.

A New Perspective on Excellence

The big step in thinking about excellence is to realize that it is something you build, not something you are occasionally given.

Work Check with Writing

When checking written work, it is important to separate two different functions:

- **Copy Editor**: The copy editor is responsible for producing clean copy – spelling, punctuation, etc.
- **Editor-In-Chief**: The editor-in-chief is responsible for the coherent development of ideas.

You are better off farming out the copy editing as much as possible so you can focus on being editor-in-chief. Copy editing is not only time consuming for you, but it also produces "bleeding papers" which students find most discouraging. If the students can do the copy editing without the paper getting bloody, they will be happier, and you will be free to focus on content.

Check Groups for Copy Editing

Imagine that you have organized your class into partner pairs for partner learning. Combine two sets of partner pairs to make a "partner square." For copy editing, each student's paper would be checked by one member of the square and then, again, by another member of the square.

Work check can be simplified in the early grades by focusing on one aspect of writing like the use of quotation marks in dialog. More advanced students can be taught the hypercritical markings used by copy editors so that writing can be checked in a systematic fashion that is understood by all.

Reducing Your Work Load as Editor-In-Chief

Much of your editor-in-chief work can be done *in-production* as you "cruise and check" during Guided Practice. You can scan written work without an answer key, and because you are mobile, you can confer with a student several times during Guided Practice. This helps you shape the final product as it is being written. Such brief interactions might sound something like this:

"You have two ideas in this topic sentence. Let's make *this* one the topic of one paragraph, and *that* one the topic of the following paragraph."

The students can do much of the work of the editor-in-chief when it is included in the writing process. As mentioned previously within the context of Say, See, Do Teaching, the teacher could employ their work groups to implement Read Around Groups. In this format the teacher would have students read each other's papers marking strong passages in the margin. The teacher could then read the best papers to the class and brainstorm those features that make a particular paper stand out. From this collaboration the class could construct a model to use for writing the second draft.

Training with "the writing project," usually sponsored by a local university, will give you many additional options for making writing an interactive process that includes both checking and editing. Such training for an entire faculty will help them to implement writing across curriculum areas.

New Perspectives

The more the teaching format resembles a series of Say, See, Do Cycles, the more work check and corrective feedback can be integrated into the learning process to be performed by the students. In contrast, the more the teacher monopolizes the learning process, the more work check and corrective feedback are separated from learning to be done by the teacher as a separate job.

In addition, the more adept you become at quality control, the more you teach the students to be independent of you as they learn. Rather than doing all of the work yourself, they do not only the work but also *the work check* while you supervise.

Section Five

Building Classroom Structure

Chapter Eleven

Succeeding from Day One

Preview

- Students are astute at assessing the absence of effective structure. They can tell whether their teachers are proactive or reactive, whether they are "old pros" or rookies.
- The rules in any classroom are defined by reality - "whatever any student can get away with."
- Much of the management in a typical classroom is by default. Students fool around because the teacher has not structured anything better for them to do.
- Structure begins as the students enter the classroom.
- Well-developed routines including Bell Work, signal from the beginning that the classroom is both a work environment and a friendly, personal environment.

A Quick Start

Scoping You Out

Let's imagine that it is the first day of your teaching career. You are as green as grass.

Imagine a departmentalized setting. You will begin the day a half-dozen times before the final bell. You are teaching World History in Room 101 at the local high school.

Classroom management gets off to a quick start. If first period begins at eight o'clock in the morning, the students will know how good you are at classroom management by eight o'clock. They are very astute.

However, the students will give you a 48-hour honeymoon. They gamble conservatively until they have had time to "scope you out." After the honeymoon, you will find out what the real rules in the classroom are.

Reality Is the Law

You may, of course, have rules of your own. Teachers love to tell students about their rules.

In some classrooms the teacher's desires actually become implemented, but in most classrooms they don't. Students know that words are cheap and actions are expensive. The real rules in any classroom are defined by *reality* – by what the teacher allows. So, the students watch.

If, for example, you ask the class to pay attention while you are speaking, but you fail to deal effectively with side conversations, students know that paying attention is optional. If you ask the class to take turns as they speak, but you occasionally recognize a student who interrupts because he or she has a good idea, students know that they are free to cut each other off during a discussion.

Classroom rules are ultimately defined by whatever any student can get away with. So the students just watch. Everything you do is a lesson. You will have taught a half-dozen lessons by the time first period *begins.*

First Lessons

Entering the Class

Imagine that you have *thirteen* minutes before the bell rings for first period. The first student enters your classroom. You have just taught the *first* lesson of the school year: *You may enter my class however you wish.*

How does the student know this? Because, he or she just did it! Remember, your rules are defined by reality.

There was no greeting, no communication of expectations, nothing specific to do. Since you have abdicated structuring this situation, structure is left to the student.

Do not be surprised if, after the honeymoon is over, the students come rolling into your classroom joking, laughing, and pushing each other. You asked for it.

Much of the management in a typical classroom is by default. Students fool around because the teacher has not structured anything better for them to do.

A Second Student Enters

You have *twelve* minutes before the bell rings, and a second student enters the classroom. You now have *two* students in your classroom. What do you think they will do?

"Hey, Jackson, where have you been?"

"Hangin' out. I heard you were out of town."

"Naw. Just for a week. Say, I hear you're goin' out with Sharon again..."

Big surprise! They are socializing. You have just taught the *second* lesson of the school year: *After you enter my classroom, you may socialize.*

The kids have important events to catch-up on. Do *you* have anything important for them to do?

Now it is *ten* minutes before the bell rings. Eight kids are in the classroom standing around, talking, and laughing.

Now it is *five* minutes before the bell rings. Twenty kids are in the classroom standing around, talking, and laughing.

It is *one* minute before the bell rings. *Everybody* is standing around, talking, and laughing. Now that you have allowed this gab-fest to start, how will you stop it?

"Students fool around because the teacher has not structured anything better for them to do."

The Bell Rings

The eight o'clock bell rings. You just taught the *third* lesson of the school year: *Do not even think about being in your seat when the bell rings.*

Why should they worry about it? You don't. There is no routine to get the students seated and ready to work *before* the bell rings, is there? Do not expect the students to take Classroom Structure more seriously than *you* do.

Getting Them into Their Seats

Since the students are not in their seats when the bell rings, how will you get them there?

> "Class, the bell has rung. Let's all take our seats. We have a lot to cover today, so let's get started. Everybody, let's take our seats!"

The students have just observed your first *overt* act of classroom management. But what classroom management "technique" did they see? It was the most widespread management technique in the world: *Nag, nag, nag.* You have just taught the *fourth* lesson of the school year: *In order to get you to do things, I nag.*

While nagging may be the most widespread management technique in the world, it is also one of the least effective. Most students learned to tune it out before they went to kindergarten.

A Lesson about Killing Time

The students will now give you a lesson about killing time. For the record, students like *brief lessons with great big breaks in between.*

Consequently, no matter how much time you give the students for a lesson transition, it will never be long enough. If you give the students three minutes, they will need five. If you give them five minutes, they will need seven. Students know how to stretch a break by *dawdling.*

Being Proactive

Proactive people know how to get organized, and they get organized well in advance.

So, when you tell the class to take their seats, three students interpret this to mean, "Now is a good time to sharpen pencils." Where does this leave you?

> "Those of you over at the pencil sharpener, please take your seats. You had plenty of time to sharpen your pencils before school. Everyone, just find a seat so we can get started."

You have just taught the *fifth* lesson of the school year: *If nagging does not work, I will nag some more.*

Giving Away the Furniture

"Everyone, just find a seat." Are you kidding? You just *gave away the furniture!* The *sixth* lesson of the school year is: *You may sit wherever you want.*

Now, imagine the biggest troublemaker in your class – the one who will make you question your career choice. Let's call this student Larry. Every classroom has a "Larry."

If you say, "Everyone, just find a seat." where do you think Larry will end up sitting? Larry knows that the farther he is from you, the more he can get away with. Consequently, he will end up sitting in the *back of the class* along with his buddies. That's where the goof-offs always sit if you give them the chance.

This is not looking good. Your "green" is showing. The students are rubbing their hands together thinking, "All right! In first period we get to *kick back.*"

The students are rating you on your skills of classroom management, and, so far, they have not seen much *style.* They are rating you along the most basic dimension of leadership ability – *proactive* versus *reactive.*

Proactive vs. Reactive

Getting Organized

Proactive means "active ahead of time." Proactive people are the natural teachers, the natural parents, the born leaders. They know how to get organized, and they get organized well *in advance.*

Let's imagine, for example, that you have a four-year-old and a seven-year-old, and you are planning to visit grandmother next week. She lives three hours away.

What will you do to get ready for this trip? I remember my wife, Jo Lynne, doing it. She had an entire routine.

A week before the trip she bought some coloring books and new crayons. At the grocery store that week she stocked up on apples and oranges and the makings of a picnic.

On the morning of the trip, the coloring book and crayons along with pencils and tablets went into one paper bag while pieces of apple and orange with some crackers went into another paper bag. In addition she collected some story books and games plus the Etch-a-Sketch for good measure.

The kids were occupied with their new crayons and coloring books as we backed the car out of the driveway. The snacks were given out as we rode along accompanied by praise for "behaving so nicely." In addition to the snacks, we stopped for a picnic halfway to grandmother's at our favorite roadside park that had a swing set.

Jo Lynne was in charge, and she was actively planning and organizing the trip to grandmother's well in advance. She's no fool. She knew what the trip to grandmother's would be like without some *organization.*

But some people don't think this way. They just put the kids in the back seat and take off down the road.

Before they have gone half a mile, the big kid takes something from the little kid, the little kid lets out a shriek and grabs it back, the big kid shoves the little kid, the little kid hits the big kid (a bad idea) and the big kid whacks the little kid who starts crying.

Reactive management always sounds the same: Nag, nag, nag.

One of the parents turns around and snaps:

> "I want you to stop this fighting *right now!* You sit on *your* side, and you sit on *your* side, and I want both of you to keep your *hands to yourselves!* I do not want to listen to that fussing all the way to grandmother's!"

The parents might not *want* to listen to "that fussing," but they *will*. Having no plan to prevent it, they must now live with it.

The Sound of Reactive Management

There is a pattern of speech that is endemic to reactive management. That pattern of speech is: *Nag, nag, nag.*

When you nag, you label the procedure that you have failed to train the other person to perform. For example:

> "I am *sick and tired* of coming into your room and seeing your clothes *all over the floor!* Let me tell you something! I was not put on this earth to spend my life *picking up after you.*"

Have you ever heard this speech? What procedure has this parent failed to train the child to perform? How about: *Pick up after yourself. It either goes in the closet or in the hamper.*

Focus on Procedure

What sets *proactive* people apart is not their goals and objectives, but, rather, their *procedures*. Proactive people know how to organize an activity in order to get things done. Reactive people either *do not know how* to organize an activity or are *too lazy* to go to the trouble. Consequently, they must *react* to the disaster that has been created by a lack of structure.

Classroom Structure

Getting a room full of young people to do things quickly and smoothly will place the structuring of behavior on a plane far above normal, everyday family life. In detail and precision it will exceed what you remember from your parents. Your parents, after all, were not trying to manage thirty children. And they were not trying to manage one complex activity after another all day long.

Getting accustomed to the level of structure required in the classroom is a big step for a new teacher. Chances are you have never acted or sounded like this before. You have never given yourself permission to be this "controlling."

Let's give our green teacher another crack at starting the school year. In so doing, let's take a close look at proactive management by examining a few of the routines that might be most helpful.

Starting Over Again

The Day Before

When the students show up, it is too late to be proactive. The day before school begins, stand at the front of your classroom and look around. How big is the room? Space can be your friend by giving you elbow room, or it can be your enemy by running your legs off. The first feature of the classroom that you must take responsibility for structuring in order to facilitate learning in *space.*

Room Arrangement

Where will you place the furniture? Can you get around easily? The first crucial element of Classroom Structure is room arrangement. This topic has been dealt with thoroughly in Chapter 3, "Working the Crowd" and Chapter 4 "Arranging the Room." By way of review, the biggest single variable that governs the likelihood of students goofing off in your class is their physical distance from you. *Proximity* is the name of the game.

Teachers who make classroom discipline look easy *move.* They produce proximity through mobility. They *work the crowd* because they know that *either you work the crowd, or the crowd works you.*

The biggest obstacle to mobility is the *furniture.* You need *walkways* – nice, broad walkways so that you can move among the students easily. Room arrangement is the art of producing walkways within the normally crowded conditions of the classroom. The optimal room arrangement allows you to get from any student to any other student in the fewest steps.

One of your first jobs in structuring the classroom is to take responsibility for where the furniture goes. This may require a conference with the principal and the custodian to gain their understanding and cooperation.

Desk Creep

What do you think will happen to your lovely room arrangement when thirty students occupy those desks? Students are full of energy, and they move. They twist and turn and squirm and scoot, and their desks move with them.

The next obstacle that we must overcome in working the crowd is *desk creep.* A desk can block a walkway by creeping less than a foot.

To contain desk creep, you will need *visual markers* to show the students where the furniture goes. Furniture must be "straightened up" during each lesson transition, or the walkways will disappear. With clear visual markers, you can say during a lesson transition:

> "...and after you have handed in your papers and sharpened your pencils, put your desks back on their marks before you take your seats."

One of the cheapest visual markers is a "tape dot." A tape dot is simply a small piece of masking tape that you tear off the end of the roll and stick on the floor. It is no bigger than the end of your finger. Two dots where the front legs of a desk touch the floor locates the desk.

On the day before the students show up, you may be placing tape dots all over the floor after you have arranged the furniture. But rest assured that this is the *last* time *you* will ever do it. When tape dots have to be replaced due to normal wear and tear, you will have the *students* do it. It will be one of their regular classroom chores.

Sometimes administrators and custodians get apoplectic when they see tape dots suddenly appear on their newly polished or carpeted floors. This is another reason for having a preliminary conference with the interested parties. If you do not do a little team building proactively, you will get the hassles that go with reactive management.

Incidentally, there are alternatives to tape dots. By fifth grade, if the teacher is using horizontal rows (see chapter 4), students can line up their desks with a few marks on the wall. I have also seen teachers use different colored dots for different room arrangements within the same classroom. The stationery store carries packages of different colored dots for pricing items at yard sales. Whatever the specific method, you will need *visual prompts* for locating the furniture.

Greet Them and Put Them to Work

Where do you stand at the beginning of the class period? Let me make a strong suggestion that you stand *in the doorway.*

In the hall, students laugh and joke and flirt as they pass from class to class. This is normal behavior for the hallway. The classroom, in contrast, is a *work* environment.

Students would love to bring their *social* environment from the hall into the classroom. They would love to spend the first part of the class period finishing their con-

Define the entrance to your classroom as a doorway between two different worlds.

versations. And they will, unless you clearly structure a change in behavior.

Do everything you can to define the doorway into your classroom as a threshold between *two different worlds.* Clearly separate the social world from the world of schoolwork.

You can only define a work environment through *work.* Stand in the doorway, greet the students warmly, and, above all else, *give them a job.*

But what job will you give them? This brings us to the topic of *Bell Work.*

Bell Work

Bell Work, as the name implies, is the schoolwork that students are doing *when the bell rings.* It is always the first task of the class period.

When you describe Bell Work to your students on the first day of school, instruct them never to ask you whether there is Bell Work today. There is Bell Work *every* day. It will always be posted on the board in the same place. Tell the students,

> "As soon as you reach your seat, look at the board for today's Bell Work, and get started."

Bell Work, as you might imagine, is a bit of a misnomer because many students enter the class minutes before the bell rings. Say to the students,

> "If you want to talk and socialize, stay out in the hall. That is what halls are for. When you are ready to work, come in."

Bell Work consumes the first five minutes of the class period. Structuring work at the beginning of the class period eliminates a serious problem in classroom management. That problem is "settling in."

Bell Work and "Settling In"

A typical class period is not on task until five to seven minutes *after* the bell rings. Teachers take roll, and students talk, sharpen pencils, and listen to announcements over the P.A. as they amble toward their seats. This daily ritual is called "settling in."

Settling in is so ingrained in the daily life of the classroom that few teachers regard it as a problem. It is just the normal way of starting class. But I regard it as a problem – a *big* problem.

If, for example, a class period lasts fifty minutes, and you take five minutes for settling in each day, you thereby consume *one-tenth of your total instructional time with this class period for the entire year.* That is a high price to pay for the privilege of settling in.

But, what if you try to start on time *without a plan*? When are you going to take roll? At the elementary level you don't just take roll – you collect lunch money, milk money, book club money, and money for the field trip on Friday. The district should issue you a cash register. In addition, there are announcements over the P.A. that interrupt you just as you are starting the lesson. And then a student comes in late with a note from the nurse.

The school district is not organized to start when the bell rings. That's why nobody does it. Try starting on time, and see how far you get. How many days in a row can you juggle all of the distractions listed above before you say, "Oh, forget it! Let's just settle in."

The fact of the matter is that you *do* need to take roll and collect lunch money, milk money, and so on. The question is, how can we do this without wasting the first five minutes of instruction? What you need is a meaningful learning experience that *does not require your active teaching*. You need Bell Work.

What Do You Do for Bell Work?

First, keep it simple. *Second,* make sure that it serves a purpose in getting the day's instruction started. Use it as a warm-up activity. It probably incorporates review that you would have done anyway *after* settling in.

If you are a science teacher, how about four questions from yesterday? If you are a math teacher, how about four problems from yesterday? Make them doable. This is not the midterm exam. If the students were here yesterday and were not comatose, they can start answering those questions or doing those problems.

But review is just one of many possibilities for Bell Work. Some teachers use journal writing or silent reading. Others put word games or mind benders on the board. I remember one teacher who had a student read to the class from a library book while he took roll. The sky is the limit as long as it makes sense in terms of your classroom.

> **Bell Work**
>
> **Bell Work begins as soon as a student enters your class and continues until five minutes after the bell rings. It provides a useful learning activity while you look after the organizational chores.**

Do *not* saddle yourself with an extra stack of papers to grade. Some teachers flip through Bell Work quickly and put an "X" in a column of the grade book for those students who gave it a decent try. Other teachers farm this job out to students who are on the "clerical work committee" this week. Some teachers collect the papers with due seriousness, glance over them, and then drop them into the circular file after school. After all, the purpose is to start kids thinking, not to assess performance.

Bell Work on Day One

What will you do for Bell Work on the first day of school? You will need something.

You may already have a routine that works for you. I have seen, for example, social studies teachers get off to a quick start with a political opinion survey or questionnaire. I know primary teachers who have the children draw pictures of their families, sort blocks by color, shape, and size, or assemble a puzzle.

You might also consider handing out 3-by-5 cards as you greet the students at the door. On the blank side of the card is a seat number. All of the desks have numbers taped to them. Greet the student and say:

> "This is your seat number. Find your seat, then turn the card over and fill it out according to the instructions on the board."

On the board is a picture showing students how to fill out the card – name, birthday, home address, home phone number, and so on. It may sound basic, but at least you put the kids to work. And they get a message that can only be conveyed behaviorally: *When you enter the room, expect to get right to work.*

Introduce Yourself

On the first day of school the *first* question in the students' minds is, "Who are *you*?" You will introduce yourself, of course, but you might also talk about yourself a little bit.

Deal with obvious questions like, "Why are you here?" Sometimes students show surprise when you confide to them that you get great pleasure from seeing young people learn. Eyes may widen when you tell them that school should be fun. Don't beat it to death. But, a few words from the heart are in order.

Icebreakers

On the first day of school, the *second* question in the students' minds is, "Who are *they*?" If you think the students all know each other, think again.

I used to have teachers hand out a blank seating chart in mid-November and ask the students to fill in the first and last names of everyone in the class. Rarely did the number of correct papers exceed 25 percent. Teachers were typically shocked, but most had to admit that they had invested little time in making it otherwise.

Students do better in class both academically and socially when they are comfortable, relaxed, and "at home." They do not do so well in an impersonal environment.

The question facing the teacher is, *"Do you care?"* Is it worth your time in order to make the students feel at home? I would strongly suggest that you devote the lion's share of the first class period of the year to creating comfort. Spend at least a half-hour doing an "icebreaking" activity.

Many teachers feel that it is all-important to "set the tone" of the class by getting right into a meaty assignment during the first class period. While well intentioned, this objective is not aligned with the students' needs.

Think of yourself suddenly thrown together with a group of your peers, some you know and some you don't, plus a few good friends that you haven't seen in months. Some social "settling in" is needed.

If you invest time and energy in producing comfort, you signal to the students that you care about them as people. If you do not invest, you signal that they are nothing but warm bodies occupying chairs in your class. Do not expect a lot of warmth and consideration coming back to you from students who are treated in this fashion.

Since the objective of breaking the ice is social, have some fun with it. Anything that gets the students to interact with each other and laugh is golden.

Sample Icebreakers

Here are some sample icebreakers that you can use on the first day of school. Customize them to fit your needs. Your colleagues can give you even more.

Games

- **Scavenger Hunt**: Hand out a sheet of paper with ten questions about things the students are likely to have in common (the last movie you saw, your favorite sport, your favorite flavor of ice cream, how you get to school, etc.). To the right of these questions are four columns. Students write the answer to each question in column one. They must then find three students who have the same answer for each question. These students sign the sheet in one of the three remaining columns. Give the students a time limit and watch them go. Be a participant yourself. Any activity of this kind will work better when you are part of it.
- **Name Game**: In the name game, students form a circle with their desks and hang a 3-by-5 card on the front of the desk with their first name printed on it. Pass out magic markers so the names can be written in big, bold letters that can be read from across the room.

  The first person begins the game by giving his or her first name plus a rhyme, an adjective, or a nickname that describes him or her. This part is always good for laughs.

  The second person does the same, and then repeats what the first student said. The third person does the same, and then repeats what the second and first students said. By the time the game has gone around the room, the person who is "it" has a lot of names and nicknames to remember, but the name cards on the front of the desks serve as reminders. Class members are directed to quickly supply missing information if a fellow student gets stuck.

  As simple as it sounds, this game usually generates a lot of kidding around while it helps students associate names with faces. Of course, the teacher goes last and learns the students' names in the process.

Class Introductions

- **Partner Introductions**: Students pair up and introduce their partners. Structure the interview by providing a list of topics. Interviewers typically get specifics about their partner's favorite movie, food, activity, etc. Go around the room and have each student introduce his or her partner to the class.
- **Group Sharing**: Have each student share with the group the best thing they did over the summer, their biggest fear, their biggest hope for the new school year, and so on. You supply the list of topics.

Art and Graphics

- **Design a T-shirt**: Have each student design a T-shirt press-on that tells about him or herself. Each student then stands up to display and explain the design.
- **Photos**: If you have a digital camera and printer, take the students' pictures on the first day of school and print them on 3x6 paper. Have the students list five things that describe themselves on the bottom half of a sheet of notebook paper. Then, have the students read their lists to the group prior to your mounting their photos on the top half of the paper. Post the photo sheets around the room.

  This activity can be extended throughout the first week of school by having each student bring a baby picture. Number the baby pictures and post them on the bulletin board. Have a contest in which points are given for matching current pictures with baby pictures.

Personal Characteristics

- **Guess Who**: Hand out a sheet with ten questions about personal characteristics of the students. Have the students answer the questions and hand them in. The teacher reads the first item on a student's list, and the entire class has to guess who the person is. Additional items on the list are read until the student is identified. The rest of the students follow in turn.
- **Place in the Family**: Have students form groups according to their place in the family (oldest, middle, youngest). The students in each group list the things they have in common and the advantages and disadvantages of their place in the family. Each group makes a list and shares it with the class.

Proactive Relationship Building

First Impressions

Students will have a well-formed impression of you by the end of the first day of the school year. They will know whether your classroom is a work environment or a place to kick back. And they will feel at home in your classroom – or not.

The students can always tell what is important to you just by watching. Things that are important are worth your time and effort. Things that are not important are either put off or dealt with in passing.

> **Things that are important are worth your time and effort.**

Do not worry, however, if you are already in the middle of a semester when you learn about the power of proactive relationship building. Tomorrow can always be the first day of school. Jump in and get started.

Tell your students what you are doing. They will know anyway. You might say:

"Class, you know that I went to a workshop last week. The workshop was about classroom management. I learned how to use our class time a lot more effectively.

"So, let's imagine that this is the first day of school. As you saw, I met you at the door, and I had a mind bender on the board for you to begin as soon as you got to your seats. This was an example of a Bell Work activity. Next, I would like to..."

Follow Through

Relationship building is a continuous process. But, if you want to make sure that it happens, you need to have a plan.

One simple follow through activity is "life space interviewing." Simply call students up to your desk one at a time as the rest of the class is working independently, and ask them about themselves. Ask about their families, their hobbies, their pets, and their special interests. Take notes. They will know that you care who they are, and you will have personal insights that will be invaluable as the school year progresses.

Chapter Twelve

Teaching Routines

Preview

- Classroom routines train the students to carry out procedures with a minimum of wasted time.
- Each routine must be taught with the care of any other lesson. This is time-consuming at the beginning, but it pays large dividends for the remainder of the semester.
- By doing chores, students learn to take pride in helping out around the classroom. The rule of chores is, "Never do anything for students that they are thoroughly capable of doing for themselves."
- Structuring communication with parents is crucial. They will either be your allies or your adversaries depending on the nature of your first contact with them.
- Sending work home on a regular basis with provision for feedback helps involve parents in proactive problem solving.

Rules, Rules, Rules

"You and your stupid rules! I can't do anything!"

Rules have never been terribly popular, particularly among young people. It is not too surprising that young teachers, new to the "parent role," approach making rules for their classrooms with some ambivalence.

"I remember all of the rules my teachers used to have. I thought most of them were dumb. Don't do this, and don't do that."

In fact, rules are typically stated in terms of "Don't do this, and Don't do that." I had to chuckle recently when I read the rules posted at the entrance to a state park:

- No fires
- No liquor
- No glass containers
- No littering
- No dumping
- No dogs
- No camping overnight

On the bottom of the sign someone had scratched, "No breathing."

This tradition of stating rules in terms of "Don't do this," and "Don't do that" is nowhere more evident than in our school discipline codes. A high school principal friend of mine once told me,

> "Our School Discipline Code explicitly prohibits every outrageous thing that any kid has ever done in the history of the school. It takes up four pages of the student handbook. It serves as the legacy of the student body."

I was consulting at a juvenile corrections facility in a small town in Michigan, and the administrators and I were trading stories after the workshop. They too had a student handbook that contained an endless list of the things that students should never do. One administrator said,

> "I got a call last year from some guy at the local airport. One of our kids was over there running around on the runway, and nobody could catch him. So I drove over there. The kid finally ran out of wind and gave up. By that time there were four or five Cessnas anxiously circling overhead. I asked the kid, 'What were you thinking?' He said, 'Hey, Mr. Donaldson, you didn't say we couldn't do it.'"

There must be a better way to approach classroom rules than making a list of do's and don'ts. These lists have never had a major effect on behavior anyway.

Types of Rules

When we speak of "rules," we are addressing a broad topic that is far more complex than "do's and don'ts." Different kinds of rules serve different functions. In the classroom, there are two basic types of rules.

- **General Rules**: General rules spell out the teacher's overall expectations for good work and good behavior within the classroom.
- **Specific Procedures**: Specific procedures spell out exactly "how to do this" and exactly "how to do that" in the classroom.

General Rules

General rules deal with broad classes of behavior and are best stated in positive rather than negative language. Typical examples are, "Treat each other with respect." and, "Pay attention when the teacher is speaking."

It is time well spent for a faculty to devise a list of general rules that all teachers can share. The discussion that accompanies this process can produce some important consensus building.

> **The only way to make procedures affordable is to make them a matter of routine.**

The following guidelines for general rules will be helpful during this discussion.

- There should be relatively few general rules (five to eight is most common).
- Only make rules that you are willing to enforce at any time. (Failing to enforce your rules defines them as hot air.)
- General rules should be simple and clear.
- They should be posted.

These general rules might best be understood as part *behavioral guideline* and part *values clarification.* A discussion of each general rule at the beginning of the semester gives the teacher a chance to convey his or her goals and expectations to the class.

Specific Procedures

As mentioned previously, procedures describe exactly *how to do this* and *how to do that.* As such, they are the nuts and bolts of Classroom Structure.

The only way to make the implementation of procedures *affordable* is to make them a matter of *routine.* Procedures must be taught as thoroughly as any other lesson – complete with Say, See, Do Cycles, Structured Practice, constant monitoring, and repetition to mastery. A routine is automatic when it can be carried out quickly and correctly in response to a simple verbal prompt.

Pay me now, or pay me later. Do it right, or do it all year long.

A School Site Procedures Manual

One of the most cost-effective forms of faculty collaboration is the development of a School Site Procedures Manual. This manual shares the wisdom and experience of teachers in the form of protocols for each routine that faculty members regularly employ.

Writing the manual stimulates sharing among teachers. This helps solidify commitment to key routines as it hones the most efficient way of implementing each one. Uniform procedures pay additional dividends whenever students transition from teacher to teacher or from one grade level to another.

Teaching Procedures and Routines

Making the Investment

The teaching of classroom procedures is time-consuming. *First,* each routine must be taught thoroughly. And *second,* there are many of them to teach.

Yet, in spite of this initial investment, classroom routines are one of the teacher's *primary labor saving devices.* They reduce effort and stress each time the teacher has the class do something as a group. Over the long run the investment in training pays for itself many times over.

Research has repeatedly shown that teachers with the best run classrooms spend most of the first two weeks of the semester teaching their procedures and routines. Teachers who do not make this investment deal with the same behavior problems over and over all semester long. It is a case of:

Pay me now, or pay me later.
Do it right, or do it all year long.

As logical as this might sound, few teachers actually make the investment. In fact, the older the students, the less investment we make.

The teachers who make the greatest investment are, of course, the primary teachers. They spend half of their time teaching procedures and routines.

The investment is still considerable in the middle grades. But by junior high and high school, the teaching of procedures has typically become perfunctory – just some announcements on the first day of class.

They Should Know By Now

When secondary teachers are asked why they don't spend more time on the teaching of procedures, they say, "They should know how to behave by now." When pressed, these teachers say such things as:

> "Spend the first two weeks on rules – you have to be kidding! I don't have two weeks for that. I would never make up the time."

or

> "I can see doing it with the little kids. But doing it with older kids seems like a complete waste of time. How often do they have to be taught these same routines?"

Consequently, the teaching of classroom procedures and routines is one of the most neglected areas of classroom management. This lack of proactive management will cost teachers dearly as the semester progresses.

Whatever The Students Can Get Away With

While these teachers' concern with "losing valuable instructional time" is sincere, it is also naive. The students know exactly how to behave in class. They always have. The question is, *do they have to?*

You should know from your own experience that students don't act the same in every classroom. They adjust their behavior to match the standards of each teacher. If their second period teacher lets them talk and fool around while their third period teacher does not, they will act up in second period and cool it in third period.

The standards in any classroom, to put it bluntly, are defined by *whatever the students can get away with.* If teachers do not take the time to carefully teach their rules, routines, and standards, they will get whatever the students feel like giving them.

"The standards in any classroom are defined by whatever the students can get away with."

This is a classic example of *proactive* versus *reactive* management. A wise teacher knows that spending time on procedures early in the semester saves time in the long run. Prevention is always cheaper than remediation.

A Sample Procedure

Let's take a typical procedure as our laboratory for examining the teaching of a classroom routine. By the time you have taught your first routine of the year, the students will know you a lot better.

Imagine that you are a fourth grade teacher, and it is the first day of school. Today, you will take the class to the library to meet the librarian. But, before the class can get to the library, they must pass through the hall. So, today you will give the lesson on *passing through the halls quietly.*

First we set the stage by talking about how noise in the halls prevents students in other rooms from learning. You know the tune.

Next, before you go out into the hall, you must develop visual cues so you can pantomime instructions to the students once you leave the room. A finger to the lips or a zippering of the mouth is standard fare. You will also need "stop" and "start" signals. But one signal you *must* have is the signal to *stop, go back, and start all over.* You probably remember it. The teacher turns solemnly, holds both palms toward the students, and then, with a circular motion, points both index fingers back toward the classroom.

Next, you will have to line the students up. Assign places in line for the same reason that you assign seating. Place the students who disrupt right under your nose, and place the orderly students at the back of the line. Separate best friends to reduce talking. Students should be able to name the person in front of them and behind them. A double line rather than a single line keeps the group more compact.

Before going out into the hall, you will need to rehearse each of your signals one last time to be sure that you can direct the students with nonverbal cues. Only then are they ready, with a final zippering of the lips, to go out the door.

... until we get it right.

Out in the hall, with due seriousness, you check the lines for straightness before giving the signal to "follow me." The little band heads down the hall.

Now, let's interject a note of reality. What, do you think, are the odds that this collection of fourth-graders will make it all the way to the library in complete silence? If your guess is "zero," you show real promise as a teacher.

Halfway down the hall you hear a giggle from somewhere in the group. Do you care who giggled? *No.* Do you care how loud it was? *No.* Do you care whether students in nearby classrooms were actually pulled off task? *No.*

You turn, hold palms toward the class, make the circular motion with your hands, and point back toward the classroom. Brace yourself for a pained look on those little faces. Some show disbelief for a moment before they realize that you are not kidding. Keeping a straight face is the hardest part of this routine.

The class shuffles back to where they began, and you repeat your signals; straight lines, zippered lips, follow me. Off we go again.

This time the class makes it two-thirds of the way to the library when you hear some talking at the back of the line. Do you care who talked? *No.* Do you care how loud it was? *No.*

You turn, hold palms toward the class and give your now well-known "about face" signal. This time you see serious pain on the faces of students.

Several students mouth the words, "I didn't do it," with pleading hands and looks of exaggerated sincerity. Keep a straight face.

Back to the beginning. Line straight, lips zipped, follow me. Off they trundle one more time.

This time they *almost make it* to the library when you hear some whispering from behind. You know what to do by now, don't you? Turn solemnly, palms to signal stop, and then about face.

The pain registered on faces the third time around is almost too much to bear. Bite your lip. They shuffle back, some under protest.

Old pros know that this is the only way to play the game. Green teachers need to be reassured that they are doing the right thing.

While the students' faces may register displeasure at practicing until mastery is achieved, your mood is always upbeat. If you were practicing a routine, like lining up, *inside* the classroom where you could speak instead of pantomime, you might give feedback in the following manner:

> "Class, we did better that time. Gina, Cameron, and Samuel, you walked just as I asked. Now, class, we are going to practice it again, and I want you to focus on facing forward after you line up. We almost have it."

Through simple practice to mastery, you are signaling to the students by your investment of time and energy that this piece of behavior is important. And, you are teaching the students that you are the living embodiment of two timeless characterizations of a teacher:

I say what I mean, and I mean what I say.

and

We are going to keep doing this until we get it right.

It is only through training such as this that students learn to take you seriously. They learn that, when you say something, they need to listen.

Establishing Standards

High Standards Are Easier

It is easier to have *high* standards in your classroom than to have *low* standards – strange but true. To understand how this works, first realize that most of the reinforcement for deviant behavior in the classroom comes from the *peer group*.

A student makes a silly remark, and four kids giggle. The student who made the silly remark has just been reinforced for playing the "clown" by four peers.

In the management trade, this peer reinforcement for deviant behavior is called "bootleg reinforcement." As in the bootlegging of booze during prohibition, the goods are being delivered "around the law."

You will have a hard time putting the lid on any type of deviant behavior as long as bootleg reinforcement is allowed to operate. The peer group will reinforce the goofing off as fast as you can set limits on it.

So, here is a piece of advice for the management of disruptive behavior. *Get a monopoly on reinforcement.*

How can you get a monopoly on reinforcement in order to eliminate bootlegging? First, let me list some things that don't work.

- Nag
- Threaten
- Punish

Now, let me list what does work.

- Practice
- Practice
- Practice

Keep doing it until you get it right. *Practice to mastery.* As you practice, practice, practice, a transformation occurs within the peer group.

Typically, "the many" are sheep in the face of the deviant behavior of "the few." After all, criticizing a peer for goofing off is *most* uncool. Consequently, *the many* tend to remain silent and mind their own business in the hope that someone else will deal with the problem.

In the classroom, that someone else is *always* you. But you will have a hard time enforcing standards without the help of *the many*.

Now, let's return to our example of teaching the class to walk quietly through the halls. After you stop and start over for the third time, *the many* start losing patience. They want to get to the library, and they are tired of trekking up and down the stupid hall. When they finally lose patience with this repeated practice, they also lose patience with the few who are causing them to do it.

The next time down the hall when one of the class clowns begins to do something silly, he or she immediately gets "dagger looks" from fellow classmates. Sensing that it is now "uncool" instead of "cool," the goof-off thinks better of it.

Finally, the class makes it to the library. And, in the process, the students learn that "quiet means quiet," and that when you tell the class to do something, you mean it. Only in this way do the students learn to take you and your standards seriously.

This assessment of you by the students will need to be strengthened through the learning of many routines. But each new routine will be easier to establish.

The next time down the hall when Larry begins to do something silly, he immediately gets "dagger looks" from his classmates.

Words Have the Meaning You Give Them

For those teachers to whom this level of investment seems strange, it is worth emphasizing at this point that *not one word* in the English language has any fixed meaning in your classroom on the first day of school. Words will only have the meaning that you give them.

Take, for example, a simple three-letter word: "now." What does "now" mean? Well, in some families "now" means "Now." In other families "now" means, "Just a second!" In other families it means, "Okay, in a minute!" In other families it means, "Okay, as soon as I'm done with this!" In other families it means, "Okay, as soon as this show is over!" And, in some families it means, "In your dreams!"

Each family is a subculture. The kids in your classroom come from all kinds of family subcultures. As you can see from the above example, words mean very different things to different people.

Kids will bring all of these different meanings into your classroom on the first day of school. As a result, a word as simple as "now" means nothing until you teach your students what *you* mean by it. The same could be said of the word "quiet" or the word "walk." None of these things have any fixed meaning until you teach the class exactly what they mean *in your presence.*

Incidentally, don't expect these meanings that you establish at such effort to magically transfer from one setting to another. The students can easily discriminate what will be tolerated in one teacher's classroom as opposed to another. That is why students can change their behavior so readily when they change classes or have a substitute.

"It is easier to have high standards than to have low standards."

Simplifying Rules and Routines

One way of simplifying rules and routines is to group them into clusters. One primary teacher, for example, had a cardboard stoplight prominently displayed in the front of the classroom where she could place an arrow pointing to the red, yellow, or green lights.

The *red* light condition meant "walk quietly and work quietly." The *yellow* light condition meant that only one person could leave his or her seat at a time, and only one person could talk at a time. The *green* light condition signaled that the class could move about and talk freely.

The stoplight served as a form of shorthand for conveying an entire set of rules and expectations. As usual, the investment in training early in the semester was repaid many times over through sheer efficiency of communication.

Classroom Chores

Certain classroom routines engage the students in helping you out around the classroom. These routines are traditionally referred to as "chores."

Frazzled Parents, Lazy Children

Where do children learn that it is important to help out? It certainly does not come from being waited on hand and foot.

Some parents do all of the work around the house. They clean, straighten up, prepare meals, do the dishes, and pick up after the kids all day long. Their only reward is to become exhausted from serving a house full of lazy ingrates.

Owning a servant, be they parent or teacher, does not seem to transmit a sense of selfless giving to children. Quite the contrary, it trains them to expect much and give little.

How often have you heard a parent say, "You know, it is just easier to do it myself." In fact, doing the job yourself rather than supervising a child's doing it *is* easier – especially when the child tries to avoid the work by whining and heel-dragging. It's easier, that is, in the *short run*.

But, what is easy in the short run becomes exhausting in the *long run*. Picking up after a child right now might seem easy, but picking up after them *forever* will not be so easy.

Never do anything for students that they are thoroughly capable of doing for themselves.

The Value of Being Needed

Effective parents train their children to help and to take pride in helping. Effective teachers do the same.

You could use some help, of course. But, more importantly, the children *need* to help.

Children who are neither asked nor expected to contribute to the well-being of the group are, by definition, not needed. They are excess baggage.

Being peripheral members of the group tends to bring out the worst in children. It feeds into laziness and dependency while denying them a way of demonstrating their worth.

Whether at home or at school, children need jobs that contribute to the well-being of the group. They need to feel proud because they have pulled their own weight. They need "chores."

The Rule of Chores

In the classroom dozens of routine jobs need to be done on a daily basis. Only when these jobs are done will the teacher have time to respond to students' special needs.

Effective teachers delegate. The size and complexity of the teacher's job require that they train the students to carry some of the burden.

Since chores are good for both the teacher and the students, I would suggest the following "rule of chores:"

Never do anything for students that they are thoroughly capable of doing for themselves.

Organizing Classroom Chores

I have known teachers, particularly in the upper elementary grades, who had a job for each student in the class. These teachers rarely had to lift a finger to do anything but teach. They had a gift for organization.

If they were teaching a small group and suddenly felt the need for their grade book, they would say to their "grade book monitor,"

"Tyler, may I please have my grade book?"

Tyler would quickly deliver the grade book and return to his seat. What a deal!

Frankly, I doubt my own ability to keep thirty classroom chores straight. A simple way of reducing the complexity of chores is to group them into four clusters and assign a team of students to each cluster of chores. Rotate the chores every week so that each student does every chore during a four-week rotation.

Of course, the chores will be different in World History than in wood shop. The clusters listed on this page are typical of a self-contained classroom and serve only as food for thought.

Cleanup

- Clean up paper and litter in the classroom.
- Arrange books and materials on the shelves.
- Clean up work areas and take care of equipment.
- Clean the chalkboard and erasers.
- Clean up a portion of the yard. If all classrooms are involved, the yard can be kept in good shape.

Bulletin board and decoration

- Make bulletin boards. Why do teachers spend so much time making bulletin boards themselves when, with a little structure, the students can have fun doing it and learn in the process?
- Decorate the classroom. Holidays, special events, and new social studies units provide a perennial source of inspiration.
- Plan art projects for the class.

Enrichment

- Plan enrichment activities and learning games.
- Help construct learning centers.
- Provide suggestions for preferred TV viewing each week.
- Present current events on a daily or weekly basis.

Clerical work

- Collect and pass out papers.
- Correct papers and record grades under the teacher's supervision (insofar as you are comfortable with this). Students often take care of recording Bell Work.
- Help with attendance and collecting lunch orders, milk money, paperback book orders, and so on.

The main investment in building routines is simply the practice required for mastery. For example, the first time the students are on the cleanup committee, you will have to teach them how you want your boards erased. And, the first time your enrichment committee presents current events, you will need to rehearse them. As always, the investment in Classroom Structure is greatest at the beginning, but it yields dividends for the entire semester.

> **If your first meeting with a parent is about a problem, you have just made an adversary for the remainder of the year.**

Helping with Instruction

While most chores have to do with mundane matters, make your students responsible for as much as they can handle. They can help you teach by developing visual aids for lessons and writing lists of test questions. Student learning groups can carry out skill practice, test review, and the editing of written work.

Peer tutoring can be considered part of the group's self-management. You model Praise, Prompt, and Leave as well as Say, See, Do Teaching every day. Teach the class these key instructional skills so they can help each other more effectively. It will make them better tutors.

Communicating Your Standards to Parents

No Second Chance

You will have dealings with the parents of your students sooner or later. The helpful parents will often contact you as soon as the school year begins to volunteer as aides or chaperones. But the parents of the troublemakers tend to avoid contact with the school.

If, however, your first meeting with these parents is about a problem, you have just made an adversary for the remainder of the year. They do not want to own the problem, and they will often blame it on you or any other convenient target if given the chance. These are the parents you least want to have as adversaries.

It will be to your advantage to be proactive rather than reactive in getting to know the parents of your students – particularly the parents of the problem students. You will need a plan for structuring your first contact.

A Self-Contained Classroom

I have known elementary teachers who sent out invitations to a barbeque or picnic at their homes as soon as they received the class list in August. Most of their colleagues expressed admiration while declining to do the same. Yet, these teachers had a level of help and cooperation from parents that was on a different scale from that of their colleagues.

Many teachers at the elementary level send out a letter before the school year starts welcoming the parents and their children, listing books to read over the summer, and giving a brief preview of the curriculum for the coming semester. This type of communication can also take place during the first week of school, accompanied by a copy of the classroom rules and a brief "mission statement" to set the tone.

As a follow-up to this contact, it is extremely important to be proactive in structuring your first personal conversation with the parents of your students. Do it early before problems force you into a negative first contact. Beginning in the second week of school, call the parents of each student. This is a brief conversation of roughly five minutes duration. Call five parents a night.

The structure of the conversation is as follows:

- **Introduce yourself.**
- **Briefly describe the highlights of your curriculum:** When I say brief, I mean *brief.* Just give a flavor of the coming year, as in:

  "This is the year the students learn about the age of steam and the industrial revolution, so you will be hearing a lot about that. In addition, we will begin writing essays of several paragraphs in length."
- **Say something positive about the child:** This conversation deals with *good news only.* If there is already a problem with the child, save it for another day.
- **Discuss the classroom standards that you sent home:** You get the opportunity to express a commitment to high standards while answering questions about the classroom rules that you sent home. In addition, you find out which students do not take things home. In such cases, tell the parents that you will send another copy home tomorrow. This level of follow-through often convinces students that messages sent home are intended to get there.

- **Ask about any special needs of the child:** Begin by asking if there are any *medical* problems that you should know about. Asking about medical problems helps the parents relax rather than jumping to the conclusion that you are asking about academic or emotional problems. The sharing that follows will often alert you to things that are not in the student's folder. Perhaps the most significant communication, however, is that you care.
- **Emphasize that you need their help:** Stress the fact that successful students have both their parents' and their teachers' support. You might say something like this:

  "As students go through school, there are usually some bumps in the road. It might be something to do with schoolwork, but it might be something hurtful that a classmate said. You might hear about it before I do.

  "The kids who do best in school have both their teachers and their parents behind them. If you hear about something that is worrisome, please call me. And if I hear about something that is worrisome, I would like to feel free to call you. If we work together, we can usually iron out these bumps before they become 'real problems.'

  "Before I hang up, I would like to invite you to 'Back-to-School night.' I will be sending an announcement home next week. This year it is the evening of..."

As a supplement to this first phone contact, some teachers "randomly" call the parents of one student per week to give a full report. This simple program seems to give the teacher a great deal of leverage over behavior in the classroom since some calls are less random than others.

A Departmentalized Setting

A teacher in a departmentalized setting, such as a high school, may see over 150 students in a given day. Such settings obviously need a different plan for reaching out to parents.

Some schools have highly elaborate outreach programs which include a welcoming picnic or special assembly for the parents of incoming freshmen, faculty ombudsmen assigned to each student, a student body welcoming program (i.e. Link Crew), connections to community churches and service organizations that make regular announcements of students on the honor roll, awards assemblies which include parents, and so on.

The development of such a plan, however, is an issue of *school site* management that involves the *entire faculty* rather than an issue of *classroom* management that you can implement by *yourself.* For your own good, however, you may wish to augment the school site program. It would be a good investment to make a welcoming phone call during the second week of school to the parents of the five students in each class whose misbehavior will most likely produce a parent conference before long.

Ongoing Communication with Parents

Sending Work Home

Sending work home regularly with a provision for parental feedback opens a communication link that will produce increased parental involvement in problem solving. This program takes on a somewhat different form at the elementary and secondary levels.

At the elementary level, send a folder of the child's work home every Thursday. The first writing assignment of the year might be the following:

Dear Mother and Father: This is the folder work that I have done in school this week. It will show you the kinds of assignments that I have been given and the kind of work that I have done. Some of the papers have been graded and some have not been graded. Please look over my work and sign your name in the space at the bottom of the page. If you have any comments, write in the space provided.

The folder system does more than simply send work home so that parents can monitor their child's performance. *First,* it says to the parents that the school wants their involvement. *Second,* it establishes an open communication link with parents. This can serve as an early warning system to the teacher.

At the secondary level, teachers usually send work home when a project or major assignment has been completed. Whatever the occasion for sending home work, the value of regular communication with parents will be no less at the secondary level than at the elementary level.

Commendations

When students do a good job, they need to hear about it, and so do their parents. While commendations are sometimes overdone to the point of being meaningless, they can also be an important part of teacher-parent communication. A personal note is probably the most meaningful form of commendation. For a teacher who regularly sends folders of work home, these communications represent very little additional work.

Preventative Conferences

Teachers and parents will either be allies or adversaries when they meet to deal with a student's problem. A conference with a parent when the problem is *small* can be a fairly relaxed exercise in problem solving. A conference with a parent whose child is in deep trouble is unlikely to be either relaxed or constructive.

Dealing with problems proactively when they are small can save you angry confrontations later on. Parents almost always perceive a large problem with their child as a failure on the teacher's part to deal with the problem before it became so serious.

A Final Note on Being Proactive

Most of us are capable of being either proactive or reactive in our approach to problem solving. Very few people are consistently proactive.

Focusing on potential problems can be disquieting. It is easy to give in to denial and procrastination. When we do, we back ourselves into "reactive management."

Proactive management is more than a set of procedures. It is a mindset. It is the way a person thinks when success is not negotiable, and it just happens to be easier in the long run.

The First Days of School

Our treatment of classroom structure is not intended to be comprehensive. Rather, it sets the stage for the chapters on discipline management that follow.

Our friends, Harry and Rosemary Wong, have written a wonderful book, "The First Days of School," which deals with classroom structure in a more thorough fashion.

Contact them at: www.firstdaysofschool.com

Section Six

Learning To Mean Business

Chapter Thirteen

Understanding Brat Behavior

Preview

- Tradition and common sense equate discipline with punishment.
- The school discipline code is organized as a hierarchy of consequences – the larger the crime, the larger the punishment.
- Only 5 percent of the student body produces 90 percent of the office referrals for the duration of their academic careers.
- For chronic disruptors, the worst consequence is that they are suspended or expelled from school. For kids who hate school, this is not a bad deal.
- Saying "no" to children and then giving them what they want if they act out builds brat behavior.
- Discipline management has always been a blind spot in teacher preparation. Consequently, we lose over a third of new teachers within their first two years.

Defining Discipline

Prevention vs. Remediation

It is most useful to organize *Tools for Teaching* as a program of discipline management with everyday goofing off in the spotlight. All previous sections of the book have dealt with the *prevention* of discipline problems in the classroom. In this section, "Learning To Mean Business," we deal with the *remediation* of discipline problems.

In this chapter, we will look at discipline management as it has traditionally been done both at the school site level and in the classroom. Our traditional way of dealing with discipline will serve as the backdrop for examining the skills of the "natural teacher" as they set limits on unacceptable behavior.

We will refer to these skills collectively as "Meaning Business." Subsequent chapters will deal with the nuts and bolts of Meaning Business – the emotions, the thoughts, and the actions.

Our Number One Concern

Nearly every educational poll of parents and teachers over the past four decades has placed "discipline" at the top of their list of concerns. While sensational topics make the news, parents worry most about everyday classroom events that effect their child's learning and happiness.

Parents hear about "being picked on," and when they visit the classroom they see "fooling around" and "wasting time." Parents ask themselves, "What does this teacher allow?"

Discipline and Consequences

Natural teachers have orderly and productive classrooms, and they never raise their voices. Parents know when their child has a natural. Their child is excited about learning and looks forward to going to school.

Naturals are experts at the *prevention* of discipline problems. Very little of their time and energy is consumed in remediation, and when problems do occur, Meaning Business "nips it in the bud."

But very few teachers are naturals. Most teachers will spend much of their energy trying to remediate typical classroom disruptions while loosing valuable learning time.

Discipline as remediation has a very different flavor from discipline as prevention. Discipline as remediation focuses on *consequences.*

"Common sense says that discipline equals punishment."

The School Discipline Code

Discipline Equals Punishment

If you were to ask fifty people on the street what it means to "discipline a child," they would give a very predictable answer. Fill in the blank yourself. *When you discipline a child, you* __________ *them.*

Indeed, common sense and common usage equate the word discipline with *punishment.* Disciplining children means "punishing them for what they did wrong."

This common sense definition of discipline as punishment produces our common sense approach to discipline management. When dealing with a specific infraction, we usually ask ourselves, "What punishment should the child receive for having done that?"

The Hierarchy of Consequences

Look in your local high school's student handbook under the heading "Discipline Code" to see what form it takes. The logic of all discipline codes is timeless – *the punishment fits the crime.* The larger the crime, the larger the punishment.

The resulting "hierarchy of consequences" has one simple purpose – to put the lid on – to eliminate disruptions – to say "no" to unacceptable behavior and make it stick. This approach has characterized discipline management in schools and classrooms since time out of mind.

Since it is the job of the school discipline code to "put the lid on," it is appropriate to observe it in action to see if it works. If it works, we should by all means reinstitute it next year just as we did last year.

The Mock Freshman Assembly

In order to get a quick overview of the school discipline code, imagine your first day of high school as you attend the Freshman Welcoming Assembly. This will not be a real assembly, of course. Rather, it will be a *mock* freshman assembly to allow us a level of candor that is foreign to such events.

This assembly is an annual rite of great seriousness for it establishes the "tone" for student behavior at the school site. A hush falls over the auditorium as the principal mounts the podium.

"Freshmen, welcome to high school. Now that we have taken care of that, let's get down to business. Our business today is the *school discipline code.* The discipline code spells out what goes and what *doesn't* go around here.

"First, I want to say that this is one of the finest high schools in the entire region, and a high school is no better than its faculty. We value our faculty above everything else. Consequently, I will not tolerate *for one moment* the abuse of any member of our faculty.

"Having said that, let me cite a statistic. There is nothing like a good statistic to rivet people's attention. At any school site, 90 percent of the office referrals are produced by 5 percent of the student body!

"Let me give a name to that 5 percent – *Troublemakers!* That's what you are, a bunch of troublemakers! Maybe I've been in education too long, but to me, *once* a troublemaker, *always* a troublemaker.

"My message for today is simple. We are *not going to put up with it!*

"Of course, I know that some of you jokers are laughing up your sleeves right now thinking, 'Yeah, right. What are they going to *do* about it?'

"Some of you think you can use foul language or throw a punch or tell a teacher to do an unnatural act and get away with it. Well, I'm here today to tell you, *you can't.*

"The logic of all school discipline codes is that the punishment fits the crime."

"On the other hand, we *love children.* We are not going to cut you off at the knees right away. So, here's how it works.

"The first time you pull some stunt around here, we are going to give you a *verbal warning.* It is our sincere hope that you *repent* right there on the spot. But, I know what most of you jokers are thinking. 'Big deal. I'm *so scared.*'

"Listen up! The next time you pull some stunt around here, you will be sent to *detention after school.* This is a special *honor system* that we operate. We take some smart-mouthed kid who gave his third period teacher a hard time and ask him to report to the office at the end of the day to *do time.*

"Believe it or not, we have often been 'stiffed' with this program. The doggone kid *didn't show up*!

"Quit laughing! Listen up!

"Now, if you pull *another* stunt around here, we will schedule a *conference with your parents!* Let me explain exactly what that means. We will spend *hours* of professional time in an attempt to collaborate with those members of the community who have already demonstrated their total *incompetence* by rearing *you.*

I know what you're thinking. 'Oh yeah, get my old man to a conference. That'll be the day! And if my mom comes, all she'll say is, 'I can't do anything with him at home, either. He's driving me crazy!'

"Hey, pipe down and pay attention! This is no joke! Now, if you pull another stunt, you'll be *sent to the office*! Do you know what will happen to you down at the office? Well, you don't want to find out!

"If you get in trouble again, you'll be sent to the office a *second* time. And, if you get in trouble again, you'll be sent to the office a *third* time. At this point you might be thinking, 'Is that it? All I get is a ticket out of class?'

"Oh no, it is *not*! If you pull *one more stunt*, you will be *suspended from school*! Let me explain exactly what that means. For a period of 24 hours you will be denied *all* of the following privileges:

- mathematics
- social studies
- English composition
- science
- foreign languages
- gym class

"And don't bother trying to check out books from the library in order to make up missed work. You have lost library privileges as well!

"Of course, we don't have people on the payroll to supervise you once you've been suspended. So, we put you under the supervision of *your parents*.

"We *know* how effective your parents are at supervising you. By way of the grapevine, we have learned what goes on at home in place of school:

- sleep late
- watch TV
- play video games
- shoot hoops
- meet your friends
- go to the mall

Do you know what will happen to you down at the office?

"After 24 hours of total deprivation, I hope we have brought you up short! But, once a troublemaker, always a troublemaker! At least, that's the way it seems to me. You just keep pushing the rules. You never know when to quit. You think you're *above the law.*

"Well, you aren't! If you pull one more stunt around here, you will be *suspended for three days!* You will have the same loss of privileges as before, and the same supervision.

"At the end of *three* days of total deprivation, I hope you return to this school site with a humble demeanor and an entirely new attitude toward education. Do I make myself clear?"

Imagine "Larry"

Does this sound as nuts to you as it does to me? Am I making this up?

Now I would like you to imagine a particular student – *Larry.* Do you remember Larry – the student who will cause you to question your career choice?

Larry is the student you have been hearing horror stories about for *two years* before he finally reaches your grade level. Larry is the student you *prayed* would be home schooled. Larry is a royal – well, let's just say that Larry is a difficult child.

Let me ask some deep and probing questions concerning Larry's psyche. Does Larry *like school?* Yeah, right! According to Larry, school _______. (Fill in the blank.)

What is the one thing Larry wants more than anything else as far as school is concerned? How about, *O-U-T!*

Would you believe that we have a management program whereby Larry can achieve his *heart's desire*? Larry *can* get out. But, there is one thing that Larry must do first. Larry must *abuse the faculty.*

However, occasional abuse won't get the job done. It must be *frequent* abuse. In order to get out of school, Larry must be such a constant pain that he works himself all the way up the hierarchy of consequences in order to get the boot. Only then does Larry get *O-U-T.*

Reinforcement Errors and "Brat" Behavior

Let's imagine a four-year-old child who is whining in order to get something. The parent says, "No." The child keeps whining and the parent says, "No." again. The child whines and whines, and the parent finally says, "All right! You can have it. I'm tired of listening to your whining!"

You know what will happen the next time the child wants something. They will whine because *whining pays off.* By giving in, the parent has inadvertently reinforced the child's obnoxious whining – a form of "brat" behavior.

But the parent *did* get rid of the whining – at least, in the short run. What a relief! For this reason the parent will probably repeat the same mistake the next time they confront the same dilemma.

There is a technical name for this pattern – a *reinforcement error.* A reinforcement error is a specific error in management that causes the problem to *go away* in the short-term but guarantees that it will *get worse* in the long-term.

Management procedures that contain reinforcement errors inadvertently provide a schedule of reinforcement for the very problem behavior that they are trying to eliminate. The school discipline code is riddled with reinforcement errors for abusing the faculty. It will maintain Larry's brat behavior for *eight straight semesters*?

But the office is not the only source of reinforcement errors for brat behavior at the school site. In fact, it is not even the primary source. To find the "mother load" of reinforcement errors, we must leave the office and walk down the hall.

Following the Problem to Its Source

A "Blow-Up" with Larry

Problems that end up in the office begin in the classroom. So let's begin at the beginning. How did Larry end up at the office in the first place?

Let's imagine that you are a high school teacher who is unlucky enough to have Larry in third period. Today Larry is in rare form. He is smirky and flippant, and he has continued talking to his buddy even after you have *twice* asked him to stop.

You cruise over to where he is sitting and stand there for a second or two as he finishes chatting with his friend. He then looks up as though to say, "Oh, you again."

You say,

> "I'm tired of this constant talking. I want you to turn around in your seat right now and get some work done."

Larry looks up and says,

> "F____ you!"

You see red! That's the last straw! Enough! Done! Finished!

> "That's it, young man! I will not tolerate such language in my class for *one instant*! You may pick up your things and leave this room *immediately*. You may *report to the office*!"

Several of Larry's buddies let out with mock "Oohs." Larry stands slowly and defiantly, acknowledging their attention, and strolls toward the door.

More Reinforcement Errors

Enough is *enough*! You have drawn the line and *laid down the law*! Or have you?

Well, not really – not when you consider the number of reinforcement errors that have just taken place. You may think that you are dictating the terms, but Larry is the man in charge. Let's count the payoffs that Larry has just received for jerking your chain in class:

- Who picked the time?
- Who picked the place?
- Who picked the victim?
- Who picked the language?
- Who could easily predict the outcome of such language?
- Who used the language in order to get the outcome?
- Who just made himself look "bad to the bone" in front of all of his buddies?
- Who just made you lose your cool?
- Who just got out of class?
- Who just made a defiant gesture as part of his exit?
- Who is now unsupervised in the hall?
- Who will now join his "jailbird" buddies in the office to shoot the breeze for the next 20 minutes or more as they wait to be seen?

We have just counted a *dozen* payoffs or "secondary gains" for Larry's using the F-word. That is a lot of power wrapped up in a monosyllable. You can't give Larry that much power and not expect him to use it.

"Straighten That Kid Out!"

The Revolving Door Policy

When we send Larry to the office after a really ugly piece of behavior, we want something *done*! What do we get? Larry is gone for the remainder of the period and shows up tomorrow "as cocky as a jaybird."

What do they *do* down at that office – a citizenship lecture? Is that it? Make him promise not to do it again? How many teachers have said,

"I am sick and tired of sending students down to the office only to have *nothing happen*. All they have down there is the 'revolving door policy.' I want them to *straighten that kid out*!"

What Do They Expect?

Ask administrators about the revolving door policy, and they'll say,

"What do they expect me to do? I have six kids outside of my door, and we're not even through *first period* yet. If I spend enough time with a kid to find out what's really going on and then *do* something about it, I'd finish in the middle of second period. By that time the office would be full of rowdy kids, and they'd be hassling the secretaries.

"This isn't an outpatient clinic with a dozen professionals on staff. It's just me, and if I don't deal with these problems quickly, I'll be *buried* in them."

"Insanity is doing the same thing over and over and expecting a different result."

A Dysfunctional System

The Oldest Myth

The oldest myth in the management of severe classroom discipline problems is that someone down the hall can fix it. We keep acting as though the office *should* be able to help us, and the office keeps demonstrating that we hope in vain. This persistence reminds me of the Chinese proverb that defines insanity as *doing the same thing over and over and expecting a different result.*

Blaming

When a social system is not working properly, the first symptom is *blaming*. Blaming always takes the same form – "If they would do *their* job, I could do *mine*!"

Teachers blame the administrators, and administrators blame the teachers. Everybody blames everybody. But, if a management system consistently fails to live up to expectations, the only cure is to *redesign the system.*

The predicament of redesigning "the system" was poignantly stated by a vice principal inquiring about our program. She said, "We know that the system doesn't work, but we don't know what else to do."

The Discipline Task Force

From time to time, out of sheer frustration, school sites confront the obvious short-comings of their discipline management program. One common exercise is to create a "discipline task force" – a committee of teachers, administrators, and parents who spend an entire year attempting to redesign "the system."

While some upgrades might be possible depending on what was there before, the committee usually ends up about where they started. After all, there is nothing that can be done to Larry legally that every educator in the state hasn't known about for the past fifty years.

Focusing on the Classroom

No Plan, No Execution

How exactly do you respond to a student who is *way* out of line? Did you receive specific strategies during your teacher training? Did you practice them to mastery?

Quite the opposite. Almost every new teacher who enters the field has to "wing it" when confronted. They have vague notions of what to do, but they have no idea of how the game is played.

Larry is not winging it. He knows exactly how to play the game. In the preceding example, Larry set the teacher up. The teacher went for the bait. Game over.

A Fast Game

Dealing with classroom provocations is a fast game. The game is lost on the basis of the teacher's immediate response to Larry's provocation. It is over in seconds.

Until teachers know how to play the game, they will be "had" whenever Larry feels like it. And nobody in the office can undo the fact that, if you can be "had" today, you can be "had" tomorrow.

You Must Mean Business

Since most discipline problems begin in the classroom, the redesign of our management system must begin there too. The teacher is the first line of defense in dealing with student provocations. If the teacher "blows it," provocations spin out of control, and small problems become big problems which end up in the office.

Natural teachers can go an entire semester without sending a kid to the office. They never raise their voices. They never get upset. But they always get their way. Effective teachers will tell you,

> "When you send a kid to the office, you publicize the fact that you can't handle the situation."

When you send a kid to the office, you publicize the fact that you can't handle the situation.

But how do natural teachers "handle the situation" and do it with a *light hand* so both they and the students enjoy coming to class? These are the skills of *Meaning Business.*

We must come to understand these skills. Only when teachers succeed with discipline management at the classroom level can administrators succeed with discipline management at the school site level.

Building Expertise

A Lovely Seminar

In chapter one, I described how I learned about Meaning Business from natural teachers. It was obviously very powerful, and I wanted to share it with the faculty.

I did exactly what I was programmed to do – a Bop 'til You Drop seminar every Tuesday afternoon for five weeks. It was a lovely seminar I was told – *very* relevant, *very* interesting, and *very* useful.

I would have been *very* happy were it not for the data. Our data showed that the seminar had *no effect whatsoever* on the teachers who were taking the seminar, to say nothing of their students. The whole effort had been a complete waste of time.

Our little research team became very depressed and naturally blamed the teachers – you can't teach an old dog new tricks, blah, blah, blah... After we had our little tantrum, our minds slowly turned to what *we* had done. Could it be possible that the teachers' failure to learn was caused by *our teaching*? Oh my!

Discovering Skill Practice

We went back to the drawing board. Meaning Business was obviously a matter of skill. Had our trainees practiced any skills? Did we ever get them on their feet?

Our stunning insight was that we had utterly omitted *skill practice* as a means of producing performance. What were we thinking?

We apologized to the faculty and added skill practice to the seminar. We got teachers on their feet and coached them through key elements of Meaning Business. In three hours of training, the rate of student disruptions in the classrooms of the "control teachers" (the ones who were not naturals) matched that of the naturals.

Meaning Business can be taught! It is not something you are born with! It is just a matter of skill.

Training Teachers

Over the past 35 years, I've been continuously engaged in training teachers in the skills of classroom management. Our understanding of management has grown into *Tools for Teaching*, and our understanding of training has grown apace.

When training teachers, we have constantly labored under the pressure of *time*. There is never enough time for the workshop you would *like* to give. There are so many skills.

Training teachers, therefore, has always driven me toward increasing my efficiency as a teacher. The first half of *Tools for Teaching* is not just the result of working with teachers in their own classrooms. It is also the result of years of training teachers to train other teachers in the skills of classroom management.

My focus was, of course, on performance. But we also wanted to build a *context of understanding* that gave those skills meaning. I learned that understanding came quickly in conjunction with skill building and very slowly in its absence.

The Study Group Activity Guide

You will find as I did that skill mastery requires training. You will probably train each other because I probably won't be there. You will begin by arranging your room, and you will present new skills using Say, See, Do Teaching.

The training protocols for every skill in *Tools for Teaching* are contained in the **Study Group Activity Guide** – a free download from **www. fredjones.com**. You will also find a plan for implementing training at your school site under the heading, "How To Use Tools for Teaching."

The following chapters will describe Meaning Business in detail. In order to *learn* to mean business, however, you will need to get up on your feet just like our original trainees.

Learning To Meaning Business

Meaning Business can be taught! It is not something you are born with! It is just skill building.

Chapter Fourteen

Staying Calm: Our Emotions

Preview

- Any classroom disruption will trigger a mild fight-flight reflex.
- This reflex not only makes you vulnerable to becoming upset, but it also stresses you physically.
- Triune Brain Theory helps to explain how the brain "downshifts" during a fight-flight reflex so that you end up functioning out of your brainstem instead of your cortex.
- To lead under pressure, you will need all of your knowledge, experience and understanding. The complex social skills required for leadership reside in the cortex.
- Thus, the fundamental rule of social power is, "Calm is strength. Upset is weakness."
- Remaining calm under pressure is achieved through relaxation. Relaxation is a skill that can be mastered with training.

Self-Preservation

When the Well Runs Dry

Teaching is one of the most stressful jobs on the planet. It has been estimated that a teacher makes more decisions in an hour than an air traffic controller. Being tired at the end of each day is considered by most to be just part of the job.

Being tired at the end of each day is also a prescription for burn-out. If you give more than you get day after day, the well will eventually run dry. When the well runs dry, you will have nothing left to give. You will suffer, your students will suffer, and your family will suffer. There has to be an easier way to do this job.

Stress Management

Since stress is part of the job, stress management is also part of the job. It is your responsibility because it is your life.

As mentioned in chapter one, stress management must occur moment by moment *in the classroom.* It must be proactive. You cannot allow yourself to be stressed all day long and then somehow undo it once you get home.

Trying to undo stress after it has occurred is more damage control than stress management. You may exercise or meditate, but most of the time you will just poop out. As always, reactive management fails where only proactive management can succeed.

Teaching Without Exhaustion

Meaning Business is on-the-job stress management. It deals with student disruptions and provocations calmly and efficiently. It makes us a better teacher. It makes our classroom a happier place. But first and foremost, it preserves us.

Natural teachers have told me, "I'm glad they pay me to do this job because I would do it anyway." These teachers find life in the classroom to be invigorating and enriching rather than exhausting.

That is the way we all wanted it to be when we entered teaching. Natural teachers show us that it can be done. But their level of success will not come for free. First, we must master our craft. We must learn to mean business.

Biology and Behavior

The Fight-Flight Reflex

Imagine that you catch some goofing off out of the corner of your eye. Let's begin with the very first thing that happens to you after you see the disruption. It is a reflex – a very primitive reflex that we share with all vertebrates.

We learned about this reflex in our high school biology class. It is the *fight-flight reflex.* This reflex is our natural response to anything that surprises us or threatens us. It could be a clap of thunder, a shadow passing across the window, a spider on our clothing, or a near accident with the car.

The fight-flight reflex, therefore, is the teacher's immediate and automatic response to goofing off. A room full of students can trigger the fight-flight reflex quite often during a school day.

Managing the Fight-Flight Reflex

A reflex such as the fight-flight reflex is *immediate* and *automatic.* You do not choose to have it.

Yet natural teachers rarely become upset in the classroom. They remain cool, calm, and collected in response to goofing off. Yet, they have the same reflexes as everyone else. They just manage stress more effectively.

We will need to find out how they do it. But first, we must become more familiar with the fight-flight reflex.

Anatomy of the Fight-Flight Reflex

The fight-flight reflex involves our entire body as it "revs up" as fast as possible to deal with threat. This mobilization occurs in two phases:

- **fast** (muscular tension)
- **slow** (adrenaline)

By understanding these two phases of the fight-flight reflex, we will lay the ground work for our own stress management.

The Fast (Neuromuscular) Phase

The fast phase of the fight-flight reflex has to do with the *tensing of muscles.* Within a fraction of a second our bodies begin to mobilize – to get ready to move quickly if need be. The fight-flight reflex tenses muscles that you can *feel:*

- Eyes open wide (to maximize field of vision)
- Teeth clench
- Diaphragm flexes as we inhale (to oxygenate the blood)
- Skeletal muscles tense (to get ready for action)

The fight-flight reflex also tenses muscles that you may *not feel:*

- Blood vessels in the stomach contract (to shunt blood to the muscles). This interrupts digestion which leaves acid in the stomach.

- Heart rate increases rapidly (to prepare for exertion). This increases blood pressure.

The fight-flight reflex is crucial to survival – at least, for an animal in a state of nature. To experience the fight-flight reflex several times in the course of a day is normal for any wild animal, and it is not damaging.

But, our species left "nature" a long time ago to create an alternative – civilization. Civilization is accompanied by physical crowding and complex social organization. It requires us to constantly interact in order to solve problems, resolve conflict, negotiate solutions, and generally stress each other out.

The fight-flight reflex is our natural response to anything we dislike or do not expect.

Some of us even place ourselves in a room full of young people all day long in order to teach. In biological terms you might think of this as the petri dish for growing stress.

Within the classroom the fight-flight reflex is triggered not every few hours as it might be in nature, but rather, every few *minutes*. In this environment, every aspect of the fight-flight reflex becomes a potential symptom of chronic hypertension. Observe the ads on television to see how many are simply attempting to ameliorate the stress of a day on the job.

- Will it be aspirin or Tylenol or Advil or Aleve to help with that tension headache?
- Will it be Tums or Rolaids or Mylanta to help with stomach acid?
- Will it be Sominex or Nytol or Tylenol PM to help you relax enough to fall asleep?
- Will it be a glass of chardonnay – or two?

How many millions of dollars do we spend just trying to "come down" after a day at work? We pay a high price for working in a stressful environment. But stress just goes with the territory, right?

The Slow (Biochemical) Phase

The slow phase of the fight-flight reflex is more damaging. Within tenths of a second our bodies begin to dump adrenaline into the bloodstream.

Adrenaline *intensifies* the physiological mobilization of the fight-flight reflex and *maintains* it over time. It makes sure that the intensity and focus of the fight-flight reflex will stay with us throughout the crisis. The more upset we become, the more adrenaline enters the blood. Here are some things to know about adrenaline:

- It increases your metabolism, the rate at which your body burns sugars. This is where "nervous energy" comes from.
- It takes roughly 27 minutes for adrenaline to clear the blood stream. Consequently, it takes only two "squirrely" behaviors per class period to keep you "wired" all day long for the remainder of your career.

Everybody knows that you have to be "on your toes" to manage a classroom, right? It's only common sense.

While it might seem like common sense, I would not recommend that you try to earn a living that way. Being "on your toes" for hours on end means that you constantly use adrenaline to create that extra energy needed to cope with the demands of students. In so doing you build up an *energy debt* during the school day that must be paid back later.

Reflexes are immediate and automatic. You do not choose to have them.

Do you experience this energy debt when the kids go home? No, you still have another 27 minutes on adrenaline before it clears the bloodstream. Consequently, you have enough energy after dismissal to scurry around organizing books and materials for tomorrow's lessons.

The energy debt hits you about a half-hour *after* the kids go home. A wave of exhaustion comes over you, and you look for a place to sit down. *What a day!*

Recovering from an energy debt that has been building for the past six hours will take you well into the evening. Who then pays for the fact that you are exhausting yourself in the classroom? As the song says, "You only hurt the ones you love, the ones you shouldn't hurt at all."

Your spouse says,

"Honey, we need to talk about something,"

and you say,

"Do we have to talk about it *right now?*"

Your child says,

"I just broke this,"

and you say,

"You broke it *already?* You just got it *last week!*"

You can't be very good with your own family when you come home day after day with the tank empty. I don't know what your pay package includes, but I doubt that anybody pays you enough to compensate for your physical well-being or your family's well-being or your own personal happiness.

Fight-Flight by Different Names

Nag, Nag, Nag

When you have a fight-flight reflex, your mouth tends to pop open. It may be a scream if your life is in danger. But in less emotionally charged social situations like the classroom, it sounds like this:

> "All right class, there is *no excuse* for all of this talking! When I look up, I expect to see people working!"

> "*Where* are you going? Would you please *take your seat?* I am sick and tired of looking up only to see you wandering aimlessly around the room!"

> "Would the two of you keep your hands *to yourselves* and *pay attention* to what is going on in class? If I see any more of this behavior, you will see me after the bell."

You remember *nag, nag, nag* from earlier chapters? Let me give you a *technical* definition of nagging: Nagging is nothing more than *a fight-flight reflex with dialogue.* If you open your mouth while you are upset, you will nag.

Nagging is nothing more than a fight-flight reflex with dialogue.

We *all* nag. Nagging is normal biological behavior. If you have a friend who claims to never nag, you have a liar for a friend. The question that is relevant to classroom management is not, "Do you nag?" but, rather, "How often do you nag?" For some teachers it is a rarity. For others it happens constantly.

Pheasant Posturing

We talk with our *hands* as well as our mouths. When we talk with our hands while nagging, we engage in "pheasant posturing."

Pheasant posturing is a term from anthropology that refers to *a lot of squawking and flapping that produces no damage.* Male pheasants do a dramatic job of squawking and flapping during their mating combat without ever touching each other.

In the classroom *squawking* is the same as *nag, nag, nag.* We do the *flapping,* however, with our *hands.*

We are not attempting to fly, of course. We just want to kick up a little dust around the barnyard so the chickies know that we're serious. In such situations we use only *one wing.*

The two most common one-wing flaps are the "circular" and the "vertical." We use the circular flap as we motion for students to turn around in their chairs. We use the vertical flap as we motion for students to sit down.

When both wings become involved, the situation is obviously serious. Imagine a teacher, upset and impatient, standing in the front of the classroom with both arms raised announcing to the class,

> "The longer it takes all of you to get *into your seats* and *settle down,* the longer I will be standing here… uh… with my arms up."

Snap and Snarl

A trainee from the court schools of Los Angeles (you can imagine the student body in the court schools of Los Angeles) said,

"I have a different name for it. I call it 'snap and snarl.' You *snap your fingers* and point when you say, 'Take your seat!' or 'Stop talking!'"

We all had a laugh as we practiced snapping and snarling. It gives a feeling of primitive power. A dinosaur comes to mind with eyes narrowed, teeth flashing. These thoughts of primitive power reminded me of an interaction I had with my younger son not long before.

Snap and Snarl with My Son

The altercation had to do with backpacks – the kind that kids take to school with their books and stuff inside. Patrick (my older son) and Brian (my younger son) used to drop their backpacks as soon as they came home from school – right at the bottom of the stairs. This was a dangerous place to put backpacks. I had taught the boys (I thought) to place their backpacks out of the way so nobody would trip over them.

One day, when I was jet-lagged from a flight home the night before, I found myself in a rotten mood. I was in the kitchen when Brian came home from school. He waltzed in the back door, dropped his backpack right at the foot of the stairs and started up to his room.

I snapped,

"Brian! Where is that back pack supposed to go?"

Brian said,

"Aw, Daaad!"

I must have been in good form to combine snapping and snarling with a silly question. And, I hadn't seen Brian in four days. Some greeting!

I felt bad. After I collected myself, I went upstairs to apologize and have a decent conversation. But later I thought at length about how inappropriate I'd been.

Let me put this whole thing into perspective. I have a Ph.D. in clinical psychology. At this point in my life, I had spent over three decades learning to understand peoples' *needs* and *feelings*, to solve interpersonal problems *constructively*, to structure *win-win* solutions for people, to be *therapeutic!* Where were all of these skills when I needed them?

A common variant of the fight-flight reflex is "snap and snarl."

Actually, I knew exactly where the skills were. I had studied it in great detail during graduate school.

Upset Changes Brain Function

Triune Brain Theory

Triune Brain Theory explains what happens in the brain when we become upset. It helps to describe why we snap and snarl when we have a fight-flight reflex.

For starters, there have been three great epochs of brain development over the eons. These epochs of brain development produced characteristic structures. You can see them in a cross-section of the brain.

Triune means "three in one." The "three brains in one" that we all possess are:

1. **Reptilian Brain (Brain stem):** These are the lower brain centers which regulate basic life functions. They include the spinal cord, the cerebellum (muscular coordination), the visual cortex plus ganglia that regulate bodily functions.
2. **Ancient Cortex (Paleocortex):** These are the mid-brain centers referred to irreverently by graduate students as "doggy-horsey brain." To see what these brain centers do, compare the social behavior of a lizard with that of your dog. Can your dog love you and be loyal? You won't get that from a lizard.
3. **New Cortex (Neocortex):** These are the brain centers that are responsible for "higher intelligence." This refers to Plato and Socrates, Bach and Beethoven, Einstein and Fermi – and us. These brain centers give us the capacity to reason.

Downshifting

The fight-flight reflex is extremely predictable and reliable. Animals that failed to execute it properly over the past 500 million years became someone else's lunch.

Reflexes are made reliable by fail-safe mechanisms. Triune Brain Theory explains the fail-safe mechanisms of the fight-flight reflex. How does the brain insure that, when your life is on the line, you "get it in gear" rather than dithering?

You can't dither without a cortex. So, your brain eliminates its own cortex. This process is called "downshifting."

Under *mild* arousal, the brain shifts from the neocortex to the mid-brain. This change can be disconcerting. Have you ever "blocked" on people's names when you were a little nervous? Downshifting plays havoc with long-term memory.

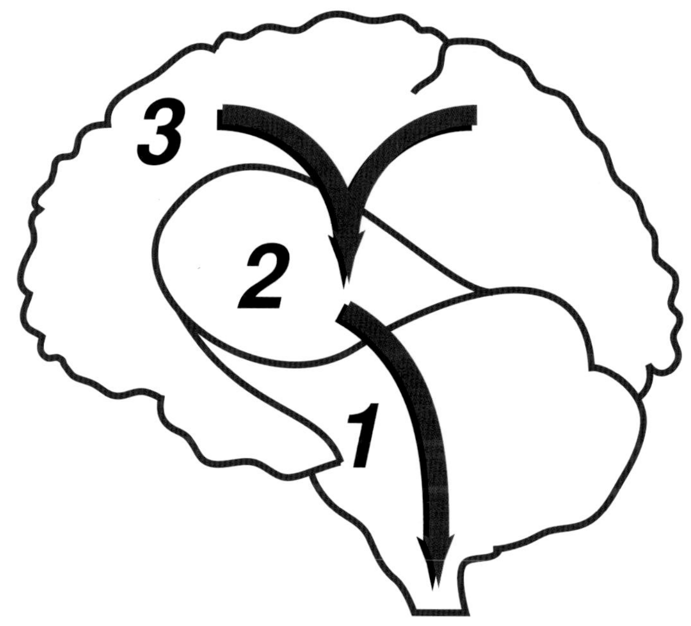

When we become upset, the brain "downshifts" from the cortex to the brainstem.

Under *moderate* to *severe* arousal, the brain downshifts all the way to the reptilian brain and spinal cord – referred to irreverently by graduate students as "going brainstem." We have all "gone brainstem" at some time, haven't we? Have you ever blown up, gone ballistic, flown off the handle, lost your cool?

Now, let me give you a piece of advice about discipline management in the classroom. You will do a much better job *with a cortex*. When you downshift, a classroom suddenly becomes thirty cortexes manipulating one brainstem. These are not even odds.

"When you downshift, a classroom suddenly becomes thirty cortexes manipulating one brainstem."

Social Power

Power and Control

Downshifting brings us to the real issue underlying this discussion of brain function, namely – *power*. Who runs your classroom, anyway?

Power is one of those words that leaves a bad taste.

"He is really on a *power trip*."

In fact, power is value-neutral. It simply refers to *control*. But control is another word that leaves a bad taste.

"She is a real *control freak*."

"He is the most *controlling person* I have ever met."

We subconsciously translate these words into "overpowering" and "controlling" – terms that denote threat. Without this "spin," however, they are just words that describe what is happening in the classroom. Take, for example, the management of a simple disruption.

You look up to see two students *talking* when they should be working. You cruise over to them as you work the crowd, and you ask them to get back to work.

Chances are, they *will* get back to work. This, however, does not signify a scholarly bent.

Rather, it signifies the fact that these students have the brains to cool it when the teacher is standing over them. To find out whether or not the students actually get back to work, you will have to wait a minute or two.

Imagine that two minutes have passed, and, from the far side of the room, you look up to see these two students *still working*. Who is controlling their behavior?

Simply look at what they are doing as a result of your interaction with them. Since they chose to pursue *your* agenda (working) rather than *their* agenda (talking), *you* are controlling their behavior.

Power is simply control. Who is controlling whom? Who calls the shot? Who gets his or her way?

Now imagine that the situation with *talking to neighbors* turned out differently. When you look up two minutes later the two students who "shaped up" when you were standing over them are *talking again*.

Who is in control now? Are they doing what *you* want them to do, or are they doing what *they* want to do?

As you can see, the outcome of this interaction is public knowledge. Any student in the classroom can look up to see whether or not you are capable of getting two students to shape up. There is no place for you to hide.

The Art of Getting Your Way

Power is control, and *control* is power. However, these two terms do not denote the "dark force." Rather, they describe who is leading and who is following. The person with more power leads. The person with less power follows.

However, when some people try to lead, they rub everybody the wrong way and people resist their leadership. They lack the necessary skills.

Other people are born leaders. They lead gracefully, and people follow. They definitely have the skills. Leading skillfully is an art – the art of *getting your own sweet way*.

Leadership is often described as "getting things done through people." It is the art of employing *social* power in order to achieve a *social* objective. In this sense leadership is synonymous with terms like "effective management" and diplomacy.

In political science, diplomacy is often described as "the art of getting the other person to do what you want them to do and *thank* you for it." Skillful diplomacy is definitely the art of social power – the art form by which *you* as a teacher earn your living.

All day in the classroom you will attempt to get students to do what you want them to do and thank you for it. You will take children during their sweetest years of youth and incarcerate them in a school building where you will require them to do one assignment after another all day long. And you will want them to like it so much that they do their best and look forward to doing it again tomorrow.

This will test your social skills to the limit. You will definitely need your cortex at all times.

Two Types of Power

Primitive Power

- Fight-Flight Reflex
- Force and Counterforce
- Reflex Behavior
- Brain Stem

Social Power

- Social Skills
- Leadership and Management
- Learned Behavior
- Cortex

Power Conflicts

Two Types of Power

There are, it would seem, *two* types of power within us – *social* power and *primitive* power. They compete with each other to control our behavior.

Primitive power is the power that we have used since time began in order to insure our physical survival. It is a direct expression of the fight-flight reflex. In social situations primitive power is expressed as *upset*. It is *aggressive*.

Social power, in contrast, is not natural – it is *learned*. It is not instinctual – it is *skillful*. Rather than being simple, it is *subtle* and *complex*. It is *nonadversarial*.

The conflict within us concerning these two types of power centers upon the fact that *you cannot do them both at the same time.* As we downshift to the brainstem when upset, we lose the cortex. We lose it for 27 minutes!

Calm Is Strength

This competition between two different types of power in governing our actions brings us to the most fundamental principle of social power:

Calm is strength.
Upset is weakness.

When you are *calm,* you can bring all of your wisdom, experience, and social skills to bear in solving a problem. When you become *upset* and downshift, none of that knowledge or wisdom is available to you. As the saying goes:

"My life is in the hands
of any fool
who can make me angry."

Who Is Controlling Whom?

To put primitive power and social power into perspective, ask yourself the following two questions:

- If you are *upset,* who is in control of your mind and body? (Trainees respond in unison, "They are.")
- If you are *calm,* who is in control of your mind and body? (Trainees respond in unison, "You are.")

Before you can ever hope to mean business, you must be in control of the situation rather than the situation being in control of you. You will never be able to control a classroom until you are first *in control of yourself.*

"Calm is strength. Upset is weakness."

One of the hardest lessons to accept about Meaning Business, therefore, is that it is first and foremost *emotional.* Unless you can be calm in the face of provocation, your fancy management strategies will avail you nothing. They will be in the cortex while you are in your brainstem.

But the biological game is played very quickly. Have you ever "flown off the handle?" How long did it take? The game is over before most teachers know that it has begun.

Calm Is a Skill

It's a Matter of Breathing

When you look up in the classroom to see disruptive behavior, you will have a fight-flight reflex. No amount of training can *prevent* the reflex. But you can *abort* it.

It takes only a few seconds for the concentration of adrenaline to build in your bloodstream. This gives you a brief window of opportunity in which to "put on the breaks."

During this brief period you can override the fight-flight reflex with a learned response. That learned response is *relaxation* – the physiological opposite of fight-flight.

But how do you relax in the face of a provocation? For starters, you relax by learning to *breathe* properly. Relaxed breathing is part of any training program that involves stress reduction. It is used in prepared childbirth training, therapy for anxieties or phobias, yoga, and the training of baseball umpires. Learning to relax is an indispensible survival skill for anyone who works in a stressful environment.

A relaxing breath is slow and relatively shallow. It is the way you would breathe if you were watching television or reading a magazine. It lowers your heart rate and your blood pressure. Your muscles relax, and your face becomes calm and expressionless.

Learning to relax is an indispensible survival skill for anyone who works in a stressful environment.

Calm Can Be Learned

Relaxed breathing is learned like any other skill – with effective coaching and practice, practice, practice. It can eventually replace fight-flight as your *dominant response* to student provocation.

The more skillful you become at relaxation, the more quickly you can relax in response to something upsetting. With mastery, relaxation can be almost instantaneous.

Emotions Are Contagious

If you are calm, you will have a calming effect on those around you. If you are upset, you will tend to upset those around you. During training, teachers learn: *Emotions are contagious. You will get exactly what you give.*

Our objectives in managing classroom disruptions are two-fold:

- *Calm* the student.
- Get them back *on task.*

These objectives are two sides of the same coin. You must calm students in order to get them back on task. Adrenaline makes people jumpy. If you raise your voice to a student, they stay jumpy for quite a while.

If students are upset, they will not be able to concentrate. If they cannot concentrate in order to study, they will probably find something else to do. It will most likely be some form of disruption. This disruption will then become your next discipline problem.

Our goal is to make problems smaller, not larger. If we remain calm, we contain the problem while preserving ourselves. If we get upset, we become our own worst enemy.

Chapter Fifteen

Being Consistent: Our Thoughts

Preview

- There are no degrees of consistency. You are either *consistent*, or you are *inconsistent.*
- If a student is disrupting in the classroom and you fail to intervene, you have just taught that student that their goofing off is acceptable behavior.
- When you see unacceptable behavior, therefore, you are on the horns of a dilemma. You either act and your rules become reality, or you fail to act and your rules are nothing but hot air.
- Consequently, in your classroom at all times *discipline comes before instruction.*
- You must have absolute clarity in your own mind as to where your behavioral boundaries lie. Without *mental* clarity you cannot have *behavioral* clarity.

No Means No

Being "In Charge"

In the classroom you are in charge. You make the rules and establish the behavioral boundaries. If you are not in charge, no one is in charge.

Often you will have to say "no" to misbehavior. When you do, you want the problem to stop. If it doesn't, that small problem is on its way to becoming a big problem.

How do you say "no" and make it stick? Perhaps a story about my mom will help. She was an ex-school teacher, and for all I know, she wrote the book on Meaning Business.

A Story about My Mom

When I was a little kid, we lived next door to the Smoyer family. Tommy Smoyer was my playmate, and Mrs. Smoyer (his mom, whose first name was none of my business) was dearly loved by us kids.

Not only was Mrs. Smoyer a nice lady, but she was also a compulsive baker. On a typical afternoon our play would be interrupted by Mrs. Smoyer opening the screen door to her back porch and calling, "Kids, come in now!" This meant that we were about to have a treat – something she had baked. Maybe it would be chocolate chip cookies or, better yet, brownies!

But some days Mrs. Smoyer would open her screen door and say, "Tommy, come in now!" This meant that she had baked a pie and would be serving it to her family rather than to the kids in the neighborhood.

One afternoon as we were playing in the backyard, I began to smell gingerbread wafting from Mrs. Smoyer's kitchen. I love gingerbread! I could hardly wait for my piece. As dinner time approached, Mrs. Smoyer opened her screen door and said, "Tommy, come in now!"

My heart sank. I wanted gingerbread! Life was unfair! Why couldn't I have gingerbread too? I wanted justice.

So, I ran across the driveway into my mother's kitchen where she was preparing dinner. I opened my negotiations where all children open negotiations, at *whine level number one.*

"*Mom,* may I have something to eat? Tommy's getting gingerbread."

My mother turned from the stove and said,

"Fred, I'm going to have this meal on the table in 45 minutes. Now, I don't want to ruin your appetite."

This was a clear communication. But I was young. I escalated the negotiations to *whine level number two.*

"But *Mom,* can't I have *something*? Don't we have some ginger snaps? I'm hungry!"

My mother said,

"Fred, I am not going to give you a snack now and then watch you sit at the dinner table and just *peck at your food.*"

My mother always used bird analogies when describing my eating habits. I was obviously getting nowhere. But I knew exactly what to do. I went to *whine level number three.*

"But this isn't *fair!* Tommy gets gingerbread. Can't I have something?"

Suddenly the mood in the room changed. My mother put down her spatula and turned slowly to face me. She looked at me intently as she wiped her hands on her apron. Then she said,

"*Fred,* I said *no,* and *no* means *no.*"

I couldn't just give up. After all, life had been unfair.

"But why can't I? Tommy gets..."

I was cut off in mid-sentence. My mother, with eyes squarely focused on mine, said,

"Fred, I am *not* going to stand here and listen to your *yammering.* ('Yammering' was my mother's code for, *You are really pushing it.*) You may either go outside to play until I call you, or you may open your mouth *one more time* and end up sitting on the stairs."

My sense of injustice must have been profound.

"But, why can't I..."

Those were the last words spoken. My mother stood before me with eyes fixed and finger pointing to the stairs. I knew it was over. I felt something inside wilt. I was silently ushered to the stairs to sit.

Rules To Live By

Rule #1 - No means no.

Rule #2 - I am not going to stand here and listen to your yammering.

Mother finished preparing dinner, and Dad came home from work. My older brother, Tom, came home from playing at a friend's house and was given a quick gesture to leave when he started to ask me why I was sitting there.

No means no.

Mother set the table, and then called Dad and Tom to diner. When they were seated, Mother turned to me and, without a trace of upset in her voice, said,

"Fred, you may join us now."

I was relieved! And I was more than a bit humbled. But I learned to think twice before trying to badger my mother.

Rules To Live By

I have no idea how many times I was sent to the stairs during my early childhood, but I am sure that it was more than once. From these experiences I learned two very important lessons that made my subsequent growing up much easier:

Rule #1 – No means no.

Rule #2 – I am not going to stand here and listen to your *yammering*.

Weenie Parents

Years later I found myself on the faculty of the University of Rochester Medical Center training interns and postdocs to work with families. The majority of our cases in the child outpatient clinic had to do with "brat" behavior. A typical case might have a father, age 37, a mother, age 35, and a single child, age 3. Who do you think was running the household?

"Therapy," in these cases, involved training parents in behavior management. It consisted of Say, See, Do Teaching with lots of practice and immediate feedback.

As you might imagine, one of the cornerstones of discipline management was, "No means no." With practice my clients even became adept at saying, "I am not going to stand here and listen to your yammering."

But, some parents just couldn't bring themselves to set limits. To begin a session, I would ask, "How did it go this week?" Then the excuses would start.

"Welll... We were in the supermarket, and he kept pulling the cans off the shelf. The faster I put them back, the faster he pulled them off. Then they all fell down. I didn't know what to do."

"Welll... We were in a restaurant, and we had already ordered our food when he started to throw the hard rolls. We couldn't just leave, could we?"

"Welll... We were at grandmother's, and I didn't want to make a scene. She is an old woman, and she is easily upset."

"Welll... It was his birthday party, and I didn't know what to do when he started running around and hitting the other children. I couldn't send him to his room in the middle of his birthday party, could I?"

These parents just couldn't bring themselves to say "no" and "make it stick." The nickname for these parents around the clinic was "weenies." You will have conferences with many "weenie parents" in the course of your career.

Consistency

Kind of Consistent

The mental part of Meaning Business centers on a clear understanding of *consistency* – consistency in setting limits on children's misbehavior. Consistency is a word that everyone knows but few people really understand. We all know that consistency is crucial to child rearing. But, exactly how does it work?

One of my weenie parents said, "But, Dr. Jones, I think we are being *pretty consistent.*" When I told this to my colleagues, we had a big laugh. We had a bigger laugh when one of my other weenie parents said, "But, Dr. Jones, I think we *are* consistent *most of the time.*"

What weenies fail to understand about consistency is that it does not permit *degrees.* You are either *consistent,* or you are *inconsistent.* There is nothing in between. There is no such thing as "pretty consistent" or "very consistent" or "extremely consistent."

Building Brat Behavior

In previous chapters we discussed the building of brat behavior through reinforcement errors. Reinforcement errors occur whenever you are consistent "most of the time."

Imagine, for example, that my mother, instead of being consistent, had been *pretty consistent. Four* out of *five* times, *no meant no.* But, *one* out of *five* times she "cracked." Maybe she had a good excuse – she was busy or stressed or distracted. In a moment of weakness, she blurted,

Weenie parents have a hard time saying "no."

"*All right*! Take some ginger snaps, go outside, and leave me alone! I'm tired of listening to your yammering!"

If my mother had cracked, she would have taught me the following lessons:

"When the going gets tough, the tough get *yammering*."

"If at first you don't succeed, *yammer, yammer again*."

"*Never give up*! Have hope! Today might be your *lucky day*."

When parents crack, they teach children that *yammering pays off*. Children learn that, by yammering, they can *get their way*. But first, they must wear their parents down by acting like brats.

The Irony of Consistency

The irony of consistency is that the closer you come to being consistent before you fail, the worse off you are. If the parent cracks easily, the child does not need to be a world-class yammerer in order to succeed. But, if the parent does *not* crack easily, the child must learn to play hardball. By making kids work hard in order to win, the parent inadvertently trains the kid to be both ruthless and persistent.

Kind of Consistent?

There are no *degrees* of consistency. Consistency permits only two conditions:

- You are *consistent*.
- You are *inconsistent*.

Consistency in the Classroom

Focus on Small Disruptions

In the classroom we will begin by focusing on the small everyday disruptions such as "talking to neighbors." We will do this for two reasons:

- **Small disruptions are more costly.** As we mentioned in previous chapters, small disruptions occur at a much higher rate in the classroom than large disruptions. Consequently, they account for the lion's share of lost learning time and teacher stress.
- **Big disruptions grow from small disruptions.** While a crisis can sometimes erupt from out of the blue, most big problems are just small problems that have been allowed to fester. When, for example, we see a seven-year-old acting like a tyrant, we strongly suspect that this child has been "getting away with murder" for quite some time. Similarly, when we see a student who is outrageous in the classroom, we suspect that the problem did not begin yesterday.

The most common disruption in the classroom, as we have mentioned earlier, is *talking to neighbors*. When you respond to goofing off in the classroom, you will be dealing with *talking to neighbors* eighty percent of the time.

Of course, different lesson formats have different rules. But, "talking to neighbors" serves well as our prototypical disruption because it is both common and simple, and it has all of the ingredients necessary for discussion.

Therefore, let's assume that, during the lesson under examination, students clearly understand that they are to be doing their own work. When the teacher looks up to see two students on the far side of the room chatting instead of working, it clearly represents goofing off.

Discipline Before Instruction

Let's deal with your *priorities* before we consider your actions. In the classroom, the following priority must govern your decision making at all times:

Discipline comes before instruction.

It is not optional. It is a cornerstone of effective management.

Placing discipline before instruction is something that most teachers would readily accept. After all, it's only logical. Does this make sense?

"If students are goofing off, they are certainly *not* doing your lesson."

How about this?

"Get your rules and routines straight at the *beginning* of the semester. If you don't, you'll be chasing after those kids for the next eighteen weeks.

Indeed, most teachers would agree, at least at a *logical* level, that discipline should come *before* instruction. Why, then, do so few teachers *act* that way.

Discipline comes before instruction.

The Moment Of Truth

A Difficult Choice

Beware! Weenieism can be far more subtle in the classroom than it is at home.

Let's imagine, for example, that you are helping a student, Robert, with a complex piece of work like a geometry proof. He is lost somewhere in the middle of the proof among the theorems and axioms and corollaries.

You have been working with Robert for a couple of minutes, and you are nearing closure. Given another *thirty seconds*, Robert will be able to progress on his own.

At this moment out of the corner of your eye you catch two students on the far side of the room *talking* instead of working. It is not a big disruption. It isn't even bothering other students nearby.

Now, be *utterly candid* with yourself as you imagine *what to do next.*

- Do you want to abort the teaching interaction in which you have invested several minutes and in which you are nearing closure? or,
- Do you want to finish helping Robert before you deal with the problem?

During training, a roomful of experienced teachers will respond in unison, "Finish helping Robert."

Of course you want to finish helping Robert! After all, you have made an *emotional* investment and an *intellectual* investment as well as an investment of *time.* You are *so close* to completion. Robert almost *has it.*

Consequently, most teachers will return to helping Robert. In the "moment of truth" most teachers will choose instruction over discipline.

The Students' Perspective

Now, let's look at this situation from the *students' perspective.* It is the beginning of the school year, and they are trying to figure out who you are.

The class just saw you make a choice. They saw you look up to observe two students goofing off, and then they saw you return to Robert.

From the students' perspective, answer this question:

"In this classroom, is discipline management on the *front* burner, or is discipline management on the *back* burner?"

You may as well make the following public announcement to the students:

"Class, do you remember what I said at the beginning of the school year about high standards and time-on-task. Well, as you know, *talk is cheap*.

"What you just saw was *reality*. As you may have noticed, when I have to choose between discipline and instruction, I will choose *instruction*. I find discipline management to be... oh, how can I say this... *inconvenient*. Consequently when I am busy with instruction, I will turn a *blind eye* to goofing off as long as it is not too bothersome.

"I would *like* for there to be no discipline problems, of course, but, as you can see, dealing with them is simply *not worth my time*. In spite of this, let me express my sincere hope that we will have an orderly and productive school year together."

The Horns of a Dilemma

When you look up to see one of your rules being broken, you are on the *horns of a dilemma*. If you act, your rules become reality. If you *fail* to act, your rules are nothing but hot air.

This is your *moment of truth*. Equivocation has a high price. If you waffle, you become a "weenie." A weenie is a magnet for brat behavior.

See and Then Act

Don't Think

Thinking when you should be acting is fatal. If the student has stepped over the line, you either do something about it or you "pull your punch."

It is too late to start thinking about what to do. You must know what to do.

Thinking at this juncture produces *dithering* instead of *doing*. To eliminate dithering, *don't think*. Discipline always come before instruction – period!

If you stop to think at this point, your thoughts will usually be rationalizations for staying with Robert. Here are some truly *irrelevant* thoughts that may come to mind.

- **How big is the disruption?** This is *irrelevant*. When you see unacceptable behavior, you either deal with it or not. The disruption will typically be small – *talking to neighbors* in most cases.
- **How important is the assignment?** This is also *irrelevant*. If the assignment were not important, you wouldn't be teaching it.

Of course the problem is small. *Of course* the lesson is important. *Of course* discipline management is inconvenient. But you cannot turn a blind eye to disruptions. No means no *every time*, or it means less than nothing. Stop dithering and do your job, or quit kidding yourself and admit that you really *are* a weenie.

Don't Consult Your Feelings

Discipline management is a game that you play out of your *head*, not out of your *gut*. Your boundaries coincide with your definition of unacceptable behavior. They have nothing to do with how you feel.

Feelings are inconstant by their very nature. If you respond based upon you feelings, you can *never* be consistent.

You cannot respond, for example, because you feel yourself "losing your patience." Your patience will be a function of:

- How much sleep you got last night.
- Whether you are upset about something else in your life like a sick child or a marital problem.
- What some other kid in class did five minutes ago.

You must, therefore, have mental clarity as to where your behavioral boundaries lie. Without *mental* clarity you cannot have *behavioral* clarity.

Without mental clarity you cannot have behavioral clarity.

Classroom Rules

You Make the Rules

I don't make the rules for your classroom. *You* do. Different lesson formats have different rules. In spite of using *talking to neighbors* as our prototypical disruption, having a rule against it may make absolutely no sense for a given activity. Partner teaching, for example, bombs without it.

Classroom rules also vary from one setting to another. What works in your classroom may not work at Juvenile Hall.

But I have also observed enough schools to know how widely differing expectations can be from one teacher to another in the same building. While rules may vary from place to place, it is dangerous to have them "up for grabs" – purely a matter of personal preference.

Far better for faculty members to discuss rules and reach consensus on the basics. The discussion among faculty members that leads to the development of the School Site Procedures Manual (chapter 12) typically spills over into classroom standards.

Teachers who have been part of this exercise have often described it as the most productive faculty activity of the entire school year. It is useful not only in consensus building but also in communicating school values to new faculty members.

Pick Your Battles

Green teachers often think of classroom rules as a kind of behavioral wish list. More experienced teachers know that each classroom rule comes with a high price tag attached.

If you are to be consistent, you must respond *every time* you see a rule infraction. Consistency, therefore, requires that you adhere to the following "rule of rules:"

Never make a rule that you are not willing to enforce every time.

Enforcement will always be an intrusion that requires you to stop what you are doing. Before you make a rule, therefore, imagine yourself enforcing it – *every* time. Then, ask yourself, "Is it worth the price?"

Firmness and Nurturance

Dealing With Larry

When you set limits in the classroom, you are establishing behavioral boundaries for the students. You know from developmental psychology that children establish reality by testing boundaries. If the boundaries never change, testing extinguishes as the child accepts the limit as being part of his or her reality. If the boundaries change, the child keeps testing.

Many of your students will come from homes in which "no" does *not* mean "no." Weenie parents create kids who will test your resolve to the limit because they are used to winning.

If they do not win, they will extinguish *very slowly* because they expect to win eventually. If you are *at all* inconsistent like their parents, these children will *never* extinguish.

Weenieism Can Sneak Up On You

Weenieism in the classroom can sneak up on you. While confrontations with Larry produces *drama*, typical goofing off produces *no drama* at all. It's usually just innocent looking chit-chat.

Since the challenge to your rules is both indirect and mild, it is seductively easy to turn a "blind eye" to the problem and just keep teaching. But, when you turn a "blind eye" to chit-chat, you allow *talking to neighbors* to self-reinforce. Don't be surprised when the problem reoccurs – and reoccurs – and reoccurs. When you have finally "had it" and intervene, you will be attempting to suppress a behavior that you participated in building.

> **"The price we pay for our own inconsistency is a reduction in our capacity to nurture."**

Inconsistency and Harshness

Green teachers who have not yet raised a family have a particularly hard time taking consistency as seriously as they should. Their primary focus is usually relationship building. Rule enforcement tends to take a back seat.

Teachers who have raised a family know all about "infantile omnipotence." They have learned to combine *affection* with *firmness and consistency* in order to create stable boundaries. For teachers who have little experience with this balancing act, the notion that boundaries cannot move, that there are no "degrees of consistency", seems overly rigid.

Nevertheless, your ability to be nurturant will ultimately be a function of your ability to be consistent. The management of behavior problems will follow one of two paths:

If you are consistent,
you can use smaller and smaller
consequences to govern misbehavior.

But, if you are inconsistent,
you must use larger and larger
consequences to govern misbehavior.

Inconsistency generates strife of increasing intensity. At some point, dealing with the same provocations from the same students over and over will become personal. In the final analysis, the price you pay for your own inconsistency is a reduction in your capacity to nurture.

Chapter Sixteen

Setting Limits: Our Actions

Action Signals Commitment

Focus on Action

Thoughts are free and talk is cheap, but action will cost you. Something has to be important to be "worth your time." Action, therefore, signals *commitment.*

In the preceding two chapters we focused on our response to one of the most typical classroom disruptions, *talking to neighbors.* We dealt with our *emotions* as we learned to relax in the face of provocation, and we dealt with our *thoughts* as we learned the importance of consistency.

In this chapter we will examine our *actions* as we continue to manage our prototypical disruption, *talking to neighbors.* In following chapters we will describe the handling of student escalations all the way to nasty backtalk and beyond.

Focus on Body Language

During our initial observations of the "natural teachers," we could not see what they were doing. It was so subtle that it was invisible to us. Nor were the naturals aware of what they were doing. They could not begin to describe it.

Only after months of observation, hours of brainstorming, and considerable trial and error did *Meaning Business* become visible to us. Yet, it was always visible to the students. They had been reading it since early childhood. Meaning Business is conveyed primarily through *body language.*

Preview

- We instinctively read each other's body language in order to predict what the other person is going to do next.
- Body language "telegraphs" our real thoughts, feelings, and intentions whether we want it to or not. The students read us like a book.
- Since we telegraph our intentions, the students are really reading our *minds.* They usually know what we are going to do before we do it.
- Our priority at all times is that discipline comes before instruction. Until this issue is resolved in our minds, our body language will betray our ambivalence.
- In this chapter, we examine the body language of Meaning Business – the signals by which students know whether or not they need to take us seriously.

Body Language Is Genetic and Generic

The whole human race speaks the same body language. Happiness, sadness, anger, and boredom look the same on any continent. The cultural differences in body language are trivial compared to the similarities.

Such uniformity of behavior can only come from its being "inborn." Body language is biology. It is "human nature."

We will bring body language to a conscious level so we can use it as a tool for helping students to succeed. In this chapter we will begin to decode that language.

Body language is the language of emotion and intention.

Decoding Body Language

Body Language Conveys Emotion

Long before children have speech, their eyes follow us and study us. They read our emotions. They know whether we are calm or upset, happy or sad, pleased or displeased.

We never lose that capacity. We can read the body language of our friends and loved ones and know immediately how they feel. We can tell by the facial expression, the posture, the way they walk.

Body Language Conveys Intention

We also read body language in order to know what other people will do next. One of the most common examples is sports. The offense reads the defense, and the defense reads the offense. What is the other player going to do next? Subtle signs tip us off.

Imagine, for example, a basketball player catching a pass and throwing the ball to a teammate. The player who catches the ball, however, immediately looks at the teammate for whom the pass is intended.

Can you imagine where the ball is going to go? So can the defense. In the second that it takes the player to turn and release the ball, do you think a defender can get a hand up in the passing lane?

The coach says, "You *telegraphed* your pass!" More than anything, body language "telegraphs" what we are going to do next.

Consequently, students in the classroom are not simply reading your body language. They are reading your *mind.* They usually know what you are going to do before you do it.

Body Language Conveys Change

Body language signals *change* in people's emotions and intentions. How can you tell that a friend is sad today? We pick up signs of change. Is it the sagging posture, the downcast eyes?

These signs have a name in learning theory. Since they are stimuli that help us discriminate change, they are called *discriminative stimuli.*

Within the context of Meaning Business, how can the students discriminate that, in response to seeing a disruption, your commitment has changed from *instruction* to *discipline*? They will study your body language for clues.

Signal Clarity

Here is how it works. If all of the signals that you give say, "I am *done* with instruction, and I have *gone* to discipline," then even your dog and cat can read it. If, on the other hand, half of your signals say, "I have gone to discipline," and half of your signals say, "I am still at instruction," then no one could be sure of your intention.

When behavioral boundaries are unclear, children *test* to find out where the boundaries lie. By lack of clarity you have obligated the students to test you.

As you can see, it all comes down to *signal clarity.* If you want the disruptive students to "shape up" when you first respond to their goofing off, you'd better give clear signals. Within the context of Meaning Business, signal clarity brings us to the topic of *ambivalence.*

Ambivalence

When we are ambivalent we are "of two minds." We are *torn* between two conflicting choices.

What are the two choices that confront any teacher when it is time to mean business? It is always the choice between *discipline* and *instruction.* Which one is worth your time?

Mixed Messages

If you are ambivalent – of two minds – your body language will signal *both* states of mind. When you signal two messages at the same time, you send a "mixed message." Mixed messages represent the body language of *ambivalence.*

What choice causes teachers to be ambivalent when allocating their time and energy in the classroom? As

When we are ambivalent we are "of two minds."
In the classroom we are most often torn between discipline and instruction.

always, the ambivalence is between *discipline* and *instruction.* When we are helping a student and look up to see some mild disruption on the far side of the room, part of us wants to continue with *instruction* while part of us knows that we should deal with the *discipline* problem instead.

As a result, teachers are very vulnerable to sending mixed messages at the very moment in which they need to be clear, unequivocal, and convincing. The outcome will be continued testing by the disruptive students.

> **Mixed messages represent the body language of ambivalence.**

Nowhere To Hide

Children Read Us Like a Book

Body language is a constant in our make-up. It has not changed in a million years. Nor, can you change it by an act of will.

In a classroom the students study *you,* and they become more astute with each passing day. At any moment they will know whether or not they need to take you *seriously.* They will know *exactly* what they can get away with and *exactly* how far they can push you.

Do not ever think that you can fool a child. The language of the body does not lie. A skilled athlete might be able to fake going right or left, but you cannot *fake out* an entire classroom full of children hour after hour with something as complex as Meaning Business.

You have two choices concerning body language. You can learn about body language in order to help you manage the classroom. Or you can be ignorant of it, in which case the students will always be one step ahead of you.

Learning a Language

We are learning a new language. Eventually we will learn enough of the language to express ourselves effectively. Body language is, after all, a *conversation.*

We participate in this conversation either knowingly or unknowingly. Our objective is to be *knowing* participants.

We will begin to learn this new language as one would learn any new language – with simple words. Then we will move to phrases, then sentences, then paragraphs.

Worst-Case Scenarios

At the beginning, pieces of body language look like techniques. We ask ourselves, "Is this the answer?" "Is this going to stop kids from goofing off in my classroom?"

When new learning confronts old habits, our defenses go on alert. We tend to confront change before we embrace it.

We often fend off change with the "Yeah, buts." These *Yeah, buts* typically take the form of worst-case scenarios.

"Yeah, but I have a kid in my class who would..."

"Yeah, but I've tried things like that and..."

"Yeah, but you don't know the kinds of homes our kids come from..."

Let me reiterate that we are learning a *language*, not a series of packaged remedies for classroom problems. We will learn to be an effective player in a game that never ends.

We will use a *typical* situation, talking to neighbors, between two *typical* students to paint a picture of a *typical* conversation in body language. The only thing remarkable about this situation is the fact that it accounts for 80 percent of the lost learning time in the classroom. For that reason alone, this unremarkable situation is pivotal.

The only thing remarkable about talking to neighbors is the fact that it accounts for 80 percent of the lost learning time.

Miss Haines and Larry – A Preview

Larry Acts Up

Miss Haines was my fifth grade teacher. She was young and pretty, and most of the guys had a crush on her, although nobody would admit it. She was also sweet and kind. But she was nobody's fool.

Larry was in that class. I'm sure you remember Larry from previous chapters – the student who will age you three years in one. I went all through school with Larry. I can still see him in my mind's eye.

One day Miss Haines was called to the office unexpectedly, and the class was left unattended. Larry, seeing that the coast was clear, began to show off.

The longer Miss Haines was gone, the more outrageous his showing off became. Miss Haines seemed to be gone forever. Finally, Larry was standing on Miss Haines desk doing a dance.

Suddenly from down the hall came the clip, clip, clip of high heels. Larry was down off that desk in a heartbeat! By the time Miss Haines appeared in the doorway we were all in our seats with hands folded. Miss Haines could mean business from down the hall.

Miss Haines Deals with Larry

One day Miss Haines was describing something to the class in an animated fashion when she caught Larry goofing off out of the corner of her eye. In mid-sentence Mrs. Haines stopped dead and slowly turned her head toward Larry as though to say,

"I beg your pardon."

Complete silence descended upon the class. All eyes turned to Larry whose face seemed to say, *Whoops*. As Mrs. Haines waited. Larry came around in his chair, faced forward and looked very sheepish. After a pause, Mrs. Haines turned to the class and continued as though nothing had happened.

Miss Haines nailed Larry in mid-sentence with no upset whatsoever. Miss Haines had *finesse.* She was one of the only teachers I had in elementary school who did not want to kill Larry by the end of the year.

Keeping It Cheap

Looking Students Back to Work

Have you ever turned toward disruptive students and simply *looked* them back to work like Miss Haines? Most teachers will answer, "Yes."

It is not as though Meaning Business was just invented, and it is not as though you have never done it. When you have gotten a result like this, chances are you did a pretty good job of Meaning Business.

On the other hand, have you ever had to *walk* over to the disruptive students in order to get them to "shape up?" Most teachers will again respond, "Yes."

Now, let me ask you the *practical* question. Which one was *cheaper?* Obviously, the trip across the room was very expensive while "the look" was very cheap.

Focusing on "The Turn"

Considerations of *cost* focus our attention on the *beginning* of your interaction with the disruptive students – on the *turn.* If the turn is utterly convincing, the students will usually "cool it" and save you the trip across the classroom. If the turn is not convincing, you will have a much more complicated situation to manage.

In order to analyze the body language of Meaning Business as we turn toward the disruptive students, we must see the action in *slow motion.* Body language is subtle. By the time you have turned toward the students, the game is usually over.

The following sections will deal with *the key discriminative stimuli for Meaning Business* as we turn toward the disruptive students. These are the signals students read in your body language that tell them whether or not they need to take you seriously.

Stop and Relax

Discipline on the Front Burner

You know from the previous chapter that when you see the problem, you have to immediately stop what you are doing in order to *commit.* If you fail to respond, you signal that instruction is on the *front* burner and discipline is on the *back* burner.

Sometimes the transition is sudden. Miss Haines stopped "dead" in the middle of a sentence when she caught Larry goofing off out of the corner of her eye. Stopping in that fashion said to the entire class,

> "This lesson will *not* continue until *that* behavior stops."

A hush fell over the class because we all knew what that body language meant. We knew that Miss Haines was in "discipline mode," and Larry was on the hot seat.

Slow Down

Calm is *slow,* and upset is *fast.* But instruction is also fast as we move and talk in an animated fashion. A sudden change of speed is the first cue that students pick up signalling a change in your priorities.

> **Taking You Seriously**
>
> **Only when you commit your time and attention to the problem will the students begin to take you seriously.**

For example, when we help a student our minds are *racing*. We are thinking about what the student knows, what the student needs, how we can best explain the concept, and what is going on in the rest of the class. When we look up and see a disruption, the fight-flight reflex *speeds us up even more.*

Everything is driving us through the transition from instruction to discipline *too fast.* The students see this speed of movement and conclude that we are impatient to return to instruction.

We need to practice coming to a dead stop. This clear discontinuity of motion signals a change of mind on your part.

Hit the "Relax Button"

Miss Haines not only stopped in mid-sentence, but she also hit her "relax button" so fast that her entire mood changed. The weather in the room was transformed. The whole class came to attention.

Like Miss Haines, your response to disruption will be the *opposite* of a fight-flight reflex. Instead of revving up, you will shut down. This sudden transition provides an unmistakable discriminative stimulus to the students that *everything has changed.* You are in "discipline mode."

You must practice until you get good at it. When you get as good as Miss Haines, you will be able to transition quickly and effortlessly. But at the beginning we will slow things down.

Excuse Yourself from Robert

To slow things down, let's imagine that you are helping a well-behaved student, Robert, when you look up to see two students goofing off on the far side of the room. In this situation you don't need to switch from instruction to discipline as dramatically as Miss Haines did. Rather, you can take a moment as you excuse yourself from Robert to relax and refocus.

Lean over and whisper, "Excuse me, Robert." Then *stay down* and take *another* relaxing breath. When you stay down to take that second relaxing breath, you do several things at once:

- **You turn away from the problem.** Since the problem triggers the fight-flight reflex, getting the problem out of your field of vision eliminates the trigger. This helps you relax.
- **You model common courtesy.** It is important to model *common courtesy* whenever possible in the classroom. It is something that many students need to learn. Besides, if you don't excuse yourself, poor Robert has no idea as to why you suddenly quit talking to him and turned your back.
- **You give yourself time to refocus.** Give yourself a moment to center yourself before you stand up. When you stand and turn toward the disruptive students, it is "show time." You might get some smart-mouth before you even come around.

  "What? I wasn't doing anything."

  If you are not relaxed before this happens, you don't stand a chance.
- **You breathe in.** If you excuse yourself from Robert and immediately stand up, your lungs will be *empty* because you just spoke. Then you will be forced to *breathe in* as you face the disruptors. When you breathe in, you *flex* your diaphragm. You will not be able to relax peripheral muscles while flexing the most centrally located voluntary muscle in your body.

Turn in a Regal Fashion

The Six Second Turn

During training, as an advance organizer, I demonstrate two different turns. Then I ask the group to choose which one means business more.

- **The First Turn**: The first turn takes *three* seconds. I begin by leaning down slowly to say, "Excuse me, Robert." Then (imagining a fluid motion):

  A thousand and one: I straighten up.

  A thousand and two: I point one foot toward the disruptive students and bring my body half-way around.

  A thousand and three: I bring my other foot around to complete the turn as I square up to the disruptive students.

  After I have completed this turn, the trainees typically look at me as though to say, "Okay, big deal. Let's see the next one."

- **The Second Turn**: The second turn takes *six* seconds. I begin in the same way by leaning down slowly in order to say, "Excuse me, Robert." Then:

  A thousand and one: I stay down and breathe in gently.

  A thousand and two: I begin to straighten up (about halfway) as I look toward the disruptive students.

  A thousand and three: I finish straightening up as I continue looking at the disruptive students.

  A thousand and four: I slowly rotate my shoulders and waist toward the disruptive students.

  A thousand and five: I point one foot toward the disruptive students as my hips come around.

  A thousand and six: I bring my other foot around to complete the turn as I square up to the disruptive students.

  As I am turning in this fashion, there is almost always a sprinkling of nervous laughter from the group. By the end of the turn the teacher who volunteered to be my "target" is often holding up his or her hands saying, "Okay, okay, that's enough."

Speed Kills

What is the difference between Meaning Business and *not* Meaning Business when you turn toward two disruptive students in the classroom? *Speed,* of course. *Three seconds* to be exact.

> **What's the difference?**
>
> **The difference between Meaning Business and *not* Meaning Business when you turn toward two disruptive students in the classroom is about three seconds!**

As a means of creating some additional visual imagery to accompany the turn, I have the trainees picture Queen Victoria, the regent of the empire upon which the sun never sets. Then I ask, "Which of these two turns would be right for Queen Victoria?" I repeat the two turns.

The group is unanimous since the slow turn is so clearly "regal" while the faster turn is so utterly ordinary. Consequently, my prompt when we practice turning toward the disruptive students is, "Turn in a *regal* fashion."

Turn from the Top Down

A three-second turn is a normal turn. A six-second turn is something you have to practice. It is unnatural.

Normally when you turn, you turn your entire body at once. You lift your foot and turn in a single motion.

Try doing it this with a six-second turn and see what happens. After you lift your foot, you still have five seconds to go. You will fall flat on your face.

When a drama coach trains an actor to turn with a regal bearing, there is a set routine. You turn from the *top down* in four parts:

- Head
- Shoulders
- Waist
- Feet

This not only slows you down, but it also keeps you balanced until the turn is completed. If you do not turn in this fashion, you will be forced to speed up. You will end up with a very ordinary and unconvincing three-second turn.

When you slow down in order to turn in a regal fashion, you discover an additional dividend. You have plenty of time to observe the students and to think, and the students have plenty of time to read your meaning.

Often, when you slowly turn your head to look at the students, they catch your "drift" and "shape up" before you have to turn the rest of your body. That's how Larry responded to Miss Haines. The less work for you, the better.

Point Your Toes

The Full Turn

Next during training, I model two additional variations of the turn. Both are done at the proper speed. In both I turn from the top down. The difference is in the *feet.*

The *first* turn is a *partial* turn. Imagine that I am turning toward disruptive students to my *right.* I slowly stand and turn my head, shoulders and waist toward the disruptive students. However, when it gets to my feet, I only pick up my right foot and point it toward the students. I leave my left foot planted as I complete the turn from the waist up.

The *second* turn is a *complete* turn. I do the same turn as before, but I also bring my left foot around so that *both* feet are pointed squarely toward the disruptive students.

Once again, there is no doubt among the trainees as to which turn means business more. A partial turn is a classic example of a *tentative gesture.* Tentative gestures bring us back to the topic of *ambivalence* and *mixed messages.*

Are you *really* finished with instruction mentally and emotionally so that you can commit yourself fully to dealing with the discipline problem? It is easy to say yes, but the body does not lie.

One Foot In and One Foot Out

In a partial turn your feet are only halfway around. During training, I will relax in this half-turned position and say, "Looking just at my body, predict which way I will move next; to the right (toward discipline) or to the left (toward instruction)." Of course, the group cannot predict. It is a 50/50 call.

Next, I remind the group that there will be a half-dozen students in any classroom who will *have to* test you in order to find out whether or not you will commit to problems like this. After all, they need to know the price of doing business, don't they?

We have been reading each other's body language for eons. Not too surprisingly, we have many common expressions that refer to the body language of commitment. Here is a figure of speech referring to ambivalence that is particularly relevant to the present discussion.

> "Well, he has one foot in and one foot out. I wish he would make up his mind!"

With a partial turn, teachers become a living embodiment of this old expression. They literally have one foot in instruction and one foot in discipline. You might say that they are, "riding the fence" or "neither here nor there."

With a partial turn, the teacher has "one foot in and one foot out."

With a complete turn, teachers resolve any ambiguity concerning their commitment. They then embody this old expression:

"It is time to face up to the situation."

In sports terms, your body *telegraphs* your next move. As you can see, it also telegraphs tentativeness. It signals any *ambivalence* you might have toward dealing with the problem.

Nagging Signals No Commitment

Nagging is the opposite of commitment. It is a "cheap shot" at discipline management when discipline is not worth your time. That lack of commitment is signaled with every part of the body. Look at the teacher's feet during "snap and snarl." They stay planted. Pheasant posturing involves only the hands and the mouth.

Make it a rule in your classroom *never* to use a partial turn when dealing with a discipline problem. If you do, your tentativeness will force you to deal with the same problem again very soon.

Get a Focal Point

Good Eye Contact

Next during training, I model two additional variations of the turn. These two variations are differentiated only by the degree of eye contact with the disruptive students.

During the first turn, my eyes glance around the room at other students. My head does not move – only my eyeballs. And the glances are quick – nothing exaggerated. I am just "checking things out" in the rest of the room as I turn.

During the second turn, I make fixed eye contact with *one* of the disruptive students throughout my standing

With a complete turn, the teacher has "faced up to the situation."

and turning. There is no doubt among those trainees in my line of vision as to which turn is more convincing.

Furtive Eye Contact

Have you ever talked to someone who wouldn't look you in the eye? Typically, furtive eye movement is interpreted as anxiety. We might conclude that the other person is lying or is worried about something.

In the classroom, such body language usually means that the teacher is worrying about the rest of the classroom while attempting to deal with the disruptive student. The teacher's attention is *split.*

The resulting fragmentation of eye contact undermines the perception by the student of cool, calm commitment on the part of the teacher. The disruptive student usually just looks at the teacher impassively as though to say, "What?" Sometimes the student actually says it out loud.

With good eye contact there is a tension between the teacher and the student that builds with each passing second. This tension represents an *expectancy* on the part of the teacher. The student understands this expectancy perfectly well – *get back to work.*

When the tension builds to the point where it finally dawns on the student that the teacher is thoroughly committed and is *not* going away, the student typically breaks off eye contact and gets back to work. As usual, by *clearly* signalling commitment, teachers can save themselves a trip across the classroom.

Hands Down

Relax Your Upper Body

When you flex your bicep, you raise your forearm. If you are sick and tired, your hands usually end up on your hips or folded across your chest. Therefore, if you gesture with your hands while agitated, your gestures will typically be waist-high. You have to "go ballistic" before your hand gestures become shoulder-high.

If you relax your upper body, your hands will be *down* at your side. However, many people feel awkward with their hands just "dangling." You need to have a plan, or those hands will be on the hips before you know it.

Get Comfortable

You could put them in your pockets, of course. This is a relaxed-looking gesture. For women, however, many items of clothing, such as pleated skirts, lack pockets. Pick a gesture that will be constant and predictable rather than one that must be altered depending on your dress for the day.

There are some advantages to simply putting your hands behind your back.

- *First,* this is a semiformal posture rather than a casual posture and, therefore, more in keeping with setting limits on disruptive students.
- *Second,* you turn your palms away from your clothing which reduces cleaning bills due to chalk dust and paint.
- *Finally,* the students cannot see your arms. This is particularly helpful in the beginning when you are still learning to relax since the last vestige of nervousness is usually some fidgeting with the fingers.

Jaw Relaxed

Check Your Jaw

As the final step in a regal turn, I will give the prompt, "Check your jaw." Setting our jaw or clenching our teeth is one of the most predictable signs of tension in the body.

Nervous tension remains in the jaw muscles even after we think we have relaxed. Unfortunately, the students can see this signal from the other side of the gymnasium.

Not a Time To Smile

While some teachers will set their jaws while setting limits, others will *smile.* Sometimes this is a sign of ambivalence as the teacher is torn between "good guy" and "bad guy" roles that have never been sorted out. This body language says, *"Please forgive me for Meaning Business."*

But there is another trigger for smiling when our jaw should be relaxed. We often smile without knowing it because the disruptive students *cause us to smile.*

Trigger Mechanisms

Smiling is what biologists call a "trigger mechanism." When a person smiles at us, it triggers our smiling back. It is part of parent/child nurturing. Smiling also serves as a submission signal. In social situations a slight smile or submission signal shows that we are friendly. This facial expression is referred to as "greeting behavior."

When we catch students goofing off, they typically look up and give us *smiley face* – that ingratiating mixture of surprise and feigned innocence that all children use to "get off the hook." "Smiley face" tends to trigger a mild inadvertent smile from us in response.

You may not feel this gentle smile. It is just a softening of the face around the mouth and eyes that says, "I am your friend, and everything is okay."

The last thing you want to do while attempting to mean business is to signal to the students that everything is *okay.* Rather than shaping up, they *relax.*

"We are not amused."

When you are relaxed, you have no facial expression at all.

We Are Not Amused

This brings us to a well known story about Queen Victoria, our model for *regal* behavior. As the story goes, someone at the royal dinner table told a slightly off-color joke. Since Queen Victoria had little patience for such humor, she looked impassively at the would-be-comedian as the table fell silent. Then she coldly stated to the offending guest the immortal words, "*We* are not amused." That was the "Royal We," of course.

You would do well to think of yourself as Queen Victoria when attempting to mean business. *Relax* your jaw. This is no time to give tacit approval to misbehavior with a slight smile. Nor, does upset serve any constructive purpose. As students go through their little antics to get off the hook; relax, wait, and give them your best Queen Victoria look that says, *"We are not amused."*

Only when the students realize that their antics are getting them nowhere will they consider an alternative strategy. The alternative that you are waiting to see is well understood by the students – *get back to work.*

The Stages of "Cute"

As a footnote, you should know that "smiley face" is only the beginning of a *series* of ingratiating gestures that have gotten kids "off the hook" since time began. Here are the *three phases of cute.* Watch kids play them like a violin.

- Smiley face
- Raised eyebrows
- Head tilted to the side

Have you ever had students in your class who thought they could skate through life just by being cute? Obviously it works for them at home. You need to teach them that this game will *not* get the desired result in your classroom.

Commitment and Power

The Strength of Our Convictions

Calm is strength, but it is not the only form of power conveyed by you. Commitment is also power. We speak of people having "the strength of their convictions."

During training teachers will often wrongly attribute the power that comes from commitment to irrelevant aspects of facial expression. Trainees will sometimes refer to the whole process as "staring them down."

You convey *the strength of your convictions,* however, not by your facial expression but, rather, by the *totality* of your body language. Having committed, you simply relax and wait to see what choice the students make. They will do one of two things. They will either get back to work, or they will not. You will know soon enough.

Power and Passivity

"Staring them down" represents the *active* voice – the language of confrontation. Meaning Business is done in the *passive* voice – the language of calm commitment.

However, the fight-flight reflex has a voice of its own that shouts into your ear, "You can't just stand there! *Do* something!" Teachers often struggle with this inner voice. If your thoughts are adversarial or your feelings agitated, your body language will show it.

Practice Makes Perfect

Body language can only be mastered through practice. The main limitation of a book as opposed to a workshop is its inability to build skills through practice. Nowhere is this difference greater than in learning the body language of Meaning Business.

The **Study Group Activity Guide** structures the same skill practice that you would receive at a workshop. The protocol for each practice exercise contains every prompt for Say, See, Do Teaching along with my "asides" and introductory remarks. You *can* have quality training at your school site that is affordable. The Study Group Activity Guide is a **free download** from www.fredjones.com.

Study Group Activity Guide
Skill Building Exercises

Study Group Activity Guide appendices D, E, F, G, and H provide practice for the skills of Meaning Business and for troubleshooting extreme behavior problems.

Chapter Seventeen

Following Through

Preview

- With pseudo-compliance, students give you just enough compliance to get you "off their case."
- Pseudo-compliance is about cutting deals. It is how disruptive students establish the price of doing business with a particular teacher.
- The question that disruptive students ask about getting back to work is, *"Do I have to?"* Their asking that question and your answering it constitute the conversation in body language known as *Meaning Business.*
- This chapter takes us beyond "the turn" as we deal with disruptive students who are playing games at every opportunity.
- When done properly the body language of Meaning Business is invisible. Consequently, it protects disruptive students from embarrassment in front of their peers.

Beyond "The Turn"

No Guarantee

The conversation in body language described in the preceding chapter was complex but brief. The teacher has done nothing more than terminate instruction, relax, turn, and commit to dealing with the disruption.

Let's assume that the students see *the turn* and respond by looking at the teacher – usually with a bit of *smiley face*. Often they will get back to work. Or, at least, they may *appear* to get back to work.

But discipline management is an indoor sport. Basketball players know how to fake, and poker players know how to bluff. Students know how to do both at the same time.

Maybe the students would just like you to *think* that they are getting back to work. How could you know what the students *really* plan to do next? You must be able to see into the future.

Fortunately, you *can* see into the future. You can predict the students' behavior by reading their body language just as they read yours.

The Conversation Continues

The turn is only the beginning of a conversation in body language. If the students decide to test you, the conversation may become quite lengthy and complex.

In this chapter we will assume that the students *do not* intend to get back to work. We will also assume that they know how to *appear* to get back to work. They would love to fake you out so that you would leave them alone.

This little battle of wills between teacher and student is part of everyday classroom life. It will provide a vehicle for analyzing the complex dialogue in body language that often accompanies Meaning Business.

Predicting Noncompliance

Look at the Feet

In the two pictures to the right, both students in each picture have gotten back to work after *the turn.* Can you tell which pair will keep working and which pair will start talking again as soon as your back is turned?

It's not much of a mystery, is it? When I have two teachers model these positions during a workshop, the whole room will pick the students on this page as having no intention whatsoever of getting back to work.

What is the critical feature of body language that allows every teacher in the room to predict the future? It is the lower body – *knees* and *feet.*

The body language above the desk top is called "window dressing" – a pretty display that is intended to impress potential "consumers." In this case, the students are *faking* compliance with their upper bodies while their lower bodies signal their true intent.

In sports such as basketball and football, every coach and player knows that you *fake* with the upper body and *commit* with the lower body. After all, the body must follow the feet. That is why the coach tells the players to *watch the body, not the ball.* Discipline management is an indoor sport, and savvy teachers will watch the body.

Pseudo-compliance

In the picture of window dressing below, the students are giving you the *appearance* of compliance while actually *withholding it.* In chapter one, we called this partial compliance *pseudo-compliance.*

Pseudo-compliance lulls you into a false sense of closure so that you prematurely terminate supervision and abort follow-through. By way of review, the four phases of

If the students intend to continue talking, their body language will usually give it away.

pseudo-compliance to look for as you observe students getting back to work are:

- **Smiley face:** They give you the look of repentant angels as though asking, "*Who, me?*"
- **Book posing:** They open their books and look back at you as though to ask, *"Does this fulfill the requirements of formal education?"*

If the students are focused on the assignment, their body language will telegraph that too.

- **Pencil posing:** They get out a pencil and touch it to paper before looking back at you as though to say, "*Look, I'm writing.*"
- **Pseudo-scholarship:** They start to write, but they look up periodically to see if you are still paying attention.

Let me emphasize that I do not care how students sit in class while they are working. Rather, the topic being addressed here is how you as a teacher discriminate *change* in the students' behavior *from* goofing off *to* time-on-task.

The present chapter extends our analysis of Meaning Business begun in the preceding chapter. Now that you have turned toward the disruptive students and they seem to have gotten back to work, how can you tell whether they will *continue* to work? Have you accomplished your objective yet, or are the students just "playing you?"

Cutting Deals

Children love to *cut deals* with adults. Pseudo-compliance is all about cutting deals. You might say that pseudo-compliance is how children establish the price of doing business with their parents and teachers.

Imagine, for example, that you ask your four-year-old daughter to pick up the blocks. She picks up half of the blocks and then stops and turns to you as though to say, "Is this good enough?"

If you say, "Thank you for helping. Let's go have lunch," you have just defined with your actions the meaning of the phrase, "Pick up the blocks." And you have given your daughter a good idea of what "finishing a job" entails. The next time you ask her to do a job, you will be *lucky* if she does half of it.

Imagine, instead, that you persist, aware that you are teaching your child what it means to *do a job.* "Now, pick up the rest of the blocks," you say. Your daughter, of

...Until We Get It Right

If you turn a blind eye to a half-finished job because it is not worth your time and effort to follow through, you will have a child who believes that half-baked is just fine.

course, will protest the higher cost of doing business with some fussing and whining.

But if you keep your toes pointed and your mouth shut at this critical juncture, the protestations will slowly die down. Eventually, your daughter will grudgingly pick up some more blocks.

Imagine that, with two-thirds of the blocks picked up, your daughter again stops and turns to you as though to ask, "*Is this good enough?*" As always, pseudo-compliance has to do with cutting deals.

In body language your daughter is saying, "I have just done you a *big* favor by picking up some more of these stupid blocks. This is a deal I only cut for preferred customers. You should be thrilled. I recommend that you take this offer."

If you say, "Oh, good. That is enough for now. Let's go have lunch," you have just defined two-thirds of the job as the equivalent of "done." This child knows she has a sucker for a parent.

Children are little power junkies. They want their way. Call it *infantile omnipotence.* And, if they cannot get *all* of their way, they will fight to get at least *some* of their way. If you persist until your daughter does 90 percent of the job, but she withholds doing 10 percent of the job, in her little child's mind, she didn't *have to.* Do not be surprised if she "steps over the line" as soon as your back is turned just to prove to herself that she didn't have to.

But what if you hang in there until *all* of the blocks are picked up? It takes time, of course. And, you will need a few relaxing breaths to get you through the fussing. But, your daughter will eventually learn that, when you ask her to do a job, you expect it to be done *right.* Life in this household embodies these timeless elements of child management wisdom:

I say what I mean, and I mean what I say.
and
We are going to keep doing this until we get it right.

Doing it *right* is, in fact, an act of *submission* on the part of the child – submission to the will of the parent. As such, it is the end of the struggle – for now.

Over time, your daughter's fussing and whining when asked to do something will weaken as she learns that such efforts are futile. You will have to go through this process more than once before you teach your child to help around the house without a lot of fussing.

But if you want your child to be a fusser and whiner, all you have to do is *crack* once or twice. Be a *weenie.* Turn a blind eye to a job half-finished because it is not worth your time and effort to follow through, and you will have a child who believes that half-baked is just fine.

As we continue our conversation in body language with disruptive students in the classroom, we will learn a lot more about pseudo-compliance. The disruptive students continually ask, "Is this good enough?" as they attempt to cut deals. Their asking and your answering constitute the heart of the conversation in body language.

Move the Body, Not the Mouth

Your Next Move

Let's imagine that, after committing to the disruptive students, you see only window dressing. You rightly conclude that the students have no intention of continuing to work. What next?

Actually, the next move is no strategic tour-de-force. You will have to go over to the disruptive students in order to deal with the situation.

As obvious as this response may seem, it is very common for teachers to act *tentatively* at this critical point in the "conversation." No doubt this is because walking over to the students is both distracting and time-consuming.

Beware of Silly Talk

"Silly talk" is our label for silly things that parents and teachers say to wayward children instead of swinging into action. It is a form of *pheasant posturing*. It is very tempting for adults to try to talk their way out of management. After all, talk is cheap. Maybe the students will repent in response to some hot air?

We described silly talk in chapter one. By way of review, here are some time-honored examples:

"Billy, what are you supposed to be doing?"

"Billy, this is the second time I've had to talk to you."

"Billy, am I going to have to come over there?"

Walk, Don't Talk

If we could do discipline management with our mouths, all children would be nagged to righteousness before their third birthday. Shut the mouth, take two relaxing breaths, and move toward the disruptive students.

Now, let me ask you a question. Have you ever started to walk toward disruptive students only to have them turn around in their seats and face forward before you had even taken three steps? What just happened?

As you might imagine, you have just communicated with the students in body language. The question for the students was, "Do we have to?" In their experience, parents often do a little pheasant posturing in situations like this and then turn away. They want to know, "Are you like those other adults, or do I have to take you seriously?"

Obviously, the only way to find out is to *test* you. They will give you a little pseudo-compliance to see if it will get them off the hook. If it does, they now know that they can "blow you off" with impunity.

When you keep your mouth shut and walk toward the students, you answer the question that they were asking with pseudo-compliance. They asked, "Do I have to?" and you answered, "Yes." When they turned around in their seats to face forward, they said, "That's all I wanted to know. I'm not in this for high stakes."

The Body Language Poker Game

Students Are Gamblers

The best analogy to the conversation in body language between teacher and disruptive students is a *poker game.* Poker, as you know, is a form of gambling. You do not have to condone gambling to understand the analogy.

Students are born gamblers. When they disrupt, they are betting that they can get away with it. But, they have to test the teacher in order to find out the exact odds in this classroom.

If the students can win easily, they will gamble like bandits all year long. But if they cannot easily "get away with it," they must gamble conservatively. As a teacher, you want a roomful of very conservative gamblers.

Basic Rules

Poker is a simple game. You are either *in* or you are *out*. If you are in, you either match or raise the bet. If you are out, you fold.

In the body language poker game, the teacher folds when he or she *turns away* from the disruptive students *before* the students have folded by getting back to work. When the teacher folds prematurely, the students soon return to goofing off.

Bluffing

Pseudo-compliance is bluffing on the part of the students. They may not want to stay in the game until the stakes become high, but they can afford a modest raise to see if you are ready to fold. You will have to stay in the game and meet raise with raise if you ever expect to see the students give up the game and return to work.

Nagging and pheasant posturing represent bluffing on the part of the teacher. The teacher seems to be doing something about the problem when, in fact, nothing of any consequence is being done.

> **Nagging and pheasant posturing represent bluffing by the teacher.**

A note to the uninitiated. You cannot fool a child. Children can smell a bluff a mile away, so don't try.

You play this game *straight up*. You raise with your time and effort. Talk is cheap. It gets no respect at the poker table.

Moving In

We will slow down the action as the teacher walks over to the disruptive students. We will examine the moves of the poker game in their logical sequence as we give them labels.

As in *the turn*, the conversation in body language as the teacher walks toward the disruptive students is very rich and subtle. The analogy of the poker game holds up quite well as both the teacher and the students make decisions to raise or fold.

For this generic walk-through, we will, as usual, imagine typical students who are engaged in *talking to neighbors*. Students with histories of child abuse whose personal space is quite large will have a "hair trigger" in response to a teacher approaching. We will deal with these students in a later chapter. For now, think *typical* child.

Say Their Names

Imagine that you are "moving in" on the two students pictured earlier, call them Tameka and Kathy. Sometimes the students are so consumed with their conversation that they fail to notice you. In this case, say their names. Use a flat tone of voice, neither sweet nor upset.

Shrewd gamblers, however, keep an eye out for the teacher. When you look at them, they will usually catch you out of the corners of their eyes. However, do not get hung up on direct eye contact at this point. Cultural norms vary.

Smiley Face

Imagine that, in response to seeing "the turn" or hearing their names, Tameka and Kathy give you smiley face followed by what appears to be scholarship. You instinctively check their knees and the feet. Their knees and feet haven't moved, and you realize that you have so far accomplished *nothing*.

Students know when to hold 'em, and they know when to fold 'em.

Walk

Take two relaxing breaths, omit silly talk, and walk slowly over to Tameka and Kathy. Pick one of them as your focus, preferably the instigator. In this case it happens to be Kathy.

Walk to the edge of her desk so that you can barely touch her desk with your legs. Stand relaxed but upright and take two relaxing breaths. Check your jaw.

It is now Kathy's move. She has two choices. She can either fold by turning forward and getting back to work, or she can continue to play.

Half a Loaf

We will imagine throughout this example that the students continue the game by raising the teacher. However, we will look at the subtle, incremental raises of the shrewd gambler rather than the clumsy play of the dysfunctional student who raises wildly. Clumsy players make rash moves like backtalk.

The next move of the shrewd gambler is pseudo-compliance. Kathy raises you by scooting her chair *half-way around*. We will call this move "giving the teacher *half a loaf*." Rather than giving you what you want, Kathy has given you only *part* of what you want. In the language of negotiations, she just said, *"I will give you half of what you asked for. I am gambling that you want out of here badly enough to take my offer."*

Imagine that you, also being shrewd, notice this partial gesture, even stepping back to look under the desk to see feet if necessary. Rather than being satisfied with *half a loaf*, you realize that you have just been *raised*.

Raising with Pseudo-compliance

By now, you probably see the pattern emerging. The way in which students typically up the ante is with *pseudo-compliance*. Pseudo-compliance is a less risky strategy than defiance. For this reason, we must become astute observers of *partial gestures*.

Visual Prompt

Seeing a raise rather than a fold, you instinctively up the ante. You *raise* Kathy in this situation by giving her a prompt. A prompt is simply a message that tells her what to do next.

Lean over gently, resting your weight on one palm, and gesture with your other hand for Kathy to bring her chair around. Stay down, wait, maintain eye contact, and take a relaxing breath.

Begin with a *visual* prompt because it is safer than a *verbal* prompt. Speech, like smiling, is a *trigger mechanism*. The most predictable way of getting another person to speak to you is by speaking to them. A verbal prompt, therefore, raises the odds of a verbal reply by the student. This would make the situation unnecessarily complicated.

"The way in which students up the ante is with pseudo-compliance."

Another Partial Turn

Typically, the student would bring his or her chair all of the way around. But we will assume, for the sake of analysis, that Kathy once again gives *partial* compliance. Her chair comes three-quarters of the way around.

You could, of course, repeat the visual prompt. Let's assume, however, that after one or maybe two visual prompts, you are still looking at partial compliance. Seeing this, you up the ante once again.

Verbal Prompt

You now *tell* Kathy to bring her chair *all of the way around*. Speaking to Kathy increases the risk of backtalk, but you have little choice. A simple sentence in a kindly tone of voice is sufficient.

"Please bring your chair all of the way around."

You can probably remember a teacher when you were a kid who told you to bring your chair *all of the way around*. That teacher knew a thing or two about pseudo-compliance.

Usually the student complies. The specificity of the teacher's prompt leaves little room for "playing dumb." To stay in the game with one more raise, the student must engage in a blatant act of *defiance*. The student has pushed pseudo-compliance about as far as it can go.

Student Choices

Blatant noncompliance in this situation usually takes the form of backtalk.

"I wasn't doing anything."

"He was talking to me."

"Hey, leave me alone."

With backtalk, the price of playing poker escalates dramatically. Instead of pennies, nickels, and dimes; backtalk gets us into serious betting. Backtalk will be the subject of the next two chapters. It is a sufficiently taxing subject to be worthy of its own space.

For now, it is enough to realize that most students, even the mouthy ones, are penny-ante gamblers. They just look brave because they have been winning with penny and nickel bets at home and at school for so long.

We will assume, therefore, that Kathy has concluded, as most students do in this situation, that discretion is the greater part of valor. She has turned all of the way around in response to your prompt, and she is working.

Palms

It would seem at this point that you have achieved your objective and that the game is over. Far from it, you have just arrived at a crucial juncture, one which dooms the efforts of many teachers.

After the verbal prompt, rest your weight on both palms and lock your elbows as though to say, *"I have all day."* Relax your hands, making sure that you are neither up on your fingertips (I want out of here) or making a fist (I am anxious).

Take two relaxing breaths as you *watch* and *wait.* Watch the student work long enough to see a *stable pattern of work that represents a commitment to time-on-task.* Wait long enough, for example, to see Kathy write a few sentences or do a math problem.

It is not too late for pseudo-compliance on the part of the student. Kathy may actually get to work, or she may just *appear* to get to work. As you watch and wait, look for signs that the student is still "gaming" you.

> **"When students finally give up the game, they will focus on their work instead of the teacher."**

Eyes Up – Eyes Down

If Kathy is still more concerned with testing you than with the assignment, she will keep checking to see what you are doing. When Kathy finally gives up the game, she will focus on the work and quit worrying about you.

The most predictable sign that the student is still "playing off of the teacher" is "eyes up – eyes down." Kathy looks up briefly as though to say, *"Oh, are you still here?"* When she sees that you have not budged, her eyes typically go back to her work.

As you watch and wait at "palms," Kathy may check you out several times. Each time she does, her behavior tells you to *hang in there.* The game is not over yet.

Eye Prompts

A variation on *eyes up – eyes down* is for the student to look up and *not* look down. This could mean any of a number of things from defiance to simply waiting for another prompt. It is hard to tell. However, this leaves you and the student eye to eye. The situation becomes more awkward the longer you are locked into looking at each other.

Finesse the situation by giving the student an "eye prompt." The simplest eye prompt is to look down at the student's work. The student typically follows your eyes down. You have said, in effect, *"All I care about is the work."*

To make an eye prompt more convincing, turn your upper body if you are in front of the student so that you can read his or her work. This more clearly says, *"All I care about is the work."*

Thank the Student and Stay Down

After the gaming has stopped and Kathy is fully engaged in working, thank her for getting to work. A simple sentence is sufficient, and touching is optional. Your emotions go from *neutral* to *warm* as you thank the student so that your tone of voice is gentle.

"Thank you for getting back to work."

After you thank Kathy, *stay down* and take *two relaxing breaths* as your emotions again become neutral. Watch and wait until Kathy once again recommits to time-on-task and demonstrates a stable pattern of work.

The most common error is to thank the student and then *stand up.* If you do this, do not be surprised if the student quits working. Thanking the student is not only common courtesy, it is also a *closure message.* It says, "That is what I wanted."

Many students, unfamiliar with both common courtesy and closure messages, misinterpret this communication. They think it means, "You have done everything that you need to do, and I am now finished dealing with you." Consequently, I have seen students look up with relieved smiles and lay their pencils down.

Therefore, after you thank Kathy, *stay down.* Watch and wait until she *recommits* to the task. Her behavior then says, *"Oh, I guess I had better keep working, huh?"*

Repeat the Process with the Second Student

Give both students equal time. If you do not, the first student feels picked on, and the second student feels as though he or she has faked you out.

Move gently to Tameka and stay at palms. Tameka will probably be on task when you get to her since she is trying to disappear. Watch her work until you get the definite feeling that she is "into the assignment."

While at palms, double check how Tameka is sitting. If she is not facing all of the way forward, reprompt her to bring her chair around. Finally, thank Tameka and *stay down* just as you did with Kathy. Wait until both students are fully at work.

Typical Error

The typical error in *moving in* is for teachers to *leave too quickly.* As you can see from the preceding example, the greatest investment in *moving in* is *staying after you arrive.*

It takes time to wait out the gaming. The students are struggling with the issue of submission – sacrificing their agenda (socializing) to your agenda (time-on-task). They do not want to give up their entire agenda, so they test to see how much of it they can retain. There is no way to speed up this process of testing.

Moving Out

The Game Continues

Even after the game *appears* to be over, it may continue. Pseudo-compliance can be reformulated into the question, "How long do I have to keep working?" As any parent knows, it is not uncommon for children to go back to what they *were* doing as soon as your back is turned.

We will choreograph your *moving out* just as carefully as your *moving in.* Moving out is straightforward in this simple scenario. It does not get complicated until the next chapter when we deal with backtalk and "cheap shots."

Move Out Slowly

Stand slowly after thanking the second student, and take *two* relaxing breaths. If you get "eyes up – eyes down," take an extra relaxing breath and wait until it is clear that everyone is working.

As you leave Kathy and Tameka, you may momentarily turn your back toward them as you walk away. Before you become involved with another student, however, turn *fully* and *point your toes* toward the two disruptors. Should they glance up, they will see a teacher quite willing to return.

As you begin to help the next student, buttonhook so that the students you just left are in your *direct line of vision.* It is not uncommon to get *eyes up – eyes down* at this late stage of the game.

Summary

The plan underlying *moving in* and *moving out* is really quite simple. You relax and kill time from a logical series of locations as you move toward the students, waiting at each location for them to make a decision. When you are working the crowd this pattern of movement is nonchalant and all but invisible.

Slowing Down

Slow Is Difficult

After practicing *moving in and moving out* during training, I will ask the teachers, "Did you feel that the entire process took a *huge* amount of time?" They will respond in unison, "Yes!"

The contrast between our normal speed of movement in the classroom and the speed of Meaning Business is so great that it must be experienced to be appreciated. With the Study Group Activity Guide, practice with a colleague. A few repetitions will get your internal clock recalibrated.

Yet, while slowing down is difficult, the relaxing breaths *pace* you. Relaxed breathing, however, is the *first* skill of Meaning Business to be *lost* after training. The result is a gradual increase in the speed of performance.

School site trainers are taught to look for the following comment from trainees in the weeks immediately after training.

> "You know, I am using body language to set limits, and it works. But, I have to keep doing it over and over with the same students."

When teachers go to the trouble of *moving in* only to leave too quickly, they literally undo what they just did. The students look up to see the teacher gone and think, *"Gee, that wasn't as big a deal as I thought it was going to be."*

Slow Is Expensive

It is impossible to practice the Limit Setting sequence without realizing how *expensive* it is. More than the effort involved, it takes *time!* It is natural, therefore, to want to *economize.* Discipline management, after all, needs to be affordable.

How can something so expensive ever be cheap? The way in which you achieve the necessary economy will determine whether or not you are successful at Meaning Business in the long run.

False Economies

Nag, Nag, Nag

The most common way in which teachers save themselves the time and effort of "moving in" and "moving out" is *nag, nag, nag.*

> "Philip and Peter! Would you please quit talking and turn around in your seats?"

We know that nagging doesn't work in the long run, but it is quick.

Speeding Up

Another false economy is to *speed up,* often done unconsciously in order to get the whole thing over with. As we just discussed, this naturally occurs following training unless we continue to work on our skills.

True Economies

An Ounce of Prevention

The commitment of time that Meaning Business sometimes requires will make us want to do it as *seldom* as possible. Prevention, therefore, is the name of the game.

The entire first half of this book has as its primary objective prevention of the goofing off that requires Meaning Business. The context for Meaning Business, therefore, includes:

- Room arrangement
- Working the crowd
- Praise, Prompt, and Leave
- Visual Instructional Plans
- Say, See, Do Teaching with adequate Structured Practice.

Imagine, in contrast, a Bop 'til You Drop teacher who lectures for 25 minutes. During all of that time, half of the class is in the green zone with nothing to do. They will find something to do – goofing off!

If this teacher attempts to set limits on the goofing off that results, he or she will have to set limits every 30 seconds. This teacher, when queried, will say, "If I were to set limits every time a student is out of line, I would get nothing else done."

Training Larry to "Fold"

A second form of prevention has to do with the way in which Meaning Business is administered. When you are consistent you become highly predictable.

Let us imagine, for example, that it is the first day of school, and Larry is in your class. Larry, naturally, will be the first student to test you. All of the other students know this. Consequently, Larry serves as their "point man."

Larry is looking for answers to important management questions. Will you see me goofing off? Will you pretend that you do not see me? Will you do anything about it? Will you do anything effective? Everybody wants to know who you really are, and Larry wants to know right now.

So, early in the day, you look up to see Larry goofing off when he should be working. Having spent the summer with weenie parents, Larry may not even track your presence as he fools around. Consequently, after the turn and a relaxing breath, you may have to say his name. Larry looks up as though to say, *"Who, me?"*

To make a long story short, you set limits exactly as we described earlier in the chapter complete with *moving in* and *moving out*. Larry cools it for now. Yet, while Larry is impressed, he is not yet convinced. He will have to give you another try.

Later on, Larry pulls the same stunt, and once again, you commit, willing to pay whatever price it takes. You turn in a regal fashion and say his name. Larry looks up to see a familiar sight. He is beginning to understand that the first time was no fluke.

Larry must now make a choice. Does he want you to stay where you are, or does he want you to walk over to where he is? At this point, the fact that children are power junkies comes to your aid. Larry wants to control the situation. Larry wants you to stay where you are. What is the only possible way in which these objectives can be achieved? You guessed it - *get to work!*

The Fruit of Consistency

If Larry knows that he cannot win with any of his tricks, all he eventually needs to see is a sign that "the inexorable process" has begun in order to know that it is time to fold.

When Larry finally wises up enough to make this decision, you have saved yourself the trip across the classroom. The size of your response is getting smaller. It has gone from a *physical* response (moving in and moving out) to a *verbal* response (*the turn* plus saying Larry's name). This is a major economy.

But, Larry, being Larry, will have to try you again. Only, by now he is tracking you visually. You have made yourself "significant," so to speak. When you see Larry, Larry sees you.

This time you can dispense with saying his name as you just turn in a regal fashion and wait. Since Larry folded on this raise the last time, chances are he will fold again this time. Your response has now gone from *physical* to *verbal* to *nonverbal.* You have looked Larry back to work.

The time may come when you can look Larry back to work without even standing and turning. But your ability to do this is predicated on Larry's *belief* that you will pay whatever price you need to pay at any time in order to create time-on-task.

Larry's behavior, therefore, is based not so much on what you are doing now, but rather on your *history* with him. You have taught him to fold early because he *believes that you will pay* – any time and anywhere.

As you can see, there is no mystery to this process. Once you shape the response you want, you can fade the prompts without losing the response.

"Larry's behavior is based not so much on what you are doing now, but, rather, on your history with Larry."

Meaning Business Self-Eliminates

As payback for your willingness to invest up front *every time* in order to make a believer out of Larry, the amount of work required on your part steadily decreases. If Larry knows that he *cannot win* with any of his tricks, all he eventually needs to see is a sign that "the inexorable process" has begun.

The time will eventually come when the unwavering enforcement of your standards becomes synonymous with your physical presence. *You* are the discriminative stimulus that says, "The entire management system is in effect because I just walked into the room."

Only through this process of training does Meaning Business finally becomes *invisible.* Unfortunately, a green teacher observing your classroom would learn next to nothing by watching you.

Working the Crowd Is Prevention

An entirely different way of thinking about prevention is to realize that *moving in* and *working the crowd* are related. Walking toward disruptive students is always a powerful intervention. That is why they often "shape up" before you get half way there.

Think of working the crowd as the *preventative* version of moving in. What this chapter describes is the *remedial* version. The more you use your body language to prevent disruptions by working the crowd, the less often you will have to stop what you are doing in order to mean business.

Camouflage

The Big Shootout

As a closing thought, let's imagine moving in on a couple of tough kids, maybe seventeen years old, with reputations and a few buddies in the class. After you turn in a regal fashion and say their names, you walk slowly toward them.

Can you imagine some of their buddies chiming in as you walk closer?

"Hey Larry, here he comes."

Does this remind you of "The Shootout At The O.K. Corral?" Are you getting uncomfortable yet? You should be.

You have just made a blunder by turning discipline management into *theater*, and Larry's peer group is the audience. Larry cannot back down now. You have just violated one of the most basic rules of Meaning Business:

Don't go public if you can help it.

You need *camouflage*. Camouflage allows you to mean business without making it into a public spectacle.

How can you mask what you are doing so that you do not embarrass Larry and back him into a corner? Fortunately, you have all of the camouflage you need. The natural cover for moving in is *working the crowd.*

Moving In with Camouflage

Imagine that, as you are working the crowd, you catch Larry goofing off on the far side of the room. He catches your eye as you look up.

You excuse yourself as you stand slowly and turn in a regal fashion. Larry has seen this before. But as you begin to cruise toward Larry, you stop casually and look at another student's work. You may not care about that student's work right now, but you act as though you do. For now, spending a moment with that student is camouflage – your normal pattern of interaction as you work the crowd.

Don't go public if you can help it.

After pausing for a moment, you turn and stroll toward Larry, maintaining eye contact with Larry for an extra split second as you move. You are talking to Larry with your body language, and, chances are, Larry is reading it very accurately. You are saying, "I see you fooling around, and it is the main thing on my mind right now. I am coming over there as I normally would. Is there something better that you might be doing by the time I get there?"

You walk a few steps more and casually interact with another student. As you turn to leave, you once again point yourself toward Larry a little more directly than usual and maintain eye contact for an extra split second. You are asking Larry the same question you asked a moment earlier.

Now, ask yourself, how stupid would Larry have to be to get "caught" fooling around? He can see it coming *a mile away*. To get into trouble, he would have to *want* to get into trouble.

Most students, even Larry, do not *want* a hassle. They just want to socialize instead of work. Even with Larry, most gambling is penny-ante gambling.

By the time you get to Larry the problem will, in all likelihood, be gone. It usually evaporates as you enter the "red zone." When you get to Larry's desk, the two of you share a knowing look. Enough said.

Win-Win Management

Your skill and finesse allow you to teach that "no means no" while protecting students from embarrassment.

At the level of everyday fooling around, there is no such thing as a "win-lose" situation. It is always "win-win" or "lose-lose."

If you embarrass students in front of their peer group, they will embarrass you in front of the same peer group to get even. And, you won't have to wait until tomorrow.

Win-Win or Lose-Lose

Larry has played this game long enough to appreciate what you just did. Your skill and finesse allow you to teach him that "no means no" while protecting him from embarrassment.

Over the years I have come to appreciate a simple truth about discipline management. With everyday goofing off, there is no such thing as a "win-lose" situation. It is "win-win" or "lose-lose." If you embarrass students in front of their peer group, they will embarrass you in front of the same peer group to get even. And, you won't have to wait until tomorrow.

Natural teachers have *finesse*. They have the social skills to get their way without embarrassing students and becoming embroiled in expensive consequences. Much of that finesse comes from the subtle body language of Meaning Business.

Chapter Eighteen

Eliminating Backtalk

Preview

- To understand the management of backtalk, think in terms of two time frames – a short-term response and a long-term response.
- The short-term response is measured in seconds. It has to do with the fight-flight reflex. If you go to your brainstem instead of relaxing and staying calm, all is lost.
- Backtalk is sudden and threatening and public. Both the fight-flight reflex and the fact that speech is a trigger mechanism set you up to do one thing – speak.
- The Cardinal Error in dealing with backtalk is to speak. The student will play off of whatever you say in order to create a melodrama.
- If you keep your mouth shut in the short-term, backtalk will usually die out. In the long-term you can do whatever you think is appropriate.

Setting You Up

Fight-Flight Reflexes Again

Imagine that you walk over to Larry who is goofing off, and you give him a prompt to get back to work as described in the preceding chapter. Instead of facing forward as most students would, Larry looks up at you and says:

> "I wasn't doin' anything. Why don't you just get out of my face and leave me alone?"

All eyes in the class immediately snap toward you. On every student's face is an expression that says, "Wow! What are you going to do about that Mr. Jones?"

To say that you feel *vulnerable* right now is probably an understatement. Larry has just "gone public" – exactly what Meaning Business tries to avoid. He has made *theater* out of discipline management, and his classmates are all eyes and ears.

There are very few things that a student can do more calculated to upset the teacher than backtalk. By challenging you in front of the entire class, the student says, in effect:

> "Hey, you guys! Look over here! This teacher is trying to tell me what to do. I want you all to know that he *can't* because he isn't in control of this situation. *I am!*"

If you fail to have a fight-flight reflex under these conditions, you may need to consult a mortician. The rest of us will be sucking in a deep breath.

Setting You Up to Speak

If you have a fight-flight reflex, you are predisposed to speak. *Nagging, pheasant posturing,* and *snap and snarl* are simply the names we have given to it. In addition, speech is a *trigger mechanism.* The most predictable way of getting someone to speak to you is for you to speak to them.

When students confront you verbally, everything they are doing seems calculated to *get you to speak.* Could there be a method to this madness?

The Cardinal Error

Having the Last Word

Let's begin with an example of the *garden variety wheedling* that is most common in the classroom. This will be a less emotionally charged situation than the one described above.

The simplest form of wheedling is denial. Denial requires perhaps three neurons.

"I wasn't doin' anything."

"Was not."

To denial we will add its companion, blaming.

"He was asking me a question."

"She started it."

It takes one fool to backtalk. It takes two fools to make a conversation out of it.

Finally, to this display of garden variety wheedling, we will add a teacher who is committing the *Cardinal Error.* The Cardinal Error when dealing with backtalk is *backtalk.* Taking the scene from the top, it might go like this:

Teacher: "Kathy, I would like you to bring your chair around and get some work done."

Student: "I wasn't doing anything."

Teacher: "You have been talking this whole period, and I want it to stop."

Student: "No I wasn't."

Teacher: "Every time I look up, I see you talking to Tameka."

Student: "She was just asking me a question."

Teacher: "I don't care who was asking who what. When I look up, I expect to see you doing your own work."

Student: "Yeah, but..."

Have you had enough yet? Who do you think will look foolish by the time this conversation winds down?

When you were four years old, you already had the social skills required to have the last word in an argument if you wanted it badly enough. All it takes is perseverance.

The First Rule of Backtalk

Two children arguing is a fairly common sight. But watching a child and a *teacher* argue is more than a bit disconcerting – which brings us to our *first* rule of backtalk:

It takes one fool to backtalk.
It takes two fools to make a conversation out of it.

The first fool is the *child*. Children will be foolish sometimes, but the normal immaturity of children does not worry me. What worries me is the *second* fool. The second fool is always the *teacher*. It is the teacher's backtalk that will get this student sent to the office.

One of the most common scenarios for a student being kicked out of class is the following:

- The student mouths off.
- The teacher responds.
- The student mouths off.
- The teacher responds.
- The student mouths off.
- The teacher responds.
- The student mouths off.

Open your mouth, and slit your throat.

By this point in the conversation, teachers usually realize that they have dug their hole so deep that the only way out is to "pull rank." That is why backtalk is the most common complaint in office referrals.

Roles in a Melodrama

Think of backtalk as a melodrama which is written, produced, and directed by the *student*. In this melodrama there is a speaking part for *you*.

If you accept your speaking part in the melodrama, it is "show time." But if you do not, the show bombs. This brings us to our *second* rule of backtalk:

Open your mouth, and slit your throat.

Imagine the conversation between teacher and student described earlier if the teacher had had the good sense to keep his or her *mouth shut*.

Teacher: "Kathy, I would like you to bring your chair around and get some work done."

Student: "I wasn't doing anything."

Teacher: (silence)

Student: "Well, I wasn't."

Teacher: (silence)

Student: "But…"

Teacher: (silence)

Student: (silence)

Students may try to keep the scene going for a while, but, as they say in showbiz, "There's nothing worse than playing to a dead house." When backtalkers run out of material, embarrassment sets in. That is when they fold. Getting back to work suddenly becomes the quickest way to disappear.

If you talk, you actually *rescue* backtalkers from their dilemma. It is like throwing a lifeline to a drowning person. By playing off of whatever you say, he or she can keep the show alive and avoid "going down for the third time."

A Comedy Routine

Think of backtalk as a comedy routine – a classroom comedy duo. There are many duos in the history of comedy: Laurel and Hardy, Abbot and Costello, Burns and Allen, Martin and Lewis.

Comedy duos all have a predictable format. There is a "clown" and a "straight man." The straight man sets up the jokes by delivering "straight lines" like:

"How bad was it?"

"Then what happened?"

"Why did you do that?"

In the classroom comedy duo, the *student* is the *clown* and the *teacher* is the *straight man.* The clown plays off of the lines delivered by the teacher.

Ironically, no matter how much you may hate backtalk, when you speak, you become the disruptive student's *partner.* This brings us to our *third* rule of backtalk:

If students want to backtalk,
at least make them do all of the work.
Don't do half of it for them!

Think of backtalk as self-limiting. You have to feed it to make it grow. If you do not feed it, it will starve. Or, think of it this way. Opening your mouth is like throwing gasoline on a fire. Do you want it to die down or blow up in your face?

"If the students want to backtalk, at least make them do all of the work."

Types of Backtalk

Few things trigger a fight-flight reflex more predictably than *surprise.* The backtalk itself is usually a surprise, but what the student says can also be a shock.

If we can reduce the surprise factor inherent in backtalk, we can reduce the probability of a fight-flight reflex. For that reason, it is useful to know exactly what to expect.

Fortunately for us, backtalk is one of the *least* creative endeavors of the disruptive student. Mouthy students have been saying the same things since little Babylonian kids went to school.

With adequate preparation, you can respond to backtalk with emotional nonchalance. When you relax your jaw in this situation, you look *bored* – a lack of expression described by trainees as "withering boredom." Backtalkers find this lack of response most disheartening.

We will look at the types of backtalk that students typically use. Backtalk can be grouped under three general headings:

- Switching the agenda
- Whiny backtalk
- Nasty backtalk

Switching the Agenda

Seducing the Teacher

There are three agendas in classroom management: discipline, instruction, and motivation. As you know from previous chapters, these three agendas represent very different management procedures. While these procedures compliment each other, they do not greatly overlap.

Consequently, if students can seduce the teacher from discipline into either of the other two agendas, discipline management is left behind. This is a very shrewd move for disruptive students since they get off the hook with almost no risk of provoking the teacher.

Switching to Instruction

The most common switch is from discipline to instruction. It delivers maximum benefit at minimum risk.

Have you ever prompted a student who is *talking to neighbors* by saying,

> "I would like you to turn around and get to work,"

only to have the student look up and say,

> "But, I don't understand how to do this problem"?

You ought to give the student extra credit for knowing how to play the game.

Recognizing Backtalk

The way you recognize backtalk is by the fact that the kid's mouth is open.

Now, let me show you a naive teacher taking the bait. In response to the student's help-seeking, the teacher says,

> "What part don't you understand?"

It's over! You lose! You may as well say to the class,

> "Class, let me explain what just happened so you will all understand. Go ahead and *talk* to your neighbors. If I see you goofing off, and if I walk all of the way over to your desk in order to deal with it, this is what you do. Look up innocently and say, 'But, I don't understand how to do this problem.' The worst thing that will ever happen to you in my class is that I will do part of your assignment for you."

Not too surprisingly, most backtalk in any classroom is switching the agenda to instruction. Switching the agenda to instruction is such a cool plan that I sometimes wonder why students would do anything else. It is a no-lose strategy. Students run no risk of getting into trouble because teachers never identify *switching the agenda* as backtalk. Teachers seem to think that backtalk has to be obnoxious. It does not.

At this point you may be wondering, "Well, then, what is backtalk?" Let me give you a simple answer to save you confusion. The way you recognize backtalk is by the fact that *the kid's mouth is open.*

"So, what should I do?" you might ask. This is a very tricky question, which is another reason why students love to use "switching the agenda" as their strategy of choice.

Let me give you the easy answer first. Take two relaxing breaths, check your jaw, clear your mind, and keep your mouth shut as you kill time. When the backtalker runs out of gas, take two more relaxing breaths and then, if you need to, give a nonverbal prompt to get back to work.

Sometimes this actually works. Chalk it up to finesse and luck. But, if the student wants to up the ante, all he or she has to say is,

"Well, I don't know how! What am I supposed to do? Are you just going to look at me?"

This move exposes the vulnerability of our previous strategy. Maybe the student really *does not* know how to do the problem. Or, maybe the student *does* know how and is just "messing with you." How would you know?

The student has you over a barrel, and the student knows it. Consequently, teachers who have not caved in by now usually fold at this point by saying,

"What part don't you understand?"

When trying to get off the hook, students act like lawyers. They think, "Do I have a case?" This student obviously has a good case. How can *you* say that they *do* know how to do the problem when *they* say that they *don't*?

The only satisfactory answer to this question lies in all of the instructional procedures described in the first half of the book – *weaning the helpless handraisers, Praise, Prompt, and Leave, Visual Instructional Plans,* and *Say, See, Do Teaching with adequate Structured Practice.* With all of this, you know very well that the students "knew how" before you made your transition to Guided Practice.

Consequently, the students don't have a leg to stand on when making a case for needing help. They know it, and they know that you know it. As a result, they will not even try to switch the agenda. Or, if they do, they will lack the self-righteous zeal required to withstand a dose of withering boredom.

In contrast, if you teach in the Bop 'til You Drop style, you will not have a clue as to what the students know after your transition to Guided Practice. The students know this. The students therefore have a good case for pleading ignorance, and you may expect them to pursue their case with panache.

Let's add another level to the student's game playing. Students know *why* we went into teaching. We want to see students *learn.* We love students who *want* to learn.

Clever students will use this insight to get off the hook when they get cornered. They will look you in the eye and, with utter sincerity, give you exactly what you want to hear. They will ask for help, as though to say, *"This is the magic moment. I am burning with curiosity. Teach me! Teach me!"*

When a teacher says, "What part don't you understand?" the visual image that comes to mind is a fish with a hook in its mouth being reeled in.

Switching to Motivation

While not as common as switching the agenda to instruction, switching to motivation has one big advantage. It gives the student *control.* It is the *power* move.

"I'm not doing this."

"This is dumb."

"We did this last year."

To clarify the issue of power and control, you cannot *make* students work. You cannot make them think. You cannot even make them pick up a pencil. The students control their own nervous systems. Students will think and write when they direct their own bodies to do so.

Therefore, *forcing* unmotivated students to work is a dead issue. You cannot intimidate them. You can only flunk them, and they don't care. Not caring gives them their power.

Switching to Instruction

Even if students do not get off the hook, which they almost always do, they run no risk of getting "into trouble." It is a no-lose strategy.

Switching to Motivation

As a simple issue of power and control, you cannot *make students work.* You cannot make them think. You cannot even make them pick up a pencil.

In the long run, if you want students to do schoolwork, you must give them a *positive* reason to do so – something that they *choose.* You will have to answer the question, "Why should I?" This will require some real expertise in the technology of incentive management. (See Chapters 9 and 10 for a discussion of motivation.)

In the short run, in lieu of incentives, you can always cut your losses. Whisper privately to the student,

> "If you are not going to do your work, we can talk about that later. For right now, I will at least expect you to allow your neighbors to do *their* work."

Most students will take this opportunity to cut their losses. Escalating at this point represents a student who is looking for an altercation.

Whiny Backtalk

Whiny backtalk is what I referred to earlier as "garden variety" backtalk. It is the common, unremarkable, everyday self-justification that students most often employ when trying to get off the hook. These are the types of backtalk that "good kids" have used since the beginning of time. The main types are as follows:

Denial

"I wasn't doin' anything."

"We weren't talking."

"I'm not chewing gum."

As you can see, this is a *very* simple strategy. It does, however, raise an important question. That question is, *Are you blind?* If you are a sighted individual, there is nothing to debate. You *saw* it.

Take two relaxing breaths, kill some time, and *keep your mouth shut.* This too shall pass.

Blaming Your Neighbor

"She was talking, not me."

"They started it."

"He was just asking me a question."

Blaming, also known as "ratting on your neighbor," is where students go when denial is not working. You can hear the absurdity of a lame excuse if you *paraphrase.*

> "Gee, teacher, we weren't goofing off when we were talking. We were operating a peer tutoring program to further our education."

Seeing the humor in backtalk is a wonderful defense against having a fight-flight reflex. Instead of thinking, *"Say, what?"* you think, *"Yeah, right."*

Blaming the Teacher

If you can't blame the person sitting next to you, blame the teacher. After all, the teacher is handy.

"I had to ask him because you went over it so fast."

"I had to ask her because I can't read your handwriting."

"I had to ask him because you didn't make it clear."

The student always blames the teacher for the same shortcoming – *professional incompetence.* Now, the absurdity of the excuse is even more palpable.

"Gee, teacher, we weren't goofing off back here. We were operating a peer tutoring program in order to compensate for your methodological deficiencies in the area of instruction."

An accusation of incompetence can make a person defensive. I have seen teachers bite on this bait.

"I went over this material step by step not ten minutes ago. It is written right up there on the board if you would care to read it. Now, I am sick and tired..."

The hook is firmly set. Reel 'em in.

Excusing You to Leave

With this version of whiny backtalk, the student is telling you, in effect, to go take a hike. Of course, only a high-roller would say, "Hey, teacher, go take a hike." With whiny backtalkers, the message takes the following variations:

- **Short Form:** "All right, I'll do it."
- **Long Form:** "All right, I'll do it if you just leave me alone."
- **Nasty Form:** "All right, I'll do it if you just get out of my face! I can't work with you standing over me like that!"
- **Emotionally Handicapped Form:** "Geez, what are you, some kind of pervert? Leave me alone!"

As always, relax, be quiet, and wait. Do not allow yourself to be suckered into the Cardinal Error. If you succeed in the short-term, you can do anything you want in the long-term.

Compliment

Sometimes a student will give the teacher a "goodie-two-shoes compliment." This student is attempting to get off the hook while scoring a few brownie points by diverting the teacher's attention. Think of it as just another flavor of baloney.

I have seen teachers thrown off by this tactic. I remember one fourth grade girl who said,

If denial doesn't work, you can always try ratting on your neighbor.

> "Oh, Mrs. Johnson, what a beautiful pin."

Mrs. Johnson stood up, looked at the pin and said,

> "Why, thank you, dear. I got that for my birthday. Now, you get some work done."

Mrs. Johnson wandered off with a contented smile on her face. Before long the student was talking again.

Nonverbal Backtalk

This may sound like an oxymoron, but it is an apt title for control tactics that function like backtalk without the risk of "lipping off." Here are some common variants:

Cry

If all else fails, try blubbering. If crying gets kids off the hook at home, they may try it at school. Some parents start apologizing as soon as the tears flow.

Stay down, relax, and wait. If you hang in there, blubbering students will eventually dry up. Then they will look up to see if you are still there. When they realize that the gambit did not work, the cheapest way for them to cut their losses is to get back to work.

While the whole process may take some time, consider it a good investment. If the tears are interminable, however, you can always cut your losses. Similar to cutting your losses when a student plays the motivation card, lean over and whisper gently,

> "We can talk about your crying later. For right now, the least I will expect from you is that you get your work done."

Leave, but return soon after the student's head comes up. Rather than getting rid of you, the student who used crying to get off the hook receives some follow through and "instructional supervision" from close range.

Push You Aside

Sometimes students will push your arm away if you lean on the desk. Is this a big deal or not?

You could, of course, make a big deal out of it. It was, after all, a rather impudent thing to do. But, chances are, it was more reflex than strategy on the part of the student. No point in making a mountain out of a molehill.

Try "rubber arm." Relax the arm that has been pushed aside and *stay down.* Hang in there and wait without backing off.

The student, confronted by an immovable object, must now finally deal with your presence. At this point he or she usually realizes that getting back to work is the cheapest way out. You can always talk to the student later if you wish.

A Kiss on the Nose

This has only happened once in my experience, but it is a good story for highlighting the power of doing nothing. It comes from a first-rate female junior high teacher in a suburb of Minneapolis who was a trainer for me in her school district.

She had the original "Joe Cool" in her classroom – three sport letterman, good looking, liked by the girls and a bit of an imp. He was talking to his buddy to the extent that the teacher finally moved in to "palms" on his desk. He looked up at the teacher, leaned forward, and *gave her a kiss on the nose.*

We had not practiced this move during training, of course. But, she remembered to take two relaxing breaths, stay down and *do nothing.* Joe obviously expected to get a "rise" out of the teacher. All eyes were on him. It came as a surprise when nothing happened. It became embarrassing when nothing *at all* happened.

Some classmates giggled. Joe blushed. The teacher just looked at him and waited, but her lack of emotion came across as nonchalance, as though to say, "This happens to me all of the time."

Joe wilted. He looked for a place to hide but had to settle for getting back to work. I am told that he never tried anything like that again.

This story highlights our general strategy for dealing with the unexpected:

When in doubt, do nothing.

This may not seem like much of a strategy, but, in the heat of the moment, it can be a life-saver. Would you rather respond impulsively or have some time to think?

Basic Short-Term Moves

What do you do with your body in the short-term when a student backtalks? Imagine that you are giving a prompt or are at "palms" when the student mouths off. Also, imagine typical kids and whiny backtalk. We will deal with nasty situations later.

The simplest thing to do, of course, is nothing. Just remain at palms. This provides enough proximity for the student to "feel your presence." Kill some time and wait.

However, if the student keeps talking in order to gain the upper hand or "back you off," you may wish to signal to him or her that this is a foolish strategy. The easiest way to signal this is by *moving closer.*

Camping Out in Front

In response to continued backtalk (i.e., the student's *second sentence*), bend one elbow and gently move down so that your elbow is resting on the table. This gets you closer to the student and improves eye contact.

Take two relaxing breaths, keep your mouth shut, and wait. This move usually dashes the student's hopes.

In response to continued backtalk, bend one elbow and gently move closer.

Camping Out from Behind

In sports (and discipline management is an indoor sport), offensive strategy can be summarized as follows: *Two good athletes can beat one good athlete.* Consequently, successful offense is synonymous with "two-on-one," "overloading the zone," or "the power play." Different sports have different names for it.

You may prefer Camping Out from Behind if you want to isolate the backtalker.

In the classroom, therefore, do not be surprised if backtalking students try to go two-on-one if you fail to rise to their bait. When whiney backtalk is failing, they may turn to an accomplice in order to "double team" you.

"Tameka was just asking me a question, (turning to Tameka) right?"

Often, the second student will "cool it" because he or she would rather disappear than up the ante. If you hang in there and wait quietly in this situation, the first student usually folds.

But, if the second student chimes in, you have two-on-one. You have a more serious problem if they start to feed off of each other. Kill some time in order to check it out. Often, the gambit will fizzle after a few whiny self-justifications.

If, however, the gambit takes wing so that the two students are working you over, you will have to switch strategies. You need to reestablish "one-on-one" with the backtalker, and you *cannot separate* the two students with your *mouth.*

Rather, you will need to *separate* the students with your *body.* Stand slowly and walk slowly around the desks so that you are standing behind and between the two students. Then, slowly move down between them so that your elbow is on the table and you are facing the first student. This isolates the backtalker.

Once isolated, the backtalker usually folds. Stay down and wait until you have a stable commitment to work. Thank the student as you normally would, and then stay down to ensure that he or she keeps working. Then, turn toward the second student and repeat the process. Next, stand between them for two relaxing breaths before moving around to the front. From there, move out as usual.

Camping out from behind actually happens most often as a low-key interaction when you are working the crowd. If, for example, you were *behind* the disruptive students, you would probably just stroll over and stand between them. You might even lean down to give a prompt just to make your presence felt. I can remember teachers doing this when I was a kid. Camping out from behind has been around for a long time.

Curve Balls

Sometimes, just as you relax, thinking that the backtalk is over, a student hits you with something that you did not expect. If your relaxation is less than it should be, this jolt may send you over the edge. As always, to be forewarned is to be forearmed. The two most common curve balls are: *the last hurrah* and *the cheap shot.*

The Last Hurrah

After the backtalk dies out and the disruptive student returns to work, thank the student as a closure message to indicate that the "incident" is over. Sometimes, however, the student does not want the "incident" to be over. At such times, your "thank you" may trigger a "snotty" comeback from the student that I have named "the last hurrah." See if you recognize any of these examples.

Teacher: "Thank you, Donna."

Donna: "Yeah, right," *or*

"You didn't help me any," *or*

"Just leave me alone," *or*

"Whatever," *or*

"Thank you, Donna." (mockingly)

This mouthy student would love to have the last word, and if you were to "lose it," that would be just icing on the cake. Instead, stay down, take two relaxing breaths, and deliver some withering boredom as you wait.

If the kid had kept quiet, you would be gone. Instead, you are still at "palms," or "camping out." As always, if backtalk fails to get a "rise" out of the teacher, it backfires.

After the student once again returns to the assignment and shows a stable pattern of work, thank him or her once again just as you did before. The student will most likely remain silent this time. This "thank you" is rich in meaning. Call it *metacommunication.* It says:

- *That* is what I wanted;
- You can relax now;
- We will do it my way, won't we?

As always, finesse allows you to be gentle while being powerful. In addition, it places you above the student's pettiness and game playing.

The Cheap Shot

Sometimes as you *turn your back* to walk away after thanking the disruptor, the student hits you with a parting "cheap shot." It is usually just a word or two muttered under the breath, such as:

"Big deal," *or*

"Ooooh." *or*

"I'm scared."

You need a plan. If you are trying to figure out what to do as classmates giggle, you will probably overreact.

Naturally, you cannot allow the student to have a mocking "last word." On the other hand, it would be nice to keep your response cheap. The most efficient response, called "Instant Replay," simply repeats *moving in* and *moving out* with a few slight alterations.

Stop when you hear the *cheap shot,* take a relaxing breath, and turn slowly to face the student. The student already knows at this point that the gamble has backfired. The gamble was that you would pretend not to hear the remark and *keep walking* while the student got the last word.

It is just as foolish to turn a 'deaf ear' to disruption as it is to turn a 'blind eye.'

It is just as foolish to turn a *deaf ear* to disruption as it is to turn a *blind eye.* You will have to deal with the *cheap shot,* and you will have to invest enough time to convey that it is serious.

Walk to the edge of the student's desk so that you barely touch it with your legs as you normally would in *moving in,* and take two relaxing breaths. Then, slowly move down to "palms." Now, just kill time from close range. The longer you stay, the higher the cost of *the cheap shot* becomes. Had the student remained quiet, you would be gone.

After you get a stable commitment to work, thank the student and stay down. Then, stand, take a relaxing breath or two, and move out. It is extremely unlikely that the *cheap shot* will be repeated. You have made your point. Cheap shots are *not cheap.*

One wrinkle in this plan occurs when the disruptive students are of the same gender so that you cannot tell from the voice who made the remark. Never overplay your hand by pretending to know more than you actually do. The students know that you couldn't tell who spoke.

Finesse the situation by going to palms between the two students so that you camp out "in the general vicinity." Then, when you thank the students for getting back to work, speak collectively. Just say,

> "I appreciate your getting back to work."

If one of them says, "I didn't do it," relax and give them a dose of withering boredom.

Post Script

As a post script to this detailed discussion of camping out, you should know that having to camp out is an extreme rarity. I felt obligated to go into detail so that you would not find yourself in the middle of an altercation thinking, "Oh great, Dr. Jones! Now what do I do?"

However, if you have established that you mean business, management is done with subtle gestures and small consequences. One of my trainees spoke for many others when she said,

> "I finally went to camping out just to see what it felt like. When you are using the rest of the system, you almost never even have to walk over to the students."

Nasty Backtalk

Nasty backtalk definitely increases the price of playing poker. We will refer to it as "high-rolling." The student is risking all in order to get control.

What separates nasty backtalk from whiny backtalk is not so much the words, but rather, the fact that it is *personal.* The backtalker is probing for a nerve ending. Experienced teachers know the following:

Never take anything a student says personally.

If you take what was said personally, you are very likely to overreact. If you do, the student has succeeded.

There are two major types of nasty backtalk: *insult* and *profanity*. Once again, to be familiar with them reduces the element of surprise.

Insult

There are a limited number of topics that students can use for insults. The main ones are:

- **Dress**

  "Say, where did you get that tie, Mr. Jones? Goodwill?"

  "Hey, Mr. Mickelson, is that the only sport coat you own?"

- **Grooming**

  "Hey, Mr. Gibson, you have hairs growing out of your nose. Did you know that?"

  "Whoa, Mrs. Wilson! You have dark roots! I didn't know you bleached your hair. Ha ha ha."

- **Hygiene**

  "Hey, don't get so close. You smell like garlic."

  "Hey, Mrs. Phillips, your breath is worse than my dog's!"

Are you ready to ring the kid's neck yet? That is the point, after all.

Take two relaxing breaths. When the sniggering dies down, the kid is still on the hook. If you are in your *cortex*, you can make a plan. Right now I am not so much concerned with your plan as I am with the fact that you are in your cortex.

Profanity

There are a limited number of swear words that students can use in the classroom. Chances are, you are familiar with all of them. There are your everyday vulgarisms, and then there are your "biggies."

Now, ask yourself, what is the real agenda underlying vulgarity? As always, it has to do with *power*. The question of power boils down to a question of *control*. Who controls the classroom? This in turn boils down to the question of who controls *you*.

Can a four-letter monosyllable control *you* and determine your emotions and your behavior? If so, then the student possesses a great deal of power packaged in the form of a single word.

Relax, tune out, and make the student do all of the work.

You know that, if you give Larry this much power, he will use it. And, if control comes quickly and predictably, he will use it again and again.

Responding to Nasty Backtalk

To understand the management of backtalk, and especially nasty backtalk, you must conceptualize your response in terms of *two* time frames, *short-term* and *long-term.* The short-term time frame is *very* short: two or three seconds.

Short-Term Response

The correct short-term response, as you might imagine, has to do with the fight-flight reflex. Take two relaxing breaths, remain quiet, and deliver some withering boredom.

If you are in your cortex, you can use good judgement and choose a long-term response that fits the situation. If, however, you are in your brainstem, judgement is out of the question. Consequently, if you succeed in the short-term, you will probably succeed in the long-term. But, if you fail in the short-term, all is lost.

Your *lack* of an immediate response is very powerful body language. It tells the student, among other things, that you are no rookie. You have heard it all a thousand times.

If the student runs out of gas and takes refuge in getting back to work, you have "finessed" the incident (and gotten somewhat lucky). Count your blessings, and consider getting on with the lesson. You can always talk to the student after class.

"It is hard for students to blame anyone else when they are the only ones 'out of line.'"

Do not worry that students will think, "Mr. Jones didn't do anything about Larry's profanity." Give them some credit for social intelligence. They just saw Larry try "the big one" and fail. They saw you handle it like an old pro. And they learned that profanity is useless in this classroom as a tool for getting the best of the teacher.

They will certainly know that profanity is not taken lightly when, on the way out of class, you say, "Larry, I would like to speak with you for a moment." Of course, you need to be standing in the doorway when you say this.

Long-Term Response

Your short-term response does not foreclose any management options. It simply gives you time to think while avoiding the Cardinal Error.

In the long-term, you can do whatever you think is appropriate. You know your options. If in your opinion the student should be sent to the office or suspended, then *do it.* Just do it calmly.

If you are calm, your actions come across with an air of cool professionalism. You are above the storm.

This calm helps students accept responsibility for their own actions. Of course, this is the last thing they want to do. They would love to have a nail upon which to hang responsibility so it is not *their* fault. If you are the least bit "out of line" by becoming upset, you have just provided that nail. However, it is hard for students to blame someone else when *they* are the only ones acting badly.

The Clinical Dimension

Imagine a situation in which a student says some ugly things in the middle of class, and you finesse the situation so that the student falls silent and returns to work. Imagine also that you keep the student after class for a talk. What do you say?

For starters, let's consider the context. When the student used insult or profanity, was he or she acting in a typical or an atypical fashion? Let's imagine a student who was acting *atypically*.

If you take the student's remarks personally, your upset will get in the way of your thinking. If, on the other hand, you are in your cortex, you can engage in problem solving. With even some simple clinical skills, you can do a lot of good.

The student is upset about something, but that something is probably *not you* since you have not seen this student for the past 23 hours. Chances are, he or she is upset about something that happened outside of class.

I would certainly want to know what that something was before I went to "consequences." Otherwise, I would run a very high risk of heaping one hurt on top of another.

A Therapeutic Conversation

When you have a conversation with the student after the others have left, you become a clinician. Being a clinician is straightforward in a simple situation like this.

People seek therapy for one reason; they are in *pain*. They seek one outcome: the *alleviation* of pain. These two simple realities give you your starting point for a conversation about the inappropriate behavior in class.

> "Vanessa, what you said in class today was not at all like you. Tell me, what is really going on?"

Take two relaxing breaths and thwart the desire to say anything else. This is called "wait time." You do not know what will happen next. You can open the door, but you cannot make Vanessa walk through it. She might say,

> "Nothing! I just want to leave!"

But, before you go to "consequences," play for time. Silence is truly golden since young people have a very low tolerance for it. If you wait calmly, the whole story will probably come spilling out. Do not be surprised if the lip starts to quiver. Have some tissues handy.

After Vanessa spills her story, you may want to give her a pass to the nurse's office so that she can pull herself together before reporting to her next class. Make sure she knows that you will be available after school. Do not be surprised if she shows up.

> **Minimizing Stress**
>
> **While there are many types of backtalk, fortunately, there is only one immediate response.**
>
> **Take two relaxing breaths.**
>
> **You protect yourself from stress while you protect the student from making matters worse.**

A Different Relationship

Over the years, I have had more than a few trainees who, when faced with exactly this situation, had the presence of mind to "open the door." One teacher spoke for them all when she said,

"I would be lying if I were to say that I was relaxed after what that student said to me in class. I kept him back as you suggested, but part of me just wanted to send him to the office. I forced myself to ask him what the 'real' problem was. I took some semi-relaxing breaths. Then, he began to spill the beans.

"I kept the next class in the hall for a minute while he pulled himself together. That was the turning point in our relationship. He has been a different child in my class from that day until now."

Young people need adults to look up to. Sometimes, all they get from the adults at home is verbal and physical abuse. But their hunger for positive adult role models can be used for healing if you know how.

Vanessa was upset in class today, obviously enough. But, she was also instinctively testing you to see if you were as uncaring as other adults in her life. She probably expected the worst – an angry teacher and a trip to the office. It would not have surprised her.

What does surprise students in this situation is to find a teacher who says, "I can see that you are hurting. Tell me about it." It catches them off guard. Sometimes their defenses crumble because they are so unaccustomed to anybody caring about whether or not they hurt.

Sometimes, healing is mediated by simply taking the time to ask and to listen. Without going that far out on a limb, you can answer the defining question in your relationship with the child, *"Do you even care?"*

The ultimate goal of Meaning Business is reconciliation.

Reconciliation

Power is not the goal of Meaning Business. Power is a means to an end. It is simply a tool that can be used for good or ill.

The goal of Meaning Business is *reconciliation.* Our calmness and skill allow us to say "no" to backtalk while potentially *strengthening* the fabric of our relationship with the student rather than tearing it.

An interaction with another human being is more pregnant with possibilities the more emotionally intense it is. A student's crisis in class, therefore, presents us with a rare opportunity. Depending upon our calmness and skill, we can often turn this crisis toward a constructive end.

In everyday child rearing, the heart-to-heart talks that are remembered usually come on the heels of a crisis of some kind – usually accompanied by tears. These heart-to-heart talks are some of the most precious moments between adult and child. They teach important lessons within a context that says that being "bad," while it leads to real consequences, cannot threaten the bond of caring.

If we react from our brainstem, as the student's parents might, we confirm the student's worst expectations. But if we have the presence of mind to simply ask and listen, we can open the door to a different way of relating.

Chapter Nineteen

Dealing with the Unexpected

Playing with Finesse

Adjustments

The description of Meaning Business presented up until now is both illuminating and limiting. In order to get a clear picture of the dialogue in body language between teacher and student, the flow of events in the classroom has been simplified. In real classrooms life is unpredictable.

Adjustments are part of playing any game – just as a football or basketball player must continually adjust to changes in the other team's offense or defense. The present chapter deals with some of the adjustments you may need to make with the general pattern of Meaning Business.

No Prescriptions

This book, and this section of the book in particular, is free of *prescriptions.* Most other discipline management programs are comprised of prescriptions. "If the student does *this,* you do *that.*"

Instead of laying the groundwork for good decision making, prescriptions preempt decision making by dictating consequences. They actually prevent adjustments to the specifics of the moment.

Fundamentals and Basic Plays

Rather than being prescriptive, effective discipline management is dynamic. It involves the complex give-and-take that we have characterized as an indoor sport.

Preview

- Sometimes with body language you get the opposite of what you expect. You may think, *It's not working.* But body language is always "working."
- People act in a bizarre fashion for a reason. Atypical responses to *Meaning Business* can teach us a great deal about the student if we know how to read the message.
- This chapter describes variations of Limit Setting for use when *needy* students or *explosive* students do the opposite of what you expect. It also describes adjustments to Limit Setting for *group* disruptions that allow you to remain in control.
- This chapter also examines the natural limitations of body language in managing behavior. Understanding these limitations will allow us to transition seamlessly to other procedures when they are better suited to the task.

This book clarifies both the fundamentals of the game and the basic plays. During the game, however, you must react and adjust as the game unfolds. If your management system gives you an adequate range of options, and if you are in your cortex, you will probably make a good call.

Crucial choices cannot be made from the sidelines. I certainly cannot sit in my office a thousand miles away and prescribe exactly what you should do with a student I have never seen in a classroom I have never visited.

However, some anomalies are more common than others. Here are some examples of Meaning Business that are "outside of the box." Hopefully, they will serve as useful precedents when it comes time to improvise.

> **Body language is always "working." But sometimes it produces a surprising result.**

Proximity Triggers Clinging

The Opposite of What You Expect

It was the first week of school, and the first grade teacher was just getting to know her students. She was working the crowd as the students did an art project at their desks. One little boy, who seemed quite immature, was fooling around at his desk, off in his own little world. The teacher stood at the child's desk for a moment waiting to be noticed.

When the boy failed to look up, the teacher bent down and rested one hand on the desktop in order to give him a prompt. When the student looked up and saw the teacher's arm in front of him, he wrapped his arms around her forearm and rubbed his face against her sleeve. He continued to do this for nearly five seconds.

Sometimes in body language you get the opposite of what you expect. If you only know the basics of body language, you may think, *"It's not working."* But body language is always "working." Sometimes, however, it produces a surprising result.

A Neon Sign

Israel Goldiamond, a psychologist at the University of Chicago, used to have a saying concerning the symptomatology of clinical disorders. He would say, "A symptom is a neon sign pointing to its own cure." To our group of young psychologists he explained, "If a person is acting in a bizarre fashion, it is for a reason. What do they get for this behavior? Whatever it is, they must want it very badly. Find out what it is, and make sure that they can only get it by acting appropriately."

Dr. Goldiamond's analysis proved unerringly true. You would do well to take it to heart.

When a child in your classroom acts in a bizarre or atypical fashion, the child is telling you a great deal about his or her life. If you can decode the message, you can understand what would otherwise seem inexplicable. And you will have the beginning of a treatment program.

Terry Cloth Mothers

When the child described above wrapped his arms around the teacher's forearm and rubbed his face on her sleeve, the image that came to mind was of baby monkeys and their terry cloth mothers. This image is embossed in the memory of any student who has ever taken an introductory course in psychology.

Baby monkeys who were deprived of their mothers' presence made surrogate mothers out of the softest object they could find. That object was a terry cloth towel. They would curl up on it and rub against it in an effort to derive the touch that they were being denied.

Like the baby monkeys, children who are socially deprived often seek attention and touch in ways that we might consider bizarre. As a result, they read body language differently than normal children do.

Indiscriminate Responding

To understand the behavior of the needy first-grader in our example, think of him as being "starved for attention." Starvation provides us with the perfect analogy.

Imagine yourself going to a new restaurant. Have you ever read through the entire menu two or three times before finally making your selection? This is the behavior of a well-fed person. You are *highly discriminating.*

Imagine, in contrast, that you had not eaten in a week. Someone offers you some food – the only food available – a turkey sandwich. Can you imagine yourself saying, "No, thank you. I prefer roast beef."?

To the contrary, you would probably "wolf it down" caring only that it was food. Under conditions of severe deprivation, we become *indiscriminate* consumers.

When children suffer from severe neglect, they become indiscriminate consumers of adult proximity and attention. They fail to read the nuances of body language that would signal approval versus disapproval – something that normal children do automatically. Rather, they "wolf it down" caring only that an adult is close enough to provide touch.

Goldiamond's Rule

"A symptom is a neon sign pointing to its own cure."

Dealing with Extreme Attention Seeking

When things go completely awry, it makes even the most experienced teachers feel as though they have somehow done something wrong. However, these situations are laden with information that can give us more effective ways of responding to that situation the next time.

The little boy's strange body language told us much that was sad about his life. His extreme neediness has neglect written all over it. As Dr. Goldiamond said, "People are bizarre for a reason."

Understand the reason, and you will have the beginning of a treatment program. Unfortunately, the treatment program is not always pleasant for us.

When we perceive the extreme neediness of deprived children, we instinctively want to heal them. We want to somehow give them the attention and love that they have been denied in order to make them whole. This is *magical thinking* on our part, and it can be destructive.

Since these children are so needy of human interaction, literally *any* interaction that you have with them will be *reinforcing.* Beware! It will reinforce whatever is happening at the time of the interaction.

If, for example, you were to interact with the boy described above because he was whining or crying or hitting, you would inadvertently reinforce whining or crying or hitting. The intent of your interaction is irrelevant. The fact that these children are indiscriminate consumers of your attention means that normal behavior on your part can easily function as a reinforcement error.

Meaning Business, therefore, can produce the opposite of what we would expect. Not being able to discriminate disapproval, the child may act inappropriately *more often* in the future in order to get the proximity that comes with your limit setting.

As students get older, their attention seeking can acquires a more antisocial flavor. Yet, whether clingy or acting out, students with an extreme need for attention will probably be present in any classroom in which you teach. Rather than giving your attention to these children unconditionally, you must be *very guarded.*

Since Meaning Business can produce a paradoxical response from such children, you will need a different way of dealing with their misbehavior – one that does not rely on the physical proximity of Meaning Business. The following section of this book – Responsibility Training – will give you an alternative approach.

Explosive Students

Invading Personal Space

Meaning Business could be seen as an invasion of the student's personal space. This invasion is subtle when you lean down to give a prompt, but it is beyond subtle by the time you go to "camping out."

In previous chapters we have imagined a *typical* student. However, some students have an atypically large personal space. They go on "alert" before you even reach their desks. Put any child with a history of physical abuse into this category.

If you go to "palms" with these students, they may get extremely agitated to the point of "losing it." Your use of physical proximity has now become a liability rather than a useful tool.

Parry Reflex

Fortunately, you can usually tell when you are dealing with students who have a history of physical abuse because their body language warns you. When you get too close, they exhibit a *parry reflex.* Parry reflexes have a lot to do with children being hit.

To parry a blow is to deflect it so that it misses you. A parry reflex is a characteristic human reflex to ward off a blow to the head. Raise your arm suddenly so that your

The parry reflex wards off a blow to the head.

forearm shields your head as you duck, and you will have mimicked a parry reflex.

The beginning of the parry reflex usually consists of clenched fists and a flexing of the pectoral and shoulder muscles, particularly on the dominant side. The student's facial expression is typically grim with eyes fixed on you. If you are right-handed, you can mimic this part of the response by bringing your right elbow into your side and raising your right shoulder slightly as you tense the muscles across your chest.

While you rarely see the student's hands as you *move in* because they are under the desk, you can usually see tensing in the chest and shoulder area, especially if the student is wearing a T-shirt. This preparation to raise the arm in defense should serve as a warning to you. This student will get highly anxious if you get much closer.

Adjusting Your Proximity

You do not *need* to approach the edge of the student's desk, nor do you *need* to bend down to give a prompt, much less stay at "palms." These are choices you make.

You could stand a foot away from the student's desk as you take your relaxing breath. And, you could prompt from a standing position. You could even turn your body slightly to make the interaction less confrontational.

Remember, body language is not a technique that must be repeated in the same way every time as in a practice exercise. Rather, it is a form of communication that must be tailored to the needs of the specific situation.

Proximity is simply a tool in body language. Any human interaction is more *intense* the closer two individuals are to each other. If the interaction needs more intensity, proximity is a good way to get it. Getting a "typical student" to quit playing games and get to work is a case in point.

If, however, the intensity of the interaction is already higher than you want, you can limit intensity by limiting your proximity. Time is on your side even though less intense interactions take a little longer to get results.

Proximity

Any human interaction is more *intense* the closer two individuals are to each other. If the interaction needs more intensity, proximity is a good way to get it.

If, however, the intensity of the interaction is already higher than you want, you can limit intensity by limiting your proximity.

Rude Surprises

Imagine that you lean down to give a young man a prompt only to have him bolt out of his chair and yell, "Get out of my face!" His chair clatters across the floor as he fixes you in his stare.

You don't always see it coming. Some students can stifle their emotions up to the last moment. A situation can sometimes blow up in your face without the warning that body language usually provides.

What do you do? Actually, this is a simple question, and, by this point in the book, you can probably give me the answer. Take two relaxing breaths, stand slowly, check your jaw, and wait. Follow the general strategy for dealing with the unexpected, *When in doubt, do nothing.* Your emotions are contagious. If you are calm, you will have a calming effect.

As you relax and wait, the young man will give himself the extra space that he needs. He will typically pace nervously as he settles down. At some point the student usually begins to feel awkward as he stands in the middle of the room with everyone watching. You may wish to reduce the awkwardness by gently motioning toward his seat.

Of course, the student could just bolt out of the room. Who can predict?

Do not feel as though you have done something wrong. Bolting and running is simply a primitive coping mechanism. The choice of coping mechanisms reveals the level of the student's social-emotional development. You have just received a lot of diagnostic information about this particular student.

Initiate the school policy for a student leaving class without permission, and continue to take your relaxing breaths. You can assess your long-term strategy in a minute.

Adjusting As You Go

No amount of experience can prevent some rude surprises during your years of teaching. The needy student and the explosive student are just two of the more predictable types that will require you to make adjustments in the heat of the moment. Here are some additional examples of improvising that will stretch our understanding of the body language of Meaning Business.

> **What Do I Do When...**
>
> In any surprise situation, the answer is always the same: *Slow down, take two relaxing breaths and remember:*
>
> *When in doubt, do nothing.*

Multiple Disruptions

Sometimes when a student makes a joke or wisecrack, everybody tries to get in on the act. In seconds laughter and "smart" remarks are coming from all directions. What do you do?

This dilemma does not fit neatly into any management niche. If the banter is good-natured, which it often is, you can afford to "go with the flow." Then you might try the following gambit which is cheap, although a little unorthodox.

Before you get into setting limits, try disrupting the disruption by talking over it. Simply place your body in the middle of the action and start expounding in some intelligent-sounding way.

> "What you said was pretty funny, Mark. And, it looks like the group thought so, too. But, your remark made a point. You'll remember, class, that we were talking about..., and the issue before us was... Let's go back to the point Jennifer made just a minute ago...."

By the time you have finished with this intelligent-sounding *blah, blah, blah,* you probably have everyone's attention. Having wrestled the attention away from Mark, you can then direct it to whichever topic or student you choose.

Heckling from Behind

Imagine that you are at palms with a disruptive student when you hear heckling from behind you.

> "Hey, what are you picking on her for? She wasn't doing anything."

This situation may seem outrageous, but it is really just a variation on a theme. Two students are double-teaming you. The accomplice who is going two-on-one just happens to be somewhere in the room other than sitting next to the backtalker.

We described your response to being double-teamed in the previous chapter. You isolate one of the students so that you can go one-on-one. Deal with the two students in sequence, one at a time.

Use the same strategy with heckling from behind. Rather than responding to the heckling when it occurs, stay with the first student until you have closure, complete with "thank you" and some additional monitoring. Then, stand slowly and turn in a regal fashion toward the second student.

In most cases the second student will have already fallen silent because the strategy to "divide and conquer" failed. When you face the second student, relax and wait to see if he or she will return to work. Usually the heckler will return to work since there is nothing to be gained by upping the ante at this point. If the heckler returns to work, you can afford to simply cruise in that direction as part of working the crowd rather than "moving in" to set limits.

Repeat Disruptions

Some students are what I will call "repeaters." No matter how effectively you deal with the disruption in the short-term, they start up again as soon as your back is turned.

These kids typically come from homes in which "no" *never* means "no." Rather, the parents just nag and then go about their business without ever following through to make sure that the child did what they were told.

These children learn to simply pause for a moment until the parent turns away before resuming their activity. They cannot imagine that they have to actually *stop* what they are doing because an adult tells them to.

When you have to set limits on a student again for the same behavior within a short period of time, a warning flag should go up in your brain. When you see it for a third time, you have a pattern. Meaning Business is obviously not working. It is time to switch strategies.

Meaning Business Is Part of a System

Different Procedures for Different Jobs

Meaning Business as we have described it in the preceding chapters is only one element among many in an effective discipline management program. It is not a cure-all.

Successful classroom management will always require a system. This system must have different procedures that do different jobs. When you reach the limit of a procedure's effectiveness, you will want to transition seamlessly into a new procedure.

Beyond Meaning Business

The next section of the book is entitled Responsibility Training. Responsibility Training performs those tasks that Limit Setting is not designed to perform.

For example, our research data showed that, as soon as teachers sat down to do small group instruction, disruptions in the remainder of the class tripled as time-on-task plummeted. When you sit down, both *working the crowd* and *limit setting* are "out the window." To manage this situation you will need Responsibility Training.

Here's another management dilemma. How do you train students to be ready to start class when the bell rings and to hustle during lesson transitions? These two things could save you ten minutes of learning time per class period. Once again, you will need Responsibility Training.

Responsibility Training might well be regarded as more central to discipline management than even Limit Setting. When you train students to be responsible, they learn to manage themselves. Isn't that our real objective? Besides, it's cheaper. When students manage themselves, you don't have to do it for them.

Section Seven

Producing Responsible Behavior

Chapter Twenty

Building Cooperation

Preview

- A teacher needs cooperation many times a day from every student in the class. Whenever students fail to cooperate, the teacher's job is made more difficult.
- Cooperation is voluntary – a gift. Before students will give the teacher all of the cooperation that is required during a school day, the teacher must repeatedly answer one simple question, "Why should I?"
- The answer to the question, "Why should I?" is called an incentive. Teachers will need incentives that teach the entire class to be responsible – even the oppositional and highly irresponsible students.
- This incentive system must increase learning time while costing the teacher almost nothing in terms of time and effort.
- This incentive system is called Responsibility Training.

Teachers Need Cooperation

Starting vs. Stopping Behavior

Behavior management is conceptually simple. There are only two things you can do with a behavior. You can *increase* it, or you can *decrease* it. If you consistently increase the behaviors you want and consistently decrease the behaviors you do not want, sooner or later you will be left with what you want.

Getting students to *stop* disrupting, therefore, is only half of discipline management. Getting students to *start* doing what they *should* be doing is the other half.

This section of the book will focus on getting students to do what they *should* be doing. How do you train the class to be in their seats ready to go when the bell rings – to hustle rather than dawdle during lesson transitions – to do what you ask the first time you ask for it? How do you build cooperation?

Teachers Need Cooperation Often

Imagine that you want all of the students in your class to:

- Show up on time
- Walk as they enter your classroom
- Bring pencils and paper
- Bring books and lab manuals
- Be in their seats when the bell rings
- Be working when the bell rings

You have just made six requests for *cooperation* from thirty students, and the class period has barely begun.

Imagine that you are a high school teacher with thirty students in each of five instructional periods. Before beginning instruction in all of these periods on a single day, you will have made *nine hundred* requests for cooperation. By the time these class periods end, you will have made *thousands* of additional requests for cooperation.

Teachers Need Cooperation from Everyone

You need cooperation from *every* student in the class, not from just the few difficult students. Even the nicest kid in your class can be far from perfect when it comes to being responsible.

Sometimes good kids are just a little flaky. Maybe when they were in the third grade and they forgot their lunch money, a parent ran it to school. And when they were in the fifth grade and forgot their homework, a parent ran it to school. They are nice kids, but they often show up without homework or lab manuals or pencils. These students collectively can cause you just as much stress and extra work as Larry.

Teachers Need Perfection

Simply *improving* the level of cooperation from students is a hollow victory. Let's imagine that you have four students who repeatedly forget to bring pencils. Let's imagine that you institute a management program that reduces the problem by 50 percent. You could publish that result in any journal.

So what! You still have to hassle with pencils at the beginning of every class period. But, now you have an extra management program to operate. As a result of the intervention, your workload has *increased.* At a practical level your life does not get any better until the problem goes away.

Consequently, in the building of cooperative behavior, I am not much interested in *improvement.* Rather, I am interested in *solving the problem* so that the problem disappears. I am interested in *every* student in the class being responsible *all of the time.*

Remedial Child Rearing

Consider the Starting Point

To gain a perspective on the scope of your job in training the class to be responsible, take a quick mental survey. Before your students came to school this morning, how many of them, do you think, did the following?

- Made their beds as soon as they got up
- Hung up their pajamas
- Helped set the breakfast table
- Cleaned up their breakfast dishes
- Hustled getting ready for school so they would not make themselves or their parents late

After your students get home this evening, how many of them, do you think, will do the following?

- Hang up their jackets
- Do chores without having to be reminded
- Help set and clean up the dinner table
- Start their homework without an argument
- Head up to bed on time
- Put their dirty clothes in the hamper

Let's See You Do Any Better

Here is a depressing statistic – *half of the human race is below average.* Not surprisingly, this statistic applies to the *parenting skills* of the parents of the students in your class. Some parents are *one* standard deviation below average.

Some parents are *two* standard deviations below average. And Larry's parents are *way* below average. They can't get Larry to the dinner table in a timely fashion without nagging, even though the kid is already hungry and the parents are using food as a reinforcer.

On the first day of school, members of the community will bring all of their accumulated childrearing problems into your class, dump them on your desk and say, in effect,

> "Let's see if *you* can get that kid to do some work. I can't even get him to make his bed!"

With your class of thirty students, you will be expected to get more cooperation out of them every day than their parents can get under the best of circumstances. And you will want it for the asking.

The Joys of Irresponsibility

Cooperation Is a Gift

If students do something as simple as showing up to your class on time, do not take it for granted. They have cut short several pleasurable activities in order to do it. They have cut short joking around in the lavatory. They have cut short talking with their friends at their lockers. They have cut short saying goodbye to their boyfriends or girlfriends for the fourth time today.

They have cut short all of these innocent pleasures so that they could show up to your class on time where you will *put them to work*. You should be grateful.

> **Is Virtue Its Own Reward?**
>
> In the classroom goofing off is its own reward. Goofing off is always the easy, pleasurable alternative to being "on the ball."

The difficult thing about managing cooperation is that cooperation is *voluntary*. It is a gift. You cannot *force* someone to cooperate. If you tried, you would get *coercion*, the opposite of cooperation.

Cooperation requires a *decision* to cooperate on the part of the student. The management of cooperation in the classroom, therefore, focuses on supplying the students with a good reason to make that decision.

Is Virtue Its Own Reward?

Are you familiar with the saying, *"Virtue is its own reward?"* I simply want to impress upon you the fact that this statement *does not apply to classroom management.*

Quite the opposite is true. *Goofing off* is its own reward. Goofing off is always the easy, pleasurable alternative to being "on the ball."

Consider the problems that teachers face in getting students to do something as simple as bringing pencils to class. Put yourself in the students' shoes.

Remember on the first day of the semester when your English teacher said,

> "Class, we write almost every day in this class, and I do not want a constant stream of students going to the pencil sharpener. One of my basic expectations is that you bring *three sharpened pencils* to class each day."

Now it is the second day of class, and the teacher says,

> "Class, let's all get out pencil and paper."

A hand immediately goes up.

> "Yes?"

> "I don't have a pencil."

"Do you remember yesterday when I asked you to bring three sharpened pencils to class every day?"

"I forgot."

"Well...here. You can borrow mine, but I want it back at the end of the period."

Is this teacher ever going to see that pencil again? The teacher may as well kiss it good-bye before giving it to the student.

However, supplying pencils is *nothing* compared to the management of pencil *sharpening*. Imagine Larry sitting in first period on his first day of high school. Larry knows what he has gotten into. At the welcoming assembly the principal made some remarks that were interpreted by Larry as follows:

"Freshmen, let me explain high school to you. We expect you to sit in your seats for the next four years and pay attention to everything that is said because it might be on the test."

Larry has been sitting in first period for *twenty minutes,* and he is already *suffering*. Larry suffers from multiple quasi-neurological deficits like "ants in the pants." Larry looks at the clock and says to himself,

"I won't make it. I need to move. I have to move! I have 3 years, 179 days, 5 hours and 40 minutes to go. I need to move now! How can I get out of my seat and move without getting into trouble?"

Larry casts his eyes upon the lead of his pencil, and a light goes on. Larry snaps his lead as his hand raises.

"May I please sharpen my pencil?"

The teacher responds,

"Use one of your other pencils."

Larry casts his eyes upon the lead of his pencil, and a light goes on.

Larry responds,

"I don't have another pencil."

The teacher says, pointing to the pencil sharpener,

"Well then, hurry!"

This is not looking good. On the first day of school the teacher was *telling* the students to bring three sharpened pencils to class. It is only the second day of school, and the teacher is already *begging* students to hurry.

Does Larry hurry? It is a comedy routine.

Larry may have the state record in the 100 meters, but the speed with which he moves toward the pencil sharpener is known in Hollywood as "slow-mo." On his way to the pencil sharpener, Larry forgets his goal in life and stops to whisper to a friend.

"Larry, would you please leave him alone and simply get your pencil sharpened and get back to your seat?"

"What?"

Have you ever looked at the work kids turn in these days and wondered, *"What will happen to this country in the next 50 years?"* When you watch Larry sharpen his pencil, you know that the future is in good hands. It's inspirational.

He cranks the handle and then holds the pencil up to the light to check the point. He sharpens it some more. He checks it again. Larry is working to tolerances of 1/1000th of an inch. He could go to work building jet engines tomorrow.

When the pencil lead finally passes rigid quality control standards, Larry heads back to his seat – by the most circuitous route imaginable.

"Larry! Would you get away from the window and return to your seat?"

"What?"

When Larry finally takes his seat, watch how long it takes him to get going. The shoulders need to be stretched. Every knuckle needs to be cracked. The writing hand makes several passes over the paper as though on a reconnaissance mission. Finally, he begins to write. It has been *five minutes* since Larry asked to sharpen his pencil.

Now ask yourself, why would Larry bring three sharpened pencils to class if it meant that he would no longer have an excuse to stretch his legs whenever he felt like it? Larry may not be a whiz in school, but he is not *stupid*.

Why Should I?

If Larry and all of his classmates are to give you all of the cooperation that you need class period after class period, day after day, you must answer one simple question. That question is: "*Why should I?*" As you may remember from chapter 9, "Creating Motivation," the answer to the question, "Why should I?" is called an *incentive*.

In the classroom, you will need incentives for work productivity, and you will need incentives for rule following. Chapter 9 dealt with incentives for *work productivity*. This section will deal with incentives for *rule following*. (Since the fundamentals for both are the same, this would be a good time to reread chapter 9.)

He's Not Stupid

Why would Larry bring three sharpened pencils to class if it meant that he would no longer have an excuse to stretch his legs whenever he felt like it? Larry may not be a whiz in school, but he is not stupid.

Incentive systems that you would currently find in classrooms have changed very little since the 1970s. These management programs typically represent a lot of work for the teacher while accomplishing only limited objectives.

If we want to answer the question, "Why should I?" for the *entire class* throughout the *entire school day*, we must become far more sophisticated in the design and implementation of classroom incentive systems. These incentive systems must accomplish *multiple objectives* simultaneously, and they must be *cheap*. The entire program must represent a *reduction* of the teacher's workload.

To achieve this level of cost-effectiveness, we will need to break new ground in the design of classroom incentive systems. In order to gain a fresh perspective, let's think for a moment about raising responsible teenagers.

Traditional classroom incentive systems typically represent a lot of work for the teacher while accomplishing only limited objectives.

A Model for Building Responsibility

Learning to Be Responsible with Money

Imagine that you have a teenage son, and you want him to be responsible with money. After all, soon he will have to manage his own affairs. What is the first thing that your teenager must have before he can learn to be responsible with money? When I ask this question to a roomful of teachers, they respond in unison,

"Money."

Indeed, in order to learn money management, you must have money to manage.

Where does the teenager get the money? In fact, that is the *least* critical aspect of the incentive system. Your teenager can work after school, or you can give him money in the form of an allowance. Both will work just fine if critical aspects of the incentive system are in place.

My parents gave me an allowance when I was in high school. I remember the lecture.

"Your job is going to school. With your extracurricular activities, you barely have enough time for homework as it is. We will give you an allowance. Payday will be Sunday. You will have to pay for school lunches, dates, burgers with your buddies, and tux rental for your winter and spring formals."

When my wife, Jo Lynne, and I had teenage sons, we used the same system. It worked fairly well, but not without a few glitches. Imagine the following scene. One Friday after dinner our older son Patrick approached me with a proposition.

"Dad, can I have ten bucks until Sunday? I'm just a little short this week. I'll pay you back, I promise. You can just take it out of next week's allowance."

To the uninitiated, this sounds like a reasonable proposition. My son was shocked at my response.

To learn money management, you will first need money.

"I'm sorry son, but I don't lend money. I *give* you money, but I don't *lend* money."

With apparent disbelief and imploring hand gestures, Patrick said,

"But, Dad, you don't understand. It's only until Sunday."

A teenager's first assumption at times like this is that you must be stupid.

"I *do* understand, son. But I still don't lend money."

"But, Dad, there's a party at Tracy's house after the game Saturday, and he just told me about it today. I need to help with food."

What's a poor guy supposed to do when things come up at the last minute?

"Sorry, son. I don't *lend* money."

"Aw, Dad...Then what am I supposed to do?"

A teenager's desperation tactic is to get you to prescribe the solution to the problem. Then you become responsible for how things turn out.

"I have no idea."

"Aw, man! I can't talk to you about anything."

Now I am a clinical psychologist with a communication problem.

"Yes, son. You *can* talk to me about anything. For example, you just asked me about a short-term loan, and you learned that the answer is, 'No.'"

As you might imagine, we shared a rather grumpy weekend with our son. "Grumpiness" is often a by-product of confronting an inconvenient reality.

Incentives Teach Lessons

Before we attempt to train a roomful of young people to be responsible, we must be clear about how to train *one* young person to be responsible. To begin with, the only thing that young people take seriously is *reality.*

You can preach, you can teach, you can beg or cajole. You can share your personal experiences or the wisdom of the ages. It will be met with a roll of the eyes that says, *"Yeah, right."* Before young people will take it upon themselves to act responsibly, they must confront a reality that demands responsible behavior.

Effective parents and teachers do not leave this reality to chance. It is possible for us to construct a somewhat artificial reality that teaches responsibility quickly and efficiently. This somewhat artificial reality is called an *incentive system.* It can teach teenagers to be responsible with small bills during high school, for example, rather than having them learn the same lesson with thousands of dollars worth of credit card debt years later.

Learning to Manage Impulses

Let's return to my son and the learning of money management during high school. In addition to understanding the pitfalls of lending, I also knew a thing or two about Patrick's spending habits.

My son's high school had an "open campus." Many students would leave campus for lunch. My son and his buddies were spending their money at "Jack's Burger Shack" rather than slumming it in the far more economical school cafeteria. To my son's youthful mind, taking out a loan to subsidize "Jack's Burger Shack" seemed reasonable.

Only when this line of reasoning "hit the wall" was my son forced to develop a new plan. The following week when his buddies said, "Hey, Pat, let's go to Jack's," my son had to consider more factors than he had the week before, not the least of which was tux rental for the upcoming winter formal.

What is crucial in money management is learning to live within a *budget.* We all want more than we can afford. The key is learning to say "no" to things we want. But impulse control requires practice. To work at it, we need a reason that is at least as strong as the impulse.

We Are All Incentive Managers

Almost everything you do as a parent or teacher creates some kind of incentive. The example of my son hitting me up for a loan is a case in point. If I say *"yes,"* I create one set of incentives. If I say *"no,"* I create another set of incentives.

If, for example, I had given Patrick an extra ten bucks on Friday, I would have:

- spared him from experiencing any new "mind-altering" reality that might lead to long-term planning.
- paid him for running out of money early as a means of increasing the money supply.

I may have a soft heart, but I don't have a soft head.

As you see from this example, we can exploit incentives to do two things at once. The *first* is to supply the children with something that they need and which, in our opinion, they should have. The *second* is to teach a lesson. The better the incentive system is designed, the quicker the lesson is learned.

Classroom Objectives

Students Waste Time

Students are expert time-wasters. They waste time all day long. They stroll into class at the last minute rather than being in their seats when the bell rings. They sharpen pencils during class time rather than sharpening them during the break. They use hall passes rather than going to the bathroom between classes. They make stretching a lesson transition into an art form.

Students could easily save enough time during a day to allow you to teach an extra lesson by doing two things:

- being in their seats with proper materials ready to begin when the bell rings instead of "settling in."
- reducing the duration of lesson transitions from five minutes to one minute.

But students have no vested interest in saving time. If they were to save you enough time to teach an extra lesson, they would get an extra lesson.

Teaching Time Management

What is the first thing that students must have in order to learn to manage time? Using money management as our analogy, the answer is, of course, *time.* The students in your class cannot learn time management until they have *time to manage.*

We must, however, teach time management to the *entire* class. Any one student can waste time for the group. It is hard to get started, for example, until everyone is seated.

Consequently, we must devise a system of *group management.* Furthermore, it must have sophisticated fail-safe mechanisms that give *every* student a reason to cooperate, *especially* Larry. We will name this system of group management *Responsibility Training.*

> **The students in your class cannot learn to manage time until they have time to manage.**

Preferred Activity Time

We Give an "Allowance" of Time

In order for the class to have time to manage, we must give the class an "allowance" of time. As with money management, the purpose of this allowance is to teach a lesson. If we structure the incentive system properly, we will be able to teach time management quickly and efficiently.

Our incentive will, of course, be built around a reinforcer – something that the students want. The time that we give them must be desired or "preferred" by the students so that, as a group, they will work for it. The only type of reinforcer that fills time is an *activity.* The allowance of time that we give to the class will, therefore, be referred to as "Preferred Activity Time" or PAT.

One question that is always asked by someone in a workshop at this point is, "What do the students have to do in order to *earn* PAT?" This question is conditioned by decades of classroom incentives that are built around Grandma's Rule: *You have to finish your dinner before you get your dessert.* It seems wrong to give the "dessert" without first seeing some work.

We have used the analogy of teaching a teenager to be responsible with money in order to get enough distance from Grandma's Rule to allow us to see incentive management through new eyes. In the design of an incentive system, sometimes you *give* in order to *get.*

I *gave* my son his allowance. He did not earn the allowance by being paid, for example, for doing chores around the house. I did not want to train him to think, "What will you pay me?" every time I asked for a little help. Chores were handled separately from the allowance.

The allowance was given for two reasons: *first,* teenagers need money, and *second,* I could exploit that need to teach money management. But the money itself was a *gift.* It was a gift with an educational purpose – as is PAT.

PAT Increases Learning Time

I have no intention of losing learning time as the price of supplying the students with PAT. Quite the opposite, I am supplying the students with a PAT in order to *increase* learning time.

As I mentioned, you can gain nearly a full instructional period during the day by simply training the class to manage two routines more responsibly: starting class on time and hustling during lesson transitions. You can gain additional instructional time during the day by eliminating traditional forms of foolishness such as showing up without pencils or sharpening pencils during class. There are many additional chores and routines during a school day that can increase learning time and reduce teacher stress if done quickly and responsibly by the group.

All of the time that you set aside for PAT, therefore, is "found time." You will *not* relinquish *one minute* of time from your instructional program. Quite the contrary, if you do not *give* the class PAT in order to teach them time management, they will *waste* the time as usual, and you will have *nothing to show for it.*

There is a second dividend to be gained from giving PAT, lest you think that this program will cost you anything. The PAT itself will *not* be time *away from* learning. Rather, you will use PAT *for* learning.

In subsequent chapters you will find that you can teach any lesson as a PAT – from skill drill to test review to vocabulary. In addition, since I cannot give you an extra planning period, it must require no extra planning time.

The Time Frame for PAT

How much time does your class need for PAT? To put it simply, you need enough time in order to do something worthwhile. Teachers might begin with 10 to 30 minutes depending on *how often* they have PAT during the week.

In the design of an incentive system, sometimes you have to give in order to get.

How often *should* you have PAT? Let's begin by defining a *time frame* for Responsibility Training. The time frame for the program runs from the *beginning* of one PAT to the *beginning* of the next PAT. Consequently, the students are always on the program, even during PAT.

The time frame for students of a given age is keyed to the amount of time that they can *delay gratification* and *exert impulse control.* It is, therefore, a function of *social maturity* rather than chronological age. Consequently, the following norms should be thought of as general guidelines that you may need to tailor to the social maturity of your particular students.

- **Kindergarten:** Kindergarten students usually have to get up and move every 15 to 20 minutes, and their level of impulse control is nothing to write home about. Consequently, a kindergarten teacher may want to have PAT every 15 or 20 minutes.

The very notion of having PAT that often would be overwhelming if PAT required much planning and effort. It is apparent from the outset that PAT must be cheap and easy for the teacher to implement.

- **First Grade:** To be conservative, you would probably want to start the first grade year with three PATs in the morning and two PATs in the afternoon. However, by midyear most first grade classes only need three a day – mid-morning, end of morning, and end of afternoon. Do not attempt to get by with only one in the morning before lunch, or you will find that the students "lose it" after 10:30.
- **Second and Third Grades:** At some time during second or third grade, most classes can go to two PATs a day – one before lunch and one at the end of the day. Fading the schedule of PATs, however, is always a judgment call. You can tell if you have been premature in thinning the schedule if you find the students "losing it" during the hour prior to PAT.
- **Fourth and Fifth Grades:** At some point during fourth or fifth grade, most classes can go to a single PAT at the end of the day. While PATs become less frequent as the students mature, it would be inaccurate to think that we are attempting to reduce the amount of PAT.

  As PATs become less frequent, they become longer. While a first grade teacher might set aside 10 minutes for each PAT three times a day, a fifth grade teacher might set aside 20 or 30 minutes for a single PAT at the end of the day.

- **Middle and High School:** While sixth grade often retains the same pattern as fifth grade, sometime before high school most classrooms go to one PAT per week. As an interim pattern, teachers may have PAT twice a week, on Wednesday and Friday.

  An alternative pattern in departmentalized settings is to have 5 to 10 minutes of PAT at the end of each class period. As such, it is typically an integral part of that day's lesson. Often, students play a learning game to review what was just taught.

Found Time

If you did not give the class PAT in order to teach them time management, they would waste the time, and you would have nothing to show for it.

Learning to Be Considerate of Others

Cooperation is a gift. In order to learn cooperation, children must be taught to give. A teacher cannot teach giving except through giving.

To say that children tend to be self-absorbed is something of an understatement. For children to consider the needs of others, they must be taught to consider the needs of others. Maturity does not come from the simple passage of time.

Responsibility Training teaches students to be considerate of others. When students waste time, they not only make the teacher's job more difficult, but they also take time from their classmates, most of whom are just sitting and waiting for activities to begin.

As teachers, some of the most important lessons we teach are lessons about life. If we understand how to design incentive systems, these lessons about life can be learned reasonably quickly and with a sense of joy. The following chapter will focus on the nuts and bolts of the design of Responsibility Training.

Chapter Twenty One

Teaching Responsibility

Preview

- While Preferred Activity Time (PAT) lays the groundwork for Responsibility Training, it is the bonus PAT that empowers students to increase the duration of PAT.
- Hurry-up Bonuses produce hustle. The time that students save by hurrying during lesson transitions and other routines is added to PAT.
- While students can earn time by hustling, they can also lose time by dawdling. This causes students to become active in managing each other's behavior.
- Automatic Bonuses eliminate the time wasting of "settling in" by giving students extra PAT for being in their seats ready to go when the bell rings.
- Responsibility Training gives teachers an effective means of managing the class during small group instruction when they are seated.

Nuts and Bolts of Training

This chapter will focus on the nuts and bolts of implementing Responsibility Training. But, for Responsibility Training to succeed, the other elements of our classroom management system must also be in place. In this chapter, therefore, we will see how the pieces of the system fit together to produce success.

The Teacher's Role

A Giver

In training students to be responsible, the teacher is first and foremost a *giver*. We give in order to teach giving – the giving of cooperation.

We will give generously. If we err, we will err in the direction of giving. If we give a little extra, no damage is done. But if we do not give enough, we can starve the program.

The teacher will give three gifts:

- **PAT:** The *first* gift that the teacher will give is *Preferred Activity Time (PAT)*. PAT does not change behavior. Rather, it sets the stage for the use of bonus PAT. Think of PAT as a "pump primer."
- **Bonus PAT:** The *second* gift that the teacher will give is *bonus PAT*. Bonus PAT changes behavior while empowering students. Bonus PAT is the heart of Responsibility Training.

- **Structure for PAT:** The *third* gift that the teacher will give is *structure for PAT*. PAT is structured time, not free time. PAT is time that is structured for learning. Its objective is to make learning fun.

A Timekeeper

Responsibility Training teaches students to be responsible with everything they do in the classroom from bringing pencils to hustling during lesson transitions. However, all of these various forms of responsible behavior can be organized under a single heading: learning to be responsible with *time*.

As mentioned in the previous chapter, students are expert time-wasters. If students were to use their time efficiently, much of the goofing off in the classroom would immediately disappear. Responsibility Training, therefore, achieves many different management objectives simultaneously by training students to manage time wisely.

As part of time management, the teacher must keep track of time. In all cases it will be *real* time – time that any student in the class could read off of the wall clock.

The Students' Role

Making Choices

The teacher gives the students time, and the students decide how the time will be spent. Students learn to take responsibility for their actions by making choices about the use of time and then living with the consequences.

Squander or Save

While students are given the power to choose how their time will be spent, their range of choices is very limited. They can:

- **Squander and be selfish:** Students can squander time by being out of their seats when the bell rings, by sharpening pencils during class, or by dawdling during lesson transitions. These various forms of time-wasting constitute little vacations from work that students take at will.

  But, these mini-vacations are not shared by the class. Rather, they are taken by individuals while the rest of the group waits. This is very selfish.

- **Save and share:** Members of the group can always choose to forego the selfishness that squanders class time, but they must have a reason to do so.

  What if the students got to *keep* the time that they usually squandered so the *whole group* could use it for something they enjoyed? This would create a vested interest in saving rather than squandering.

The time that the students save is called "bonus PAT." It is the bonus PAT that empowers the students to increase PAT by saving time.

Hurry-up Bonuses

Learning to Hustle

Hurry-up Bonuses achieve one of the most difficult objectives in all of behavior management – *training kids to hustle*. Training kids to hustle is particularly difficult when work can be avoided through dawdling.

To get a sense of how difficult it is to train kids to hustle, consider the varsity basketball team at your local high school. These kids are dedicated to basketball. They love to play.

> **Hurry-up Bonuses**
>
> Hurry-up Bonuses achieve one of the most difficult objectives in all of behavior management – training kids to hustle.

Yet, coaches throughout the country are routinely reduced to yelling in frustration,

"Come on, hustle! Let's go! Let's go! Let's go! You're just going through the motions out there!"

If you think it is difficult to get the varsity to hustle during practice, try gym class. Try math class. Try social studies.

> **People will only take responsibility for things that they control.**

An Analogy from Family Life

Hurry-up Bonuses are familiar to most of us from everyday family life. Moms and dads have used them since time began.

The most common example of a Hurry-up Bonus around the house is *the bedtime routine.* In chapter 9, "Creating Motivation," I described the bedtime routine that my parents used when I was a little kid. My mother would say:

"All right kids, it is 8:30 – time to get ready for bed. Wash your face, brush your teeth and get your pajamas on. As soon as you are in bed, it will be story time. But lights out at nine o'clock."

My brother and I well understood that the faster we moved, the more time we would have for stories. And we also knew that dawdling reduced the length of story time.

Teaching Responsibility through Empowerment

In the bedtime routine the PAT is, of course, story time. But, during the bedtime routine, who is in control of the *amount* of story time that the children receive? During training, teachers respond in unison, "The children."

Indeed, the children are in complete control. If they choose to hustle, they will maximize the duration of story time. But, if they choose to dawdle, they will reduce the duration of story time. My brother and I got into the habit of being ready *before* 8:30 so that we could have a full half-hour of stories.

Understanding the nature of a simple choice made by children at bedtime teaches us one of the most important lessons about learning to be responsible: *People will only take responsibility for things that they control.*

Making choices implies that we have some control over our destiny. If we do not control the outcome of our actions, then choice is a sham since our efforts are to no avail. Before people will learn to make wise choices, therefore, they must:

- have power
- know how to use it

Our job as teachers is *first,* to empower the students to make choices, and *then,* to teach them to make good choices. Responsibility Training, therefore, is a teaching paradigm.

Lesson Transitions

The Mechanics of a Hurry-up Bonus

One of the greatest hemorrhages of time-on-task in any classroom is the lesson transition. A lesson transition usually takes about five minutes.

During these lesson transitions students move in a most unhurried fashion as they hand in papers, sharpen pencils, get drinks, move furniture into or out of groups, and get out materials. There is utterly no sense of urgency. Obviously, students like nice big, unhurried breaks with brief lessons sandwiched in between. They know that, as soon as the transition is over, it will be time to get back to work.

Your average lesson transition can easily be accomplished in half-a-minute if the students choose to hustle. But, why would the students hustle if hustling only puts them back to work sooner?

In contrast, let's walk through a lesson transition that contains a Hurry-up Bonus.

"Class, before you get out of your seats, let me tell you what I want you to do during this lesson transition. First, hand in your papers by laying them on the corner of my desk. Then, if you need to sharpen your pencils, this is the time to do it. If you need a drink of water, this is the time to get it.

"I want my clean-up committee to erase my boards and straighten up the books on the shelf. I want everybody to pick up any paper you see laying around the room and get your desks back on their marks.

"I will give you two minutes to get this done. But you know from past experience that you can get it done in half-a-minute. So, let's see how much time you can save. All of the time you save will be added to your PAT.

"Let's check the clock. (Pause until the second hand passes the six or twelve.) Okay, let's begin."

Being Generous with Time

While it takes students half-a-minute for a typical lesson transition if they hustle, in the preceding example I gave them two minutes. As I mentioned earlier, be generous in the giving of time. If you err, err in the direction of generosity. My rule of thumb for determining the amount of time allotted for the completion of a routine is to:

Socializing is a bootleg incentive that competes with your incentive system.

- Estimate how long it would take if they hustled.
- Round that number up to the next minute.
- Double that number.

If it would take 2 to 3 minutes to clean up after a project, round up to three minutes and then double it to six.

Bootleg Reinforcement

As the students get up from their desks, you immediately begin to *work the crowd.* Your primary objective as you work the crowd is to eliminate the "bootleg reinforcement" that is part of any lesson transition.

As described in chapter 12, "Teaching Routines," bootleg reinforcement is an incentive for goofing off that is delivered by the *peer group.* Imagine, for example, three students standing around the pencil sharpener talking. The reinforcer for socializing is socializing. It is a self-reinforcing behavior.

By working the crowd, you disrupt the disruption.

This bootleg incentive system is competing with *your* incentive system, the Hurry-up Bonus. In this competition, the bootleg incentive usually wins.

One of the main characteristics of a reinforcer that determines its power is *immediacy of delivery.* The bootleg incentive usually wins the competition because it is being delivered *now,* whereas the PAT will not be delivered until much *later.*

One of your primary objectives in classroom management is to get a *monopoly on incentives.* This is done by suppressing the goofing off that is self-reinforcing. If you fail to do this, the students' bootleg incentives will constantly neutralize your management program.

Teachers get a monopoly on incentives primarily through "management by walking around." Just walk up to the students who are chatting and wait patiently. The students, well aware of what they should be doing, typically give you a self-conscious grin accompanied by some silly talk.

"I was just going to sharpen my pencil."

As the students "get on the ball," you stroll over to the four students standing around the drinking fountain and repeat the drill. As always, by working the crowd you "disrupt the disruption." In addition, by sheer proximity, you continually prompt the students to *get on the ball.*

The nemesis of working the crowd during a lesson transition is a student who says to you, "May I ask you a question?" This student could be a future Rhodes Scholar or the biggest "clinger" in the classroom. It makes no difference. Your answer is always the same.

"As soon as we are back in our seats."

During a lesson transition, you have far more important jobs to do than instruction. If you want a quick lesson transition, you must work at it. A lesson transition is perhaps the most concentrated example of classroom management during the entire school day. Thinking of it as a "break" represents a classic rookie error.

All for One, and One for All

As the lesson transition nears completion, you head to the front of the room. Imagine, however, that, as you make a final check around the room, you see some crumpled paper on the floor over by the door. Most of the students are already seated, but one student is standing near the paper. As you point, you say:

"Class, there is a piece of paper over there on the floor."

Can you imagine the student who is standing near the paper saying,

"It's not mine."

Simply look at the student and shrug. After all, it is not your problem. What do you think several classmates seated nearby will say to the student standing near the paper?

"Pick it up! Pick it up!"

Welcome to "all for one, and one for all." You have just observed peer pressure in the form that it almost always takes with Responsibility Training – *urgent whispers.*

Wrapping Up the Transition

As the last student sits down, you say,

"Thank you class for doing such a good job of cleaning up and arranging your desks. Let's check the time. You saved one minute and seventeen seconds. Let's add that to our PAT."

You walk to the board and add a minute and seventeen seconds to the PAT. The students are all smiles.

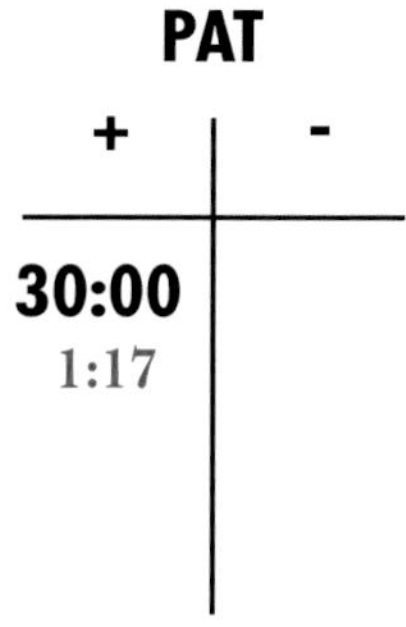

The teacher gives a Hurry-up Bonus for a quick lesson transition

The role into which you are consistently placed by Responsibility Training is *benevolent parent*. You give time, you protect time, and you congratulate the group for saving time. Your benevolence, however, is tempered by the next component of Responsibility Training, *time loss*.

Time Loss

The Lord Giveth, and the Lord Taketh Away

Our first bonus in Responsibility Training, the Hurry-up Bonus, provides us with our first view of the inner workings of discipline management as a system. The system is far more complex than the simple giving of bonuses.

The first complication with Hurry-up Bonuses results from the fact that *you can't win 'em all*. Some days, in spite of your best efforts, the Hurry-up Bonus bombs as the students run overtime. This can happen for legitimate reasons which may include any combination of the following:

- A storm front is blowing through.
- It is two days until the beginning of vacation.
- It is the full moon.

As you work the crowd during the lesson transition, you feel the time slipping away. You work the crowd and prompt the students with increased urgency, but to little avail. The students seem to be moving in slow motion.

With fifteen seconds left in the allotted time, you head to the front of the classroom. You stand calmly facing the students and look at the clock as the time runs out. Then, as you point to the clock, you say,

> "Class, you're on your *own* time now."

Relax and wait for the last student to be seated. Then say,

> "Thank you, class, for straightening up the room and getting back in your seats."

Then, after taking a second to look at the clock, walk to the board and record the time consumed under your PAT tally. The tally has two columns, one for time *gain* and one for time *loss*.

The tally in the example below would indicate that the students have saved time during two previous lesson transitions but have lost five seconds during this one. This example is actually quite representative of the proportion of time gain versus time loss in Responsibility Training.

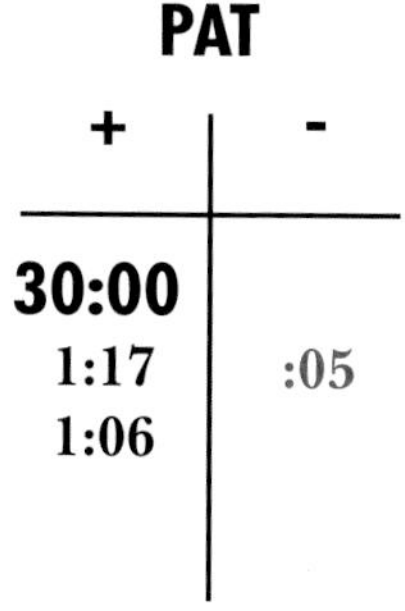

On rare occasions students lose some time due to dawdling.

As you can see, the system is *rigged* so that the students *come out ahead*. When they gain, they gain in minutes. But, if they lose, they only lose in seconds. Five seconds actually represents a rather large time loss. It usually takes only two or three seconds for students to get into their seats when several of their classmates are urgently whispering,

> *"Sit down! Sit down!"*

The time loss component of Responsibility Training is both necessary and the bane of my existence. It is necessary because Responsibility Training *does not work consis-*

tently without it. And it is the bane of my existence because it *opens the door to abuse* by poorly trained or negativistic teachers.

Time Loss Produces Consistent Success

First, let's deal with Responsibility Training working *consistently.* Responsibility Training is *group management:* all for one, and one for all. Turning management over to the peer group has significant advantages:

- Kids will do things for their peer group that they would never do for you.
- You side-step the resentment that some students harbor toward adult authority.

However, without the time *loss* component within Responsibility Training, the peer group lets you down just when you need them. The *many* do not stand up for themselves as their time is being wasted by the *few.* They just sit there and let it happen.

This tendency of the many to act like sheep comes from the natural awkwardness of any student taking a public stand for righteousness. Imagine, for example, that during a typical five-minute lesson transition, some student were to stand up and say,

> "Class, some of us are dawdling and wasting valuable learning time. I wish everyone would just hurry-up so that we could get back to work."

While voicing a noble sentiment, this "goodie-two-shoes" has just distinguished him or herself as being the biggest dweeb on the continent.

If you want students to enforce your classroom standards, you must give them a reason for doing so that does not make them look like a bunch of "goodie-two-shoes." Enlightened self-interest is the ticket. The time loss component of Responsibility Training gives the students a plausible vested interest in enforcing your standards. A student does not have to be a "suck-up" to say,

> "Sit down! You're wasting our PAT."

Of course, you would not want students to become *overzealous* with rule enforcement so that they would get nasty. Nor would you want to make any student into a scapegoat.

Don't worry. There is much less of a tendency in that direction than you might think. Here are some of the reasons that overzealousness is all but nonexistent:

- **Students will not allow it.** They look at the overzealous student in an irked fashion and say something like, "Chill out."
- **You will not allow it.** You immediately set limits on it just like you would with any other form of disruption.
- **There is little reason for it to occur.** When the few can no longer abuse the many, you find that there is much less latent animosity between students that might surface at such times in the form of rude remarks.

Time Loss Opens the Door to Abuse

Next, let's deal with the fact that the time loss condition within Responsibility Training is the *bane of my existence.* Can you imagine a colleague who is a bit *negative* or *burned-out* eventually saying to the class,

> "All right, class, it is only Wednesday, and you have already lost *half* of your PAT. If we continue like this, there will be *no* PAT this week!"

This teacher is obviously using Responsibility Training as a *weapon* by abusing the time loss condition. When used properly, time is lost in seconds rather than in minutes, and even then, time is lost only rarely. Furthermore, time loss typically self-eliminates in a matter of days or weeks so that thereafter it exists in the students' minds as a *potentiality* rather than as an actuality.

For teachers to take large amounts of PAT from the students, they must be:

- **Poorly Trained:** This can easily occur when a teacher hears about parts of this system second-hand – often from a well-intentioned colleague who has been to a workshop. Since the manipulation of PAT smacks of "instant cure," teachers are tempted to try it without other elements of the program being in place. When time loss is used for high-rate behaviors such as *talking to neighbors* and *out of seat* that are the proper domain of working the crowd and Limit Setting, excessive time loss is the natural outcome.

When time loss becomes excessive, students become resentful, and cooperation ceases.

- **Extremely Negative:** Teachers can be negative for a variety of reasons ranging from exhaustion to career burn-out to a personality problem. When negativism is chronic, abuse of time loss will be chronic. When time loss becomes excessive, students become resentful and cooperation ceases.

Layers of Management

A Foundation for Successful Incentives

You consistently place yourself in a position to congratulate the group for its success because success was not left to chance. Each piece of behavior needed for an efficient lesson transition was carefully built and supervised.

The clean-up committee erased your boards properly because you had *trained* them to do so during the first month of school. And, they knew that, had they done a sloppy job, they would have done it over because you were supervising their work. The students moved their desks properly rather than dragging them across the room for the same reasons.

In addition, you systematically eliminated bootleg reinforcement as you worked the crowd. And, finally, as you worked the crowd, you set limits on any goofing off that you encountered.

The incentive of extra PAT for hustle was only *one* layer of management among *many* during the transition. Indeed, the incentive was not even the main one. Rather than saying that the students succeeded because of the incentive, it would be more accurate to say that the incentive succeeded because of the solid foundation of management upon which it was built.

A Slice of Life

To understand how discipline management works as a *system*, let's first list the four layers of discipline management. (See chapter 2, "Focusing on Prevention.")

1. Classroom Structure
2. Limit Setting
3. Responsibility Training
4. Backup System

The strategy for solving a problem is very simple:

- Extract as much management from Classroom Structure as you can before moving on to Limit Setting.
- Extract as much management from Limit Setting as you can before moving on to Responsibility Training.
- Extract as much management from Responsibility Training as you can before even considering the Backup System.

Think of discipline management as a four-layer cake. We would never serve a birthday cake by cutting off the top layer and serving it one layer at at time, would we? Rather, we would cut through all four layers to serve a slice of cake.

Similarly, we will never serve up one layer of our management system all by itself. Rather, think of every management dilemma as a "slice of life." The solution will potentially contain all four layers of the management "cake."

Management Deferred

By far, the greatest investment of time and energy in a well-managed classroom is in *Classroom Structure.* The teacher will first rearrange the furniture in the room in order to *work the crowd.* In addition, the teacher will invest heavily in the *teaching of routines* early in the semester. During the teaching of a lesson, *working the crowd* will be facilitated by additional elements of Classroom Structure which include *Say, See, Do Teaching* plus *Visual Instructional Plans* plus *Praise, Prompt, and Leave.*

Success with Incentives

Rather than saying that the students succeeded because of the incentive, it would be more accurate to say that the incentive succeeded because of the solid foundation of management upon which it was built.

Any management task that is not taken care of with Classroom Structure will be shifted to the next level, *Limit Setting.* Consequently, as we mentioned in Chapter 12, "Teaching Routines," teachers who do not spend enough time teaching classroom routines will find themselves constantly setting limits on the misbehavior that occurs during those routines.

Any management task that is not taken care of by Classroom Structure or Limit Setting will be shifted to the next level of management, *Responsibility Training.* Herein lies the problem.

If teachers get only a brief explanation of Responsibility Training without the rest of the program, they will have little choice but to use it as a "solo" management procedure. When used solo, Responsibility Training comes across as a cure-all. The natural tendency, then, is to use Responsibility Training, and especially *time loss,* to manage *everything* – talking to neighbors, out of seat, wandering around the classroom, dawdling, not having pencils – you name it!

The proper domain of Responsibility Training is relatively *narrow.* It builds behaviors such as hustling or showing up on time with books and pencils – those jobs for which Classroom Structure and Limit Setting are poorly suited.

If you were to ask Responsibility Training to bear the entire burden of discipline management, it would collapse under the weight of that burden. You would back yourself into continually *taking* time rather than *giving* it. As a result, the system would become a weapon rather than a gift, and its entire intent would be perverted.

Automatic Bonuses

Right Place, Right Time, Right Stuff

Automatic bonuses are used when you cannot measure the amount of time that the students have saved. Imagine, for example, that the students are in their seats ready to go when the bell rings. How much time did they save? You have no way of knowing. You can only measure time *loss.*

When the students are on time, *automatically* give them a bonus of a predetermined size. The size of the bonus is up to you, but one minute is the norm.

Automatic Bonuses

Automatic bonuses are used when you cannot measure the amount of time saved.

They are most commonly given for students being at the right place at the right time with the right stuff.

Automatic bonuses are most commonly given for students being at the *right place* at the *right time* with the *right stuff.* They are most useful in training students to begin class on time rather than wasting the first five minutes of the class period with "settling in."

Imagine, for example, that the students are in their seats ready to go when the bell rings. As always, they are in their seats for more reasons than one. You greeted the students at the door, the students had a Bell Work assignment, and you worked the crowd during Bell Work while setting limits on any goofing off. As a final layer of management, you provided an incentive.

Having laid the groundwork for the success of the incentive, you are now in a position to congratulate the students at the beginning of class with the daily "automatic bonus routine."

> "Class, thank you for being in your seats. That is one minute. How about pencils? (The students hold up their pencils.) Good! That's two minutes. Let me see lab manuals. (The students hold them up.) Good! Three for three."

You then walk to the board and add three minutes to the bonus column of the PAT.

PAT

+	-
30:00	
1:17	:05
1:06	
3:00	

Daily automatic bonus routines eliminate the wasting of time during "settling in."

Taking Responsibility for Pencils

Now, let's imagine that, thirty seconds before the bell rings, a girl in your class discovers that she has no pencil. That pencil is worth a full minute of PAT.

She asks the students near her for a pencil, but nobody has an extra one. As you walk by, the student says,

"May I please borrow a pencil?"

You answer,

"I don't lend pencils."

You knew that was coming, didn't you? It is now fifteen seconds until the bell rings! What should the poor girl do? What if she said to the class,

"Hey, you guys! I need a pencil!"

In a class of thirty, twenty-nine other students have a vested interest in this girl having a pencil. She will get a pencil. When the whole class wants something to happen, it will happen.

The beautiful thing about this pencil routine, apart from the girl having a pencil, is that it is not *your* pencil. Even better, you do not care whether the person who loaned the pencil gets it back. It is *not your problem!* Group management makes it *their* problem. You are no longer caught in the middle.

Learning to Help Each Other

Some students are just forgetful. Imagine for a moment a boy in your class who often forgets things. He is a good kid, but just a little flaky. He forgets homework and deadlines and pencils and notebooks.

Think of responsible people, in contrast, as having "Post-It notes" all over their brains. When my kids were in school, my brain was buried under Post-It notes, as was my wife's.

"Bring refreshments to school for Brian's birthday party at 11:00 today."

"You have to chaperone Anne's field trip, and the bus leaves the school at 1:00."

"Dinner will be late this evening because Patrick has a basketball game after school."

Some people have never learned to bother with Post-It notes – flaky kids, for example. They don't "sweat the details." You can remind them a dozen times, but they will still forget and then say, "Nobody told me."

Switch perspectives for a moment, and imagine that you are a student who shares science class with the flaky kid. Your locker is next to his, and you remember (because you have a Post-It note on your brain) that today is lab day. As you grab your lab manual, you remember that last week the class failed to get its bonus minute because "Mr. Flake" forgot his manual. To make sure that it does not happen again, you say,

"Hey, Herb. Got your manual?"

When students have a vested interest in "taking care of business," they often take care of it when you are nowhere around. Neither Classroom Structure nor Limit Setting can do that.

Bonus Contests

Contests Are Optional

When we began experimenting with PAT at the high school level, a few teachers, for no apparent reason, posted the running totals of PAT for each class period on the board. These classes consistently earned more PAT than classrooms in which the teachers did not post PAT. The difference was about five to eight minutes of PAT over the course of a week.

PAT Bonus Contest Prizes

First Place	5 bonus minutes
Second Place	4 bonus minutes
Third Place	3 bonus minutes
Fourth Place	2 bonus minutes
Fifth Place	1 bonus minute

By including bonus points for rank order, everyone has a vested interest until the end of the contest.

As an experiment, we asked all of the teachers to post running totals of PAT for each class period. Sure enough, when the teachers who had not posted PAT began to do so, their classes' net PAT immediately shot up by five to eight minutes per week. It seemed that the class periods were competing with each other without even being aware of it.

To maximize the benefit, we instituted a formal contest in which bonus PAT was the prize. During a five period day, bonuses would be given as shown in the box above. Notice that even last place got a bonus minute. You can afford to err in the direction of generosity if PAT is always used for learning.

Cutoff Point Contests

An incentive system will be more powerful if everyone participates, and it will be less powerful if people drop out. One of the problems of having prizes based on *rank order* (first through fifth place, for example) was that fourth and fifth places tended to quit trying when they saw that they could not catch up. Soon, not trying became a habit.

To eliminate this tendency, we substituted *cutoff points* for rank order. Cutoff points were the rough equivalents of the time typically earned by competing class periods, but evenly spaced. The example below is for a teacher who gives each of five class periods 30 minutes of PAT to start the week with cut-off points at increments of three minutes.

The beauty of cutoff points is that any class can earn extra minutes of PAT at any time with just a little more effort. This greatly increases peer involvement. In addition, since class periods are not actually competing with each other, they can all earn the "first place" bonus. This tends to eliminate the problem of dropping out.

PAT Bonus Cutoff Points

45 minutes of PAT earns	5 bonus minutes
42 minutes of PAT earns	4 bonus minutes
39 minutes of PAT earns	3 bonus minutes
36 minutes of PAT earns	2 bonus minutes
33 minutes of PAT earns	1 bonus minute

The beauty of cutoff points is that any class can earn extra minutes of PAT with just a little more effort.

Layering Bonuses

Teachers will often want to use a field trip, a movie, or a big project of some kind for PAT. Since these activities require an extended PAT, teachers are tempted to save PAT for several days or weeks in order to accumulate the necessary time.

This extension of the time frame for Responsibility Training typically has disastrous results as kids simply give up. However, you can have the class work for long-term goals without giving up the power of short-term reinforcement by *layering bonuses*. Simply keep two sets of books side by side.

Imagine, for a moment, that you are a fourth grade teacher who would like to have the class earn time for a field trip. Keep two PAT tallies side by side at the board – one for the normal PAT that might occur at the end of the day, and one for the field trip. Whenever you add a Hurry-up Bonus or an Automatic Bonus to the daily total, add the same bonus to the field trip total. Only bonuses add to the field trip total, not the initial gift of PAT.

Discipline from a Distance

Small Group Instruction

How do you manage goofing off in the classroom when you are *seated* during small group instruction? As soon as you sit down, the rate of disruption skyrockets. Not only do you lose "working the crowd," but Limit Setting becomes prohibitively expensive. You have to stop instruction and stand up before you can even begin. You turn toward the disruptive students, and they "shape up." As soon as you sit down, they start goofing off again. This is called, "yo-yoing the teacher."

You can have long-term goals without giving up your short-term incentives by keeping two bonus tallies on the board.

Data taken during small group instruction showed that both *talking to neighbors* and *out of seat* tripled as soon as the teacher sat down. In addition, *time-on-task* among students *not* in the small group plunged by over fifty percent. This degree of goofing off translates into the noise level that most teachers have learned to accept as the price of small group instruction.

> **Never use time to manage a behavior that you could have managed with your body.**

This dilemma of managing from a seated position produced some of the research that evolved into Responsibility Training. At the beginning, we gave the teachers a stopwatch to hold up as a warning cue when they saw a disruption on the far side of the classroom. If the disrupting students returned to work, no time was lost. But, if the disruption continued, the teacher started the watch and let it run until the students were back on task. Any time on the stopwatch was deducted from PAT.

The peer group immediately began "shushing" disruptive students. In the research, disruptions were reduced by over 80 percent, and time-on-task doubled during the first week. By the end of the second week, disruptions were down by 95 percent, and time-on-task was the same as when the teacher was working the crowd.

More importantly, time loss was small. By the end of the second week, time loss averaged about fifteen seconds during a one-hour class period. By the end of the third week, most of the stopwatches were in the drawer. After that, teachers only had to point to the wall clock when they caught the eye of a disruptor.

Later on we learned how to exploit *bonuses* so that management was more a matter of giving than of taking. Yet, from a seated position, the original version provides an effective alternative to the widespread goofing off typical of small group instruction. To put it simply, time can be substituted for proximity. Using the stopwatch from a seated position is like beaming your body across the room. Talking stops, and "the wanderer" literally jumps into his seat to turn off the stopwatch.

Beware of More Abuse

The very magic of using Responsibility Training for *talking to neighbors* and *out of seat* when you are seated can be highly seductive. It can train even the best teachers to use time loss for high-rate disruption at other times *in lieu of working the crowd.* This can be disastrous.

It is important to discriminate the *change in ground rules* for the use of time loss that occurs when the teacher is *seated* during small group instruction as opposed to when the teacher is *mobile.* When you are mobile, you *never* use time loss for high-rate disruptions like *talking to neighbors* and *out of seat.* When you are seated, you *must* use time loss for these same high-rate disruptions.

Responsibility Training is robust enough to absorb time loss for high-rate disruptions if its use is limited to *small group instruction when the teacher is seated.* Problems occur only when the teacher "steps over the line" and uses time loss for the sake of convenience when *not seated.*

To help delineate the proper use of time loss in Responsibility Training, trainees learn the following rule:

Never use time to manage a behavior that you could have managed with your body.

Open Field Settings

Physical education teachers sometimes find Limit Setting difficult due to sheer distance. When students are goofing off on the far side of the gym or at the other end of the playing field, the use of physical proximity for management becomes impractical.

Teachers in open field settings usually find themselves substituting the time loss of Responsibility Training for the physical proximity of Meaning Business more often than teachers in regular classrooms. If used judiciously, this can work.

Hurry-up Bonuses can also increase hustling in such settings to create time for a sizable PAT by the end of the class period. I know physical education teachers whose kids hustle through "dressing out" and required assignments in order to get:

- a three-on-three basketball tournament
- access to gymnastics equipment
- access to the weight room

Eliminating Annoyances

Pencil Sharpening

While automatic bonuses help us with part of "pencil management," we are still left with the problem of sharpening pencils during class. The first step toward solving this problem is to inform your class that you do not allow pencil sharpening after the bell rings.

To deal with broken pencil leads, you need a canister of sharpened pencils on your desk. They should be short, grungy pencils. If you buy nice new pencils, break them in half, sharpen both ends and break off the eraser. The little pencils used to keep score at golf courses are perfect. Instruct your students as follows:

> "If you break your pencil lead during class and have no other pencil, hold your pencil in the air so I can see it. I will nod to you at which time you may leave your seat to exchange pencils at my desk. Leave your pencil on my desk, and take one out of the canister. You may get your own pencil back at the end of class when you return mine to the canister."

Typically, this is the end of the problem. Occasionally, however, a student might take advantage of the situation by killing time at your desk looking for the best pencil in the canister. First, try a little "heart-to-heart" talk with the student to see if the problem will go away without further sanctions. If the problem persists, you may need to put students on the clock when they get out of their seats to exchange pencils. When students see that you have the situation covered, they usually "shape up" without you ever having to actually take away time.

Hall Passes

Hall passes allow administrators to know whether students they meet in the halls *should* be out of class. There are many legitimate reasons for students being out of class. The use of hall passes only becomes a problem when students use them to go to the restroom.

The flim-flammery of using hall passes to go to the restroom becomes clear in the light of one biological fact – *an average three-year-old child can sleep through the night dry.* This means that teenagers who "need" a pass out of class in order to avoid wetting themselves might have a little brother or sister who "held it" last night for *eight hours while unconscious.* Does this sound as though the teacher is being taken for a ride?

You need to understand that every institution on the face of the earth has a toilet training program. There are only two options:

- When you gotta go, you gotta go.
- When you gotta go, do it on your own time during the breaks provided.

Option number one provides an incentive for abusing use of the hall pass as a means of getting out of class. Option number two removes that incentive.

> You can run your own incentive programs along with Responsibility Training.

The simplest way to eliminate the abuse of hall passes is to eliminate their use for going to the restroom. Of course, any student with a note from a physician would be excepted. For the rest of the student body, the rule is – *go to the bathroom during the breaks provided.*

Teachers at the primary level, however, express a need for hall passes given their experience with such young children. These concerns are legitimate.

As always, management problems are solved most easily when they are solved preventatively. Let me share an observation. Primary teachers often bring their classes in from recess and march them right past the restrooms without stopping. These are frequently young teachers who lack experience with child rearing.

Anyone who has raised children knows how flaky young kids can be about having to go to the bathroom. I would ask my own kids when we were near the restrooms, "Do you have to go?" and they would say, "No." Five minutes later when we were nowhere near a restroom, they would be doing the one-legged dance. Soon parents learn not to ask. You just say, "Go in and *try!*"

Additional Incentive Options

Add-On Programs

During workshops teachers often assume that whatever is not explicitly *included* in the program is, therefore, *excluded.* As a result, teachers sometimes ask at the break whether they might be "permitted" to continue using a particular incentive program that they have found useful even though it is not included in *Tools for Teaching.*

For the sake of clarification, Responsibility Training is not the "be all" and "end all" of incentive management. Rather, it represents a breakthrough in *efficiency.* It allows the teacher to hold the *entire class* accountable for a *wide range* of behaviors *all day long* for no more effort than a tally of time on the board.

Any other incentive program that you may be using in class can be run along with Responsibility Training. They won't interfere with each other.

For example, elementary teachers often have "responsibility charts" upon which students can earn stars or points for doing basic tasks during the day. In a similar vein, primary teachers often use a point system similar to Responsibility Training for students who cannot tell time. If you have something that works, hang on to it. Here are some additional ideas for solving classroom problems that can operate side-by-side with Responsibility Training.

Tattling

How do you eliminate tattling? It can be a constant headache that puts the teacher "over a barrel."

Imagine a boy who continually comes in from recess complaining about how some student tripped him or pushed him down. If you *listen* to the tattling each day, you reinforce it. If you *don't listen* to the tattling, you appear to be hard-hearted and uncaring. What to do?

Enter *response-cost management.* The most common example of response-cost management is the legal system. The good news is that the system offers you justice. The bad news is that lawyers are expensive.

Most people will not pay $10,000 in lawyer fees to redress a $1,000 grievance. The cost of utilizing the legal system limits your willingness to use it. Cost, therefore, "manages" frivolous lawsuits so that the courts are not flooded with them.

Apply the same logic to tattling. In order to manage the rate of tattling, you will need a response that is expensive enough to eliminate frivolous tattling.

For this you will need a Tattle Box. Take a shoe box, cut a slit in the lid, and prominently label it "Tattle Box." When little Sammy comes in from recess complaining as usual about some horrible crime, look concerned and say:

> "Sammy, I want to hear all about what happened on the playground. Here is a pencil and a piece of paper. I want you to describe exactly what happened. Give me a full paragraph, and remember to put your name, the date and the time of day at the top. When you are done, I will check it for spelling and punctuation. When you have corrected it, you can put it in the tattle box. Start writing while I get things going with the rest of the class.

Many times Sammy will say, "Oh, that's all right." and sit down without writing anything. So much for that tattle.

Sometimes, however, a student will actually write out an "incident report." When they are done writing, scan it and drop it dutifully into the Tattle Box. This will allow you to pick up serious problems or patterns of conflict that need to be dealt with right away.

On Friday you will have Tattle Time. Solemnly turn the Tattle Box *upside-down* and lift the box off of the lid so that the oldest tattles are on top. Pick up the tattle on top and read the time and date.

> "Our first tattle is from Jennifer on Monday morning. Jennifer, can you tell me what happened?"

Chances are, Jennifer will give you a blank stare. This gives you a chance to be nurturant and congratulatory.

> "Well good. I am so glad that you children are learning to take care of these problems on your own."

Drop that tattle into the waste basket and pick up the next one as you continue with Tattle Time.

> "Our next tattle is from Todd on Tuesday. Todd, can you tell me what happened?"

Chances are, you will get another blank stare. More congratulations are in order. Occasionally there will be a tattle that is actually remembered. Since the tattle is obviously still a live issue, this is your opportunity to deal with it. You may initiate some group problem solving or a "human development circle." During group problem solving you can teach students to express feelings and resolve conflict. When the air is clear, proceed to the next tattle.

You can easily limit the duration of Tattle Time if you wish. Start it ten minutes before PAT, and throw in a Hurry-up Bonus.

> "If we get done with Tattle Time early, we can begin PAT early."

Naturally, I assume you can tell the difference between a tattle and a child who needs immediate attention due to being hurt or severely upset. Within the limits of good judgement, however, the Tattle Box has a perverse beauty.

Raffles

How do you get kids to turn in homework. Well, actually, you can't. Homework happens at home, and parents are in charge of managing it. But you can produce a moderate level of improvement by instituting a raffle.

When you greet students at the door, collect homework. Give each student who hands you their homework assignment a raffle ticket. Don't buy raffle tickets. Make a weird design on a piece of paper, make copies, and cut them into small pieces.

Most teachers will hold their raffle at the end of the day or week. Usually teachers raffle off food treats or junk that has been left in class. The range of things that can be raffled off is limitless. You can even make a "power pass" out of a 3x5 card that entitles the winner to turn in an assignment one day late or skip a homework assignment.

Raffles can also help with sloppy desks. First, have a class-wide house cleaning. Then, tell the students,

> "Be prepared for an 'Oink Attack.' More than once today I will simply stand up and say, 'Oink Attack!' Everyone must then open their desks. I will come around and drop a raffle ticket into each desk that is still neat."

Have "Oink Attacks" fairly frequently at the beginning, and then thin the "schedule of attacks."

Hassles with Computers

Schools that provide computers for students encounter an entirely new species of management problems – "hardware hassles." Students show up to class with dead batteries or without a power adapter or without any laptop at all.

As with pencil management, teachers have used automatic bonuses to make students more responsible. Bonuses can be given if everybody's battery is charged or if everybody has their power adapter.

However, the benefits of this approach are limited because, unlike pencils, students don't have extra batteries and power adapters that they can share. Sometimes incentives can be augmented by a change in Classroom Structure. For example, one school dealt with dead batteries by having a multi-charger in each classroom so that students could switch out dead batteries quickly. Another school ran retractable power cords from the ceiling so students could recharge during class.

Individual Bonuses

What about Larry?

Can you imagine having one student in the class who might ruin bonuses for the group just to show that he or she can? Most teachers report that they have at least one such student. As always, let's call this student Larry.

Larry is the reason that group incentives have such a poor record in the research. With group incentives, you cannot give a reinforcer to *anyone* unless *everyone* has acted responsibly. Consequently, one student can always ruin it for the group, and there always seems to be at least one of these students in every class.

Failsafe Mechanisms

Of course, we cannot allow Larry to ruin Responsibility Training. If he ruins the incentive, Larry now controls the class by being negative and oppositional.

Preventing this will require a failsafe mechanism. The following chapter will describe the failsafe mechanism designed to motivate Larry to join the group. That failsafe mechanism is called Omission Training. Larry's individualized program will, in turn, create a general pattern for dealing with students having special needs.

Chapter Twenty Two

Turning Problem Students Around

Preview

- Omission Training supplies problem students with an incentive for self-control by providing a reinforcer when they refrain from a behavior for an interval of time.
- Omission Training mated with Responsibility Training gives the teacher a powerful and flexible means of motivating the peer group to help the student with individual needs.
- If the student on Omission Training refrains from the problem behavior for a given amount of time, he or she earns bonus PAT for the group.
- Omission Training typically eliminates the problem behavior rapidly while making a hero out of an unpopular student.
- Omission Training is easy to use since it amounts to nothing more than a bonus clause added to Responsibility Training.

What about Larry?

The Confrontation

Imagine a Hurry-up Bonus in which all of the students but Larry are in their seats ready to begin as the time runs out. You point to the clock and say,

> "Class, you are on your own time now."

Larry turns to you and blurts,

> "This whole thing is stupid! PAT is stupid too! This sucks!"

Do you have a student in your class who might respond in this way? If so, you have a lot of company.

Who Is Larry?

Before we make a plan for dealing with the confrontation, let's take a moment to think about Larry. Is Larry a happy child? Is Larry a popular child?

Hardly! What kind of kid would say to the class, in effect:

> "I have the power to hurt everyone in the class by ruining PAT, and I am going to do it"?

Typically, Larry is angry and alienated. He takes it out on you, and he takes it out on his classmates. He does hurtful things, and he is often a bully. As a result, he tends to be unpopular with his classmates.

Would Larry like to be popular? Show me a child who would not.

Yet the anger gets in the way. He does not seem to know how to be popular. He keeps doing things that seem calculated to make the other students dislike him. He is his own worst enemy.

Your Immediate Response
Take a relaxing breath. Turn in a regal fashion. Take another relaxing breath. Give yourself a moment to think. Your demeanor signals to everyone that this is serious.

Walk slowly to Larry, and wait for a moment before saying anything. Allow your own calm to help Larry relax. What you then say is not what Larry expected to hear.

> "Larry, if you think PAT is stupid, we may as well forget it. I would not expect you to work for something that you did not want. I know I wouldn't."

Larry was expecting much worse. Usually he signals relief by saying something inconsequential like, "Right."

It would seem that Larry does not value PAT as an incentive. The fact that you know better is beside the point for the moment.

Rather than being a "tactic," your words simply acknowledge the realities of the situation. You cannot make students like PAT any more than you can force them to cooperate.

Your Plan
If you can finesse the short-term situation, do so. If you stay calm and wait, Larry may take his seat for a lack of anything better to do. You can talk to Larry later.

Of course, you cannot guarantee the outcome of any situation. If Larry chooses to escalate, you will probably end up using your Backup System.

Let's assume for the moment that you successfully finesse the immediate situation. Before the day is over you must have a heart-to-heart talk with Larry. During this talk, you will implement Omission Training.

> **Omission Training**
>
> **The general name given to an incentive system that *decreases* the rate of a behavior is *Omission Training.***

Omission Training

Incentives to Eliminate Behavior
As described earlier in the book, the basic strategy that underlies behavior management is quite simple. *Increase* the behaviors that you *do* want, and *decrease* the behaviors that you *do not* want. If you can do this, sooner or later you will be left with what you want.

Not too surprisingly, therefore, there are two basic kinds of incentive systems. One kind *increases* the rate of a behavior, and the other kind *decreases* the rate of a behavior. The vast majority of incentive systems used in classroom management, including Responsibility Training, are of the first kind. Yet, incentives to decrease behavior can be very helpful, especially when dealing with severe or chronic behavior problems.

The general name given to an incentive system that *decreases* the rate of a behavior is *Omission Training*. Omission Training has a unique structure.

The Structure of Omission Training
The structure of Omission Training is dictated by the simple fact that you cannot reinforce the *non*-occurrence of a behavior. It would sound stupid if you tried:

"I like the way you didn't just hit him."

The recipient of this compliment might well conclude that you were losing your mind.

You can, however, reinforce someone for not doing something *for a given length of time.* You could, for example, reinforce a student for going *ten minutes* without interrupting or for going *twenty minutes* without getting out of his or her seat or for going *an entire class period* without hitting.

Omission Training plus Responsibility Training

While Omission Training is useful in providing a means other than the Backup System for eliminating problem behaviors, it becomes especially powerful when mated with Responsibility Training. This combination of management programs mobilizes the peer group to help both the teacher and the student with special needs.

For example, you could give the group a minute of bonus PAT if Larry could go ten minutes without making an inappropriate remark. This gives the peer group a vested interest in supporting Larry's efforts and ignoring his provocations. Cheers typically erupt as the PAT is posted on the board.

As you can see, Omission Training within a group context goes beyond simply changing a behavior. It makes Larry a hero with you as his cheerleader. It gives you "the power of the peer group," and it involves the class in helping an unpopular child which is uplifting for everyone.

In addition to helping a single child, you can also reinforce the *entire class* for omitting a behavior. You could, for example, give the group a minute of bonus PAT if *no one* interrupted for a given amount of time. This allows you to eliminate a problem behavior that is brief but scattered, and, therefore, difficult to deal with using Limit Setting.

A Vested Interest in Helping

While Omission Training is useful for eliminating problem behaviors, it becomes especially powerful when mated with Responsibility Training. This combination gives the peer group a vested interest in supporting Larry's efforts to improve while ignoring his provocations.

The Heart-to-Heart Talk

Find a quiet place where you will not be interrupted for the next twenty minutes. Heart-to-heart talks usually require plenty of "wait time." Of course, you will impart your own style to this conversation. The following dialogue is only intended to map out the terrain. The heart-to-heart talk has four parts.

Enough Is Enough

"Larry, that scene in front of the classroom this morning in which you told me that PAT was stupid – that is what we call in education 'unacceptable behavior.' I will make you a promise. If one of us has to go, it will be you.

"Right now, we are looking at the Backup System. As I explained at the beginning of the semester, it goes from a verbal warning all the way to the state penitentiary and everything in between. It is not supposed to be fun. Its purpose is to raise the price of misbehavior to the point where you are no longer willing to pay for it.

"Between where we stand right now and the Backup System lies another option. It is a lot more enjoyable than the Backup System.

"Let me explain it to you. Then, if you want to do it, we will. And, if you don't, we won't."

Brainstorming a Reinforcement Menu

"This morning when you said that PAT was stupid, my first thought was that I had thoroughly failed you in explaining PAT. So, let me try again.

"First of all, you do not have to do what the rest of the group is doing during PAT. It is always possible to do your own thing as long as it is constructive. It is even possible that everyone in the class might do a different activity during PAT. The only thing that must be the same for everyone is the *duration* of PAT.

"So, let's sit down with a pad of paper and make a list of things that *you* would like to do during PAT. The boundaries are as always: It must be something that *you want,* and it must be something that *I can live with.*"

This phase of program building is known as "brainstorming a reinforcement menu." It marks a change of direction in the conversation from "enough is enough" to becoming a partner with Larry in seeking enjoyment. If the two of you can pinpoint some PAT activities that Larry really wants, you have the foundation for a win-win solution to the problem.

As you brainstorm PATs with Larry, remain flexible without giving up your focus on learning. You will never accept just "kicking back" as a PAT. But management is *the art of the possible.* If the most achievement-oriented activity that Larry lists is reading motorcycle magazines, you may want to put it on the list even though you might expect more from some other students. After all, those magazines represent fairly challenging reading.

Estimate a Time Frame for Omission Training

How long can Larry behave himself during a typical day? When in doubt, shorten your estimate. You want Larry to *succeed every day.*

The most common time frame in regular classrooms is half a class period (25 minutes). Even on days when Larry gets into trouble, he will probably give you at least half a class period without getting into trouble. Be conservative. If 25 minutes seems like a lot to ask, shorten it to something that is "doable."

Explain the Mechanics to Larry

Brainstorming a reinforcement menu usually puts Larry in a positive frame of mind. Estimating the time frame gives you the final piece of the puzzle. Now, it is time to explain what you have in mind to Larry.

"You can do any of the items on our list during PAT. That is, you could if you had PAT. But, unfortunately, you don't. You said it was stupid, and I said, 'Then, let's forget it.' And you said, 'Right.' So, I did.

"Kidding aside, I do want you to have PAT. But I also want to relax and enjoy teaching when I come to work. And that little 'altercation' we had this morning was hardly enjoyable.

"That is to say, while I want you to have PAT, I want something in return. I want something that you have given me *every day* that you have been in my class since school began – even on days in which you got into trouble. I want you to give me *half a class period* of appropriate behavior. You don't have to do anything special. Just cool it for 25 minutes.

"Think of it as a gesture that says, 'I will meet you halfway.' If you meet me halfway, I will meet you *more* than halfway. I will give you back your PAT, but that is not all. I will give you your PAT *plus a minute.* But it is not just *your* minute. It belongs to the *entire class.*"

Always rehearse your announcement of the program to the class with Larry beforehand so that there is no embarrassment when the time comes. Typically with older students, the less said the better.

The next day you begin the program. As soon as Larry earns his first bonus minute, announce it just as you rehearsed.

"Class, let me have your attention. Larry and I have devised a program that we are implementing today, and Larry is doing a great job. As a result, Larry has just earned a bonus minute of PAT *for the entire class.* I will circle the tally so you can see how many minutes Larry has earned for the group. Think of this minute as a gift from Larry to all of you."

Walk to the board and post the minute on the PAT tally. Draw a circle around the bonus minute and all other minutes that Larry subsequently earns for the class. Then say,

Larry becomes a hero by earning time for the group.

"Let's hear it for Larry. (Lead the group in giving Larry applause.) Come on, class! Let's not be shy. You just got lucky. Let's hear it for Larry! (You can always get a class to applaud if you try.)

"Okay, Larry, let's see if we can get another minute before the period is over."

As the class period comes to an end, say to the group,

"Class, let me have your attention. Larry has just earned a *second* minute for the group. Larry, you are doing a great job. Let me post your second bonus minute on the board.

"Class, you are all two minutes richer thanks to Larry. Let's hear it for Larry." (Once again, lead the group in applause.)

Let us return to our conversation with Larry for a moment. There is one more detail of the program that needs to be explained to him.

"Larry, there is one more part to this program that I need to show you. It is a *kitchen timer.*

"If anybody ruins this program, it will probably be me, not you. I may get busy teaching and forget about keeping track of the minutes. As I see you walking out of the room, I will think, 'Oh no! I forgot all about Larry's minutes.'

"So that I do not have to be a clock-watcher, I will use this kitchen timer. I will set it to 25 minutes and forget it. When 25 minutes is up, it will ring, and we will both know that you have earned another bonus minute."

In fact, the class quickly learns that the sound of the kitchen timer signals a bonus minute for them as well. Within a day or two, cheers erupt before you even make the announcement.

One final detail needs to be explained to Larry.

"With this program, you can only *earn* time for the group. You can no longer lose time.

"Consequently, if you should get into trouble in class, you will deal with me personally. After you rejoin the group, I will reset the kitchen timer so that you can immediately begin earning bonus PAT. If the period should end before you have earned the next minute, I will carry all of your time forward to the next day so that you *never lose time.*"

As you can see, Larry could not lose time for the group if he wanted to. Since Larry showed a weakness for playing the bully, we have simply removed the temptation.

A Bridge to Healing

Making Larry Popular

As we mentioned earlier, Larry is typically neither happy nor popular. But he would like to be. He just doesn't seem to know how.

Over the years these negative emotions can produce serious deficits in social skills. Larry is not very good at getting along with people because he has not spent much time trying. Omission Training serves as a "pump primer" for helping Larry learn to get along with people by setting him up for success from the very beginning.

If I needed a behavioral program to make an unpopular child popular, I would immediately pick Omission Training. I have seen it bring an outcast child into the middle of the class sociogram in two weeks!

Changing Perceptions of Larry

The peer group is in the habit of noticing what Larry does *wrong* and failing to notice what he does *right.* Unless you have some powerful way of causing the peer group to look at Larry differently, they will continue to expect the worst and fail to notice Larry's improved behavior.

Getting the Class Involved

The peer group is in the habit of noticing what Larry does wrong. Unless you have some powerful way of causing the peer group to look at Larry differently, they will continue to expect the worst while they fail to notice Larry's improved behavior – an extinction program.

For the price of a heart-to-heart talk and a few marks on the PAT tally, you have rearranged group dynamics to support Larry's growth.

Omission Training focuses the peer group's attention on Larry's new behavior and helps them see Larry through new eyes. Without the theatrical aspect of Omission Training plus the bonus PAT that the class shares, the peer group might be slow to notice Larry's improvement so that they inadvertently put his improvement on extinction. Rather than let this happen, we will make a hero out of Larry.

In Omission Training, we allow the normal hunger of young people for peer approval to serve a constructive end. And we give the peer group an opportunity to experience being part of the healing process.

It Is Cheap

In addition to Omission Training being powerful, it is *cheap*. For the price of a heart-to-heart talk and a few marks on the PAT tally, you have rearranged the group dynamics of the entire class to support Larry's growth.

It is actually cheaper to institute Responsibility Training just so you can institute Omission Training than it is to institute a traditional individualized behavior modification program. And it is far more powerful since it delivers "the power of the peer group."

The Life Span of Omission Training

How Often Do You Need It?

Upon learning about Omission Training, most trainees envision two or three students in each class period who would need it. They assume that every "Larry" will be a candidate. This misperception needs to be corrected before we can get an accurate picture of the implementation of Omission Training.

It is impossible for you to assess your need for Omission Training until you have fully implemented Classroom Structure, Limit Setting, and Responsibility Training. Only then can you count the problems that are left over.

Typically, the tally is zero. Proper Classroom Structure *plus* Limit Setting *plus* Responsibility Training will give you far more management leverage than you have ever experienced.

My biggest problem with Omission Training is that it is so seldom needed that, by the time it is finally called for, trainees have forgotten about it and have unnecessarily gone to the Backup System. While a sudden blow-up may force you to use your Backup System, Omission Training almost always provides a cheaper and more pleasant way of resolving a repetitive problem.

How Often Do You Need Omission Training?

It is impossible to assess your need for Omission Training until you have fully implemented Classroom Structure, Limit Setting, and Responsibility Training. Only then can you count the problems that are left over.

Typically, the tally is zero.

Won't Others Want It?

During a workshop, someone will always ask, "Won't other students want Omission Training if it makes Larry into a hero?" As logical as this seems, I have no memory of it ever happening.

The explanation probably has to do with the fact that Omission Training is so seldom used and then, only for problems of marked severity. To put it bluntly, the student who receives Omission Training is "way out there." He or she is so deviant that no classmate would want to be put in the same category. Consequently, while other students appreciate the extra bonus minutes, they are quite happy to let someone else get the "glory."

How Long Do You Let It Run?

Any student who needs an Omission Training program is severely damaged. Consequently, after you set up Omission Training for one of these students, let it run for a long while. You need to allow time for healing to take place.

At the regional special education facility where program development took place, we would allow Omission Training to run for six to eight weeks before we even considered eliminating it. During that time we would look for "soft signs" of healing. In addition to improvement in Larry's behavior, we would look for signs of acceptance by the peer group such as:

- being included in games and activities just like the other students
- having students sit near him in the lunchroom before all of the other seats are taken
- walking down the hall in animated conversation with classmates

When it seemed as though the target student had become integrated into the social fabric of the class, we would consider eliminating Omission Training. But we were very conservative. If you are in doubt, let it run a little longer.

Eliminating Omission Training

Fading Procedures

The easiest way to eliminate Omission Training is through a simple fading procedure. The two most common methods are:

Let Omission Training run until you see Larry integrated into the social fabric of the peer group.

- gradually extending the time frame
- fading critical features

Of the two, I would choose the second, fading critical features. Extending the time frame can backfire since the student might feel as though you are constantly changing the rules.

Fading Critical Features

The fading of critical features is a simple three-step process. Discuss it with the student beforehand:

Step 1: Eliminate time-keeping.

"I keep setting the kitchen timer, and you keep getting the bonus minutes. You have gotten all of your bonus minutes for so long that I am beginning to wonder why I bother setting the timer.

"Would you mind if I announced to the class that you had earned *two* bonus minutes at the *end* of every class period? Then I could forget the timer."

Rarely does the student object to this alteration in procedure. By this time Larry has probably noticed that the kitchen timer has become superfluous too. Besides, he is still earning the same number of bonus minutes for the group, and he is still receiving public recognition.

Step 2: Eliminate the contingency of reinforcement.

"You know, Larry, I am beginning to think that it is silly to wait until the end of the period to give you your minutes. I am usually busy with other things then. I have almost forgotten it several times.

"Why don't I just give you your bonus minutes at the *beginning* of the class period so that I won't forget? You will get the same number of minutes, and I will announce it just as I always do."

Step 3: Eliminate the program.

The arrangement described in step 2 can run indefinitely. There is no pressing need to eliminate the program, particularly if you are worried that the student might revert to his or her old habits.

If you decide that the program has finally become "excess baggage," the easiest time to eliminate it is to simply drop it at the end of the semester. Have a simple ceremony in which both you and the class recognize Larry's achievement, and then begin the new semester without the program.

When Fading Fails

Fading any management program is a calculated gamble. You won't win them all. Consequently, as you progress with the fading program described above, you must be very attentive to signs of failure.

The main sign of failure is a gradual reemergence of the problem behavior. Seeing the old problem reemerge tells you that fading was premature.

The cure is to simply reverse the fading procedure. Reinstitute the last step that was faded and wait. Typically, you only need to go back one step, although you can go back to the original program if the reemergence of the problem behavior is sudden. If you have to reverse course, remain where you have reestablished success for a long time before you risk going forward with the fading procedure again.

Protecting Automatic Bonuses

All or Nothing

Imagine an automatic bonus in which all of the students get a minute of PAT for being in their seats when the bell rings. Today when the bell rings, everybody is seated but Larry.

Obviously, you cannot give the class its bonus minute. Group management is "all for one, and one for all."

But imagine that this problem occurs again the next day. Now, the class has failed to get its bonus *twice in a row.* Are you beginning to get a sinking feeling of powerlessness? What if it happens a *third* time?

Early in our discussion of Responsibility Training, I said that I wanted perfection, not just improvement. The reason I gave was purely *practical.* What is the practical difference in terms of hassle between having two students who show up without pencils as opposed to four?

Now, let me give you the *technical* reason for seeking perfection. If Larry can deprive the class of its Automatic Bonus, Larry is not only in control of the class, but he has also placed the rest of the students on an *extinction program* for cooperation. This is a management disaster!

All or Nothing

If Larry can deprive the class of its bonus, Larry is not only in control of the class, but he also puts the rest of the students on an *extinction program* for cooperation.

You must have cooperation from *everyone,* or the entire notion of Automatic Bonuses collapses. That is why group management has such a poor track record in the research literature. It promises great efficiency and power, but there is usually at least one Larry in the class who will wreck the program just to prove that he can.

Cutting Larry Out of the Herd

We need a failsafe mechanism to keep Larry from ruining Automatic Bonuses for the class. It is called *cutting Larry out of the herd.* I will give you two versions.

In the *simple* version, you tell the class that Larry can no longer lose their bonus minute by being out of his seat. Rather, if Larry is out of his seat, you will deal with him. The *more powerful* version adds an element of Omission Training to the program. Simply add the following paragraph to your explanation.

> "However, class, if Larry is *in* his seat when the bell rings, you will *all* get a *second* bonus minute. So, class, while Larry can no longer cost you time, he can give you time if you all choose to work together."

Avoiding the Backup System

When a student consistently blocks the teacher's management objectives, the resulting exasperation naturally leads the teacher's mind toward the Backup System. But, the Backup System is both costly and prone to failure.

The use of Omission Training provides an excellent alternative. For very little effort you can protect the many from abuse by Larry. In the process, you substitute a *positive* approach to management in place of your Backup System which is adversarial by nature.

Helping Substitute Teachers

If you place Responsibility Training in the hands of a substitute teacher, you may return to find that your class has lost PAT for the next month. When stressed, substitutes tend to overuse the penalty portion of the program.

You can, however, give substitute teachers a simplified *bonus-only* version of the program. Tell the students before you leave that the substitute will keep a list of the names of cooperative students. When you return, each name on the list will be worth three bonus minutes.

Or, you could have the substitute teacher give the students a "cooperation score" of 0, 1, 2 or 3 at the end of each assignment. All of these scores will be added when you return. The total will represent the number of bonus minutes of PAT that the class earns for having cooperated with the substitute while you were gone.

Piggybacking

Omission Training can be stretched well beyond the bounds of discipline management. You can make a kid a hero for anything. Just "piggyback" the individualized program onto the group program.

Motivating the Unmotivated

A fourth grade teacher that I trained several years ago had a boy who had never turned in a complete assignment in all of his years of formal education. Yet, the student was bright. The teacher decided to use the peer group to gain some leverage over motivation. She said to her "do-nothing" student during a math assignment,

> "I know that you understand the material. But today I will give you an added reason to try. For each math problem that you complete, I will announce to the class that you have earned a bonus minute of PAT for everyone. I will be back soon to see how you are doing."

The teacher provided frequent feedback to the student at the beginning in order to keep him going. The announcement of each bonus minute was greeted with cheers from the class. Within two weeks the student was handing in all assignments.

"While Omission Training is not magic, it is as close as you will get in behavior management."

Helping the Class Pariah

A fourth grade teacher in Indiana had a boy who never bathed, never combed his hair, and slept in his clothes. He smelled. The other children tormented him, and he retaliated by hitting, tripping, shoving, and calling names.

In desperation the teacher put the boy on an Omission Training program for going a half-hour without tripping or hitting or shoving. The boy succeeded beautifully since these behaviors are almost impossible to do while seated at a desk, and the class cheered as their PAT grew. The boy's negative behavior declined, and the peer group began to treat him better. Eventually, he began to bath and groom himself.

One day the boy's mother visited the teacher after school to see what was going on. She said that she no longer had to fight with her son about showering and combing his hair and sleeping in his clothes. She was moved to tears when she told the teacher that, for the first time in his life, her child had been invited to a birthday party.

Overview

While Omission Training is not magic, it is as close to magic as you will get in behavior management. It has tremendous power to save the child who might otherwise become a casualty, and it provides a win-win strategy for dealing with severe behavior problems. In both regular and special classrooms, Omission Training all but eliminated office referrals.

Chapter Twenty Three

Initiating Preferred Activity Time

Preview

- When you use curriculum enrichment for PAT, you get "two for the price of one." You give the students a special learning activity while getting motivation for free.
- One of the best motivational hooks in education is team competition. You can teach anything by playing team games.
- The best game rules create the most time-on-task. One of the most effective ways to reduce "standing on the sidelines" is to have teams play defense as well as offense.
- When the team on offense misses a question, give the other team a chance to field the question for extra points.
- Playing defense creates peer pressure among the students on each team to look up the answer as soon as they hear the question.

Two for the Price of One

You'd Do It Anyway

The fifth grade students had just taken their seats to begin the school day when their teacher made the following announcement.

"Class, before we start the day, I want to point out the art materials on the project table over by the window. The art project will be your PAT this afternoon.

"As always, I have set aside twenty minutes at the end of the day. You know, however, that once you start a project like this, you always wish you had more time. Well, you *can* have more time. All of the bonus PAT that you earn today will be added to the art project."

The students did not know that, had their teacher never heard of PAT, they would have done the art project anyway. They only knew that all of their hustle throughout the day translated into art.

By using learning as a PAT, you get "two for the price of one." You give the students an enrichment activity to enjoy while getting motivation for free.

Self-Contained vs. Departmentalized

Teachers in self-contained classrooms have more potential PATs during a school day than they can use. They have art and music and story time and extra recess to say nothing of special projects. Add to this all of the curriculum enrichment activities that are available for the units being studied, and they have quite a list. Rather than spending a lot of time planning PAT, these teachers need only pick the best activity of the day and call it PAT.

PAT only becomes a potential headache in a departmentalized setting. Art and music now belong to other departments, and recess is just a memory. Of course, these teachers can use curriculum enrichment for PAT, but their choices are more limited since they only have their students for one subject.

With fewer "freebies" lying around, these teachers will more often have to build PATs from scratch. If you teach economics, you will repeatedly have to ask yourself, "*How do we have fun with economics?*" The answer had better be cheap. I cannot grant you extra planning time.

Team competition is the most reliable motivational 'hook' in education.

Team Competition

A Motivational Hook

Apart from curriculum enrichment activities, *team competition* is perhaps the most reliable and easy to use motivational "hook" in education. Anything can be taught in the form of a team game, and team games make terrific PATs.

The power of team competition hit me one day while I was working at juvenile hall. As I walked into one of the classrooms to make an observation, I was met with,

"All right! Seventeen to fifteen! We've got 'em!"

"Josh is up. Josh, the next word is 'mosquito.'"

"You can do it. You can do it."

"Mosquito, M-O-S-Q-U-I-T-O."

"Yes! We rule! Eighteen to fifteen!"

Slowly it dawned on me that I was watching a bunch of kids in *juvenile hall* going ape over *spelling*. Spelling!

At the time of my visit to "juvy," I was in a quandary about PAT. My high school teachers were telling me that they did not have time to plan PATs. It was too much trouble.

The classroom at juvenile hall caused a lightbulb to go on in my head. I tried to remember playing games in school when I was a kid.

I clearly remember my fourth grade teacher, Mrs. Franklin, playing a team game. It was raining, and we could not go out for afternoon recess. She divided the class in half, and we spent twenty minutes playing math baseball. She did it on the spur of the moment, and we loved it.

The strange thing about my memory of math baseball is that we only did it once. I remember wishing that we could do it again, but we never did. We would have gladly worked for the opportunity to play academic baseball over and over if we had only been given the chance.

Game Rules

The realization that you can make lessons into team games caused me to study team game rules. Did you know that there really aren't that many different games in the world? The rules to baseball, football, basketball, hangman, and Jeopardy are all the same! With a half-dozen sets of rules you can generate hundreds of PATs.

Here's what makes the best team games – *time-on-task.* Kids love to play, and they hate being on the sidelines. Consequently, the best games produce the most learning.

The kids at juvenile hall were going ape over a team game that taught spelling.

Academic Baseball

Play More, Learn More

Let's begin with the rules for academic baseball. Studying the rules for baseball will teach us a lot about game rules in general.

In baseball, your team is up roughly half of the time, and the other team is up roughly half of the time. If PAT lasts 30 minutes, your team will only be up for about 15 minutes. By having innings in which teams takes turns at bat, you *halve the length of everybody's PAT.*

How can we improve the rules of the game so that kids spend more time playing and less time on the sidelines? The answer is *defense.* If the students play defense, they will be engaged in playing when the other team is up at bat.

Double Diamond Baseball

Lay out *two diamonds* on the floor with 3x5 cards or "Post-It" notes as bases. Have the students get out of their seats to "run the bases." They have fun strutting their stuff, and you don't have to keep track of who is on base.

We will play the game with questions at four levels of difficulty; singles, doubles, triples, and home runs. These questions usually come right off the top of your head. If you want to simplify the game, make every question worth one run.

Divide the room into two teams. On the team that is "up" first, pick a student and say,

"Batter up! Do you want a single, double, triple or home run?"

The student picks a level of difficulty, and you *pitch* a question. If the student gets a *hit* by answering the question correctly within ten seconds, he or she is on base. Of course, if some other student on the same team says the answer, the batter is out. Mild showing off as the student rounds the bases is usually greeted with hoots and cheers from teammates.

If, however, the student *misses* the question, you turn to the other team and say,

"Fly ball!"

Repeat the question and then *wait* before calling on anyone. This brings us to our next element of team game structure. Do you play this game open-book or closed-book?

Aha! If you play the game open-book, the team on defense can start looking up the answer as soon as they hear the question. As a result, the team on defense frantically flips through books, lab manuals, and notes to find the answer while the student who is "up" attempts to answer the question. There is actually peer pressure to look up the answer since dropping a fly ball means that a teammate was simply too lazy to look up the answer.

There is a certain contagion to looking up the answer that fills the room. Since kids hate to sit on the sidelines with nothing to do, the students on the team that is "at bat" usually start looking up the answer as well.

After you say, "Fly ball!" wait at least five seconds or until the rustling of book pages dies down. Then, call on a student. By calling on whomever you please, you can distribute questions more effectively while assuring that the weaker students get questions that they have a good chance of answering.

Scoring

If students on defense answer the question correctly, they *catch* the fly ball and make an *out* on the other team. If, however, they miss the question and *drop* the fly ball, the batter is on base with an error, and all runners advance one base.

Normally in baseball, the team with the most runs wins, but not in *this* game. In this game the final score for each team is calculated as *runs minus outs.* Catching a fly ball nullifies a run. In the final score it is the equivalent of hitting a solo home run. Defense is serious business.

Alternate Questions between Teams

Alternate questions between the teams. Consequently, a team would be up for one question and then on defense for the following question. By alternating questions between teams, each team has the same number of at-bats, and the dramatic tension is maximized since everyone can see who is ahead at any moment and what difficulty of question is needed to score.

Alternating the questions in this fashion eliminates innings. Rather, you have two games running side-by-side like a race. It is a race to see which team can get around the bases more often before time runs out. The generic name for a game format that alternates questions between teams is "Ping-Pong."

Game Variations

Baseball Becomes Football

To change baseball to football, draw two gridirons on the board, one for each team. Begin the game by saying to a student,

"Ten, twenty, thirty, or forty yard question. What will it be?"

Questions alternate between the teams as they move their footballs down their respective gridirons.

If a student misses a question, turn to the team on defense, and say,

"Sack!"

If the student you call on answers the question correctly, he or she throws the other team for a ten-yard loss.

An alternative way of structuring academic football is to pit one team against another on a *single gridiron* as in the real game of football. Secondary students often prefer this variant. Start on the fifty-yard line. Rather than using the Ping-Pong format, each team gets three downs to score. Three downs to score forces the students to use the long yardage questions.

If a ten-yard question is missed, the teacher says, *"Sack!"* as in the previous example. A correct answer throws the offense for a ten-yard loss. If, however, a twenty-, thirty- or forty-yard question is missed, the teacher says, *"Interception!"* A correct answer gains possession of the ball at the line of scrimmage.

Academic baseball becomes academic football with the change of seasons.

Of course, teachers can elaborate this basic format to suit their pleasure. You could have extra point questions after a touchdown. You could have difficult "Hail Mary" questions when more than forty yards are desperately needed. I have even seen teachers have a classroom Super Bowl complete with a coin-toss ceremony. One teacher played football so often that she eventually made a gridiron out of felt with a felt football so she could change field position easily.

Football Becomes Basketball

Think of football as simply a "path game" like the preschoolers' "Candyland." In such games the players move down the "squares" of the path in order to reach a "goal." A gridiron is simply a path with ten squares.

Once you envision games played on courts or fields as path games, you can play basketball or soccer just as easily as you can football. By answering more difficult questions, you can move down the path several squares at a time in order to score more quickly.

Basketball is simply a path game that requires seven "moves" in order to score, whereas football requires ten moves to score. In basketball, if the team with the ball misses the question and the team on defense answers it, they "steal the ball." The game then switches directions.

Hangman
"What'll it be? One, two, three, or four body parts?"

To use the Ping-Pong format, draw two gallows on the board, and alternate the questions between the teams. Add fingers and toes to make enough body parts so that the game lasts longer.

Jeopardy
"Pick a ten, twenty, thirty, or forty point question. The category is . . ."

All games from television make great PATs. Games like *Jeopardy, Who Wants To Be A Millionaire?* and *Trivial Pursuit* can be used to review factual information. However, some older game shows such as *What's My Line?* and *To Tell the Truth* are great for history. Students love impersonating historical figures in order to fake each other out.

Generating Questions
While teachers typically come up with questions on the spur of the moment, you can involve the students in the writing of questions. You could say, for example,

"Class, as you know, our test on chapter 7 is Thursday. I want to give you some class time to prepare for the test. But, I am going to have you prepare in the following fashion.

"Take out four pieces of paper, and number them one through four, placing the number in the upper right-hand corner. Write a single, double, triple, and home run question corresponding to the number on the paper.

"As you write these questions, look through chapter 7 for those things that are most important. Imagine that you are a teacher writing test questions.

"In fact, I will use some of your questions on the test. You may get to answer your own question on Thursday if you give me a good one.

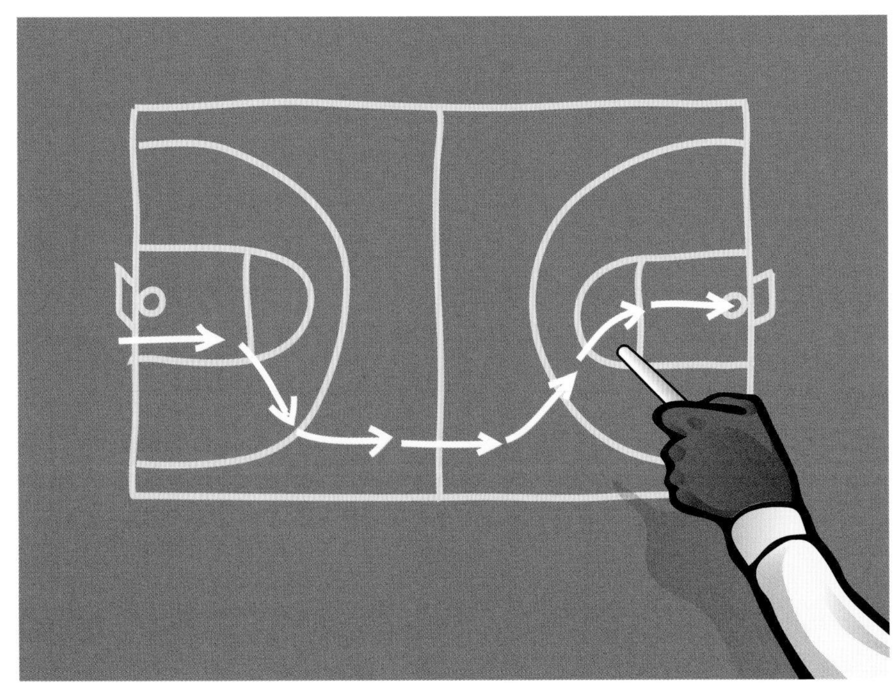

Basketball is simply a path game that requires seven "moves" in order to score.

"Don't make the singles too easy because the other team might get that question. And, don't make the home runs too hard because you might get that question.

"Below the question, write the answer. I want a complete paragraph. Beneath the answer, write the page number where the information can be found.

"You have the rest of the period to write your questions and answers. I will be coming around to see how you are doing."

In addition to structuring a good review activity, you end up with a stack of singles, doubles, triples, and home runs. Save the questions for your unit test review. *Jeopardy* is an excellent review game since the stacks of questions from different chapters supply your *Jeopardy* categories.

Academic Volleyball

Perfect for Vocabulary

In volleyball, your team can only score when *you have the serve.* When you have the serve, you can score points *in succession.* If, however, you miss, the service goes to the other team. Then, they can score points in succession until they miss.

You would not want to use questions that require explanations for answers. A team could be on defense a long time if the other team were to run off a string of points. For such questions, baseball would be a much better choice.

For volleyball, the questions and answers must come "fast and furious" to keep the game from dragging. The quick pace of questions makes volleyball ideal for vocabulary. Volleyball, therefore, is often used by foreign language and biology teachers.

The Rules

Divide the room into two teams, and say,

"I will begin by giving a word to one of the teams. Then, I will point to a person on that team. You will have *one second* to give me the first letter of the word. If you are correct, I will point to another person on that same team, and he or she will have *one second* to give me the next letter of the word.

"If someone misses, the word will come over to the other team. I will point to someone on that team, and he or she must pick up where the other team left off. The second team will keep the word as long as they spell it correctly. If they miss a letter, the word comes back to the first team. The team that gives me the last letter of the word gets the point and the next word.

"Ready? Here we go! The first word is 'photosynthesis.'"

Point to a student, and you are off and running. Drive the pace of the game so that students must be on their toes. You are a high-energy game show host.

For younger students whose attention spans are short, you can reduce the burden on memory and attention as follows. Give the word to the entire class, and have them write it down. Then, as the word is being spelled, everyone can follow along to keep track.

Keep 'em Honest

Perfect for Math

What kind of game rules work for math? The whole class could fall asleep while the person who is "up" attempted to solve a quadratic equation.

The game described below was described earlier in chapter 10, "Providing Accountability," as a method of work check. However, work check takes place in the form of a contest that can serve as a PAT.

To review, divide the class into two teams. Pair each member of Team A with a member of Team B, and have the pairs place their desks side by side. Write a math problem on the board, and give each problem a time limit as follows:

> "All right, class, you have two minutes for this next problem. (Write the equation on the board.) Ready? Go!"

Give the students a warning as time runs out.

> "Class, you have fifteen seconds."

Keep 'em Honest Work Check

When time runs out, go through the following routine:

> "Time! Exchange papers.
>
> "The answer is…
>
> "Check them and return them.
>
> "How many got it right on Team A?
>
> "How many got it right on Team B?
>
> "The score is now___ to___
>
> "You have three minutes for the next problem…"

Would people on Team A let people on Team B have extra time to work on the problem? Hardly! They'll say, "I'll take that!" and grab the paper.

Would anybody on Team A cheat for anybody on Team B? Not likely!

After the papers are returned, would students on Team B let their counterparts on Team A hold up their hands if they did not get it right? What do you think?

The whole check routine takes seconds, and each team keeps the other team honest. With every additional problem the score mounts and the tension builds.

Of course, you could give the class the same math problems on a worksheet. But, that would be a drag, and *you* would have to grade the papers.

Speed Games

Family Feud

When you call on the first person who has his or her hand up, you have a *speed game.* An example of a speed game on television is *Family Feud* in which the first team to hit the buzzer gets to answer the question.

College Bowl

College Bowl is a hybrid of a four-level/Ping-Pong format and a speed game. On the TV version, two universities were represented by four students each. Questions at four levels of difficulty were given during 10, 20, 30, and 40 point rounds.

To start the game, Team A would be given a 10 point question. The team would huddle, and the team captain would announce their answer. If they got it right, they would get 10 points. But, if they missed it, that question would go to Team B. Then, Team B would get their own 10 point question. If they missed it, the same question would go to Team A. The final part of the 10 point round was a toss-up question.

The toss-up question was the *speed* part of the game.

Television Game Formats

Television games must be of high interest or they wouldn't be successful. Be on the lookout for ones that you can adapt to your classrooms.

Join In

Teacher involvement is one of the keys to success with PAT. You must be with the students enjoying the activity and structuring it.

The moderator would read a question, and the first person to hit the buzzer answered the question. If that person answered the question correctly, he or she earned an extra 10 points for his or her team. But, if that player got it wrong, the other team could *huddle* before answering – a penalty for *buzzing in* before being sure of the answer.

This game format does not work well for large teams. Too many students become passive while the smarties dominate. Teachers commonly use their cooperative learning groups as teams with College Bowl. Some teachers keep "league standings" on the board with the students responsible for computing won/lost percentages.

Having stacks of questions prepared in advance makes this format easier to use. Since you cannot moderate several games simultaneously, have students moderate by simply pulling questions off of the appropriate stack.

PAT in the Elementary Grades

Using Curriculum as PAT

Debra Johnson, a first grade teacher from Dunlap, Tennessee, can honestly say that, after she learned to exploit PAT, she never taught another spelling lesson. Yet, at the end of one semester, all of her students passed the spelling achievement test at the second grade level, and some went as far as the fourth grade level.

How did she do it? Debra played spelling games for PAT two or three times a week. She posted lists of spelling words so that the students could prepare for Spelling Baseball. Soon, the students asked for harder words so that they could hit triples and home runs.

Spelling was not the only lesson she taught through PATs.

> "We also did math, vocabulary, art, reading, journal writing, story telling and sharing. One of their favorite activities was reading from their journals. Soon I began to see every lesson as a potential PAT."

How Much PAT?

Finding the correct time frame for PAT was a matter of trial and error, reported Ms. Johnson. At the beginning she tried one a day, but her first graders could not "hold it together" that long.

> "It all fell into place when I did three PATs a day. It was a match for their maturity level."

Debra gave the class fifteen minutes as a gift, but she was always able to bring PAT up to 30 minutes with bonuses. That meant one hour and 30 minutes of PAT a day! When asked if she lost anything by having so much PAT, she said,

> "I didn't give up *anything*. In fact, we saved enough time to do learning activities that I had not been able to fit into my schedule."

> "At one point they earned so much additional time that I had to put it into a savings account. They spent it to watch Reading Rainbow and the Magic School Bus."

Key to Success

When asked for the most important ingredient of a successful PAT, Debra said that *teacher involvement* is the key. "It does not work well if you just turn the kids loose. You must be there enjoying it with them and structuring it."

PAT for Research

Using PAT to Do Reports

The fourth grade class of Ann Owen in East Noble, Indiana frequently earned more time than it could use during its daily PAT. Ann put the unused time into a special account so that the class could eventually earn an entire day of PAT. The class used that day to present group reports on Great Britain.

From Monday through Thursday on the week of the presentations, the regular PAT was used to get ready for the big day. The class used video tapes, books, magazines, encyclopedias, and the internet to aid in their research.

The presentations showed that the students had learned about Say, See, Do Teaching by watching Ann. The geography group had everyone make maps of Great Britain. They then supplied stickers so that classmates could mark key areas and cities. The Games Group brought pancakes and skillets to reenact the famous Leeds Pancake Relay that celebrates Shrove Tuesday. Another group made transparencies showing the evolution of the Union Jack and what each part represents. They then passed out materials so that each classmate could design a flag of his or her own.

Cost and Benefit

When asked what all of this cost her, Ann said, "It was just another lesson. We would have had group presentations anyway." She added, "They owned the activity. They were responsible for earning the time and for making the most of it. They were successful, and they felt it."

PAT in Middle School

Using PAT for Foreign Language

Dale Crum of Arvada Middle School in Jefferson County, Colorado uses PAT with his Spanish classes.

"Most of our PATs are games. One of their favorites is basketball. Each of two teams sends a member to the board, and when I say a word in English, the first one to write it properly in Spanish wins. The winner gets to shoot a Nerf basketball at the trash can with more difficult shots earning more points

Share PATs

If a group of colleagues shares one PAT each week, you will all have more ideas than you can use.

"Another game they love is Pictionary. Each team sends a person to the board, and I secretly give them a word in Spanish. They have to draw a picture of it while each team tries to guess the word. The kids get excited as they call out words, but there is a penalty for using English."

Scheduling PAT

Dale uses different schedules of PAT for his seventh and eighth grade classes. According to Dale,

"The eighth graders have PAT once a week. I start them out with 15 minutes on Monday, and by Friday they have earned over a half-hour. They love Fridays.

"A couple of my seventh grade classes can be squirrely, and they could not wait until Friday if their lives depended on it. For them we have PAT at the end of each 50 minute class period. I tell them, 'Earn it today. Get it today.' We play learning games that review the material I taught that day."

PAT in High School

Using PAT for Science

Annette Patterson in Artesia, New Mexico uses a game she calls "Tag Team" in all of her science classes from

Basic Science through Chemistry. *Tag Team* combines large motor activity with review to create a high level of excitement.

"First, I divide the class into four teams and line them up. Then, I name a category of information. It could be the attributes that distinguish birds from other animals or the signs and chemical symbols for earth elements.

"Once I name the category, the first member of each team races to the board to write down an example of that category. Then they race back to hand the chalk to the next person in line who races to the board. Each round of the game lasts one minute. The team with the most correct answers wins. Since repeats don't count, everybody pays close attention."

Everybody Likes to Play

Annette finds that the advanced students look forward to PAT just as much as her Basic Science students.

"When I first started with PAT, I was afraid that the older college-bound students would not go for it. I couldn't have been more wrong. I guess kids just like to play."

Getting Started

Anxiety and Avoidance

"Our high school kids are too cool for PAT."

"I don't know what to use for English."

"If we played games, my kids would go wild."

Comments like these occur during every workshop and reflect the anxiety that we all feel about starting something new. A voice inside says, "What if I try this, and it bombs miserably?"

Those who give it a try invariably report, with a sense of wonder, "It works!" As Annette Patterson said, "I guess kids just like to play."

Assessing Maturity Realistically

Many secondary teachers scare themselves out of doing PAT by imagining that teenagers are more mature than they really are. The teacher who said, "Our high school kids are just too cool for PAT," had convinced himself that his students were seventeen going on twenty-seven.

It would be more accurate to think of the students as seventeen coming from seven. Any game that the students have ever enjoyed playing, they still enjoy playing. I have seen high school classes work up a sweat playing "Steal the Bacon" just like fourth graders.

Make a PAT Bank

Every member of the faculty has great PAT ideas. If your colleagues were to take turns sharing one PAT a week, you would have more ideas than you had time to use.

Create a PAT Bank at your school site. Have faculty members write up their favorite PATs on 4x6 cards and keep them in a file box. Also, collect books of PAT ideas, and keep them in a central location.

PAT Starter Set
www.fredjones.com/PAT

Visit our web site for learning games that are useful in all subject areas with students at both the elementary and secondary levels.

Section Eight

Positive Classroom Management

Chapter Twenty Four

Dealing with Typical Classroom Crises

Preview

- The Backup System is a hierarchy of consequences for dealing with severe or repetitive discipline problems.
- Once a student is sent to the office, management becomes expensive because it consumes the time of at least two professionals and often requires meetings and paperwork.
- It is far cheaper to nip the problem in the bud. But what, exactly, do you do when such a nasty problem first occurs in the classroom?
- Most teachers enter the profession without a clear answer to this question. Consequently, when the time comes, they must "wing it."
- Small backup response options provide strategies for nipping problems "in the bud." These responses are low-key and private. Yet they clearly communicate to the student that "enough is enough."

Beyond Limit Setting

What the...?

As you turn from writing a sentence on the board, you see something fly across the room.

"What the...?"

Your head quickly follows the trajectory back to its source. You catch Larry as his body comes around. He gives you his innocent look.

Your brainstem shouts out, "Why you little..."

Meanwhile, your cortex whispers, "Slow down. Take a relaxing breath. Turn in a regal fashion."

What Next?

Larry is trying to disappear, but he knows he's been busted. Your lesson has come to a halt. Everybody can tell that this is serious.

As you take another relaxing breath, you size up the situation. You have time to think: "I can't just go on teaching after something like that. Should I send him to the office? He's just sitting there innocently now."

Do You Have a Plan?

In your training to be a teacher, did you ever receive a clear answer to the following question? Exactly what do you do when a student pulls some stunt in your classroom that causes you to say to yourself, *"I never want to see that in here again?"*

I have asked that question to thousands of teachers in dozens of locations, and almost never does a hand go up. This should teach us something. There is no plan. Our profession does not have any straightforward, generally understood way of dealing with one of the most predictable discipline management dilemmas that will eventually confront any teacher.

With no plan of action, we are left to devise some kind of plan on our own. We read a book. We ask the teacher down the hall. We search our memories. We beg, borrow, and steal and finally we "wing it."

What do you think the odds are that thousands of young teachers will all come up with a good plan during their first year on the job? And, once they come up with a plan, what do you think the odds are that they will ever change it?

The Structure of the Backup System

A Hierarchy of Consequences

The Backup System is a hierarchy of consequences arranged in a stair-step fashion from small to large. The logic of the Backup System was discussed briefly at the beginning of Chapter 13, "Understanding Brat Behavior." This logic is timeless – *the punishment fits the crime.* The bigger the crime, the bigger the punishment.

The objective of the Backup System is to suppress the unacceptable behavior so that it does not reappear. This is done by raising the price of a behavior to a point where the student is no longer willing to pay for it. As you go up the Backup System, unfortunately, the program becomes more expensive for everyone involved.

Certain of the milder consequences are under the teacher's control *within the classroom.* Common examples that you may remember from your childhood include keeping a student in from recess, talking to a student after class, or keeping a student after school.

The remainder of consequences at the school site occur *outside of the classroom* where they are referred to as "The

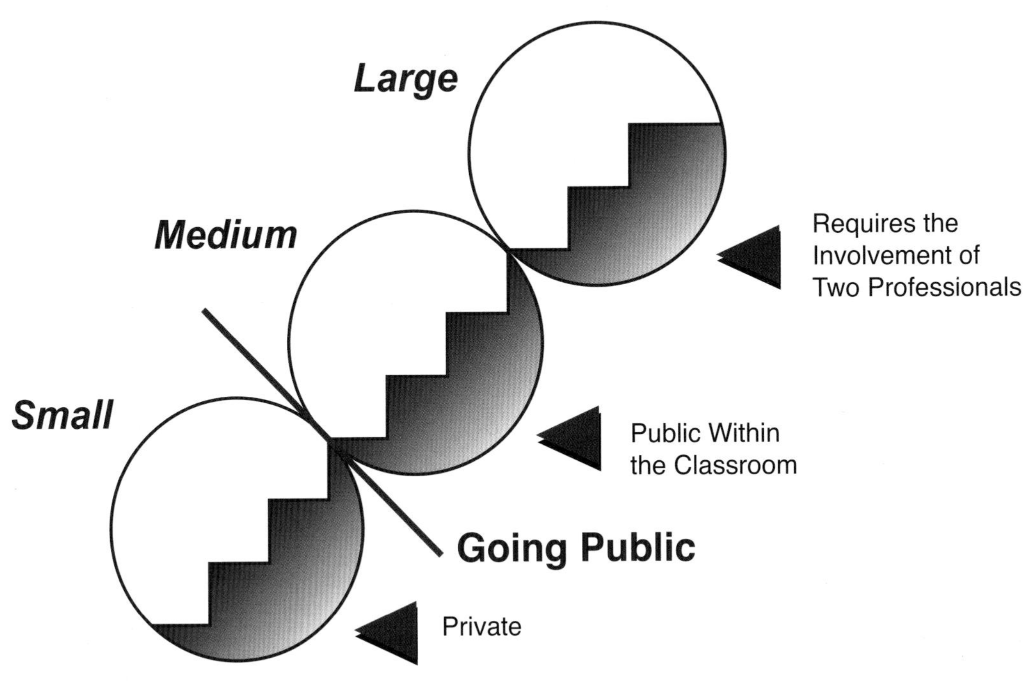

As you go up the Backup System, the program becomes more expensive for everyone involved.

School Discipline Code." These, too, have not changed much since you were a kid and include being sent to the office, detention, in-school suspension, and out-of-school suspension.

Beyond the school district, the Backup System is administered by the juvenile justice system and the criminal justice system. It is a rare high school administrator who has not had some dealings with juvenile hall.

Problems with the School Discipline Code

We had some fun with the School Discipline Code at the beginning of chapter 13 with our "mock freshman assembly." As we all know, the same 5 percent of the student body, the "Larrys," produce 90 percent of the office referrals for as long as they are in school. Year after year, we ask our school discipline system to "put the lid on." And, year after year, we are left frustrated, muttering to ourselves,

> "It should work!"
>
> "Why doesn't it work?"
>
> "What do we have to do to make it work?"

No matter how many times we convene a task force to revise the School Discipline Code, nothing ever changes. For one thing, as I mentioned earlier, there is nothing you can legally do to Larry that every educator in the state has not known about for decades. And, secondly, many of the things that we do try, like kicking Larry out of class or sending him home from school, backfire by reinforcing him for giving us a hard time.

Levels to the Game

The diagram on the opposite page is a schematic of the "hierarchy of consequences" with consequences divided into three sections, *small, medium, and large.* The three levels of the Backup System can be described as follows:

- **Large** – Large backup responses require help from outside of the classroom. Sending a student to the office, assigning detention, or suspending a student are the most common examples.

  Large backup options are expensive because they consume the time of at least two professionals and often require meetings after school and extensive paperwork. In addition, by the time you send a student to the office, you have already paid a high price in terms of stress.

  Since large backup responses can serve as stress reducers just by getting rid of Larry for a while, they have a tendency to become addictive. A certain percentage of teachers on any faculty will repeatedly "bounce" students to the office just to make them disappear.

- **Medium** – Medium backup responses occur within the classroom. Their defining characteristic, apart from being under the teacher's control, is that they are *public.*

  Most of the classroom sanctions that we remember from childhood come under this category. There is nothing private about having your name put on the board, being sent to time-out or being kept after class for a talk with the teacher.

  Medium backup responses tend to be cheaper than large ones because they consume the time of only one professional while rarely requiring extra meetings or paperwork. However, a hidden cost of these sanctions can be the revenge of an embarrassed student who was antagonistic to begin with.

- **Small** – Small backup responses provide teachers with a clear idea of what to do the *first time* they see a problem that they never want to see again. They are your first line of defense.

Small backup responses are *private*. They are *subtle*. The rest of the class usually does not even know that they occurred. Consequently, small backup responses avoid the potential for revenge from an embarrassed student.

It is the job of small backup responses to "nip problems in the bud." They say to the student, in effect:

> "You are entering the Backup System. A word to the wise. Stop what you are doing now while it is still cheap. The price will only go up from here."

If the student takes the teacher seriously and stops goofing off, management is cheap for everyone. As you can see, however, it all hinges on the student taking the teacher seriously.

Classroom vs. School Site Discipline Management

While it is important for a teacher to understand the Backup System in its totality, most of the Backup System occurs outside of the teacher's classroom. Rather than being part of classroom management, it falls under the heading of school-site management.

School-site management covers anything that happens outside of your door. It includes the management of noise in the halls, litter and graffiti, rowdiness during assemblies, and disruptions in the lunch room, on the school grounds, and at the bus dock.

Effective school-site management has been described in detail in the books, *Positive Classroom Discipline* and *Positive Classroom Instruction*. Relevant chapters are posted on our web site **www.fredjones.com** so that you may read them at will. Since *Tools for Teaching* describes the skills of *classroom* management, our discussion of the Backup System will focus upon sanctions that teachers can use by themselves within the classroom to keep small problems from becoming large.

Using Small Backup Responses

Entering the Backup System

You will typically enter the Backup System for one of two reasons:

- A sudden obnoxious incident
- A repeat disruptor

While obnoxious incidents are plain to see, it would be worth our while to spend some time with *repeat disruptors*. As I mentioned in Chapter 19, "Dealing with the Unexpected," some kids come from homes in which the parents *never* follow through after saying "no." These children learn to simply pause when told to stop until the parent looks away. Then, they continue doing as they please.

When you see the this pattern a few times, a red flag should go up in your brain that says, "We may have a repeater." When you conclude that you do, it is time to go to the Backup System. There is no point in playing this game all year. Use whatever level of sanction is necessary.

After you have employed the Backup System to teach the "repeater" that "no means no," you can probably fade your consequences back to Limit Setting. However, until you teach that lesson in no uncertain terms, repeaters assume that you are a "weenie" just like mom and dad.

Camouflage and Containment

During training I do a demonstration in which I say to the trainees,

> "I am going to model working the crowd. It is a boring demonstration because working the crowd is never dramatic.
>
> "Watch carefully though, because, when I am done, I will ask you a question. Do not guess at the answer. If you know the answer, raise your hand."

As I work the crowd, I interact briefly with a series of students just as any teacher might during Guided Practice. Then, I say to the group,

"Raise your hand if you know who is in trouble."

No hands go up – not even the hands of those sitting next to the person who is "in trouble." Then I say,

As with Meaning Business, working the crowd provides the camouflage that allows your Backup System to be invisible.

"Let me tell you why you do not know who is in trouble. Because, I don't *want* you to know. It is none of your business.

"Will the people who received corrective feedback on a math problem please raise your hands (two hands go up). Will the people whose work I checked please raise your hands (two more hands go up). Now, will the person who is in trouble please raise your hand."

Some mild laughter ripples through the group as those sitting next to the person "in trouble" realize that they were unaware of it. I then say:

"One of the things that we learn from this demonstration is that, when you are working the crowd, the students cannot tell *corrective feedback* from *work check* from your *Backup System*. They all look the same.

"When you are working the crowd, you talk to students from close range. You typically lean over to whisper so as not to pull other students off task. Consequently, it is a private communication."

As with Meaning Business, *working the crowd* provides the camouflage that allows your Backup System to be invisible. When discipline management is invisible, you have a greater ability to keep small problems small.

Just a Warning?

What I said to the student "in trouble" was:

"This is the second time I have had to deal with this talking, and I want it to stop. If I see any more talking, we will have a little conversation of our own after class. For right now, all I really care about is you getting some of this work done."

This is a verbal warning. The specific words are not critical. You will ad-lib something of this general nature when the time comes.

But there are warnings, and then, there are warnings. I could have admonished the disruptive student in front of the class, or I could have written the student's name on the board. Both are types of warnings commonly used by teachers. But they would have been *public events.*

Imagine that you are sixteen years old in a high school class full of your friends, and the teacher calls you down in front of your peer group. How would you feel toward that teacher? Would you get even?

If you were the teacher, that student's "getting even" would be your next discipline problem. Isn't it a little self-defeating to have the "solution" to one discipline problem be the cause of the next one?

Keep It Private

As I mentioned in Chapter 18, "Eliminating Backtalk," discipline management when it becomes a public event tends to be either win-win or lose-lose. If you make students look foolish in front of their peer group, they will make you look foolish in front of the same peer group.

If, on the other hand, you are protective of the students, even when they are out of line, they will probably cut you some slack when you need it. At the very least, they will have no reason for revenge.

If the warning is a public event, it is a *medium* backup response that unavoidably involves the peer group. If the warning is private, it is a *small* backup response that does not involve the peer group. It would be far more protective of the student and far less risky for you to keep the warning as private as possible.

The Function of Small Backup Responses

A Word to the Wise

Small Backup responses are communications that say to the student,

"You are entering the Backup System. A word to the wise..."

Sometimes you have to give two or three of these messages with increasing explicitness to get your point across. The objective of these communications is to get the student to fold in the poker game before the price gets high for everyone.

Goofing off in the classroom is typically a penny-ante game. Kids are rarely in it for high stakes. They just want a diversion in the midst of work. Students will usually fold before the price gets too high if you give them a chance to do so gracefully. Of course, all bets are off if you embarrass them or back them into a corner.

> **Self-Defeating**
>
> **If you make students look foolish in front of their peer group, they will make you look foolish in front of the same peer group.**
>
> **Isn't it a little self-defeating to have the "solution" to one discipline problem be the cause of the next one?**

An Invitation to Fold

Small backup responses are *communications,* not sanctions. They are "promissory notes." Their objective is to:

- inform students that they are entering the Backup System (i.e., that you have had about enough of their foolishness)
- invite students to fold (i.e., to cool it before you are forced to deliver consequences with real price tags attached)

You are making an offer that students would be foolish to refuse. Most of the time, unless students have a big chip on their shoulders, they will make the pragmatic choice and keep "the price of doing business" low.

The backup response options listed below are arranged from most private (smallest) to most explicit (largest). Most of them have been around forever, and you may be able to add an item or two of your own to the list. The two or three that you choose may differ depending on the student and the situation.

> **Students will usually fold before the price gets too high, if they can do so gracefully.**

Small Backup Options

Pre-Warning

A pre-warning clearly communicates that "enough is enough" without specifying consequences. This gives you time to observe the situation, and it gives the student time to think. A fourth grade teacher from Memphis, a "natural" if I ever saw one, described her pre-warning to me. She said,

"Students know perfectly well when they are 'stepping over the line.' Rather than letting it slide, I will confront that person privately with my most serious demeanor. I will look the student in the eye and say, 'If I see any more of this behavior whatsoever, I am going to have to start planning what to do.'

"Their eyes get big. The student knows that I am serious. Rarely do I ever have to 'start planning' what to do."

A pre-warning often elicits a short burst of nervous laughter from students. Due to the teacher's manner, students know that it is serious business. But when they process the words, they realize to their relief that they are not really "in trouble" yet.

A pre-warning is frequently all that you need. It serves as a "wake-up call" to students who are too busy "goofing off" to realize that they are being inappropriate. If the problem continues, you can always go to an explicit warning.

Warning

Warnings have already been discussed in detail. A warning describes the consequence to the student if you "see this behavior one more time." A warning is *never* a bluff.

Pulling the Card

Imagine that you have a 3-by-5 card file on your desk containing each student's name, address, and home phone. Having students fill out these cards is a shrewd Bell Work activity on the first day of school.

Imagine, further, that you have given a warning to a student, let's call him Larry as usual. You look up to see Larry doing "it" again. You catch his eye as you take a relaxing breath. He gives you his best "oops, sorry" look.

Slowly, without calling any attention to yourself, walk to your desk and casually pick up the card file. Leaf through it, and pull out Larry's card as you look at him. Lay the card on the corner of your desk face up. Look at Larry again with your best Queen Victoria face as you place the card file back on your desk. Then return to what you were doing, giving Larry one final look.

Obviously, you are communicating with Larry. He would have to be pretty dense not to realize whose name, address and home phone number is sitting face-up on the corner of your desk.

You have literally "rolled one more card" in the poker game, and now Larry must decide whether to raise or fold. Hopefully, he will "cool it" and keep the price of poker cheap for everyone.

A Note in the Grade Book

Having already interacted with the disruptive student once, you look up to see the problem reoccur. You catch the student's eye.

Walk slowly to your desk, and, making eye contact with the disruptor, sit down and pick up your grade book. Write a note concerning the incident in the appropriate place, and give the student another look. Stand slowly, lay the grade book down on your desk, and return to what you were doing. With a permanent record of the behavior in the grade book, poker is getting more expensive.

Once again, the student must make a decision to raise or fold. As always with small backup responses, you are attempting to communicate as subtly as possible that folding would be a very wise thing to do.

A Letter on the Desk

A letter on the desk is your last stop before you go to medium backup responses. It is not frequently done, but it has saved a few teachers from needing more expensive sanctions.

Having already given the disruptive student two opportunities to fold (your choice as to the options used), you decide to give small backup responses one more shot (a judgement call). You catch the student's eye and then go to your desk where you sit down and begin to write.

Write a brief letter home. It takes less than a minute to write since it only contains five sentences which cover the following points:

You have literally "rolled one more card" in the poker game, and now Larry must decide whether to raise or fold.

- Dear _____, today in class I have had to deal with (briefly describe the problem behavior).
- I need your help.
- If we work together now, we can prevent this from becoming a "real" problem.
- I will call you tomorrow at which time we can make a plan.
- Thank you for your cooperation and concern.

Sign the letter, and put it in an envelope. Address the envelope, but don't waste a stamp yet. Take the letter and a piece of tape to the student's desk. Lean over and tape the letter on the desk, and whisper to the student as privately as possible,

"This is a letter home to your parents describing exactly what I have had to put up with in here today. If I see *no* more of this behavior before the end of the (day, for young students, or week, for older students), then, with my permission and in front of my eyes, you may tear up this letter and throw it away.

"If, however, I see *any* more of this behavior, I will send the letter home even if I have to hand-deliver it. Do I make myself clear?

"For now, all I really care about is getting some of this work done. Let's see if we can keep life simple."

The letter on the desk is what you might call a visual prompt. It can serve as a continual reminder to be wise.

I am sometimes asked, "What would you do if the student just tore up the letter and threw it on the floor?" This question is almost always asked in a tone that says, "These little sanctions won't work with some of my students."

To put small backup responses into perspective, let me emphasize again that the critical variable in a well implemented Backup System is *not* your success. You will always succeed because you will always raise the ante in the poker game no matter what the stakes. The only critical variable is the *price paid by the student.* If the student forces you to deliver stiffer sanctions, then deliver them.

Medium Backup Options

Medium backup responses include those public classroom sanctions that are familiar to us from our own schooling. Some, such as public warnings and reprimands, tend to be counter-productive because they generate resentment. Others, such as time-out, can serve the teacher well by providing an unequivocal means of saying "no" that is nonadversarial.

Because medium backup responses are familiar to us, it is easy to assume that we understand them. However, as is always the case in the implementation of classroom management procedures, the devil is in the details. This section describes the details of some of the more common and useful procedures in order to maximize their success rate.

Heart-to-Heart Talk

When a problem reoccurs in class, my first instinct is to have a talk with the student to find out what is going on. Have the student do most of the talking.

"Jennifer, tell me, what was going on in class today between you and Michelle?"

Good clinicians are masters of wait time, and they are masters of making the other person do all of the work.

"What are we going to have to do to resolve this problem?"

Sometimes it is possible to have this conversation privately during class time. But, usually it will be after class.

Time-Out in the Classroom

Time-out has served as an alternative to more punitive sanctions in behavior management programs in recent decades. Time-out, however, is a prime example of a detailed procedure that is often used casually – "Like benching a kid, right?" Well, not exactly.

For starters, time-out should have the following elements:

- Two time-out areas should be prepared in the classroom since problems often involve two students. These areas need to be *visually isolated* so that the students in time-out cannot entertain each other or the rest of the class.
- Time-out should be considered an extension of Meaning Business with the same body language and the same withering boredom in response to any wheedling or arguing.
- Time-out should be relatively brief, usually not in excess of five minutes.
- Time-out should be boring. It is time away from desirable activity. There should be no "bootleg" sources of entertainment available in the time-out area.

The first problem with using time-out hits you as soon as you try to find two visually isolated areas in a classroom. It is hard enough to find just one.

The second problem in using time-out is the natural resistance of young people to being bored. If they would just sit in time-out quietly and be repentant, the whole thing would be so simple. But, instead, students who are squirrely in class tend to be squirrely in time-out.

Time-Out in a Colleague's Classroom

If a student continues to disrupt after being sent to time-out, you might consider time-out in a colleague's classroom. It often produces more reliable results than sending a kid to the office, and it sends the message that the teachers can handle serious problems themselves. The fine points of time-out in a colleague's classroom are as follows:

- The colleague to which the student is sent must thoroughly understand the program, approve of it and feel free to reciprocate should he or she need to.
- Time-out in a colleague's classroom should last for the remainder of the period or for at least 20 minutes.
- The student should be delivered to the colleague's classroom with a folder of work.
- The student must do the work in the folder during the entire time that he or she is in time-out. Academic help from the teacher should be brief and matter-of-fact.
- The student cannot join in any classroom games or activities. Usually he or she sits facing the wall so as not to be distracted or entertained.
- Last, but not least, the student should be separated from his or her peer group *by as many years as possible.*

This final condition is perhaps the *most important* of all since it almost guarantees that the student will not want to repeat the experience. Yet, it is the condition that is *most commonly violated.* It is far easier for a fifth grade teacher to send Larry to the fifth

The Key to Success

The key to success with a Backup System is not the size of the negative sanction.

Rather, the key to success is *the person who is using the Backup System.*

grade class across the hall than to deliver him to a first grade class in another wing of the building.

If, however, you put Larry in an adjoining fifth grade classroom, he will probably have a grand old time showing off for his friends. The failure of time-out in one classroom has simply been exported to another classroom.

But put a fifth grader in a first grade classroom, and he or she will feel like "a fish out of water." Or, at the high school, send the goof-off from freshman life science to physics where he or she will not get the time of day.

Staying After School

Keeping students after school can be difficult to implement due to bus schedules, to say nothing of your schedule. But, where practical, it can be powerful.

Keeping students after school to *complete their work* can be just as useful as keeping students who disrupt. Students who just "twiddle their thumbs" in class soon learn that completing assignments is not an option. Rather, it is "pay me now, or pay me later."

The key procedural element to keeping a student after school is that he or she do schoolwork rather than playing games or being the teacher's "little helper." It is not supposed to be reinforcing.

You must be particularly wary of the possibility of *reinforcement errors* with latchkey children. Sometimes just being with someone after school is preferable to being with no one.

Keeping students after school can be costly to any teacher who has other obligations at the end of the school day. One cheap solution is to keep the student for only five or ten minutes after dismissal. This provides time for some values clarification, while Larry's buddies go off and leave him behind.

Why Do Classroom Backup Responses Work?

Traditional Logic

The traditional logic of the Backup System is that *the punishment should fit the crime* as a means of suppressing crime. It seems logical. It should work.

Unfortunately, our experience tells us otherwise. The same group of "Larrys" produce the vast majority of office referrals for as long as they are in school. And, regardless of the sanctions used, the overall rate never goes down.

In addition, we know that some teachers send students to the office several times a day and have no classroom control, whereas other teachers rarely raise their voices and almost never need to send a student to the office. This seems backwards. Why does the Backup System seem to fail those teachers who use it the most while helping those teachers who use it the least?

The Key to Success

The key to success with a Backup System is *not* the size of the negative sanction as logic might dictate. Rather, the key to success is *the person who is using the Backup System.*

If, from the first day of school your students learn that *you say what you mean, and you mean what you say,* and that *no means no* regardless of the circumstances, then, when you say "enough is enough" with your small backup responses, it means something. If, on the other hand, you are not perceived as Meaning Business, you can make any threat you want, and the kids will test you further just to see what happens. Weenies get no respect.

Chapter Twenty Five

Exploiting the Management System

Preview

- A management system differs from a bag of tricks by providing a full range of effective procedures that can easily be exploited in solving classroom management problems.
- The management system described in this book is organized into three levels based upon cost: interpersonal skills, incentive systems, and the Backup System, with the Backup System being the most expensive.
- The more effective teachers become at management, the less they will use the Backup System and the more they will rely on their interpersonal skills.
- In general, the more difficult the management problem, the more reinforcement-oriented is the cure. Only a management system organized in this fashion can avoid the tendency of alienated students to "raise the ante" when confronted by the Backup System.

The Management System

Beyond a Bag of Tricks

The term "bag of tricks" accurately describes our traditional approach to classroom management. Over the course of our careers we try a little of this and a little of that in the hope that things will get better.

Every year a new crop of fads and buzz words arrive on the scene to add to our bag of tricks. Yet we know from experience that this approach will not take us anywhere that we have not already been. As a profession, we have had no "game plan."

Good News

The good news is that the methods described in this book provide that missing game plan. They represent a clear window into the world of the exceptional teacher that is both high-tech and down-to-earth. They define "working smart."

Discipline or Instruction?

Over the years I often found it difficult to get administrators to focus on instruction as part of successful discipline management. They would express the desire for "just a discipline program," adding that discipline was the main source of teacher complaints.

Yet educators know that good discipline and good instruction go together. But *how* do they go together? Educators have come up with very few specifics to define this relationship. Perhaps they are looking in the wrong place.

They have tended to focus on the *content* of instruction rather than the *process* of instruction. Through engaging curriculum they hoped to overcome the propensity of students to goof off rather than work. But this picture of the interrelationship between discipline and instruction is too simplistic.

To understand the cause-and-effect relationship between discipline and instruction, we must delve deeply into the social dynamics of the classroom. For example, we cannot even work the crowd, a precondition of effective discipline management, until we wean the helpless handraisers. And, we cannot wean the helpless handraisers until we create mastery by integrating the verbal, visual and physical modalities of learning in the teaching of a lesson.

Since everything in the classroom is interconnected, we must manage discipline and instruction simultaneously. And, to solve management dilemmas quickly, our choices must be organized so that we may review them at a glance.

Three Levels of Management

The figure to the right organizes the management system into a *decision ladder*. As you can see, our management options are arranged along two paths: *reinforcement* and *suppression*.

While reinforcement is well understood by educators, we need to spend a moment with suppression since it can be confused with punition. Suppression only becomes punitive at the top of the decision ladder

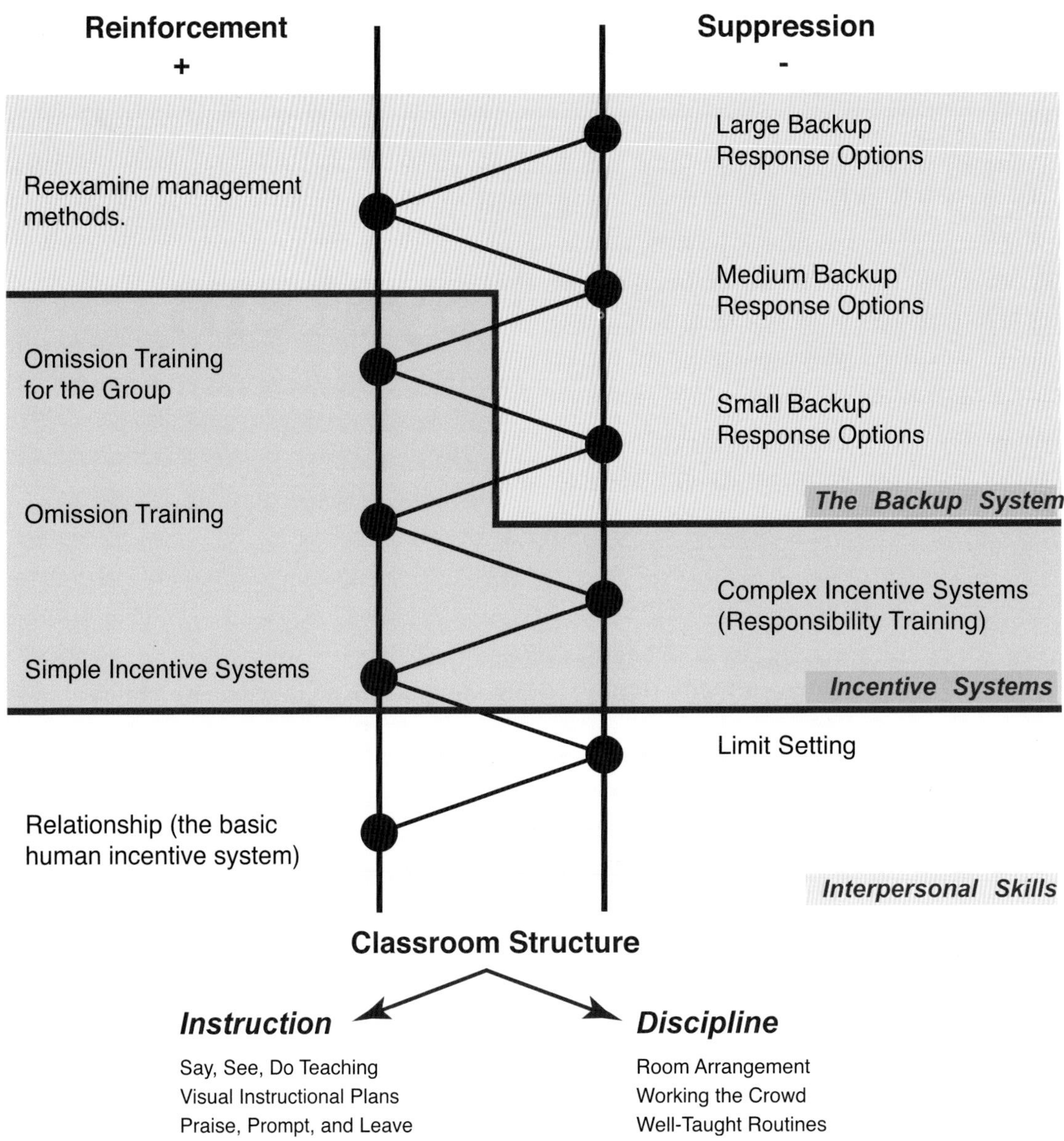

To solve problems, go up the Decision Ladder.

with medium and large backup responses. Up to that point misbehavior is dealt with in a non-punitive and non-adversarial fashion. Limit Setting (Meaning Business) and Responsibility Training give teachers the tools to deal with misbehavior without becoming negative. These tools are indispensible in making discipline management positive.

Furthermore, our management options are arranged from inexpensive to expensive as you move from bottom of the decision ladder to the top. In problem solving, we start at the bottom and move systematically *up* the decision ladder. In this way we solve management problems as inexpensively as possible.

The decision ladder is divided into three levels of management:

- **Interpersonal Skills:** This level of management describes the skills of the natural teacher. This is the *least* expensive level of management since interpersonal skills have no overhead in terms of program development and implementation. The teacher's presence is the management program.
- **Incentive Systems:** Incentive systems provide motivation. As part of *instruction,* they provide motivation for working hard and being conscientious. As part of *discipline,* they provide motivation for cooperating with the teacher and with classmates in carrying out classroom routines.

  Incentive systems add an element of cost to management since they require recordkeeping and the giving of reinforcers. However, more sophisticated incentive systems minimize these costs. Responsibility Training, for example, trains the entire class to cooperate in a wide range of management situations at almost no additional cost to the teacher.
- **The Backup System:** The purpose of the Backup System is to communicate that "no means no" to students who exhibit severe or repetitive disruptive behaviors. The greater part of the Backup System is contained in the School Discipline Code. These sanctions tend to be very expensive since they involve the time of several professionals and typically require reports, meetings with parents and special programs such as in-school suspension.

  However, some of the most important sanctions are delivered invisibly by the teacher in the classroom. These Small Backup Responses can keep little problems from becoming big by nipping them in the bud. However, for Small Backup Responses to work, the students must *already* perceive the teacher as Meaning Business.

"Classroom Structure is the ground upon which effective management stands."

Interpersonal Skills

Structure and Instruction

As you can see on the decision ladder to the left, Classroom Structure is the ground upon which effective management stands. Classroom Structure, however, is far more than room arrangement, rules, and routines.

Classroom Structure includes the process of instruction itself. It includes Say, See, Do Teaching so that students are fully engaged in learning by doing. It includes the use of Visual Instructional Plans (VIPs) so that the steps of performance are crystal clear. And, it also includes Praise, Prompt, and Leave as an indispensable tool in making helpless handraisers into independent learners.

Effective teachers invest most of their classroom management effort at the level of Classroom Structure. Any element of Classroom Structure that is omitted or overlooked by the teacher will become a problem that requires Limit Setting.

Relationship Building

The first item on the positive side of the decision ladder is relationship building. While this could be subsumed under the heading of Classroom Structure, I have placed it as a separate item on the positive side of the ladder to remind us that all other aspects of management rest upon the goodwill that teachers establish with their students.

Relationship building is not just a matter of being nice. It is a *program.* It requires an investment of time and energy for both planning and implementation. It begins with an ice-breaking activity during the first period of the school year and never lets up.

Limit Setting

Since Limit Setting says "no" to unacceptable behavior, we cross over to the negative side of the decision ladder. Staying calm and using effective body language allows you to say "no" to unacceptable behavior in a nonadversarial fashion. You must be able to set limits without producing alienation and embarrassment or you will continually undermine your relationship with students.

Most of the time-honored ways of saying "no," like nagging, criticizing, threatening, and punishing have a very negative effect on relationships. By the end of the school year, teachers and students in classrooms characterized by such methods are usually glad to be rid of each other.

Incentive Systems

Simple Incentives

Simple incentive systems represent a straightforward application of Grandma's Rule: *You have to finish your dinner before you get your dessert* (see Chapter 9, "Creating Motivation"). Simple incentives have two parts – dinner and dessert, task and reinforcer. For dessert, we cross over to the positive side of the decision ladder.

Incentives for work productivity are of this type – *as soon as you finish the assignment correctly, you may work on your project.* Incentives for discipline management commonly used in elementary classrooms such as point systems and star charts are also of this type.

However, in discipline management, simple incentive systems tend to be a lot of work for what you get. Complex recordkeeping and reinforcement exchange produce improvement but no cure. The problems still remain. To make the use of incentives for discipline management cost-effective, complex incentive systems will be required.

Complex Incentives

Complex incentive systems have more parts than simple incentive systems, most notably, *bonuses* and *penalties.* Responsibility Training represents the state of the art in complex incentive systems for discipline management.

We place complex incentives on the negative side of the decision ladder because they contain penalties. However, Responsibility Training is experienced as positive by students since bonuses are common and penalties are rare.

Omission Training

If more management leverage is needed, probably because Larry chooses to ruin PAT, we go to the positive side of the decision ladder for Omission Training. Omission Training is a bonus-only management program. Larry can no longer lose PAT for the group.

Omission Training delivers the power of the peer group in order to turn Larry around. It is extremely cost-effective because it delivers that power for no more work than a heart-to-heart talk and a bonus clause added to PAT. Yet it rearranges the social dynamics of the classroom so that Larry is now a hero rather than an outcast.

Omission Training for the Group

As you can see by looking at the decision ladder, Omission Training for the group typically occurs after you have gone to small backup responses for repeated infractions. If you find that you are using small backup responses too often, you can give the group bonus PAT for avoiding the Backup System.

The Backup System

Small Backup Responses

Small backup responses take us to the negative side of the decision ladder. Small backup responses represent a series of communications that say, in effect, "A word to the wise..." If the student takes a hint and cools it for the rest of the period, the communication has done its job. However, the likelihood of that happening is a direct function of the degree to which the student already takes the teacher seriously.

Medium Backup Responses

Medium backup responses are also on the negative side of the decision ladder because they represent the penalties that teachers have traditionally used in the classroom. In the overall scheme of discipline management at the school site, sanctions such as sending a child to time-out or keeping a student after class are typically viewed as small consequences, the kinds of things a teacher might do upon first encountering a problem.

As you can see from the decision ladder, however, medium backup responses are near the *top*. Teachers have a great many management options that they can and should employ before even considering a medium backup response.

There are serious reasons for avoiding medium backup responses. For one thing, they are expensive. Simply setting up a parent conference can cause the teacher several phone calls, to say nothing of time after school for the conference *if* the parent shows up. Even time-out can be a pain if the students in time-out choose to disrupt further.

Large Backup Responses

Large backup responses are typically contained in the School Discipline Code. When it comes to large backup responses, there is nothing new under the sun.

Reexamine

On the decision ladder between medium and large backup responses you will see an option entitled "reexamine." A sudden crisis can take even the most effective teacher into large backup responses. Yet, under normal circumstances, effective teachers rarely send students to the office. Frequent reliance upon large backup responses should serve as a signal that a teacher is in trouble. We need to help that person reexamine his or her options using the management system as our guide.

Using the Decision Ladder

The Region of Finesse

The figure on the following page shows the decision ladder with the contributions of *Tools for Teaching* outlined in red. The elements of discipline management unique to this program comprise most of the teacher's options between Classroom Structure and the Backup System. This is the region of management in which finesse solves problems in a nonadversarial fashion before they become difficult and expensive.

A Matter of Balance

Effective discipline management typically deals with *pairs* of behavior. You systematically strengthen the behaviors you want while weakening the behaviors that you do not want. If you simply suppress problem behavior without systematically building appropriate behavior, one problem might well be replaced by another.

Discipline management, therefore, should be viewed as the *differential reinforcement* of appropriate behavior rather than as simple suppression. It is *discrimination training* in which students are given both a good reason to *stop* goofing off and a good reason to *start* cooperating.

Consequently, as we move up the decision ladder in problem solving, we continually move back and forth between reinforcement and suppression. If Limit Setting isn't working, rather than upping the ante on the negative side, cross over and try incentives. If simple incentives are not enough, cross over and try Responsibility Training. If the penalty component of Responsibility Training is not working, cross over and try Omission Training.

Looking at the decision ladder in this way, you might characterize *Tools for Teaching* as "everything you can possibly do to avoid the Backup System." When using the Backup System, the larger the negative sanction becomes, the greater 1) the cost, 2) the likelihood of failure, and 3) the likelihood of negative side effects like resentment. Not surprisingly, we send the "Larrys" to the

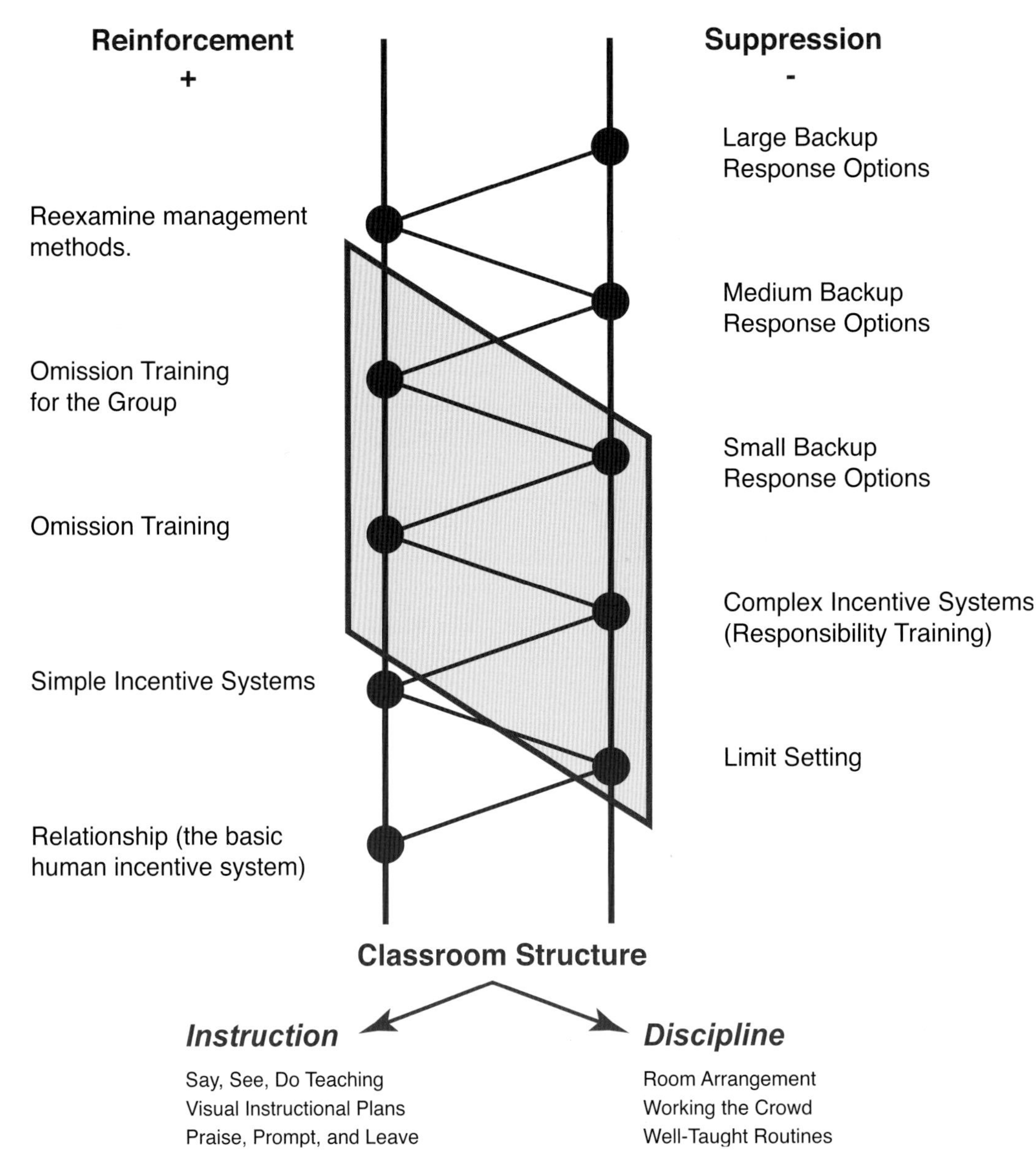

Tools for Teaching gives you nonadversarial management options.

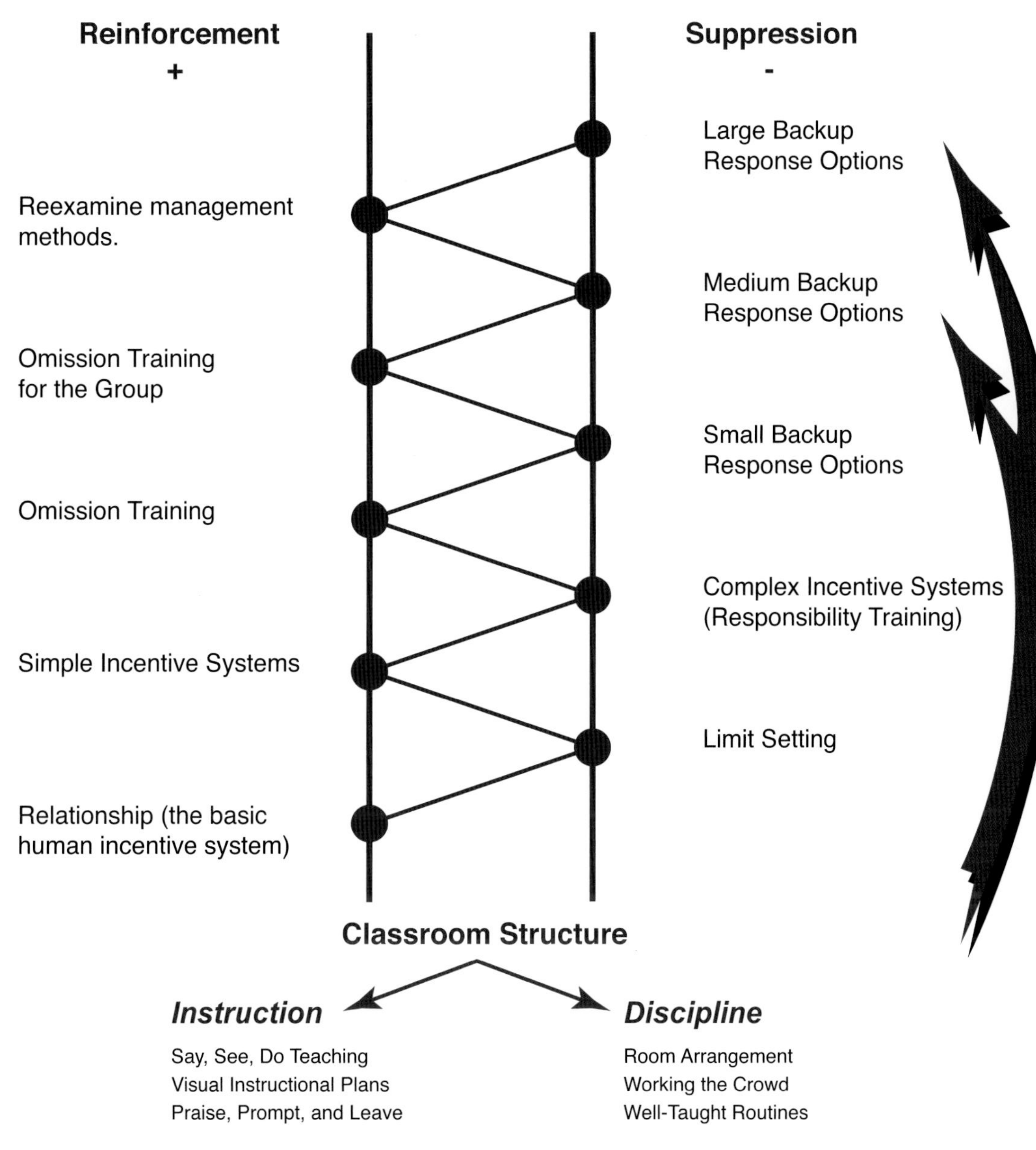

Primitive discipline management goes straight to the Backup System.

office over and over for as long as they are in school. The "solution" to this dilemma has traditionally been the fact that these kids drop out of school.

Understanding the nature of the Backup System should cause us to be very cautious concerning its use. You may be forced to go to the Backup System on occasion to deal with a crisis, but you would not want to go there very often. In training we say, "You may have to visit, but you wouldn't want to live there."

Primitive Discipline Management

Three Strikes

The figure to the left represents discipline management as it is all too frequently done. It goes from Classroom Structure directly to the Backup System with only a few reprimands in between. Sometimes it is no more than a name on the board and a few check marks followed by a trip to the office. Call it "three strikes and you're out."

It is natural when we are upset to leapfrog up the negative side of the decision ladder. When we are angry, we tend to reach for the largest of our negative sanctions.

I will refer to this simplified approach to discipline management as "primitive discipline." Primitive discipline lacks the finesse that makes discipline management nonadversarial or causes it to self-eliminate over time. If you repeatedly leap to the Backup System to solve your discipline problems, you will find yourself at war with Larry.

Working Down the Decision Ladder

To solve a problem, you move *up* the decision ladder. However, as your management system becomes established, you work your way *down* the decision ladder.

For example, on the first day of school Larry may "go for broke" in the discipline management poker game to see whether or not he is in control. But, when confronted by a highly effective teacher, Larry soon learns "not to throw good money after bad." Instead of upping the ante, Larry learns to fold early in order to cut his losses.

When you watch highly effective teachers, it becomes obvious that most of their discipline management is at the level of interpersonal skills. Large consequences have been replaced with Meaning Business.

Turning Common Sense Upside Down

Positive Sanctions for Negative Behavior

The figure to the right presents our major discipline management procedures analyzed in terms of reinforcement and suppression. The procedures are Limit Setting, Responsibility Training and Omission Training.

Limit Setting, in conjunction with working the crowd, is the most cost-effective way of dealing with typical, high-rate disruptions like talking to neighbors. Yet, as we mentioned earlier, Limit Setting is suppression. It is a gentle and *nonadversarial* form of suppression, but it nevertheless says "no" in a convincing fashion.

Next comes Responsibility Training, which is a hybrid of bonus and penalty. It is used for difficult to manage situations – dawdling, coming to class without materials, wasting time with pencil sharpening and hall passes, and management from a seated position.

Beneath Responsibility Training comes Omission Training which is a bonus-only management program. Omission Training is used for our most difficult management situations – angry, alienated students who say to the teacher, "You can't make me."

Common Sense Revisited

The common sense of discipline management holds that the punishment must fit the crime. *The bigger the crime, the bigger the punishment.*

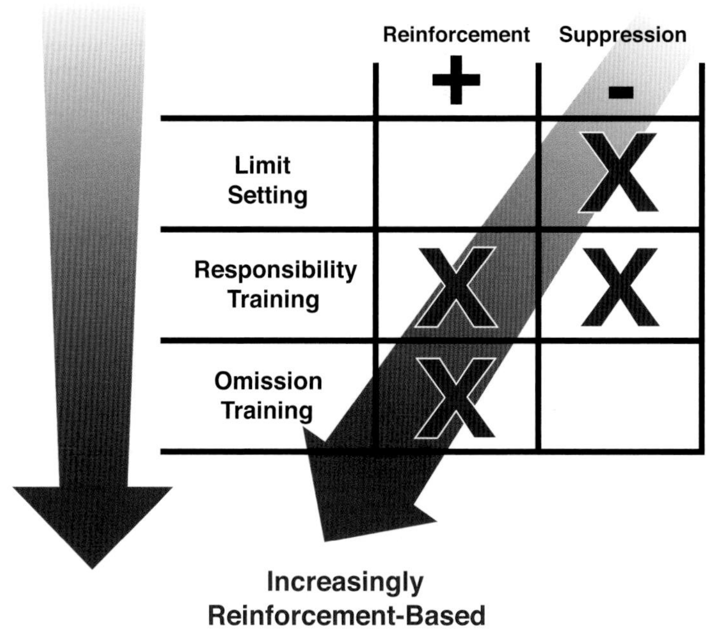

The more provocative the student, the more positive the response.

As you can see from this diagram, our management system turns common sense upside-down. The *smaller* the disruption, the more negative or suppressive is our response. However, the more *provocative* the student, the more *positive* is our response. Consequently, with the most angry and oppositional students like Larry, the management program has *no penalty component whatsoever.* Why is our system constructed in this upside-down fashion?

The Only Game in Town

I would like to say that I designed the management system in this fashion from the outset to help angry and alienated young people. But, I did not.

Rather, I simply worked with highly effective teachers and did research until I had developed solutions for all of their everyday headaches. Only after years of work did it become increasingly clear that positive management was much more *powerful* than negative management.

To understand why, consider the home that Larry comes from. The "Larrys" of the world are angry and alienated for a reason. They have been raised with the "yell, slap, and hit" school of childrearing.

When Larry and his parents come into the family clinic, I ask the parents questions in private about their problems in dealing with Larry.

> "How do you get Larry to do something that you need done?"
>
> "I wish I knew."
>
> "I mean, it *has* to be done – no ifs, ands or buts. What do you *finally* do in order to get Larry to move."
>
> "Well, I'll tell you the truth. When I take off my belt, that's when that kid finally moves."

Over the years Larry has learned to play power and control "games" for high stakes. He will test you, his teacher, because he must take stock of your power – your power to *coerce.* Coercion is the only form of power from an authority figure that Larry understands.

And when push finally comes to shove in the classroom, what will *you* do? What do you have to threaten him with? Will you pull out the School Discipline Code and say, "If I see that behavior one more time, I will..."

You will... what? Send him out of class? Send him home? Larry's old man takes a belt to him. What form of power can you employ that Larry would "respect?"

The management system described in this book treats highly oppositional behavior with positive consequences because, in the final analysis, it is the only game in town. Larry is at war with adult authority. If we do not have a program that is sophisticated enough to train Larry to cooperate in lieu of a public submission to adult authority, we will be faced with an endless war of wills.

When Consequences Work

If our hierarchy of consequences does not work for Larry, who will it work for? The answer is – good kids. They may fool around sometimes, but they are *not* at war with adult authority. Quite the opposite, they do not want to disappoint their parents. They will shape up. For Larry, you will need an approach that encompasses every aspect of his life in the classroom and is positive in nature.

Relationship Building

Beyond Behavior Management

When describing management programs, commentators tend to contrast "behavioral" approaches with programs that focus on "relationship building." Behavioral programs deal with *consequences* and *management skills,* whereas programs that focus on relationship building emphasize *bonding* and *communication skills* and *problem solving skills.*

Most text books on discipline management contain a synopsis of my work, usually labeled "The Jones Model" or "Positive Classroom Discipline" – the title of my first book. I am placed firmly in the behavioral camp which leaves me *less* than satisfied. Programs that contain a lot of "how to" are always described as behavioral.

Certainly *Tools for Teaching* is loaded with "how to." But, my desire to be specific may well have masked the relationship building dimension of the program.

Good behavior management always has relationship building as its primary objective. You want teachers to relate to children positively, and you want children to succeed in school so they will be self-confident. Behavior management is simply a means to that end.

A Clinical Perspective

Dealing with the whole child is basic to my training as a clinical psychologist. At the beginning of my career, I worked in the clinic with families having a schizophrenic parent. This is the big leagues of family therapy since, at this level of psychopathology, game playing is done for high stakes and on many levels. Analyzing the give and take of a classroom social system is simple by comparison.

Later I was trained in behavior therapy. I learned a whole new language – the language of consequences and stimulus control. Family therapy began as contingency management, but it soon evolved into parent training. In addition to managing unruly behavior, the parents desperately needed communication skills. They didn't know how to talk to their kids without criticizing and nagging.

First we had to turn the child's obnoxious behavior around, and then we had to train the parents to relate constructively to the child in order to support that new behavior. Thus, the two areas of my training, behavior management and relationship building, quickly merged.

Behavior management and relationship building remain intertwined throughout *Tools for Teaching*. There is no separate chapter for relationship building. Rather, *building* relationships with your students and *protecting* those relationships are combined in each procedure.

Junior high school gives us a particularly good venue for seeing behavior management and relationship building as they work side by side. In these classrooms, the positive and negative aspects of any teacher-student relationship are amplified.

The Trials of Junior High

Most teachers say that they would not teach junior high on a bet. The kids are just too squirrely – raging hormones and all of that. But other teachers choose junior high and would teach nothing else. How do some teachers get along famously with an age group that is notorious for torturing teachers?

The answer lies in the extreme vulnerability of young people at that age. They are changing and growing, of course, and their relationship with the opposite sex has gone from "yuck" to "wow." But that alone is not what makes kids so vulnerable in early adolescence.

What makes them so vulnerable is their discomfort with who they are in conjunction with their desperate desire to be popular. They are *afraid* – afraid of having the most zits, afraid of having the biggest nose, afraid of being too big or too small, afraid of being ugly, afraid of being rejected.

Am I Smart or Stupid?

There is one aspect of the child's self concept, however, that is learned primarily from you. They will learn whether they are *smart* or *stupid*. If you make them feel stupid, they will get even. But, if you make them feel smart and comfortable in class, they will be *so* appreciative.

Making kids feel smart must happen with every lesson, and it must happen for all of the students, not just the "smarties." What kinds of things can we do as we teach each lesson to make students feel self-confident and *smart*?

Succeeding with Instruction

Many of your one-on-one instructional interactions with students will be helping interactions. What form will these helping interactions take?

Without training, your eye will instinctively find the error, and you will end up talking about it. While talking about the error, you will give a failure message even though you try to be positive and up-beat. You will give it unwittingly and with the best of intentions – perhaps a candy coated *"Yes… but" compliment* wrapped with encouragement. But the net emotional experience for the student will be negative.

With each helping interaction you either heighten or reduce the student's sense of vulnerability. Praise, Prompt, and Leave *protects* students. It changes the flavor of helping interactions from negative to positive. It does so not by candy coating feedback, but rather, by giving a simple prompt *correctly*.

Visual Instructional Plans also reduce the students' sense of vulnerability. They provide a road map to success that any student can refer to at will. Visual Instructional Plans, therefore, provide an insurance policy against forgetting, becoming confused, and feeling overwhelmed.

However, the biggest protector of children in the area of instruction is Say, See, Do Teaching. There is no greater sense of vulnerability than walking into a class wondering whether or not you will survive the coming lesson. Say, See, Do Teaching packages learning in a way that allows students to chew and swallow each bite. It replaces cognitive overload with self-assurance.

Self-Concept

Much has been written about "self-concept" in recent decades, and we have given awards for everything imaginable in an attempt to manufacture it. But students are realists, and they are hard to fool. You cannot flim-flam them with pseudo-accomplishment.

Feeling smart – having a "positive self-concept as a learner" – can only be achieved in one way. It is based on *real* success resulting from *real* mastery. Students will experience success primarily as a result of your technical proficiency in teaching a lesson.

Motivation Sets the Tone

If you are skillful at building *motivation*, you live by the adage, "No joy, no work." Whether it is in building motivation to *work hard* or in building motivation to *follow classroom rules*, your focus is on preferred activities. To build motivation you must have a sense of fun, and fun builds relationships.

Are You With Me or Against Me?

Within the area of *discipline*, nothing increases students' sense of vulnerability more than being in trouble. In discipline management, Meaning Business allows the teacher to set limits in a nonadversarial fashion without creating embarrassment. In conjunction with working the crowd, it is all but invisible.

Why Are Some Teachers Cool?

Why do kids like some teachers so much more than others? They cannot tell you. They use vapid phrases like, "She's really nice." or "He's cool."

But the kids know where they feel safe. They feel safe where they can relax with their peer group and feel smart without any concern about being embarrassed or looking bad.

For teachers who know how to make teenagers feel comfortable and safe, junior high students can become like puppy dogs. That teacher's jokes will be funny. That teacher's lessons will be interesting. Even their clothes will be cool.

Building Relationship Proactively

We have also talked at length about the importance of being proactive in relationship building. The first period of the school year will be devoted to an ice-breaking activity that helps students feel at home in their new surroundings.

During the first week you will interview each child privately in order to make your relationship more personal. During the second week of school you will begin building a bridge to parents with a welcoming phone call. These concrete steps are a meaningful sign to students and parents alike that you care.

When you implement Tools for Teaching, relationship building will occur as a natural by-product.

Communication Skills

A Theraputic Approach

While some theorists focus on relationship building, others place effective communication at the center of classroom management. These theorists are typically clinical psychologists who have adapted therapy skills to the classroom. These modified therapy skills are typically labeled, "communication skills" or "problem solving skills."

As a clinical psychologist, I am drawn to the importance of giving new teachers training in this area. My first instinct in dealing with interpersonal problems is to talk to the other person. It seems the natural thing to do if you want to know what is going on beneath the surface.

Realistic Objectives

Before designing a training program for teachers, however, a reality check may be in order. In teacher training, we can barely squeeze a course on classroom management into the curriculum. It is hard to imagine having time to train teachers to use therapy skills effectively.

To compound the problem, therapy with children is a very specialized field. It is hard to get kids to even *own* a problem much less talk about it. And when they do talk, what do you get? Their main strategy is denial, and their favorite response is, "I dunno."

Add to this the dilemma of time. Solving problems by talking about them is *very* time consuming. You will be lucky if, during your first "session," you get a relaxation of defenses and a bit of candor. During your next session you can move on to problem definition.

Yeah, right! Maybe you can shoehorn this "therapy session" in between third and fourth periods. Or maybe you'll have time between the end of school and that parent conference.

We would do well to have modest objectives. The most we can hope to do is equip new teachers with a few basic communication skills that allow them to converse with students and parents comfortably and constructively. We should focus on basics – a few key strategies and help in avoiding the most blatant rookie errors.

Use What You Already Have

To simplify the acquisition of problem solving skills, utilize what you already know. In Chapter 6, "Simplifying the Verbal Modality," there was a section on *discussion facilitation.*

Discussion facilitation employs a simplified version of therapy skills. You will use these skills in a heart-to-heart talk with a student or during a parent conference.

Your "bread and butter" skills are 1) *open-ended prompting,* 2) *wait time,* and 3) *selective reinforcement.* These skills allow you to facilitate conversation and guide the train of thought without dominating the conversation. In Chapter 18, "Eliminating Backtalk," we gave an example of such a conversation. Keep it simple. However, keeping it simple brings us to the topic of rookie errors.

Rookie Errors

The main rookie errors for young therapists are:

- talking too much
- giving advice

Rookie therapists just can't stay away from the *expert role.* They feel as though it is their responsibility to solve the problem. Only with time and training do they learn to relax and let the patient do the work. As all young therapists learn, "Advice doesn't help." Rather, their job is to help the patient solve his or her own problem.

Problem Solving

Conversations with students will often be precipitated by some kind of interpersonal problem. Therefore, a new teacher will need a few problem solving skills. The following problem solving process is fairly standard:

- Define the problem
- Generate solutions
- Evaluate solutions
- Choose the best solution
- Implement the solution
- Evaluate the outcome

A version of this problem solving process can be found in the Study Group Activity Guide, Appendix I under the heading "Group Problem Solving Process." This Group Problem Solving Process allows teachers to bring problems of program implementation to their follow-through groups and be supported by colleagues rather than being given advice and made to feel stupid.

As a facilitator, your job is always to direct the other person through the problem solving process while making sure that *they* do the work. You can tell if you have coopted the expert role by taking note of who is doing the most talking.

A Final Note on Classroom Management

Any attempt to define classroom management as either *this* or *that* will come up short. Everything you do in the classroom is interrelated. Wherever your skills are weak, that is where the problems will emerge.

By integrating discipline, instruction, and motivation, *Tools for Teaching* provides you with the fundamental skills of being a classroom teacher. When you implement *Tools for Teaching,* relationship building will occur as a natural by-product.

Index

About the Authors

I have been working with teachers regarding classroom management for over thirty years now. I began my career as a clinical psychologist, receiving my Ph.D. from UCLA. My first job was director of the ward for autistic children at the UCLA Medical Center where I succeeded Ivar Lovaas. He had trained the staff beautifully, and they in turn trained me. It was at this time in 1969-70 that I began working in classrooms for emotionally disturbed children. There I came across two natural teachers who could make these "handicapped" students eat out of the palms of their hands. This story is recounted in Chapter 1, "Learning from the 'Natural' Teachers."

From 1972-78 I was on the faculties of both the University of Rochester and the University of Rochester Medical Center. There I was part of a large program-project grant from the National Institute of Mental Health to study "high-risk" families – families with one parent having a severe psychological disability. Soon after I arrived in Rochester, I began working with the regional Board of Cooperative Educational Services to help with severe behavioral problems in their classrooms. Working in classrooms with highly capable teachers and graduate students became my career "hobby." By 1978, it became clear to me that I was having much more fun with my hobby than with the high-risk research. In 1978, I cancelled a final site visit for a Career Development Award from NIMH and resigned from the university. I have been a consultant ever since, training teachers and writing.

Jo Lynne and I met at the University of Kansas in 1961 where she was getting a degree in education. We married two years later and have been working together ever since studying classrooms and raising a family.

Patrick (below left) received his bachelor's degree from The Colorado College and his masters in education from the University of California at Santa Cruz. He taught high school before joining me to write *Tools for Teaching.*

Brian (below right) received his bachelor's degree from Kenyon College. After doing the illustrations for this book, he attended Otis Art Institute in Los Angeles. He has recently illustrated a children's book authored by Tom Dunsmiur entitled, *You Can't Milk A Dancing Cow*, published by Tanglewood Press.

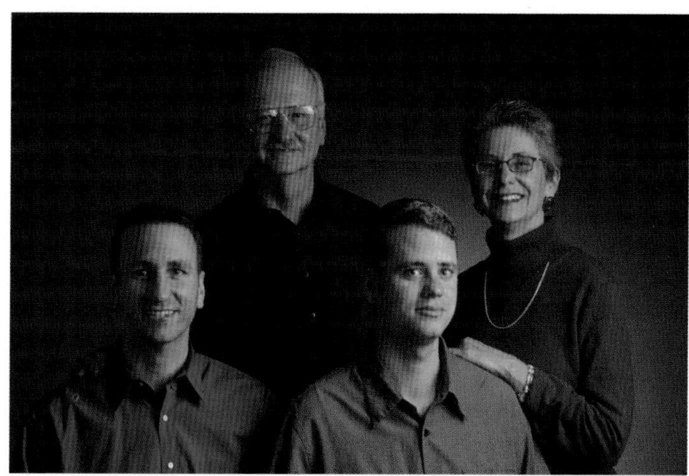

SEE FRED IN ACTION!

What's on your Overview DVD:

- Laugh with Fred as he describes life in the classroom
- Become familiar with *Tools for Teaching* and the *Video Toolbox*
- Hear how other educators use the program
- Learn how to use the free Study Group Activity Guide
- See how to help parents with the Parent Edition DVDs

Fredric H. Jones & Associates, Inc.
103 Quarry Lane
Santa Cruz, CA 95060
tel: (831) 425-8222 fax: (831) 426-8222
info@fredjones.com www.fredjones.com